ACCOUNTING FOR PROFIT FOR BREACH OF CONTRACT

This book defends the view that an award of an account of profits (or 'disgorgement damages') for breach of contract will sometimes be justifiable, and fits within the orthodox principles and cases in contract law. However there is some confusion as to when such an award should be made. The moral bases for disgorgement damages are deterrence and punishment, which shape the remedy in important ways. Courts are also concerned with vindication of the claimant's performance interest, and it is pivotal in these cases that the claimant cannot procure a substitute performance via an award of damages or specific relief.

The book argues that disgorgement damages should be available in two categories of case: 'second sale' cases, where the defendant breaches his contract with the claimant to make a more profitable contract with a third party; and 'agency problem' cases, where the defendant promises the claimant he will not do a certain thing, and the claimant finds it difficult to supervise the performance. Moreover, disgorgement may be full or partial, and 'reasonable fee damages' for breach of contract are best understood as partial disgorgement rather than 'restitutionary damages'. Equitable bars to relief should also be adopted in relation to disgorgement damages, as should allowances for skill and effort.

This book will be of interest to contract and commercial lawyers, and will be especially valuable to anyone with an interest in contract remedies and restitution. It draws on case law in a number of common law jurisdictions, primarily England and Wales, and Australia.

Volume 2 in the series Hart Studies in Private Law

Accounting for Profit for Breach of Contract

Theory and Practice

Katy Barnett

·HART·
PUBLISHING

OXFORD AND PORTLAND, OREGON
2012

Published in the United Kingdom by Hart Publishing Ltd
16C Worcester Place, Oxford, OX1 2JW
Telephone: +44 (0)1865 517530
Fax: +44 (0)1865 510710
E-mail: mail@hartpub.co.uk
Website: http://www.hartpub.co.uk

Published in North America (US and Canada) by
Hart Publishing
c/o International Specialized Book Services
920 NE 58th Avenue, Suite 300
Portland, OR 97213-3786
USA
Tel: +1 503 287 3093 or toll-free: (1) 800 944 6190
Fax: +1 503 280 8832
E-mail: orders@isbs.com
Website: http://www.isbs.com

British Library Cataloguing in Publication Data
Data Available

ISBN: 978-1-84946-251-8

Typeset by Hope Services, Abingdon
Printed and bound in Great Britain by
TJ International Ltd, Padstow, Cornwall

FSC www.fsc.org
MIX
Paper from responsible sources
FSC® C013056

To Scott, Eloise and Joshua

PREFACE

This book is a revised, updated and expanded version of my PhD thesis which was completed at the University of Melbourne between 2007 and 2010. I am grateful that I was given an Australian Postgraduate Award by the Australian Government, without which I would not have been able to complete my PhD.

In this book, I advance an interpretive theory of the law which is intended to enhance our understanding of the existing law of disgorgement damages for breach of contract. Of course, such damages are not presently available in Australia, but I argue that the award of the remedy of an account of profits (or 'disgorgement damages') for breach of contract is justifiable in some circumstances, and that an award *can* be situated within orthodox contract law principle and cases. It is important to note that disgorgement damages will not be available for *all* breaches of contract under my scheme: the availability of disgorgement depends in part upon the nature of the claimant's interest in performance of the contractual obligations and the availability of a substitute performance (either through an award of compensatory damages or through an award of specific relief).

Simply, I argue that disgorgement damages are available in two main categories of case: the 'second sale' cases, where the defendant breaches his contract with the claimant to make a more profitable contract with a third party; and the 'agency problem' cases, where the defendant promises the claimant he will not do a particular thing, and the claimant finds it difficult to supervise the performance.

I focus on the law of Australia and England and Wales, although there are references to material from all common law jurisdictions, including the recent US *Restatement (Third) of Restitution and Unjust Enrichment*. I have considered material available to me before 1 October 2011.

I am extremely grateful to my two PhD supervisors, Professor Michael Bryan and Professor Andrew Robertson at the University of Melbourne, who have given me encouragement, support, friendship and valuable suggestions as to how to improve my work. I have learned an immense amount from them, and I am very grateful for their guidance. In addition, I would like to thank my thesis examiners, Professor Graham Virgo and Professor Mitchell McInnes, for their insightful suggestions and timely, generous feedback on my thesis. Similarly, I found the suggestions and comments of Hart's anonymous reviewer extremely useful.

The following friends and colleagues have been kind enough to discuss ideas with me over the past four years: Matthew Harding, Megan Richardson, Elise Bant, Ralph Cunnington, Rob Chambers, James Edelman, Ross Grantham, 'Rip' Verkerke, David Brennan, Jeannie Paterson, Helen Dale, Anna Thwaites and Nicole Rich.

I am also very grateful for the assistance of the Law Research Service at the Melbourne Law School Library, particularly Robin Gardner, Claire Kelly, Tom Kavanagh, Tom Andrews and Chris Lum. Thank you also to the team at Hart Publishing for their professionalism and support – a pleasure to deal with!

I would not have been able to finish either my PhD or this book without the support of my parents, parents-in-law, sister, grandparents and friends. My co-authors and those who comment at my blog, www.skepticlawyer.com.au, have generally inspired me, supported me and opened my mind.

Finally, I would like to dedicate this book to my wonderful husband Scott and our children, Eloise and Joshua. Scott has held the fort at times when the thesis/book 'ate my life' and has been most understanding and supportive at times when it all just seemed too hard. Eloise, you'll be glad to hear that Mummy's book is *finally* finished!

Melbourne, October 2011

TABLE OF CONTENTS

TABLE OF CASES

TABLE OF LEGISLATION

Australia

Canada

Europe

Israel

New Zealand

United Kingdom

United States

1

Introduction

It has been suggested that disgorgement damages for breach of contract are unorthodox and potentially disastrous for contract law.[1] The aim of this book is to create a workable interpretive theory of the law of disgorgement damages according to which parties to a contract can predict with reasonable accuracy the remedy which a court will award if they breach their obligations. It is preferable if parties are aware of each other's intentions at the outset of a contract, and the threat of disgorgement remedies ensures that contractors do not make idle promises which they do not intend to keep. In some circumstances compensatory damages and specific relief are not adequate to protect the claimant's interest in performance of the contract. The award of a remedy in private law is intended to vindicate the claimant's right, in the sense that the claimant's right is made good. Disgorgement damages fill a gap in the law, as they allow for an appropriate recognition of the claimant's rights in those cases where specific performance would have been available but it is no longer possible, and where compensatory damages are inadequate. They also serve to deter defendants from breaching contracts, particularly as there is no possibility of stipulating liquidated damages to ensure performance.

I use the term 'disgorgement damages' to describe the remedy for stripping profits from a wrongdoer for breach of contract.[2] Gain-based damages for breach of contract have sometimes been called 'restitutionary damages'[3] or an 'account of profit'.[4] 'Restitutionary damages' is an inapposite label because 'restitution' is an ambiguous term with two mutually exclusive meanings, either a 'giving back' of a benefit unjustly received or a 'giving up' of a benefit made at the expense of the claimant because a wrong has been committed against her.[5] It was for this reason that Lord Nicholls in *Blake* preferred not to use the term 'restitutionary

[1] *Attorney-General v Blake* [2000] UKHL 45, [2001] 1 AC 268 (HL) 299 (Lord Hobhouse dissenting).

[2] *cf* J Edelman, *Gain-Based Damages – Contract, Tort, Equity and Intellectual Property* (Oxford, Hart Publishing, 2002). See also *Stevens v Premium Real Estate Ltd* [2009] 2 NZLR 382 (NZSC) [102] (Tipping J).

[3] See, eg D Friedmann, 'Restitution of Benefits Obtained Through the Appropriation of Property or the Commission of a Wrong' (1980) 80 *Columbia Law Review* 504, 515; G Jones 'The Recovery of Benefits Gained from a Breach of Contract' (1983) 99 *LQR* 443; P Birks, 'Restitutionary Damages for Breach of Contract: *Snepp* and the Fusion of Law and Equity' [1987] *Lloyd's Maritime and Commercial Law Quarterly* 421.

[4] *Blake* (n 1) 284 (Lord Nicholls); S Doyle and D Wright, 'Restitutionary Damages – The Unnecessary Remedy?' (2001) 25 *Melbourne University Law Review* 1.

[5] P Birks, *An Introduction to the Law of Restitution*, 2nd edn (Oxford, Oxford University Press, 1989) 12.

damages', calling it an 'unhappy expression'.[6] 'Account of profits' is also an inappropriate label. It is laden with historical baggage, as it is traditionally awarded for equitable wrongs, and not for common law wrongs.[7] By contrast, 'disgorgement damages' is a jurisdictionally neutral term which jettisons the historical baggage of the label 'account of profits' and sidesteps the ambiguity of the label 'restitutionary damages'.[8]

My theory of disgorgement damages is intended to be overarching, and to be used in any common law country. Accordingly, I will use cases from England, Australia, New Zealand, Canada and the United States to draw a general overarching doctrine.

I Method

The methodology adopted by this book is interpretive. It attempts to enhance our understanding of the existing law of disgorgement damages for breach of contract.[9] It also suggests the directions in which the law should develop, as this area of the law is still nascent.

Stephen Smith outlines four useful criteria which must be considered if a particular interpretive theory is to be comprehensive and persuasive:

1. **Fit** (the extent to which the theory 'fits' the data it is trying to explain);
2. **Coherence** (the extent to which the theory is consistent and intelligible);
3. **Morality** (the extent to which the theory justifies the law's claim to be a legitimate or morally justified authority); and
4. **Transparency** (the extent to which the theory explains the legal reasoning of legal actors themselves).

The benefit of this framework is that it can be adapted, and different emphases can be placed on each criterion. Unlike Professors Smith, Beever and Rickett, I do not adopt a corrective justice interpretation of private law, nor do I seek to establish an ordered taxonomy which explains private law generally. My aim is more modest: to

[6] *Blake* (n 1) 284 (Lord Nicholls).

[7] J Edelman, 'The Measure of Restitution and the Future of Restitutionary Damages' (2010) 18 *Restitution Law Review* 1, 7. *cf Blake* (n 1) 284; Doyle and Wright (n 4).

[8] The use of 'damages' could be criticised on the basis that accounts of profits have been expressly held *not* to be awards of damages: see *Watson v Holliday* (1882) 20 Ch D 780 (CA) (affd *Watson v Holliday* (1882) 52 LJ Ch 543 (CA)). However, it has been suggested that damages merely represent a money award for a wrong: P Birks, 'Equity in the Modern Law: An Exercise in Taxonomy' (1996) 26 *Western Australian Law Review* 1, 29. *cf* H McGregor, 'Restitutionary Damages' in P Birks (ed), *Wrongs and Remedies in the Twenty-First Century* (Oxford, Clarendon Press, 1996) 203, 203.

[9] S Smith, *Contract Theory* (Oxford, Oxford University Press, 2004) 5; A Beever and CEF Rickett, 'Interpretive Legal Theory and the Academic Lawyer' (2005) *MLR* 320, 324. Against S Hedley, 'The Shock of the Old: Interpretivism in Obligations' in CEF Rickett (ed), *Structure and Justification in Private Law – Essays for Peter Birks* (Oxford, Hart Publishing, 2008) 205 for criticisms of interpretive theory.

establish a workable, coherent set of criteria for awards of disgorgement damages which fits (by and large) with existing law, and which reflects the competing justifications for private law remedies,[10] and for contract law in particular. My view as to the relative importance of each criterion is also different. I place less importance on morality, for example, than would Smith, Beever and Rickett.

I now turn to the way in which my theory of disgorgement damages meets each criterion.

A Fit

Courts acknowledge that disgorgement damages are available for breach of contract in at least some, but not all, common law countries.[11] In *Blake*, Lord Nicholls argued that courts would award disgorgement damages according to a two-part test: first, the claimant must have a 'legitimate interest' in performance of the contract, and secondly, compensatory damages must be inadequate.[12] Nonetheless it has been said with some accuracy that, even after a number of cases where judges have applied *Blake*, 'the legitimate interest test remains hopelessly ill-defined and difficult to apply.'[13]

This book seeks to fit the theory of disgorgement damages to the existing law, and to clarify the way in which the 'legitimate interest' test can be applied. An analysis of existing case law discloses two broad categories of cases where disgorgement damages for breach of contract have been awarded:

[10] Hedley (n 9) 212 says interpretive accounts tend 'to treat disorder as a mere appearance, as showing merely that we have not reached the end of the enquiry yet.' Disorder is something which naturally arises in an incremental system like the common law because the law arises from the input of many judges dealing with many different factual situations. Nonetheless, I argue that some kind of pattern can and should be drawn out of the case law.

[11] UK: see *Blake* (n 1); *Esso Petroleum Company Limited v Niad Limited* [2001] EWHC Ch 458, [2001] All ER (D) 324 (Ch); *Experience Hendrix LLC v PPX Enterprises Inc* [2003] EWCA Civ 323, [2003] 1 All ER (Comm) 830 (CA). Canada: see *Bank of America (Canada) v Mutual Trust Co* (2002) 211 DLR (4th) 385 (SCC) [25] (Major J); *Amartek Inc v Canadian Commercial Corp* (2003) 229 DLR (4th) 419 (Ontario SC) 467 (O'Driscoll J) (on appeal held there was no collateral contract: (2005) 5 BLR (4th) 199 (Ontario CA)); *Montreal Trust Co v Williston Wildcatters Corp* (2004) 243 DLR (4th) 317 (SKQB) 122 (Vancise JA). US: see obiter in *Earthinfo Inc v Hydrosphere Resource Consultants*, 900 P (2d) 113 (Colo SC, 1995) 117–21; American Law Institute, *Restatement (Third) of Restitution and Unjust Enrichment* (2011) § 39 (disgorgement remedy for 'opportunistic' breach of contract). *cf* Australia, in which disgorgement for breach of contract has generally been rejected, apart from a sole obiter comment of Deane J in *Hospital Products Ltd v United States Surgical Corp* (1984) 156 CLR 41, 124–25 (HCA). See against *Hospitality Group Pty Ltd v Australian Rugby Union Ltd* (2001) 110 FCR 157 (FCA) 196 (Hill and Finkelstein JJ); *Town & Country Property Management Services Pty Ltd v Kaltoum* [2002] NSWSC 166 [85] (Campbell J); *Biscayne Partners Pty Ltd v Valance Corp Pty Ltd* [2003] NSWSC 874 [232]–[235] (Einstein J); *Short v Crawley* [2005] NSWSC 928 [24] (White J); PW Young, 'Recent Cases – Account of profits for breach of contract' (2000) 74 *Australian Law Journal* 817; RI Barrett, 'The "Most Wrong" Equity Cases 1990–2003: Attorney General v Blake' (presented at the Supreme Court Judges' Conference, 24 August 2003).

[12] *Blake* (n 1) 285.

[13] R Cunnington, 'The Measure and Availability of Gain-based Damages for Breach of Contract' in D Saidov and R Cunnington (eds), *Contract Damages: Domestic and International Perspectives* (Oxford, Hart Publishing, 2008) 207, 235.

1. **'Second sale' cases.** Alice contracts with Boris for the supply of property, goods or services. Boris sees an opportunity to sell the property, good or service to Conrad for a greater profit. Therefore Boris breaches his contract with Alice and sells to Conrad for a profit. Typically, the contract between Alice and Boris is no longer specifically enforceable but there is a profit for Boris to disgorge.
2. **'Agency problem' cases.**[14] Boris promises Alice he will *not do* a specific thing which relates to Alice's best interests, but Boris breaches the contract and does the very thing which he has contracted not to do, making a profit as a consequence. Breaches of fiduciary duty concurrent with breach of contract form the core of this category, but breach of negative covenant cases on the margin between contract and fiduciary duties also fit into this category in some circumstances.

Chapter four will focus on the 'second sale' cases. The concept of substitutability is the key to determining whether disgorgement damages will be available in these cases, and this produces the best fit with the few existing cases. Substitutability looks to what the claimant hoped to gain from the contract, and therefore what remedy the defendant must give the claimant as a substitute for the performance which was denied as a result of the breach. Ordinarily, damages or specific relief ensure that the claimant receives an adequate substitute for performance, but in a 'second sale' scenario, neither damages nor specific relief are available. Thus some other remedy is needed to vindicate the claimant's performance interest, namely disgorgement damages. It is sometimes suggested that disgorgement damages for breach of contract is precluded by 'efficient breach' theory.[15] This postulates that where a promisor breaches to make a more profitable contract with a third party, the breach should be encouraged because it is economically efficient. The promisee does not lose out because she gets compensatory damages, and the resource is allocated to the person who values it the most. However, while 'efficient breach' seems at first blush to fit better with the preference of contract law for compensatory damages, where the subject matter of the bargain is not substitutable, courts generally *do not* allow promisors to breach, and instead award specific relief. In addition, the theory of efficient breach does not fit with other areas of contract law.

Chapter five will consider the 'agency problem' cases, for which additional considerations must be taken into account besides substitutability. In particular, courts must consider whether the remedies for breach of negative covenants adequately protect the performance interest in certain sorts of contracts in which the claimants are particularly vulnerable. Typically such contracts seek to protect a non-financial interest.

[14] 'Agency' here is *not* intended to connote the legal relationship of agency. It is used in the *economic sense* to talk about relationships where a legal actor undertakes to act in the interests of another and where the undertaking is difficult to supervise. See J Stiglitz, 'Principal and Agent (ii)', entry in S Durlauf and L Blume (eds), *The New Palgrave Dictionary of Economics*, 2nd edn (Basingstoke and New York, Palgrave Macmillan, 2008).

[15] See, eg R Posner, *Economic Analysis of Law*, 8th edn (New York, Aspen Walters Kluwer, 2011) 149–58.

Chapter six will outline the criteria courts use to choose between full and partial disgorgement. Most cases fit with the theory that the choice of remedy depends upon the reason why specific relief is no longer available. If the defendant has put specific relief out of the claimant's hands and it is impossible to procure a substitute performance, then the defendant should be liable for full disgorgement damages. The deterrent considerations are particularly important in such a case. However, if specific relief *could* be granted but the court has chosen not to award it for discretionary reasons, then the court should award a proportion of the profit in the form of a 'reasonable fee' award.

Courts have indicated that an allowance for skill and effort may be awarded to a defendant in some cases of disgorgement damages for breach of contract.[16] This is correct, and I seek to fit these cases into the law with regard to bars to relief and allowances (which basically deal with questions of desert in one form or another). This will be considered in greater detail in chapter seven.

B Coherence

I seek to establish that disgorgement damages are coherent[17] and consistent with both contract law principles and other existing laws. I also seek to ensure that the development of disgorgement damages continues to be intelligible.

The criterion of 'substitutability' (discussed in detail in chapter three) assists in making the law of disgorgement damages coherent. Not every breach of contract gives rise to disgorgement damages. It is important to have regard to the aims of contract law and, specifically, the aims of remedies for breach of contract. The claimant has a 'performance interest', or an interest in gaining what was promised according to the contract.[18] Remedies for breach of contract seek to provide either the means by which to procure a substitute performance, or the performance itself. The primary remedy for breach of contract in common law countries is expectation damages.[19] Expectation damages do not merely compensate for loss, but also seek to recognise the claimant's performance interest in a way which is least intrusive to the defendant.[20] When expectation damages do not adequately

[16] *Earthinfo* (n 11); *Experience Hendrix* (n 11) [44] (Mance LJ).

[17] I adopt what Smith calls the 'less-demanding version' of coherence, ie a theory is coherent 'to the extent that it presents contract law as consistent or non-contradictory': see Smith (n 9) 11. I do not seek to identify a single principle which unites all cases. Nor would I take the view that we can only understand law from within, and that coherence necessarily means that one must discount other perspectives on the efficacy of the law (eg empirical work and evaluative work): *cf* Hedley (n 9) 214–15. Indeed empirical and evaluative work would be very useful in this field.

[18] D Friedmann, 'The Performance Interest in Contract Damages' (1995) 111 *LQR* 628; B Coote, 'Contract Damages, *Ruxley*, and the Performance Interest' (1997) 56 *CLJ* 537, 566; B Coote, 'The Performance Interest, *Panatown*, and the Problem of Loss' (2001) 117 *LQR* 81.

[19] NC Seddon and MP Ellinghaus, *Cheshire and Fifoot's Law of Contract*, 8th Australian edn (NSW, LexisNexis Butterworths, 2002) 1080–83, [23.6]–[23.7].

[20] See (n 18); C Webb, 'Performance and Compensation: An Analysis of Contract Damages and Contractual Obligation' (2006) 26 *OJLS* 41, 41–42, 45–49; D Kimel, *From Promise to Contract: Towards a Liberal Theory of Contract* (Oxford, Hart Publishing, 2003) 102–04.

recognise the performance interest, courts are likely to award specific relief and compel the defendant to give the claimant exactly what she bargained for. However, if compensatory damages are inadequate and specific relief is no longer available, *and* the defendant has made a profit, the 'next best' remedy to effectively vindicate the claimant's performance interest is disgorgement damages. Courts have already given extensive thought to questions of substitutability when awarding specific relief and these cases provide guidelines as to when it will be appropriate to award disgorgement damages.

Chapters four and five establish that disgorgement damages for breach of contract are coherent with existing law. The 'second sale' cases, which involve a breach of contract in order to sell the subject matter of the contract to a third party more profitably, work along the same principles as awards for specific performance. As with specific performance, the primary criterion is 'substitutability', or whether or not the claimant can procure a substitute performance from elsewhere. The negative covenant cases are extensions of the existing cases on concurrent breaches of contract and fiduciary duty, for which disgorgement damages are incontrovertibly available.

Chapter six seeks to explain the relationship between the 'reasonable fee' cases and the cases involving 'skimped performance' (ie where the defendant saves an expense by not delivering full performance under the contract). There is an overlap between some reasonable fee cases and some cases of skimped performance, because the defendant could be said to have saved himself the expense of paying a fee to the claimant for release from his obligation. The 'reasonable fee' is also the expense saved. However, we should reject the suggestion of the Court of Appeal in *Blake* that 'restitutionary damages' are 'simpler and more open',[21] and thus represent the remedy of choice in cases of skimped performance. In most cases of skimped performance, it is still possible to put the claimant in a position as if the contract had been performed by an award of damages. Often, the question is whether the measure of damages should be the cost of rectifying the performance (which provides a pecuniary substitute for performance) or simply the decrease in value of the subject matter of the contract (which merely compensates for loss in value). In rare cases it may be necessary to award disgorgement damages for an expense saved when performance is impossible, and damages are inadequate on *any* scale (whether measured by cost of rectification or decrease in value), particularly in a case where the claimant paid upfront for a contract where the purpose was to avoid risk.

In chapter seven, the existing equitable bars to relief which apply to specific performance are used as a basis for those bars to relief which should apply to disgorgement damages. The principles which govern allowances for skill and effort are drawn from fiduciary law. Accordingly, these principles are consistent with the existing law.

[21] *Attorney-General v Blake* [1998] Ch 439 (CA) 458 (Lord Woolf).

C Morality

The aim of private law remedies is to appropriately recognise and vindicate the claimant's rights in a way which reflects the moral aims behind remedies. There are a number of ways in which a claimant's right can be appropriately vindicated: through compensation, deterrence, punishment or even simply recognition of the right. In chapter two, this book identifies the two moral[22] rationales behind disgorgement damages (namely, deterrence and punishment). The primary rationale behind disgorgement damages is deterrence. Simply, there are some situations where the defendant should be deterred from breaching because the claimant's performance interest should be protected. A further rationale for awards of disgorgement damages is punishment or retribution. The basis of the retributive rationale is that the defendant has engaged in wrongful conduct, and thus ought to be punished. It is backward-looking and desert-based rather than forward looking and consequentialist.[23] It follows from this that courts must consider a variety of 'desert-based' considerations, including the advertence of the defendant's breach and the availability of bars to relief and allowances. Compensation for loss is hard to establish as a rationale for full disgorgement damages, despite the attempts of some courts and scholars who argue the contrary. Perhaps a compensatory rationale sits easier with at least some of the *Wrotham Park* damages cases (which I see as 'partial disgorgement'), but for reasons which will be explained in chapters two and three, it cannot explain all such cases.

This book treads the middle line between the polar opposite approaches towards contract theory. On the one hand, the promissory or rights-based analysis emphasises the claimant's right to performance and argues that the primary obligation arising from a contract is the claimant's right to have the contract performed. On the other hand, the utilitarian approaches, typified by those who support 'efficient breach', argue that the primary obligation arising under a contract is to pay compensatory damages for any loss occurring as a result of breach. These would seem to be incompatible theoretical approaches, but as so often occurs, the best explanation lies somewhere between the two extremes.

My theory recognises the claimant's 'performance interest'.[24] However, this right is not unqualified, as the claimant is not always entitled to demand actual performance. Sometimes the claimant's performance interest may be satisfied by an award of compensatory damages if an alternative performance can be easily purchased with damages. Thus, sometimes, the defendant *is* effectively 'free' to breach his contract, subject to the obligation to pay damages.

[22] I adopt what Smith calls the 'moderate version' of morality. I seek to establish how the law of disgorgement damages might be thought to be justified, even if it is not: see Smith (n 9) 13, 18–23.

[23] B Chapman and M Trebilcock, 'Punitive Damages: Divergence in Search of a Rationale' (1989) 40 *Alabama Law Review* 741, 780.

[24] See (n 20).

Disgorgement damages are intended to vindicate the claimant's performance interest, and to strengthen the performance interest of future claimants by deterring other future defendants from breaching their contracts. Stripping defendants of their profit when they breach a contract in certain circumstances is a 'nudge'[25] to encourage parties to either perform their obligations or negotiate a release from the contract. If compensatory damages are inadequate to protect the claimant's performance interest and disgorgement damages are not awarded, a defendant has nothing to stop him from deliberately breaching a contract and leaving the claimant without a substitute performance. However, if profits are stripped from a defendant, there is no longer any incentive on the part of that defendant or other defendants to breach a contract in the future, at least without entering into negotiations with the claimant first. Ultimately, courts use disgorgement damages as 'self-policing' rules.

D Transparency

One of the primary difficulties with the law of disgorgement damages is that there is a distinct lack of transparency[26] in the accounts of courts and commentators. My theory does not square with what courts say they are doing in many cases. Courts tend to disguise their actions in three ways. First, they seek to obscure an award of disgorgement damages for second sales of property and shares under a constructive trust analysis, as discussed in chapter four. Secondly, many of the negative covenant cases which result in disgorgement of gains are clothed in a fiduciary analysis, albeit unconvincingly, as discussed in chapter five. Finally, courts tend to obscure disgorgement, particularly 'reasonable fee' awards or partial disgorgement, in the language of compensation, as discussed in chapter six. Partial disgorgement has also been analysed as a form of subtractive unjust enrichment, but I will argue that this analysis cannot be sustained for breach of contract.

Only a few cases explicitly recognise that gains are being disgorged for breach of contract. First, there is *Wrotham Park Estate Co Ltd v Parkside Homes Ltd*[27] which, in the words of Lord Nicholls in *Blake*, shone 'rather as a solitary beacon' because of its recognition of the possibility of partial disgorgement of profit for breach of contract.[28] Secondly, the Israeli Supreme Court explicitly awarded full disgorgement for breach of contract in *Adras Building Material v Harlow & Jones GmbH*.[29]

[25] See RH Thaler and CR Sunstein, *Nudge: Improving Decisions About Health, Wealth and Happiness* (New Haven, Yale University Press, 2008) 6.

[26] I adopt what Smith calls the 'moderate version' of transparency. I merely seek to establish how judges could sincerely (even if erroneously) believe that the reasons they give are correct: see Smith (n 9) 24, 28–32.

[27] *Wrotham Park Estate Co Ltd v Parkside Homes Ltd* [1974] 1 WLR 798 (Ch).

[28] *Blake* (n 1) 283.

[29] *Adras Building Material v Harlow & Jones GmbH* 42(1) PD 221, translated in (1995) 3 *Restitution Law Review* 235 (SC of Israel, 1988).

Finally, *Blake* is the watershed case that explicitly recognised the availability of disgorgement damages for breach of contract in mainstream common law.[30]

The lack of transparency originates partially from confusion as to what the law is. Following *Blake*, the cases of *World Wide Fund for Nature v World Wrestling Federation Entertainment Inc*[31] and *Experience Hendrix*[32] indicate that there is uncertainty as to when disgorgement damages should be awarded and what their measure should be. My theory seeks to address this.

Lawyers and courts are also conservative. They prefer to clothe new legal developments in existing doctrine, which is why disgorgement damages are disguised under unconvincing fiduciary analyses, categorised as 'compensatory damages', or justified as an incident of a constructive trust arising from a specifically enforceable contract of sale. In addition, damages arising from *Lord Cairns' Act* have tended to be seen as a narrow exceptional category rather than a broader principle which should be incorporated into contract law generally.

The divide between common law and equity also encourages courts to obscure awards of disgorgement.[33] Courts are far more willing to award disgorgement for breaches of equitable obligations than for breaches of common law obligations.[34] If disgorgement damages must be pigeonholed as equitable or legal, they should be seen as an operation of equity's auxiliary jurisdiction, like specific performance for breach of contract. But, as will be discussed in chapter two, courts and commentators often attempt to fit disgorgement damages into a compensatory framework,[35] in part, perhaps, because it is considered that only compensatory remedies are appropriate for breach of a legal obligation such as breach of contract.

A compensatory analysis is appealing for commentators and judges because it results in a restoration of what was taken from the claimant rather than the

[30] *Blake* (n 1) 283.

[31] *World Wide Fund for Nature v World Wrestling Federation Entertainment Inc* [2001] EWHC Ch 482 (Ch); *World Wide Fund for Nature v World Wrestling Federation Entertainment Inc* [2006] EWHC 184, [2006] FSR 38 (Ch); *World Wide Fund for Nature v World Wrestling Federation Entertainment Inc* [2007] EWCA Civ 286, [2008] 1 WLR 445 (CA) [29] (Chadwick LJ).

[32] *Experience Hendrix* (n 11).

[33] A Burrows, 'We Do This At Common Law But That In Equity' (2002) 22 *OJLS* 1, 12.

[34] S Worthington, 'Reconsidering Disgorgement for Wrongs' (1999) 62 *MLR* 218, 235.

[35] One method is the 'lost opportunity to bargain' theory: RJ Sharpe and SM Waddams, 'Damages for lost opportunity to bargain' (1982) 2 *OJLS* 290. Implicitly accepted in *Jaggard v Sawyer* [1995] 1 WLR 268 (CA) 291 (Millett LJ); *Gafford v Graham* (1999) 77 P & CR 73 (CA) 86 (Nourse LJ); *WWF – World Wide Fund for Nature v World Wrestling Federation Entertainment Inc* [2007] EWCA Civ 286, [2008] 1 WLR 445 (CA) [29] (Chadwick LJ). See criticisms of *WWF* in R Cunnington, 'A Lost Opportunity to Clarify' (2007) 122 *LQR* 47; R Cunnington, 'The Measure and Availability of Gain-Based Damages for Breach of Contract' in D Saidov and R Cunnington (eds), *Contract Damages: Domestic and International Perspectives* (Oxford, Hart Publishing, 2008) 207, 221; C Rotherham, '"*Wrotham Park* Damages" and Accounts of Profits' [2008] *LMCLQ* 25, 36–55.

Professor McInnes has argued that disgorgement damages are compensating for a lost right: see M McInnes, 'Account of Profits for Common Law Wrongs' in S Degeling and J Edelman (eds), *Equity in Commercial Law* (Pyrmont, NSW, Lawbook Co, 2004) 416–18; M McInnes, 'Gain, Loss and the User Principle' (2006) 14 *Restitution Law Review* 76, 84–86. However, see criticisms in A Burrows, 'Are "Damages on the *Wrotham Park* Basis" Compensatory, Restitutionary or Neither?' in R Cunnington and D Saidov (eds), *Contract Damages: Domestic and International Perspectives* (Oxford, Hart Publishing, 2008) 165, 173; Rotherham, ibid 44–45.

redistribution of a 'windfall' benefit to the claimant.[36] Distributive justice is seen to be innately suspicious: it involves a moral value judgement on the part of the decision maker, as well as a decision which involves depriving one party of a right to money or property.[37] But a compensatory analysis is difficult to fit with the existing law, particularly where full disgorgement is concerned, and it will be argued in chapter two that while some prefer the view that partial disgorgement damages operate to compensate for loss, the better analysis in the context of contract law is that they strip a defendant of gain.

While courts do not like the redistributive implications of disgorgement damages, it is submitted that it is preferable if courts are transparent about their actions rather than attempting to squeeze disgorgement damages into a compensatory scheme, which results in the definition of 'loss' being unduly expanded.

II Conclusion

My aim is to create a comprehensive interpretive theory of the law which provides the best explanation of the case law to date, and which allows lawyers, judges, litigants, academics and contractors to predict more easily when disgorgement damages will be awarded. In addition, I seek to balance the interests of the claimant and the defendant, and to be sensitive to the contractual context of awards of disgorgement damages.

Broadly speaking, disgorgement damages will only be awarded in exceptional circumstances: where there is a second sale, or where there is an agency problem. Nonetheless, it is hoped that they will provide an incentive for contractors to avoid idle promises which they do not intend to keep, or to negotiate a release from their obligations. In this way, disgorgement damages serve to vindicate the claimant's interest in performance of a contract, and to protect the performance interests of future claimants.

[36] C Rotherham, 'The Conceptual Structure of Restitution for Wrongs' (2007) 66 *CLJ* 172, 189–90.

[37] D Kennedy, 'Distributive and Paternalist Motives in Contract and Tort Law, with Special Reference to Compulsory Terms and Unequal Bargaining Power' (1982) 41 *Maryland Law Review* 563, 587.

2

Rationales Behind Disgorgement Damages

I Introduction

In this chapter we examine the moral rationales for awarding disgorgement damages. It is important that a convincing moral basis be established for awarding damages under this head, not only because it reinforces the moral legitimacy of private law but also because a coherent account of the law can only be given if it rests on sound foundations of legal morality.[1]

Remedies in private law are intended to vindicate the claimant's legal right as best as possible; in this context, the relevant right is the claimant's performance interest under the contract. Sometimes the best way of vindicating a contractual right is to award compensatory damages for the loss suffered, but as I will discuss in more detail in the next chapter, awarding 'expectation damages' for the claimant's loss is not the only way to vindicate a claimant's performance interest. Compensation is not the only moral rationale which informs vindication of the claimant's performance interest. Other moral rationales are also relevant, such as deterrence and punishment. In this context, I use vindication to mean a making good of a claimant's rights.[2] When vindicating the claimant's interest arising from entry into a contract, courts look primarily to the loss suffered (compensation), which may give the mistaken impression that this is *all* they look at. However, courts also seek to acknowledge the claimant's right, prevent the conduct from occurring again at the hands of that defendant or any other defendants (general and specific deterrence) and punish the defendant for failing to respect the claimant's right (retribution).

Although punitive or exemplary damages are distinguishable from disgorgement damages, they share common motivations and a common notoriety because these awards deviate from the perceived compensatory norm.[3] Professors Chapman and Trebilcock identify three potential rationales which may underlie awards of punitive damages:

[1] S Smith, *Contract Theory* (Oxford, Oxford University Press, 2004) 5.

[2] As do Dr Witzleb and Professor Carroll: see N Witzleb and R Carroll, 'The Role of Vindication in Torts Damages' (2009) 17 *Tort Law Review* 16, 17–19. See also *Oxford English Dictionary*, 'vindication, *n.*', 2nd edn (Clarendon Press, Oxford 1989) Vol XIX.

[3] J Edelman, *Gain-Based Damages – Contract, Tort, Equity and Intellectual Property* (Oxford, Hart Publishing, 2002) 5–23.

1. **Compensatory rationale** – to restore losses suffered by the claimant at the defendant's hands;
2. **Deterrent rationale** – to deter the defendant and others from engaging in similar conduct in the future; and
3. **Retributive rationale** – to punish the defendant for the conduct that has harmed the claimant.[4]

Only two of the rationales listed above convincingly provide a moral justification for full disgorgement damages: namely, deterrence and retribution. A compensatory analysis is perhaps more convincing for *Wrotham Park* damages, but as such damages are classified as 'partial disgorgement' in my scheme, deterrence and retribution provide the best justifications.

Deterrence is the central justification behind disgorgement damages. Professors Thel and Siegelman have argued that disgorgement remedies are 'a kind of anti-remedy' because they provide incentives that prevent the breach from occurring in the first place.[5]

At present, when compensatory damages are inadequate to protect the claimant's performance interest and specific relief, obtainable when the breach first occurred, is no longer available, a defendant has no incentive to stop him from breaching and leaving the claimant without a substitute performance. The claimant's performance interest remains unprotected. However, if profits are stripped from a defendant, there is no longer any inducement for that defendant or other defendants to breach a contract in the future, at least without entering into negotiations with the claimant first. The profit-stripping causes defendants to 'self-police' their behaviour. The particular claimant's interest is recognised by the fact that the court strips the defendant of his profit to which he would ordinarily be entitled under contract law, and gives it to the claimant.

Linked to the above, disgorgement also has a retributive or punitive rationale. This is admittedly a controversial argument. It should be emphasised that disgorgement is not as strongly retributive as punitive damages; punishment is limited to the stripping of the profit made by the contract breaker and includes no additional amount to represent social disapproval. Disgorgement merely puts the promisor in the situation he would have been in if he had done what he promised.[6] It does not strip him of anything additional. And as discussed in chapter six, there may be situations where it is appropriate to award only partial disgorgement. The retributive and deterrent power of the remedy depends on the proportion of the profit disgorged. Disgorgement is more punitive than compensatory damages, as it does not just compensate for loss, but explicitly removes any benefit from the defendant. In the vast majority of cases, a promisor is allowed to keep his gains made by breach, thus removal of gains is punitive. If the retributive

[4] B Chapman and M Trebilcock, 'Punitive Damages: Divergence in Search of a Rationale' (1989) 40 *Alabama Law Review* 741.

[5] S Thel and P Siegelman, 'You Do Have to Keep Your Promises: A Disgorgement Theory of Contract Remedies' (2011) 52 *William and Mary Law Review* 1181, 1239.

[6] ibid 1230, fn 206.

rationale were paramount, courts might allow the claimant to recover both her loss *and* the gain made by the defendant. The 'double recovery' rule operates to preclude this, suggesting that it operates to prevent retribution from playing too large a role in private law.

The two goals (deterrence and punishment) may work in tandem. For example, in *Attorney-General v Blake*,[7] the House of Lords case which first explicitly awarded disgorgement damages for breach of contract, deterrence and punishment worked together to produce the outcome. George Blake was a spy who betrayed the British Government and then, in breach of an ongoing negative covenant in his contract of employment, later wrote a book about his experiences without seeking permission. Part of the reasoning behind the award of the remedy was that Blake *deserved* to be punished by being stripped of his profit because of the advertent nature of the breach. Similarly, it was important that Blake and other people should be deterred from committing a similar action in the future. However, in other cases, considerations of punishment and desert may conflict with considerations of deterrence, particularly when the remedy awarded against the defendant is weakened or reduced in some way by considerations of desert. This will be discussed in chapter seven on bars to relief and allowances.

Courts consistently attempt to explain disgorgement damages with respect to compensatory principles,[8] and although this has some attraction in the area of partial disgorgement in particular, it cannot be sustained as a general explanation for disgorgement damages across the board. There is a lack of transparency about courts' explanations of awards of disgorgement damages, in the sense that they do not identify the real reasons behind the awards.[9] Judges may sincerely (even if erroneously) believe that the reasons they give are correct, but they misuse terms such as 'compensatory' in their reasoning. A compensatory analysis is appealing for commentators and judges because it *pretends* that the court has restored what was taken from the claimant rather than redistributing a 'windfall' benefit to the claimant.[10] Restoration is more doctrinally acceptable than the controversial redistribution of wealth which occurs with disgorgement.

Nonetheless, since courts are engaged in redistribution it is better to be open about this. A compensatory rationale cannot explain full disgorgement damages, whether as compensation for loss or substitutive compensation. It does not fit with what courts actually do unless the definitions of 'loss' and 'gain' are distorted. And while it is perhaps more arguable that partial disgorgement is compensatory in

[7] *Attorney-General v Blake* (*Blake*) [2000] UKHL 45, [2001] 1 AC 268 (HL).

[8] See, eg *Jaggard v Sawyer* (*Jaggard*) [1994] EWCA Civ 1, [1995] 1 WLR 268 (CA) 291 (Millett LJ); *Gafford v Graham* (*Gafford*) [1998] EWCA Civ 666, (1999) 77 P & CR 73 (CA) 86 (Nourse LJ); *WWF – World Wide Fund for Nature v World Wrestling Federation Entertainment Inc* (*WWF*) [2007] EWCA Civ 286, [2008] 1 WLR 445 (CA) [29] (Chadwick LJ); *Smith v Landstar Properties* (2011) BCCA 44 (BCCA) [39], [44] (Finch CJ). In tort, see *Strand Electric and Engineering Co Ltd v Brisford Entertainments Ltd* (*Strand Electric*) [1952] 2 QB 246 (CA) 256 (Romer LJ).

[9] Smith (n 1) 24, 28–32. I adopt the 'moderate' version of transparency according to Smith, which looks at the reasons judges give and attempts to unpick the difficulties of these reasons.

[10] C Rotherham, 'The Conceptual Structure of Restitution for Wrongs' (2007) 66 *CLJ* 172, 189–90.

nature, I argue that it is more coherent in a contractual context to see it as gain-based relief that is grounded in deterrence and retribution.

In this chapter, I will first consider the supposed compensatory rationale and suggest that it is not an appropriate justification for disgorgement damages. I will then consider, successively, the specific operation of deterrence and retribution.

II Compensatory Rationale

The rationale of compensatory damages for breach of contract is to restore the claimant to the position she would have been in had the defendant not breached the contract.[11] This is ordinarily achieved by means of an award of expectation damages.[12]

However, it has been pointed out that compensation can have two different meanings:

1. Compensation for loss, where money is given to compensate for factual loss caused to a person; and
2. Substitutive compensation, where money is given as a substitute for a right of which a person has been deprived.[13]

Compensation for loss is subjective, and corresponds to the actual loss suffered by the claimant, whereas substitutive compensation represents an objective valuation of the right of which the claimant has been deprived.[14] The importance of this distinction is that compensation for loss requires actual harm or financial loss to be suffered by the claimant, whereas it is irrelevant to substitutive compensation whether the claimant has suffered financial loss or harm: the important thing is that the claimant's right has been infringed.[15] The nature of the right gained under a contract will be discussed in detail in the section dealing with substitutive compensation.

Compensatory analyses of disgorgement damages for breach of contract are favoured by those who see the primary or only role of monetary remedies for breach of contract as being to compensate claimants for loss.

Analyses of this sort are also associated with the corrective justice theory of private law that focuses on the need for a correlative loss and gain. Drawing on

[11] Compare C Webb, 'Performance and Compensation: An Analysis of Contract Damages and Contractual Obligation' (2006) 26 *OJLS* 1.

[12] *Robinson v Harman* (1848) 1 Ex 850, 154 ER 363; *Photo Productions Ltd v Securicor Transport Ltd* [1980] UKHL 2, [1980] AC 827 (HL).

[13] R Cunnington, 'The Measure and Availability of Gain-Based Damages for Breach of Contract' in R Cunnington and D Saidov (eds), *Contract Damages: Domestic and International Perspectives* (Oxford, Hart Publishing, 2008) 207, 215; R Stevens, *Torts and Rights* (Oxford, Oxford University Press, 2007) 59–62.

[14] Cunnington (n 13) 215–16; Stevens (n 13) 60–61.

[15] Cunnington (n 13) 215–16; Stevens (n 13) 60–61.

Aristotelian notions of corrective justice, Professor Weinrib argues that private law can only intervene if there has been a gain on behalf of one party and a loss at the expense of the other.[16] Loss and gain are understood in normative terms rather than material terms.[17] 'The defendant enjoys a normative gain when he breaches a duty owed to the claimant; the claimant suffers a normative loss when she suffers the corresponding infringement of her right.'[18] The trigger for corrective justice is Kantian normative wrongdoing.[19] The parties can be regarded as notionally equal at the beginning of their interaction because of their status as 'self-determining agents', and corrective justice restores the parties to equality.[20] Corrective justice reduces the dispute between the parties to a bilateral *private* transaction.[21] The 'correlativity' between the parties creates the liability: one person gains at the other's expense.[22] The private law intervenes only to restore equality between the parties.

For an award of contractual damages to comply with this theory of corrective justice, 'not only must the breach of contract be a wrong to the promisee but the damages must be a measure of that wrong.'[23] Weinrib argues that the reasoning of the courts in disgorgement damages cases is instrumentalist. Promisees are awarded profit not because they can show an entitlement, but because they are 'conveniently situated for assisting in the accomplishment of certain social goals'.[24]

According to corrective justice theorists, awards which do not fit within a corrective justice framework are illegitimate. The appeal of a corrective justice analysis is that it seems less harsh and more justifiable, because the claimant is merely taking back what was hers in the first place, whereas disgorgement seeks to shift a windfall from the defendant to the claimant.[25]

A Compensation for Loss

If compensatory damages are seen as compensation for factual losses suffered by a person, then, by their very nature, full disgorgement damages do not fit within such a rationale. They do not compensate for the claimant's factual loss but seek

[16] E Weinrib, 'The Gains and Losses of Corrective Justice' (1994) 44 *Duke Law Journal* 277; E Weinrib, *The Idea of Private Law* (Cambridge, Mass., Harvard University Press, 1995); E Weinrib, 'Aristotle's Forms of Justice' in S Panagiotou (ed), *Justice, Law and Method in Plato and Aristotle* (Edmonton, Academic Print & Publishing, 1987) 133–52; E Weinrib, 'Restitutionary Damages as Corrective Justice' (2001) 1 *Theoretical Inquiries in Law* 1; E Weinrib, 'Corrective Justice in a Nutshell' (2002) 52 *University of Toronto Law Journal* 349; E Weinrib, 'Punishment and Disgorgement as Contract Remedies' (2003) 78 *Chicago-Kent Law Review* 55.

[17] Weinrib, *Idea of Private Law* (n 16) 76–83; Weinrib, 'Corrective Justice in a Nutshell' (n 16) 353–54.

[18] M McInnes, 'Unjust Enrichment: A Reply to Professor Weinrib' (2001) 9 *Restitution Law Review* 29, 35.

[19] Weinrib, *Idea of Private Law* (n 16) 84–113.

[20] ibid 76–83.

[21] ibid 43.

[22] ibid 76–83; Weinrib, 'Restitutionary Damages as Corrective Justice' (n 16) 5.

[23] Weinrib, *Idea of Private Law* (n 16) 75.

[24] ibid 77.

[25] Rotherham (n 10) 189–90.

to cause the defendant to disgorge his factual gain. There is no need for the claimant to have suffered any pecuniary loss. Therefore, it would appear difficult to fit full disgorgement damages into a compensatory rationale.

It has been argued, however, that some species of gain-based damages can be fitted into a compensatory rationale by means of the 'lost opportunity to bargain' analysis.[26] Justice Sharpe and Professor Waddams argue that when a defendant wrongfully uses another's property without diminishing its value, the defendant has nevertheless caused a real loss to the claimant, namely the loss of an opportunity to bargain.[27] The argument presumes a hypothetical bargain, where the defendant would have paid the claimant a reasonable sum for release from the contract or from an injunction restraining breach. By failing to bargain, the defendant has caused the claimant a pecuniary loss. This analysis has been implicitly adopted by English courts in a number of cases.[28]

However, the 'lost opportunity to bargain' analysis has been cogently criticised.[29] Waddams himself has accepted that it cannot explain all the relevant cases.[30] It is open to two objections. First, it introduces a fiction into legal analysis (the 'hypothetical bargain'). It presumes that the defendant would have agreed to 'buy the right' to break the contract, although often the facts indicate the very opposite. There is also an associated assumption that the claimant would have agreed to 'sell the right'.[31] As a result, it fails to explain the very cases for which an explanation is most necessary:[32] those cases where there was no opportunity to

[26] RJ Sharpe and SM Waddams, 'Damages for lost opportunity to bargain' (1982) 2 *OJLS* 290; SM Waddams, 'Gains Derived from Breach of Contract: Historical and Conceptual Perspectives' in R Cunnington and D Saidov (eds), *Contract Damages: Domestic and International Perspectives* (Oxford, Hart Publishing, 2008) 187, 192. (Waddams concedes in the latter piece that compensation cannot be the sole explanation of the cases, but argues that it is still relevant.) See also A Phang and P-W Lee, 'Rationalising Restitutionary Damages in Contract Law – An Elusive or Illusory Quest?' (2001) 17 *Journal of Contract Law* 240, 252–53.

[27] Sharpe and Waddams (n 26).

[28] *Jaggard* (n 8) 291 (Millett LJ); *Gafford* (n 8) 86 (Nourse LJ); *WWF* (n 8) [29] (Chadwick LJ). See also *Strand Electric* (n 8) 256 (Romer LJ).

[29] See, eg *Surrey County Council v Bredero Homes Ltd* [1993] EWCA Civ 7, [1993] 1 WLR 1361 (CA) 1369–70 (Steyn LJ); *Experience Hendrix LLC v PPX Enterprises Inc* [2003] EWCA Civ 323, [2003] 1 All ER (Comm) 830 (CA) [45] (Mance LJ), [57] (Peter Gibson LJ) (*Experience Hendrix*); P Birks, 'Profits for Breach of Contract' (1993) 109 *LQR* 518; W Goodhart, 'Restitutionary Damages for Breach of Contract: The Remedy that Dare Not Speak its Name' [1995] *Restitution Law Review* 3, 7; J Edelman, 'The Compensation Strait-Jacket and the Lost Opportunity to Bargain' [2001] *Restitution Law Review* 104; A Burrows, *The Law of Restitution*, 2nd edn (London, Butterworths, 2002) 477; G Virgo, *Principles of the Law of Restitution*, 2nd edn (Oxford, Clarendon Press, 2006) 439–40; R Cunnington, 'A Lost Opportunity to Clarify' (2007) 122 *LQR* 47; A Burrows, 'Are Damages on the '*Wrotham Park* Basis' Compensatory, Restitutionary or Neither?' in D Saidov and R Cunnington (eds), *Contract Damages: Domestic and International Perspectives* (Oxford, Hart Publishing, 2008) 165, 169–71; R Cunnington, 'The Assessment of Gain-Based Damages for Breach of Contract' (2008) 71 *MLR* 559, 562–63; Cunnington, 'The Measure and Availability' (n 13) 220; S Harder, *Measuring Damages in the Law of Obligations* (Oxford, Hart Publishing, 2010) 180–81.

[30] SM Waddams, *Dimensions of Private Law* (Cambridge, Cambridge University Press, 2003) 108; Waddams, 'Gains Derived from Breach of Contract' (n 26) 192.

[31] Burrows, 'Damages on the '*Wrotham Park* Basis'' (n 29) 170.

[32] C Rotherham, '"*Wrotham Park* Damages" and Accounts of Profits' [2008] *Lloyd's Maritime and Commercial Law Quarterly* 25, 31; Cunnington, 'The Assessment of Gain-Based Damages' (n 29) 562–63.

bargain with the defendant, and the claimant would never have agreed to a release of the injunction in the first place.[33] *Wrotham Park Estate Co Ltd v Parkside Homes Ltd*[34] is a case in point. The question of release from bargain arose when the defendants breached a negative covenant in favour of the claimant which provided that no more than a specified number of houses could be built on certain land. The first defendants, Parkside Homes Ltd, purchased land from the claimants and built more houses than specified on the land. Brightman J said:

> On the facts of this particular case the plaintiffs, rightly conscious of their obligations towards existing residents would clearly not have granted any relaxation but for present purposes I must assume they could have been induced to do so.[35]

In addition, Brightman J noted that the claimants could not have lawfully used the covenant to demand money from the defendants.[36] Given this, it cannot be said that the claimant lost an opportunity to bargain because he never possessed it in the first place, and nor would he have exercised it if he had had it. Similarly, the loss of opportunity to bargain theory cannot explain cases where the contract or covenant would not have been specifically enforceable. Again, this was the case in *Wrotham Park*. The second defendants were the owners and mortgagees of the houses built in breach of the negative covenant. They did not complete their purchase of the property until after the building work had been completed, by which time the court was not prepared to award a mandatory injunction.[37] There never was an opportunity for the claimant to bargain with the second defendant.[38] Thus, the theory does not fit well with the factual scenarios it is trying to explain, and it lacks coherence. It follows from these criticisms that the 'lost opportunity to bargain' analysis is flawed as a general explanation for cases of gain-based damages, unless one simply sees the 'hypothetical bargain' as a yardstick for measuring the value of the right infringed rather than as compensation for an *actual* factual loss.[39] Even then, there are still difficulties with a substitutive compensation analysis, as will be discussed in the next section.

Gabriel Moss QC in *Tamares (Vincent Square) Ltd v Fairpoint*[40] suggested that *Wrotham Park* could be rationalised as compensation for the claimant's 'lost opportunity to apply for an injunction'. This works well in cases where the defendant has gained an advantage over the claimant, but it is less convincing where the claimant could have applied for an injunction but failed to do so, or where the court refused to order an injunction for discretionary reasons.[41] In those cases, the claimant did not lose an opportunity to apply for an injunction,

[33] Cunnington, 'The Measure and Availability' (n 13) 221.

[34] *Wrotham Park Estate Co Ltd v Parkside Homes Ltd* (*Wrotham Park*) [1974] 1 WLR 798 (Ch).

[35] ibid 815.

[36] Cunnington, 'The Assessment of Gain-Based Damages' (n 29) 562–63.

[37] *Wrotham Park* (n 34) 811.

[38] Cunnington, 'The Assessment of Gain-Based Damages' (n 29) 563.

[39] See, eg M McInnes, 'Gain, Loss and the User Principle' (2006) 14 *Restitution Law Review* 76, 84–86.

[40] *Tamares (Vincent Square) Ltd v Fairpoint* [2007] EWHC 212 (Ch).

[41] Cunnington, 'The Assessment of Gain-Based Damages' (n 29) 563.

but either did not take it in the first place, or took his opportunity but was refused an award by the court.[42]

Accordingly, disgorgement damages for breach of contract cannot be justified according to a compensatory rationale because they do not compensate for a factual loss.

B Substitutive Compensation

'Substitutive compensation' is where money is given as a *compensatory substitute* for a right of which a person has been deprived. In the context of contract law, the defendant gives the claimant a specific undertaking to perform a particular stipulated action. This is a voluntary right which is only exigible against the person who has made the undertaking.[43] In Hohfeldian terms, an ordinary contract creates a 'claim right'.[44] Alice can claim that Boris has a duty to do or to refrain from doing a particular act because Boris created an obligation towards Alice when they entered into a voluntary undertaking together. The contract gives rise to a 'performance interest' on the part of Alice that needs to be recognised. The question is then how the law recognises an infringement or a deprivation of that right. Specific relief attempts to grant the primary right to performance under the contract itself; by contrast, substitutive compensation attempts to put a monetary value on the deprivation of the right.

Stevens has a broader analysis, mentioned below, which does not confine substitutive damages for the right to the compensatory rationale alone, and may extend to restitutionary damages and disgorgement damages in appropriate cases.

i Compensation for a Lost Right

It is argued that some of the cases of gain-based damages or restitutionary damages are actually instances of 'substitutive compensation'.

Professor McInnes argues that the 'user principle' cases compensate the claimant for the value of her lost right of *dominium* (being the right to control access and to use her property).[45] McInnes groups together various 'user principle' cases involving an award of a 'reasonable fee', including cases of trespass arising from

[42] ibid.

[43] Stevens (n 13) 9–10.

[44] W Hohfeld, 'Some Fundamental Legal Conceptions As Applied In Judicial Reasoning' (1913) 23 *Yale Law Journal* 16; W Hohfeld, 'Fundamental Legal Conceptions As Applied In Judicial Reasoning' (1917) 26 *Yale Law Journal* 710.

[45] M McInnes, 'Account of Profits for Common Law Wrongs' in S Degeling and J Edelman (ed), *Equity in Commercial Law* (NSW, Lawbook Co, 2004) 405, 416–18; McInnes (n 39) 84–86. See J Edelman, 'Gain-Based Damages and Compensation' in A Burrows and Lord Rodger of Earlsferry (eds), *Mapping the Law – Essays in Honour of Peter Birks* (Oxford, Oxford University Press, 2006) 141, 153–58 for an attempt to reconcile this approach with restitutionary damages.

Giglio has also argued that the 'user principle' cases are compensatory: see F Giglio, *The Foundations of Restitution for Wrongs* (Oxford, Hart Publishing, 2007). For a detailed analysis and critique of Giglio's arguments, see Rotherham (n 32) 45–52.

wrongful occupation of land,[46] trespass arising from wrongful use of land,[47] detention of chattels[48] and nuisance[49] (all varieties of proprietary tort). He argues that these cases involve a violation of a property right, and that by making an award of damages, the law is assigning a monetary value to the claimant's injury to her right.[50] The hypothetical bargain used in the 'reasonable fee' cases is simply a method of valuing the claimant's right, and the focus is on why the claimant could have demanded a bargain from the defendant in the first place.[51] As will be canvassed in chapter six, I have some sympathy for McInnes' view in this latter regard; however, I see the 'reasonable fee' as a yardstick by which to measure gain instead.

McInnes extends his analysis to contract cases such as *Wrotham Park*, where he says the award of a reasonable fee is intended to protect the claimant's *dominium*.[52] He does not explain whether a 'reasonable fee' award will or should be awarded in a case where a contract is not intended to protect property rights. Presumably he considers that 'reasonable fee' awards can only be made for breach of contract when the contract seeks to protect a proprietary interest (as in *Wrotham Park*). His concept of substitutive compensation for a lost right is tied inextricably to property rights and the use value of those rights, not to a contractual right to performance.

McInnes' analysis has been criticised on the basis that it is difficult to understand what loss has occurred when a right, such as the right to performance of a contract, has been infringed.[53] The claimant has not *lost* a right: she retains the same rights she had before the wrong was committed. It has been hypothesised that perhaps McInnes had in mind the claimant's loss of opportunity to exercise the control accorded to her by her proprietary rights over the property.[54] However, McInnes' analysis does not explain those cases where the claimant did not lose the right to control her property right, but rather chose not to exercise her right or, after attempting to exercise her right, was denied that opportunity by the court.[55]

[46] *Penarth Dock Engineering Co Ltd v Pounds* [1963] 1 Lloyd's Rep 359; *Swordheath Properties Ltd v Tabet* [1979] 1 WLR 285 (CA); *Ministry of Defence v Ashman* [1993] 2 EGLR 102 (CA); *Ministry of Defence v Thompson* [1993] 2 EGLR 107 (CA); *Inverugie Investments Ltd v Hackett* [1995] 1 WLR 713 (PC); *Gondal v Dillon Newsagents Ltd* [2001] *RLR* 221, [1998] EWCA Civ 1324 (CA).

[47] *Martin v Porter* (1839) 5 M & W 351, 151 ER 149; *Jegon v Vivian* (1871) LR 6 Ch App 742; *Whitwham v Westminster Brymbo Coal and Coke Co* [1896] 2 Ch 538 (CA); *Phillips v Homfray (No. 1)* (1871) LR 6 Ch App 770 (CA); *Phillips v Homfray (No. 2)* (1883) 24 Ch D 439 (CA); *Bracewell v Appleby* [1975] Ch 408; *Jaggard* (n 8); *Yakamia Dairy Pty Ltd v Wood* [1976] WAR 57 (WASC).

[48] *Strand Electric* (n 8); *Hillesden Securities Ltd v Ryjack Ltd* [1983] 1 WLR 959 (QB); *Gaba Formwork Contractors Pty Ltd v Turner Corporation Ltd* (1991) 32 NSWLR 175 (NSWSC). See recently *Chep Australia Ltd v Bunnings Group Ltd* [2010] NSWSC 301 (NSWSC).

[49] *Carr-Saunders v Dick McNeil Associates* [1986] 1 WLR 922 (Ch).

[50] McInnes, 'Account of Profits for Common Law Wrongs' (n 45) 416.

[51] McInnes (n 39) 85.

[52] ibid 84–85.

[53] Burrows, 'Damages on the '*Wrotham Park* Basis'' (n 29) 173; Rotherham (n 32) 44–45. Against Cunnington, 'The Assessment of Gain-Based Damages' (n 29) 564.

[54] Burrows, 'Damages on the '*Wrotham Park* Basis'' (n 29) 173.

[55] ibid. See, eg *Wrotham Park* (n 34) and *Tamares* (n 40). Burrows argues that characterising such cases as compensatory on the basis of the loss of an opportunity to apply for an injunction fails for similar reasons: Burrows, ibid 171–72, referring to the reasons of Gabriel Moss QC in *Tamares*.

It also leaves unexplained those cases where a reasonable fee or disgorgement damages have been awarded for breach of contract, but no relevant proprietary right was infringed.[56]

Professor Benson has engaged in a variant of the 'compensation for a lost right argument' in an attempt to situate disgorgement damages within a corrective justice analysis. He analogises interference with certain contractual rights with a tortious interference with property rights.[57] He argues that where property rights are protected by tort, there is a 'taking from' the rights of the claimant and a 'taking by' the defendant which renders the liability correlative.[58] The 'quantitative representation of an injury' may be either the claimant's loss flowing from the interference with her property right *or* the defendant's gain made by using or disposing of the property, and the rights behind that injury have the necessary correlative structure.[59] He states:

> So long as the loss or gain can be conceived as a *quantitative determination of injury*, the remedy that cancels it, whether by repairing the plaintiff's loss or by disgorging the defendant's gain, comes under a single regulative principle. It fulfils the aim of putting the party in the same position as he or she would have been if he or she had not sustained the wrong.[60]

The defendant's gain represents what the defendant took from the claimant, and accordingly, it represents the *value* of the injury in a correlative sense.[61]

Extending this analysis to breach of contract, Benson argues that in some circumstances, non-performance by the promisor is a usurpation of the promisee's exclusive authority to possess, use or alienate the benefit received under the contract.[62] However, where the subject matter of the contract is not unique, the promisor does not violate the promisee's right: as long as the promisor pays compensatory damages, this will be an adequate reflection of the value of the promisee's right.[63] It is only where the subject matter of the contract is unique that the promisor violates the promisee's right in such a way as to demand specific performance, or, Benson argues, disgorgement damages for breach of contract.[64] As will be evident from the discussion in chapter three, I agree with Benson's analysis in this respect.

[56] See, eg *Reid-Newfoundland Co v Anglo-American Telegraph Co Ltd* [1912] AC 555 (PC); *Reading v Attorney General* [1951] AC 507 (HL); *Adras Building Material v Harlow & Jones GmbH* 42(1) PD 221, translated in (1995) 3 *Restitution Law Review* 235 (SC of Israel, 1988); *United States v Snepp*, 444 US 507 (USSC, 1980); *Blake* (n 7); *Esso Petroleum Company Limited v Niad Limited* [2001] EWHC Ch 458, [2001] All ER (D) 324 (Ch).

[57] P Benson, 'Disgorgement for Breach of Contract and Corrective Justice: An Analysis in Outline' in J Neyers, M McInnes and S Pitel, *Understanding Unjust Enrichment* (Oxford, Hart Publishing, 2004) 311, 321–30.

[58] ibid 316–17.

[59] ibid 318.

[60] ibid.

[61] ibid 320.

[62] ibid 326.

[63] ibid 327.

[64] ibid 327–30.

However, Benson engages in sleight of hand, glossing over the question of whether or not the claimant has suffered a factual loss. He is only able to justify disgorgement damages for breach of contract by saying that gain-based damages can be regarded as 'compensatory' in a broad sense, arguing that they compensate the claimant for the value of the injury *as measured from the defendant's perspective* (ie by causing the defendant to disgorge his gain).[65] By this method Benson argues that the claimant is restored to the situation she would have been in if the contract had been performed.

His analysis fails to recognise the importance of the performance interest in contract law remedies. Contract law is not simply concerned to redress harm, but to place the claimant in the position she would have been if the contract had been performed. On a factual basis, in many cases, surely the claimant would not have been in a position to recoup the defendant's gain if the contract had been performed. Of course, this may depend on the nature of the contract. In fiduciary contracts the beneficiary generally would obtain the profit but for the breach, since it was the fiduciary's duty to make the profit for the beneficiary. Nonetheless, in the vast majority of ordinary contracts, this argument perpetuates a fiction, and disgorgement damages cannot be regarded as compensatory without adopting a concept of 'loss' which is so broad as to be practically meaningless. It suffers from a lack of coherence in that the concept of 'loss' adopted lacks consistency and intelligibility.

By contrast, Andrew Botterell has undertaken a corrective justice analysis of disgorgement damages for contract which is cognisant of the importance of contractual performance.[66] He argues that a Kantian view of contract does not necessarily preclude a finding that disgorgement damages are available for breach of contract, because it can be shown that for some contracts, the promisee has a right not to the thing promised, but that the promisor is obliged to perform a particular action.[67] This leads to an implied promise that the promisor will not perform an action (such as selling the subject matter of the contract to a third party) which renders the particular action impossible.[68] Botterell says:

> In sum, the problem with Weinrib's argument is his assumption that an entitlement to the action contracted for cannot give rise to the acquisition of a right that is sufficiently fine-grained to justify awarding disgorgement damages in cases of contractual breach. To assume this, however, is to confuse having a right of ownership with having a proprietary right. Weinrib seems to assume that if there is no proprietary right to a thing, there can be no right of ownership 'nearby'.[69] But if Alice has a right that Bert contractually perform some particular action A, then, on the current view, Alice has an ownership right in A as

[65] See S Stoljar, 'Restitutionary Relief for Breach of Contract' (1989) 2 *Journal of Contract Law* 1, 3, for similar arguments.

[66] A Botterell, 'Contractual Performance, Corrective Justice, and Disgorgement for Breach of Contract' (2010) 16 *Legal Theory* 135.

[67] ibid 149–54.

[68] ibid 150–54.

[69] In Ben McFarlane's terminology, this could be said to be an equitable proprietary right, ie a 'right to a right'. See B McFarlane, *The Structure of Property Law* (Oxford, Hart Publishing, 2008).

> well as an ownership right in any action of Bert's that is incompatible with A. Consequently, where A is a particular action and where Bert's doing B is incompatible with his doing A, then Alice is entitled by way of damages to any profits realized by Bert as a result of doing B. Because doing B is something over which Alice can assert a right of ownership, any gains that result from Bert's doing B properly belong to Alice.[70]

Botterell argues that this may render disgorgement damages compensatory, as disgorgement damages return the promisee to the position she should have been in had the contract been performed (ie the claimant gets the profits deriving from the item she contracted for).[71] However, he acknowledges that whether disgorgement damages are compensatory depends on one's view of what 'compensation' means, and if it means compensation for factual loss, it is difficult to argue that disgorgement damages are compensatory.[72] Again, as with Benson's analysis, in many cases it is difficult to argue that the claimant would have been entitled to recoup the gain the defendant made if the contract had been performed, unless, as mentioned previously, the contract was a fiduciary one.

The most convincing argument in this area is that *Wrotham Park* damages are a form of compensation because they compensate for the loss of the right to performance, as (where contracts are concerned at least) the objective value of the right infringed will always be the same as the objective value of the benefit received.[73]

However, a disgorgement analysis should be preferred because one of the preconditions for an award of *Wrotham Park* damages is that compensatory damages must be inadequate, and if *Wrotham Park* damages are themselves compensatory, then one of the preconditions for their award has not been met.[74] Dr Odudu and Professor Virgo argue that any analysis of *Wrotham Park* damages must be more nuanced:

> These restitutionary awards will be made where the claimant has not suffered a pecuniary loss. Instead the courts appear willing to identify a different type of loss arising from the invasion of the claimant's rights. Indeed, in *Blake*, Lord Nicholls of Birkenhead recognises that user damages are exceptions to the general rule that damages are assessed on the basis that they compensate the claimant for loss or injury. Consequently these remedies are available where no financial loss has been suffered and so, although the terms are not expressly used, compensatory damages can be considered to be inadequate. But this analysis will only work if compensatory damages are considered to compensate for a particular type of loss, namely pecuniary loss, and the inadequacy arises simply from the fact that this type of loss was not suffered.[75]

As will become evident in chapter three, I argue that the purpose of expectation damages is twofold: to compensate for the claimant's pecuniary loss and to recog-

[70] Botterell (n 66) 150–51.
[71] ibid 157–58.
[72] ibid 158.
[73] Cunnington, 'The Assessment of Gain-Based Damages' (n 29) 565–67.
[74] ibid 567; O Odudu and G Virgo, 'Inadequacy of Compensatory Damages' [2009] *Restitution Law Review* 112, 118.
[75] Odudu and Virgo (n 74).

nise the claimant's performance interest. If there is no pecuniary loss suffered but the claimant nevertheless requires recognition of her performance interest, it is in this circumstance that compensatory damages will be inadequate and specific relief or disgorgement should be considered.

ii Rights-based Analysis

This analysis is based on the work of Professor Stevens.[76] Properly speaking, in his analysis, substitutive damages are not confined to the compensatory rationale, and may extend to restitutionary damages and disgorgement damages in appropriate cases.

Stevens argues that substitutive damages are not awarded to eradicate harm, but as the 'next best' response the law can give instead of the primary right.[77] Compensation for loss is neither the only response to the deprivation or infringement of a right, nor is it always the 'next best' response – sometimes the defendant's gain represents a better substitute for the right infringed.[78] Damages will be awarded even if there is no loss to the claimant or gain to the defendant consequent upon infringement of the right.[79] Thus, it could be argued that where the claimant has been deprived of her right to performance, the defendant's gain may represent the best substitute for the claimant's right to performance if compensatory damages and specific relief are both unavailable.

The problem with disgorgement damages is that, as Weinrib has noted, while a deterrent or a punitive rationale may establish why the defendant should surrender his gain, it fails to indicate why *this* claimant in particular should get an award of disgorgement damages.[80] Stevens argues that once an award is seen as a form of substitutive damages for the infringement of the claimant's rights, this argument falls away.[81] If one argues that the right of which the claimant has been deprived is the right to contractual performance, it is possible to argue that disgorgement damages are a substitute for the deprivation of this right which can no longer be awarded through specific relief (disgorgement damages are effectively a substitute for specific relief). It is the deprivation of this right which creates the nexus between the defendant's gain and the claimant as a suitable recipient of that gain. Stevens' arguments form an essential link in establishing the claimant's entitlement to disgorgement damages above that of any other random member of society.

Stevens notes that insofar as breach of contract was concerned, Mr Justice Holmes considered that the contracting party's duty was to perform *or* to pay damages for failing to perform, making it appear that the obligation to pay

[76] Stevens (n 13).
[77] ibid 60.
[78] Against J Edelman, 'The Meaning of Loss and Enrichment' in R Chambers, C Mitchell and J Penner (eds), *Philosophical Foundations of the Law of Unjust Enrichment* (Oxford, Oxford University Press, 2009) 221, 223–26.
[79] Stevens (n 13).
[80] Weinrib, 'Punishment and Disgorgement' (n 16) 74.
[81] Stevens (n 13) 86.

damages is not triggered by a wrong. However, Stevens argues, this ignores the fact that the secondary right to damages is the 'next best' substitute for the primary right.[82] He observes that courts have 'failed to adopt a consistent approach and it is difficult, if not impossible, to reconcile the authorities.'[83] Therefore, it appears that courts will sometimes award substitutive damages for breach of contract, but sometimes they will not.[84]

The analysis of Stevens is more convincing than that of Benson, as Stevens concedes that a claimant cannot really be restored to the same position she would have been in if she had not sustained the injury, but that substitutive damages attempt to provide the 'next best' solution.[85] Further, he does not see disgorgement damages as 'compensatory' as this would involve an illegitimate stretching of the concepts of 'loss' and 'gain'. Rather, disgorgement damages are substitutive for the right.

The main difficulty with Stevens' analysis, as he freely concedes, is the difficulty of isolating which rights can be infringed by a defendant in such a way as to give rise to substitutive damages.[86] In the context of disgorgement damages for breach of contract, however, this problem is not present. The right is the right to performance, and the infringement of this right will give rise to disgorgement damages in the situations where the subject matter of the contract is not substitutable.[87]

Burrows has criticised Stevens' analysis, saying:

> The Stevens approach is flawed in imagining that we sensibly can, or would want to, put a value on the right that has been infringed without considering the consequential impact of that infringement. In principle I would argue that the value of a right infringed should be measured by the consequences of the infringement for the victim; and that is what the traditional compensatory approach does[88]

It is important to have regard to the consequences of infringement for the victim. It is *only* if damages are inadequate to compensate for the claimant's right to performance and if substitute performance is no longer available that disgorgement damages should be considered.

The question remains whether disgorgement damages are truly substitutive. They are *not* a substitute for performance in the same way that expectation dam-

[82] ibid.

[83] ibid 70.

[84] Stevens cites *Alfred McAlpine Construction Ltd v Panatown Ltd* [2000] UKHL 43, [2001] 1 AC 518 (HL) where the court was divided as to whether to award substitutive damages for breach of contract. The case was complicated by the fact that the undertaking to take reasonable skill and care in constructing the building in question had been given to a party other than the party who had entered into the building contract with the defendant.

[85] See also S Smith, 'Performance, Punishment and the Nature of Contractual Obligation' (1997) 60 *MLR* 360 on rectification damages as pecuniary substitutes for the lost right.

[86] Stevens (n 13) 329.

[87] It should be noted that Stevens is likely to disagree with this use of his analysis, at least insofar as *Wrotham Park* is concerned: see R Stevens, 'Damages and the Right to Performance: A *Golden Victory* or Not?' in J Neyers, R Bronagh and S Pitel (eds), *Exploring Contract Law* (Oxford, Hart Publishing, 2009) 171, 192–93.

[88] Burrows (n 29) 185.

ages are, nor can they award the actual performance contracted for in the way that specific relief does. While in our notional hierarchy of remedies in contract law specific relief is awarded where compensation for the claimant's factual loss is inadequate, disgorgement damages are not awarded as a substitute for compensation for the claimant's factual loss. Indeed, whether or not the claimant has suffered a factual loss is irrelevant to disgorgement.[89] The claimant need not have suffered any factual loss at all.[90] However, it is sometimes said that disgorgement damages are awarded 'in lieu of' specific relief when specific relief has been put out of the claimant's reach by the defendant, just as *Lord Cairns' Act* damages are awarded in lieu of injunctive relief. It is in this sense that disgorgement damages could be said to be a substitute for the right to specific relief, which is in turn an award of the actual performance right made in lieu of compensatory damages. Nonetheless, they are a very imperfect substitute for specific relief, and their intention is more to vindicate the claimant's right, to deter the defendant and others from breaching such contracts in the future, and to punish the defendant for breaching this particular contract.

C Conclusion

It is difficult to argue that full disgorgement damages are compensatory, although they may be considered to be a possible substitute for the claimant's right to specific relief according to Stevens' broader conception of substitutive damages, which encompasses restitutionary and disgorgement damages.

The temptation for courts and scholars to classify disgorgement damages as compensatory should be resisted. A compensatory rationale makes the award look less controversial, but it does not actually *fit* with what courts do unless one invokes fictions such as the 'lost opportunity to bargain' analysis, or, alternatively, unduly extends the concepts of 'gain' and 'loss'. It is perhaps easier to argue that partial disgorgement damages are compensatory than it is to argue the same with regard to full disgorgement damages. However, the requirement that compensatory damages must be inadequate before 'reasonable fee' awards are made would make no sense if 'reasonable fee' awards are in fact compensatory. It therefore makes more sense to seem them as gain-based.

Duncan Kennedy has noted that courts and lawyers are deeply distrustful of distributive motives.[91] This is because it involves making a value judgement about who deserves a particular resource. Distributive awards are often 'zero sum' –

[89] MA Eisenberg, 'The Disgorgement Interest in Contract Law' (2006) 105 *Michigan Law Review* 559, 561; L Smith, 'Disgorgement of the Profits of Breach of Contract: Property, Contract and "Efficient Breach"' (1994) 24 *Canadian Business Law Journal* 121, 122.

[90] 'Factual loss' looks to the consequential losses suffered as a result of the breach and the actual losses suffered by the claimant. In this way, it differs from substitutive compensation, which seeks to objectively compensate the claimant for the infringement of a right. See Stevens (n 13) 60–61.

[91] D Kennedy, 'Distributive and Paternalist Motives in Contract and Tort Law, with Special Reference to Compulsory Terms and Unequal Bargaining Power' (1982) 41 *Maryland Law Review* 563, 587.

helping one party (the claimant in this situation) means hurting the other (the defendant in this situation).[92] Nonetheless, it is far better for courts to be transparent about what they are really doing when they make disgorgement damages awards: they are redistributing the defendant's profit to the claimant.

This redistribution can be morally justified by the fact that the defendant has deprived the claimant of her right to performance, and that some form of vindication is required. The two rationales which underlie and justify awards of disgorgement damages are deterrence and retribution.[93] It is to these that we now turn.

III Deterrent Rationale

The primary reason for awarding disgorgement damages is deterrence.[94] Perfect disgorgement strips the defendant of his profit and puts him in the position he would have been in if the breach had not been committed.[95] Because the defendant receives no gain from breach, disgorgement damages remove any incentive for future potential contract breakers to breach and thereby make a profit.

Deterrence looks to deterring future conduct. It has two aspects, specific and general deterrence. Specific deterrence is concerned only with deterring the specific defendant in question from repeating the wrongful conduct. General deterrence warns other would-be wrongdoers of the consequences of their conduct. Both species of deterrence are found in disgorgement damages. The forward-looking nature of deterrence is in contrast to the backward-looking nature of the retributive rationale.[96] Clearly, in an individual case, once disgorgement damages are awarded for breach of contract it is too late to deter that particular defendant from breaching; but that defendant or other potential defendants will be deterred from repeating the conduct in the future.

The question is then *why* breach of contract needs to be deterred in some circumstances. First, it is necessary to deter breach of contract in some circumstances in order to protect the interests of future claimants in having their contracts performed.

However, the legitimacy of the deterrent aspect of disgorgement damages depends in part as to how the obligations arising from breach of a contract are viewed, because the ambivalence towards the performance interest goes to the root of the contractual obligation itself. There are two extremes. On the one hand, some, such as Professor Daniel Friedmann, argue that '[t]he essence of contract is

[92] ibid 571.

[93] Rotherham (n 10) 189–90.

[94] Edelman (n 3) 83–86; Edelman (n 45) 149.

[95] R Cooter and T Ulen, *Law and Economics*, 3rd edn (Reading, Mass, Addison-Wesley, 2000) 234.

[96] J Berryman, 'The Case For Restitutionary Damages Over Punitive Damages: Teaching the Wrongdoer that Tort does not Pay' (1994) 73 *Canadian Bar Review* 320, 322.

performance.'[97] On the other hand, others, such as Mr Justice Holmes of the US Supreme Court[98] and the proponents of 'efficient breach',[99] argue that the only obligation arising from breach of a contract is an obligation to pay expectation damages. This book takes the middle line, arguing that in some circumstances the only obligation is to pay expectation damages, but in other circumstances, the claimant has a legitimate expectation that the contractual obligation itself will be performed.

The second reason why breaches of contract should be deterred in some circumstances is because it may result in greater efficiency. Disgorgement damages ensure that the party who is tempted to breach 'self-polices' his actions. The administrative costs for enforcing contracts are reduced and the presence of disgorgement damages as a remedy for breach ensures that a promisor is likely to perform when the subject matter of the contract is non-substitutable. Furthermore, if disgorgement damages loom as a possible remedy, a promisor is likely to hesitate before making a promise he does not intend to keep. Punitive damages would perhaps perform a similar function, but disgorgement damages are more subtle and less retributive.[100]

Not all contracts will give rise to liability for disgorgement damages. Substitutability helps to ensure disgorgement damages are not over-deterrent. I will first consider the nature of the contractual obligation and the need for a deterrent sanction in *some* circumstances. I will then go on to consider efficiency arguments for sanctions which deter breach of contract. Finally, I will briefly outline the idea of substitutability, a concept which will be explained in greater detail in chapter three.

A Deterrence and the Nature of Contractual Obligation

If performance is the essence of contract, then it is arguable that disgorgement is an important remedy because it provides an incentive to perform rather than breach.[101] Consequently, Friedmann, who coined the term 'performance interest', is an avowed proponent of disgorgement damages for breach of contract.[102] Even Weinrib acknowledges that disgorgement damages could be justified on the basis that they encourage parties to keep their bargains, a correlative duty within his

[97] D Friedmann, 'The Performance Interest in Contract Damages' (1995) 111 *LQR* 628, 629.

[98] OW Holmes Jnr, 'The Path of the Law' (1897) 10 *Harvard Law Review* 457, 462. See also OW Holmes Jnr, *The Common Law* (Boston, Little & Brown, 1881) 301.

[99] See, eg R Posner, *Economic Analysis of Law*, 8th edn (New York, Aspen Walters Kluwer, 2011) 149–58.

[100] Edelman (n 3) 17.

[101] Against Smith (n 85) 370–71. While Smith argues that the aim of contract law is to provide performance, he says that contractors should not be forced to perform by remedies such as specific performance because this would cause parties to perform *for the wrong motive*, and thus the intangible benefits of bonding and trust will be weakened.

[102] D Friedmann, 'Restitution of Benefits Obtained Through the Appropriation of Property or the Commission of a Wrong' (1980) 80 *Columbia Law Review* 504; D Friedmann, 'Restitution of Profits Gained by Party in Breach of Contract' (1988) 104 *LQR* 383; Friedmann (n 97).

scheme of corrective justice.[103] Professor Fried argues that a promisor creates rights in the promisee because the making of the promise has created an expectation in the promisee. Thus, according to Fried's promissory analysis of contract law, the disappointment of the promisee's expectation is a wrongful abuse of trust.[104] Fried himself does not consider the reasons why contract law privileges expectation damages over specific relief,[105] let alone disgorgement damages. Nonetheless, under a promissory analysis, disgorgement damages could be said to vindicate the wrongful abuse of trust occasioned by breach of contract.

On the other hand, if the primary obligation arising from a contract is merely to pay compensatory damages for loss, then there should be no incentive for a contractor to perform. As long as the breaching party pays damages, the primary obligation has been fulfilled, and it is illegitimate to force a promisor to perform.

The two ways of looking at the obligations arising from the contract are reflected in the remedies for breach.[106] There is a notional hierarchy of remedies whereby remedies such as specific performance and injunctions are seen as exceptional, and dependent upon the 'inadequacy of damages' at law.[107] It has been said that 'our law of contract is not so much about enforcing promises as compensating for their breach.'[108] Some argue that the present regime of contractual remedies does not prioritise the claimant's interest in performance.[109] Given the law's preference for damages over specific relief, it is no surprise that the explanation of the 'efficient breach' scholars has proved influential. On the other hand, the very existence of the concept of 'inadequacy of damages' and the availability of remedies such as specific performance shows that our law *does* attach considerable importance to performance, in some circumstances at least.

It will be suggested in chapter three that neither view wholly fits with the data provided by the cases (ie that contracts must always be performed or that the only contractual obligation is to pay damages). Instead, the truth is somewhere in between, depending on the subject matter of the contract. Disgorgement is likely

[103] Weinrib, 'Punishment and Disgorgement as Contract Remedies' (n 16) 73. See also R Grantham and CEF Rickett, *Enrichment and Restitution in New Zealand* (Oxford, Hart Publishing, 2000) 476 who make a similar point.

[104] C Fried, *Contract As Promise – A Theory of Contractual Obligation* (Cambridge, Mass, Harvard University Press, 1981) 14–17. See R O'Dair, 'Damages for Breach of Contract' (1993) 46 *Current Legal Problems* 113, 121.

[105] R Craswell, 'Contract Law, Default Rules and the Philosophy of Promising' (1989) 88 *Michigan Law Review* 489, 517–20; Smith (n 85) 362. See also American Law Institute, *Restatement (Third) of Restitution and Unjust Enrichment* (2011) § 39 comment c.

[106] B Coote, 'Contract Damages, *Ruxley*, and the Performance Interest' (1997) 56 *CLJ* 537, 540–42; E McKendrick, 'The Common Law at Work: the Saga of *Alfred McAlpine Construction Ltd v Panatown Ltd*' (2003) 3 *Oxford University Commonwealth Law Journal* 145, 167–68; Webb (n 11) 45–49; D Pearce and R Halson, 'Damages for Breach of Contract: Compensation, Restitution and Vindication' (2008) 28 *OJLS* 73, 79–80.

[107] M Tilbury, *Civil Remedies – Volume I* (Sydney, Butterworths, 1993) [1021]. Against D Laycock, 'The Death of the Irreparable Injury Rule' (1990) 103 *Harvard Law Review* 687.

[108] NC Seddon and MP Ellinghaus, *Cheshire and Fifoot's Law of Contract*, 8th Australian edn (Chatswood, NSW, LexisNexis Butterworths, 2002) 1021–22, [24.1].

[109] ibid; E McKendrick, 'Breach of Contract and the Meaning of Loss' (1999) 52 *Current Legal Problems* 37, 38.

to be ordered in circumstances where courts have indicated that performance would be ordered (ie specific performance, injunction to restrain breach of negative covenant or a breach of contract which is concurrent with a breach of fiduciary duty). However, if compensatory damages are 'adequate' to put the claimant in a position as if the contract had been performed, then there is no need to deter breach.

B Deterrence and Efficiency

Deterrence of breach of contract is also justifiable on the grounds of economic efficiency. Deterrence is a utilitarian principle, aimed not only at deterring the particular defendant in a particular case, but also other potential defendants generally. As a result, remedies with a deterrent effect are favoured by some law and economics scholars who wish to create efficient incentives for contract performance.[110]

Professor Cooter and Mr Freedman have argued that disgorgement remedies awarded against breaching fiduciaries provide an efficient way of policing the behaviour of fiduciaries and preventing them from misappropriating trust property.[111] The disgorgement remedies available for breach of fiduciary duty ensure that the sanction equals the gain from wrongdoing, thus ensuring successful deterrence.[112] If beneficiaries had the burden of detecting and proving the fiduciary's breach of duty, the sanction would not adequately punish the fiduciary. The fiduciary would be more likely than not to profit from misappropriating assets.[113] Far from being economically inefficient, the laws with regard to fiduciary duties are economically efficient, as they provide for 'self-policing' by the fiduciary. The same kind of argument can be extended to some kinds of contract, particularly those contracts I will discuss in chapter five which lie on the margin between fiduciary duties and contract law.

Thel and Siegelman argue that disgorgement damages for breach of contract maximise economic efficiency in a variety of ways. First, disgorgement damages minimise the administrative costs of enforcing contracts for courts.[114] When awarding expectation damages, courts have to decide what would have occurred if the promise had been fulfilled, which is often a difficult question. It is preferable if the parties can come to an agreement *without* needing the intervention of the

[110] EA Farnsworth, 'Your Loss or My Gain? The Dilemma of the Disgorgement Principle in Breach of Contract' (1985) 94 *Yale Law Journal* 1339; SW DeLong, 'The Efficiency of a Disgorgement as a Remedy for Breach of Contract' (1989) 22 *Indiana Law Review* 737; MA Eisenberg, 'The Disgorgement Interest in Contract Law' (2006) 105 *Michigan Law Review* 559. The first two authors see a limited role for disgorgement damages in contract law, but they concede that there is *some* role.

[111] R Cooter and BJ Freedman, 'The Fiduciary Relationship: Its Economic Character and Legal Consequences' (1991) 66 *New York University Law Review* 1045.

[112] ibid 1052.

[113] ibid 1052–53.

[114] Thel and Siegelman (n 5) 1224–25.

state via the court system.[115] Parties are likely to refrain from making idle promises if they know that they will have to disgorge any profits from the breach. Alternatively, the breaching party may attempt to negotiate a release from obligations instead of breaching, which means that a dispute is more likely to be resolved privately between the parties. If courts order disgorgement on a regular basis, they may prevent breaches from occurring;[116] that is to say, they will achieve general deterrence.

Disgorgement damages are also more efficient for the contracting parties because they act as a bonding device between the parties, an assurance for the promisee that the promisor will perform:

> The answer lies in the fact that expectation remedies as actually administered are systematically and unavoidably *under*compensatory. If promisees cannot count on their expectations being satisfied, *promisors* will suffer because promisees will insist on a reduced contract price in the shadow of the undercompensatory remedies that they will receive in event of breach. Promisors thus are keenly interested in assuring promisees that they will not interfere with the latter's expectations, for by doing so they will get higher prices ex ante.
>
> The disgorgement regime outlined above is thus best understood as a bonding device. By subjecting himself to disgorgement, the promisor gives valuable assurance to the promisee – for which he is presumably compensated – and suffers no risk of penalty: he will never be worse off than he would have been if he had performed.[117]

While law and economics scholars of the Chicago School would argue that 'efficient breach' is the preferable rule, it is also arguable that disgorgement damages provide an efficient resolution to contract disputes. Disgorgement damages encourage parties either to perform their obligations or to negotiate a release from the contract, rather than unilaterally breaching the contract and potentially leaving a claimant without a substitute performance.

In addition, an incentive to prevent breach is needed because the failure of a party to perform a contract not only harms the promisee herself but also undermines society's confidence in contracting generally.[118] If parties are not confident that their bargained-for interests will be protected by law, they will be reluctant to contract and the impact upon commercial activity and efficiency will be negative.[119]

However, not *all* promisors should be deterred from breaching. The role of substitutability in preventing over-deterrence will be examined next.

[115] G Calabresi and AD Melamed, 'Property Rules, Liability Rules, and Inalienability: One View of the Cathedral' (1972) 85 *Harvard Law Review* 1089, 1093.

[116] A Choi and G Triantis, 'Completing Contracts in the Shadow of Costly Verification' (2008) 37 *Journal of Legal Studies* 503 argue that liquidated damages prevent parties from breaching.

[117] Thel and Siegelman (n 5) 1227–28.

[118] J Raz, 'Promises in Morality and Law' (1982) 95 *Harvard Law Review* 916, 933; Fried (n 104) 13.

[119] Cunnington, 'The Measure and Availability' (n 13) 240.

C Deterrence and Substitutability

The addition of disgorgement damages to the panoply of remedies may allow a court to better protect the contracting parties' performance interest because they deter potential defendants from breaching contracts. We wish to deter defendants from breaching their contracts because in *some circumstances* the law considers that it is particularly important that a promise be kept. Nonetheless, there must be a limit to the deterrent effect of disgorgement damages. There is a risk of 'over-deterrence' if disgorgement damages are routinely awarded as a remedy for breach. It is important to stress that not every breach of contract will give rise to a liability for disgorgement damages, if only because not every breach results in the defendant profiting from the breach. A decision to award disgorgement damages cannot and should not rest on whether or not a particular judge thinks it was 'fair' of the defendant to breach his contract. There must be clear and predictable criteria which indicate when a defendant will be deterred from breaching his contract by the imposition of disgorgement damages.

The concept of *substitutability* is the key to the inquiry which must be made by courts, and lends coherence to my analysis. Substitutability is central to the operation of common law remedies for breach of contract. Ordinarily, the common law presumes that expectation damages will suffice to provide a substitute performance. Specific relief will be ordered in circumstances where the claimant would be unable (or find it very difficult) to procure a substitute performance.[120] Because the claimant's interest in performance will not be adequately recognised by an award of compensatory damages, she is justified in compelling the defendant to perform the contract. Various commentators have observed that if specific relief was or ought to have been available to a claimant in a contract claim, but is no longer available, and compensatory damages are inadequate, it is likely that the claimant may be able to seek disgorgement damages in lieu of specific relief, assuming that the defendant has made a gain from the breach of contract.[121]

The availability of disgorgement damages for breach of contract operates to deter a potential defendant from unfairly resiling from his obligations in a way which will prejudice the interests of the claimant. By deterring potential defendants from breaching contractual obligations, the law protects the claimant's 'performance interest' in a way which is coherent with existing law. Disgorgement

[120] *Adderley v Dixon* (1824) 1 Sim & St 607, 610, 57 ER 239, 240.

[121] SM Waddams, 'Restitution As Part of Contract Law' in A Burrows (ed), *Essays on the Law of Restitution* (Oxford, Oxford University Press, 1991) 197, 208–09; P Jaffey, *The Nature and Scope of Restitution* (Oxford, Hart Publishing, 2000) 390–94; Grantham and Rickett (n 103) 480–81; S Doyle and D Wright, 'Restitutionary Damages – The Unnecessary Remedy?' (2001) 25 *Melbourne University Law Review* 1, 11–13; Edelman (n 3) 152–55; Benson (n 57) 327–30; P Jaffey, 'Disgorgement and "Licence Fee Damages" in Contract' (2004) 20 *Journal of Contract Law* 57, 61; Eisenberg (n 110) 582; Cunnington, 'The Measure and Availability' (n 13); Waddams, 'Gains Derived from Breach of Contract' (n 26) 205–06; R Cunnington, 'The Inadequacy of Damages as a Remedy for Breach of Contract' in CEF Rickett (ed), *Justifying Private Law Remedies* (Oxford, Hart Publishing, 2008) 115; Botterell (n 66) 151–53. See also American Law Institute (n 105) § 39 comment c.

damages give teeth to the principle of *pacta sunt servanda*, and may encourage parties to keep to their bargains.[122] A deterrent rationale will not focus so much on the quality of the defendant's breach (a retributive concern) but on whether the kind of bargain is one where parties should be deterred from breach. Nonetheless, deterrence only operates effectively when a breach is conscious. An unconscious contractual breach cannot be deterred because there is no conscious decision on the part of the defendant from which he can be deterred.

Still, the way in which courts and commentators assess the quality of the defendant's breach gives us a hint that there is an underlying retributive motive behind disgorgement damages for breach of contract.

IV Retributive Rationale

The early analyses of disgorgement damages frequently emphasise that the defendant's conduct is wrongful or that the defendant has been 'unjustly enriched'.[123] It is often said that no one shall be allowed to profit from his own wrong.[124] The moral basis of the retributive rationale is that the defendant has engaged in wrongful conduct and ought to be punished.

A retributive rationale is backward-looking and desert-based rather than forward-looking and consequentialist.[125] It is essential that any punishment must be deserved. Kant argues:

> Judicial punishment can never be used merely as a means to promote some other good for the criminal himself or for civil society, but instead it must in all cases be imposed on him only on the ground that he has committed a crime; for a human being can never be manipulated merely as a means to the purposes of someone else and can never be confused with the objects of the Law of things. . . . He must first be found to be deserving of punishment before any consideration is given to the utility of this punishment for himself or for his fellow citizens.[126]

Disgorgement has a punitive rationale, but it is not as penal as punitive damages; it merely puts the promisor in the situation he would have been in if he had done what he promised.[127] It does not take more.

[122] Weinrib, 'Punishment and Disgorgement as Contract Remedies' (n 16) 73.

[123] See, eg J Dawson, 'Restitution or Damages' (1959) 20 *Ohio State Law Review* 175, 186–87; IGE Palmer, *The Law of Restitution* (Boston, Little & Brown, 1978) 438; Friedmann, 'Restitution of Benefits' (n 102); G Jones, 'The Recovery of Benefits Gained from a Breach of Contract' (1983) 99 *LQR* 443.

[124] See, eg *Halifax Building Society v Thomas* [1995] EWCA Civ 21, [1995] 4 All ER 673 (CA); *Riggs v Palmer* 22 NE 188, 190; 115 NY 506, 511 (NYCA, 1889). The new *Restatement* explicitly states 'A person is not permitted to profit by his own wrong': American Law Institute (n 105) §3. See also H McGregor, 'Restitutionary Damages' in P Birks (ed), *Wrongs and Remedies in the Twenty-First Century* (Oxford, Clarendon Press, 1996) 203, 209.

[125] Chapman and Trebilcock (n 4) 780.

[126] I Kant, *The Metaphysical Elements of Justice* (John Ladd trans, 1965) 100 [trans of: *Metaphysische Anfangsgründe der Rechtslehre*].

[127] Thel and Siegelman (n 5) 1230, fn 206.

The argument that disgorgement damages have a punitive aim is perhaps even more controversial than the argument that they have a deterrent aim. Indeed it has been said by Lord Hoffman that, 'the purpose of the law of contract is not to punish wrongdoing but to satisfy the expectations of the party entitled to performance.'[128] It could be argued that a punitive justification is inappropriate in a contractual context and unnecessary for disgorgement damages specifically because the deterrent aim explains fully the way in which they operate. However, this does not fit with the cases themselves, some of which exhibit a strong punitive aspect, and thus to ignore this justification is to close one's eyes to an important reason why courts order disgorgement.

A The Retributive Aspect of Disgorgement Damages

Disgorgement damages are sometimes said to be 'quasi-punitive'.[129] Jaffey argues that 'punishment is inflicted for the purpose of upholding the community's interest in the performance of the duty broken and of legal duties in general.'[130] Edelman has argued that *Blake* has a punitive aspect, exemplified in the refusal of the House of Lords to award an allowance for Blake's skill and effort.[131] Indeed, the opening line of Lord Nicholls' speech drips with condemnation of the defendant: 'My Lords, George Blake is a notorious, self-confessed traitor.'[132]

Questions of punishment raise a logically prior question: in the circumstances, does this particular defendant *deserve* to keep this gain? The consideration of 'desert' implies that disgorgement damages have a distributive element. Scholars such as Weinrib have argued that questions of desert should not enter into private law.[133] Punishment is said to be an inappropriate or illegitimate purpose for private law to pursue.[134] Weinrib argues that punishment is a one-sided consideration which is incompatible with notions of corrective justice and the equality of treatment required by corrective justice, because it focuses on the blameworthiness of the conduct of the defendant.[135] In addition, it is said that punishment should not be part of private law because it seeks to vindicate not just the specific relationship between the parties but the broader regime of rights. The proper

[128] *Co-operative Insurance Society v Argyll Stores (Holdings) Ltd* [1998] AC 1 (HL) 15 (Lord Hoffman).

[129] United Kingdom and Northern Ireland Law Commission, *Aggravated, Exemplary and Restitutionary Damages* (Law Com No 247, 1997) para 7.18; Jaffey, *Nature and Scope of Restitution* (n 121) 374–76. See also C Mitchell, 'Remedial Inadequacy in Contract and the Role of Restitutionary Damages' (1999) 15 *Journal of Contract Law* 1, 9–10: '[r]estitutionary damages in this sense have a punitive character – their concern is to condemn and discourage the behaviour of the defendant by removing any benefits he has gained from his wrong.' Against Grantham and Rickett (n 103) 487.

[130] Jaffey (n 129) 375.

[131] Edelman (n 3) 171–72; *cf* Cunnington, 'The Assessment of Gain-Based Damages' (n 29) 576–77.

[132] *Blake* (n 7) 275.

[133] Weinrib, *The Idea of Private Law* (n 16) 74.

[134] Weinrib, 'Punishment and Disgorgement as Contract Remedies' (n 16) 86–87; A Beever, 'The Structure of Aggravated and Exemplary Damages' (2003) 23 *OJLS* 87; S Todd, 'A New Zealand Perspective on Exemplary Damages' (2004) 33 *Common Law World Review* 255.

[135] Weinrib, 'Punishment and Disgorgement as Contract Remedies' (n 16) 86–87.

party to enforce the broader regime of rights is the state, via the mechanism of the criminal law.[136] It has also been argued that a retributive rationale requires the extra procedural and evidentiary constraints which are associated with the criminal law protections for the accused.[137]

These arguments can be rebutted. Retribution is used in a narrower sense in this area than in the criminal law, as it focuses on the infringement and vindication of a *private right*.[138] Further, the argument that compensation is solely a function of private law and punishment is solely a function of criminal law fails to 'fit' with the reality of what courts do.[139] The true division is not between punishment and compensation, but between the individual enforcement of rights and a public attribution of blame by the state.[140] Disgorgement damages are not a criminal punishment, and they do not supplement the criminal law.[141] Therefore, the stigma and approbation which attach to criminal offences enforced by the state do not apply in the case of disgorgement damages.[142]

Pey-Woan Lee has questioned Weinrib's assertion that punishment is necessarily incompatible with normative corrective justice (specifically, in relation to punitive damages for breach of contract).[143] She queries why awards which bear a correlative structure according to Weinrib are invariably compensatory rather than punitive.[144] Weinrib's arguments with regard to punitive damages reflect a 'compensate or punish' rationale, but Lee argues that normative corrective justice need not do so.[145] Punitive damages *can* fit within a corrective justice framework if one first accepts the importance of performing one's contractual obligation, and then adopts the retributive theory of Jean Hampton (which, like Weinrib's normative corrective justice, is premised on the Kantian theory of human worth).[146] A person who commits a wrong against another demeans the other, because it is implicit that he considers his rights of greater worth than those of the victim, a notion that Hampton calls 'moral injury'. A retributive response is justified as it denies the wrongdoer's moral elevation and vindicates the equality of the parties. Lee concludes that punitive damages are a hybrid remedy with both

[136] See further Chapman and Trebilcock (n 4) 782.

[137] Weinrib, 'Punishment and Disgorgement as Contract Remedies' (n 16) 100–01; Chapman and Trebilcock (n 4) 804–05; Jaffey, *Nature and Scope of Restitution* (n 121) 376–78; *Cassell & Co Ltd v Broome* [1972] AC 1027 (HL) 1100 (Lord Morris).

[138] Stevens (n 13) 85. Against Jaffey (n 121) 376.

[139] Edelman (n 3) 19; R Cunnington, 'Should Punitive Damages be Part of the Judicial Arsenal in Contract Cases?' (2006) 26 *Legal Studies* 369, 380–81; Jaffey (n 121) 378.

[140] Cunnington (n 139) 381. It has been observed that the distinction between wrongs directed against individuals and against the state is not workable or useful: Smith (n 85) 366.

[141] Cunnington (n 139); Stevens (n 13) 86. These pieces deal with punitive damages, but the same argument holds for disgorgement damages.

[142] ibid.

[143] P-W Lee, 'Contract Damages, Corrective Justice and Punishment' (2007) 70 *MLR* 887.

[144] ibid 893.

[145] ibid 895.

[146] J Hampton, 'The Retributive Idea' in J Murphy and J Hampton (eds), *Forgiveness and Mercy* (Cambridge, Cambridge University Press, 1988) 111, 131–41; J Hampton, 'Correcting Harm Versus Righting Wrongs: The Goal of Retribution' (1992) 39 *UCLA Law Review* 1659.

compensatory and retributive elements. The victim of breach is compensated for the moral injury done to her because of the violation to her liberty.[147] She argues that:

> [a]dhering to a retributive analysis is critical in emphasising the role of private law in protecting the objective worth of the human agent, and not merely her physical or psychological well being (as the traditional emphasis on compensation is wont to do).[148]

Similar arguments can be made with respect to disgorgement damages. It can be argued that by breaching a contract, the defendant has caused a moral injury to the claimant. He has done 'the very thing he contracted not to do',[149] and implicitly elevated his rights against the rights of the claimant, and thus he should be punished. It should be emphasised, however, that disgorgement damages are not designed to compensate the claimant for a moral injury, and do not reflect the harm in any sense. By contrast, it is arguable that punitive damages seek to compensate the claimant for her moral injury, and that the award reflects the harm.

Punitive damages and disgorgement damages could also be said to be vindicatory, as they vindicate the claimant's right to performance of a contract.[150] One of the functions of punishment is to express a public vindication of the claimant's rights.[151] It follows that a remedy which vindicates the claimant's rights and returns a defendant to the position he would have been in if he had performed his obligations under the contract expresses a punitive motive. The court condemns the violation of the claimant's rights by stripping the defendant's gain from him. As noted earlier, the punitive rationale is stronger if the court instead awards punitive damages, placing the defendant in a *worse* position than if he had properly performed his obligations.

It has been established that punitive rationales can be present in private law generally. However, before detailing how the punitive rationale shapes disgorgement damages, we must deal with the suggestion that remedies which are based in equity do not (or should not) have a punitive character, and the argument that punitive remedies should not be available for breach of contract.

B *Digital Pulse* and Punishment

If disgorgement damages must be pigeonholed as equitable or legal, they should be seen as an operation of equity's auxiliary jurisdiction, like specific performance for breach of contract. But this means that, in an Australian context at least, any assignment of a punitive function to such damages is inconsistent with the

[147] Lee (n 143) 898.
[148] ibid.
[149] *Attorney-General v Blake* [1997] EWCA Civ 3008, [1998] Ch 439 (CA) 458 (Lord Woolf).
[150] Some have argued that contract remedies have a vindicatory aspect, eg the making good of a claimant's right: see Pearce and Halson (n 106).
[151] J Feinberg, 'The Expressive Function of Punishment' in J Feinberg, *Doing and Deserving* (Princeton, Princeton University Press, 1970) 95, 104.

holding of a majority of the New South Wales Court of Appeal in *Harris v Digital Pulse Pty Ltd*[152] that an account of profits awarded for breach of fiduciary obligation is not punitive in nature. Heydon JA went further and suggested that equitable remedies were not explicable in terms of punitive rationales. Spigelman CJ suggested that punitive damages were not available for breach of contract or breach of fiduciary duty. Mason P dissented on both matters, and it will be suggested that his Honour's judgment should be preferred.

In *Digital Pulse*, Digital Pulse Pty Ltd ('Digital') conducted an information technology business that provided website design. The first and second defendants, Harris and Eden, were employees of Digital. Their contracts of employment contained express terms preventing them from competing with Digital during the term of their employment. They also owed fiduciary duties of loyalty to Digital. However, they were dissatisfied with Digital and set up their own business. While still employed at Digital, they diverted work from Digital towards their new business. Later, the defendants incorporated a new company called 'Juice-D' which received the payments for the work diverted from Digital. Both defendants were directors of Juice-D. Digital sued the defendants and Juice-D in a variety of causes of actions, including breach of fiduciary duty. Importantly for present purposes, Digital sought exemplary damages for breach of fiduciary duty. At trial Palmer J awarded $10,000 against both Harris and Eden, representing exemplary damages for breach of fiduciary duty.[153] Harris and Eden appealed to the New South Wales Court of Appeal.

Heydon JA's judgment is the most trenchantly opposed to the notion of equitable remedies having a punitive aspect. His Honour expressly rejected the suggestion that the imposition of an account of profits for breach of fiduciary duty had a penal aspect. It is hardly surprising that he did so, as the fourth edition of *Meagher, Gummow and Lehane's Equity: Doctrines and Remedies* (of which Heydon JA was one of the authors) contained a summary of the decision that was very critical of the trial judgment.[154]

The primary focus of Heydon JA's judgment was on whether equity permitted penal remedies. His Honour said:

> [W]hile it is true that these rules [which apply to dishonest fiduciaries] have a deterrent and prophylactic function, like the whole regime applying to fiduciaries in apposition of conflict of duty and interest or duty and duty, they are not penal in character.[155]

[152] *Harris v Digital Pulse Pty Ltd (Digital Pulse)* [2003] NSWCA 10, (2003) 56 NSWLR 298 (NSWCA). Compare *Cook v Evatt (No 2)* [1992] 1 NZLR 676 (NZHC); *Aquaculture Corp v New Zealand Green Mussel Co Ltd* [1990] 3 NZLR 299 (NZCA); *Norberg v Wynrib* [1992] 2 SCR 226 (SCC).

[153] *Digital Pulse v Harris* (2002) 166 FLR 421 (NSWSC) 449.

[154] RP Meagher, JD Heydon and MJ Leeming, *Meagher, Gummow and Lehane's Equity: Doctrines and Remedies*, 4th edn (Sydney, Butterworths, 2002) 839:

> Palmer J ('the poor man's Robin Cooke') has disregarded all this learning and principle, and decided that damages [can] be awarded in a claim for equitable compensation . . . but one hopes that this is a decision that will never be followed.

[155] *Digital Pulse* (n 152) 369 (Heydon JA).

In his opinion, the basis of the remedy was the extent to which the defendant had been unjustly enriched. With respect, this conclusion cannot be correct because the High Court in *Warman International Ltd v Dwyer* concluded that unjust enrichment was not the exclusive basis for an account of profits for breach of fiduciary duty.[156] Unjust enrichment is concerned with the reversal of transfers of value, whereas there is no need for a transfer of value from the claimant to the defendant for an account of profits to be awarded.[157]

His Honour argued that the use of the words 'penal', 'punitive', 'punishment' and 'prophylactic' to describe equitable remedies was often misunderstood.[158] He said:

> The rules relating to an account of profits are not restitutionary in the sense that they do not rest on giving back something which the plaintiff once had, or restoring the plaintiff to a state of affairs which the plaintiff once occupied but has lost because of the fiduciary's behaviour, or requiring some damage to the pre-existing position of the principal, or compensating the principal for some loss suffered. They strip the fiduciary of gains whether or not the plaintiff could ever had [sic] made the gains in question. No doubt the strictness of the rules, in tending to prevent fiduciary temptation arising and thus tending to protect the principal from fiduciary misconduct, tends to deter fiduciaries from misconduct themselves. But it does not follow that the rules are punitive.[159]

Accordingly, his Honour concluded that exemplary damages could not be awarded for an equitable wrong because they were a 'criminal sanction', giving them a penal aspect which was not appropriate to a court of equity.[160]

Mason P dissented. His Honour said:

> The discretionary remedies of constructive trust (or lien) and accounting of profits are part of equity's ample armoury when dealing with cases of breach of fiduciary duty. Their functions and purposes are the preclusion of unjust enrichment and deterrence, both general and specific. In one sense, the former function looks to the private rights of the parties whereas the latter expresses more general public concerns.
>
> The various functions of exemplary damages also inhere in the single remedial act. The 'public' function is triggered on the 'private' initiative of the affected plaintiff who pockets the fruits of the award. In such a context, the distinction between deterrence and punishment is illusory. It would be entirely lost on the defendant. This is a distinction that is not drawn with regard to the award of exemplary damages generally.[161]

[156] J Birch, 'Exemplary Damages for Breach of Fiduciary Duty' (2005) 33 *Australian Business Law Review* 429, 436–37; *Warman International Ltd v Dwyer* (1995) 182 CLR 544, 557 (HCA). Against *Dart Industries Inc v Décor Corporation Pty Ltd* (1993) 179 CLR 101, 111 (HCA), in which the High Court held that an account of profits awarded for the infringement of a patent was based on unjust enrichment.

[157] Birch (n 156).

[158] *Digital Pulse* (n 152) 406 (Heydon JA).

[159] ibid 409 (Heydon JA).

[160] ibid 422 (Heydon JA).

[161] ibid 332 (Mason P).

He said that exemplary damages exhibited a composite goal, including punishing, deterring and vindicating the injury to the victim.[162] With respect, it is submitted that Mason P's judgment is correct.[163]

The award of exemplary damages in *Digital Pulse* should not have depended upon whether equity supports punitive remedies. Exemplary or punitive damages could be available for breach of fiduciary duty in some very limited and exceptional cases, but *Digital Pulse* was perhaps not a suitable case for awarding them because the conduct of the defendants was not difficult to monitor, and there was not the requisite deterrent justification. This was illustrated by the fact that the defendants' operations were quickly found out and terminated, and that they only succeeded in making a small profit.[164]

Disgorgement damages also display a composite rationale. In any event, none of the judgments deny that an account of profits may have a deterrent character. Despite this, Heydon JA would be unlikely to approve of a deterrent *justification* for an account of profits, even if he acknowledges its deterrent *effect* in *Digital Pulse.*

Spigelman CJ also found that exemplary damages should not be awarded, but his Honour disagreed with Heydon JA in two important respects. First, he disagreed with Heydon JA's characterisation of exemplary damages as a criminal sanction.[165] Secondly, his Honour did not rule out punitive monetary awards in equity altogether. Rather, his Honour considered that a breach of fiduciary duty was analogous to a breach of contract for which exemplary damages are unavailable in Australia.[166] Thus, it followed that exemplary damages should be similarly unavailable for breach of fiduciary duty. He also drew an analogy with the rule preventing penalty clauses in contract,[167] although it is questionable how convincing this analogy is, given that penalty clauses are agreed between the parties and reviewed by the courts, whereas exemplary damages are wholly under the control of the courts, and thus entirely different in nature.

Spigelman CJ's judgment contains the assumption that punitive damages are not available for breach of contract in Australia,[168] and an inference could be drawn from this that *any* remedy with a punitive justification should not be available for breach of contract.

[162] ibid 335 (Mason P).

[163] Birch (n 156); D Morgan, '*Harris v Digital Pulse*: The Availability of Exemplary Damages in Equity' (2003) 29 *Monash University Law Review* 377; J Edelman, 'A "Fusion Fallacy" Fallacy?' (2003) 119 *LQR* 375; A Burrows, 'Remedial Coherence and Punitive Damages in Equity' in S Degeling and J Edelman (eds), *Equity in Commercial Law* (NSW, Lawbook Co, 2005) 381.

[164] It should be noted that Palmer J was particularly influenced by the consistent dishonesty of Eden and Harris, the cynical and conscious nature of the breach, and the fact that there had probably been more business which Juice-D had taken from Digital, but no evidence was available. *Digital Pulse* (n 153) 437–39.

[165] *Digital Pulse* (n 152) 303 (Spigelman CJ). Against *Digital Pulse* (n 152) 353 (Mason P).

[166] See *Gray v Motor Accident Commission* (*Gray*) (1998) 196 CLR 1 (HCA) 6–7; *Hospitality Group Pty Ltd v Australian Rugby Union Ltd* (*Hospitality Group*) (2001) 110 FCR 157 (FCA) 191, 197. Against *Flamingo Park Pty Ltd v Dolly Dolly Creation Pty Ltd* (1986) 65 ALR 500 (FCA).

[167] *Digital Pulse* (n 152) 312 (Spigelman CJ).

[168] *Digital Pulse* (n 152) 304 (Spigelman CJ).

There is American, English and New Zealand authority that punitive damages are unavailable for breach of contract.[169] By contrast, punitive damages are available for breach of contract in Canada.[170] Australian law is unclear. It has been queried whether there is binding Australian authority which operates to rule out punitive damages for breach of contract.[171] Griffith CJ said in *Butler v Fairclough* that the wilfulness of the breach should not affect the measure of damages for breach of contract, but these observations were obiter only.[172] Spigelman CJ cited *Gray*, but the High Court said in that case that the rule against awarding exemplary damages for breach of contract was only an 'apparent rule'.[173] In *Hospitality Group*,[174] a majority of the Full Federal Court held that punitive damages were not available for breach of contract on the basis of the House of Lords' decision in *Addis*,[175] but *Addis* is not binding in Australia, especially after the High Court decided in *Uren v John Fairfax & Sons Pty Ltd*[176] that it would not follow the English authority of *Rookes v Barnard*[177] on exemplary damages.

Thyssen lists the policy reasons why courts are generally averse to awarding punitive damages for breach of contract.[178] First, it is said that the law of contracts mostly governs commercial relationships, where the amount required to compensate for loss is easy to calculate, in contrast to the law of torts. The rebuttal to this is that some further remedy should be available for those breaches of contract where the loss is *not* easy to calculate. Secondly, it is argued that punitive damages are unavailable for breaches of contract because they do not cause the same kind of distress or discomfort as torts, but this is a generalisation, and there are surely circumstances where a breach of contract is more distressing than a tort. Compare, for example, the benighted family in *Whiten*, who suffered gravely because of an insurance company's breach of contract,[179] with a case like *Strand Electric*, where the defendant committed the tort of detinue by retaining the claimant's switchboards.[180] It is impossible to generalise that breaches of contract do not cause distress but torts do. Thirdly, it is argued that punitive damages for breach of contract would prevent efficient breaches from occurring. For reasons which will be raised in detail in chapter four, this is unlikely to occur with disgorgement damages for

[169] See American Law Institute, *Restatement (Second) of the Law of Contracts* (1981), § 355: 'Punitive damages are not recoverable for a breach of contract unless the conduct constituting the breach is also a tort for which punitive damages are recoverable'; *Thyssen Inc v SS Fortune Star* 777 F 2d 57, 63 (2nd Cir, 1985); *Addis v Gramaphone Co Ltd* [1909] AC 488 (HL); *Paper Reclaim Ltd v Aotearoa International* [2006] 3 NZLR 188 (NZCA).

[170] *Vorvis v Insurance Corporation of British Columbia* [1989] 1 SCR 1085 (SCC); *Whiten v Pilot Insurance Co* [2002] 1 SCR 595 (SCC).

[171] Burrows (n 163) 394, fn 56.

[172] *Butler v Fairclough* (1917) 23 CLR 78 (HCA) 89.

[173] *Gray* (n 166) 6–7.

[174] *Hospitality Group* (n 166) 191.

[175] *Addis* (n 169).

[176] *Uren v John Fairfax & Sons Pty Ltd* (1966) 117 CLR 118 (HCA).

[177] *Rookes v Barnard* [1964] AC 1129 (HL).

[178] *Thyssen* (n 169) 63.

[179] *Whiten* (n 170).

[180] *Strand Electric* (n 8).

breach of contract, and in fact, disgorgement damages are compatible with 'efficient breach' theory if substitutability is taken into account. A reason not mentioned in *Thyssen*, but raised by Griffiths CJ in *Butler*, is that the wilfulness of the breach should be irrelevant to contract law.[181] Richard Posner and other scholars have also argued that 'wilfulness' or 'fault' should not be introduced into contract law because breach should not be regarded as a wrongful act.[182] However, it is simply impossible to treat a contract as a totally self-contained document, and the wilful nature of the parties' conduct intrudes into various areas of contract law.[183]

In any case, Mason P noted in his dissent that punitive damages for breach of contract had not necessarily been ruled out by Australian authorities, and that there was no reason to use this as a basis upon which to refuse punitive damages for breach of fiduciary duty.[184]

Of course, it is easier to establish that disgorgement damages should be available for breach of contract if punitive damages are already available.[185] But regardless of whether punitive damages are available for breach of contract, courts should not be precluded from awarding disgorgement damages for breach of contract. Disgorgement damages are not as harsh as punitive damages, and do not display the same strong retributive character. As Edelman has said, disgorgement damages are 'the sharp axe' (as opposed to the 'blunt axe' of exemplary damages).[186] Disgorgement damages remove *actual profit made*, and take no more than this. The defendant will not be punished by being put in a worse position than if the contract had been performed.

Now that it has been established that punitive rationales can enter into the private law and can inform equitable, contractual remedies in particular, I will go on to consider how the punitive rationale shapes disgorgement damages.

C 'Cynical Breach' and the Retributive Rationale

In order for the defendant to be justly punished in a private law action, it is important that he is cognisant of what he has done, otherwise he cannot be said to

181 *Butler v Fairclough* (n 172) 89.

182 R Posner, 'Let Us Never Blame a Contract Breaker' (2009) 107 *Michigan Law Review* 1349. See also S Shavell, 'Why Breach of Contract May Not Be Immoral Given the Incompleteness of Contracts' (2009) 107 *Michigan Law Review* 1569. Against G Cohen, 'The Fault that Lies Within our Contract Law' (2009) 107 *Michigan Law Review* 1445; M Eisenberg, 'The Role of Fault in Contract Law: Unconscionability, Unexpected Circumstances, Interpretation, Mistake, and Nonperformance' (2009) 107 *Michigan Law Review* 141; S Thel and P Siegelman, 'Willfulness Versus Expectation: A Promisor-Based Defense of Willful Breach Doctrine' (2009) 107 *Michigan Law Review* 1517; S Shiffrin, '*Could* Breach of Contract Be Immoral?' (2009) 107 *Michigan Law Review* 1551; S Grundmann, 'The Fault Principle as the Chameleon of Contract Law: A Market Function Approach' (2009) 107 *Michigan Law Review* 1583; R Kreitner, 'Fault at the Contract-Tort Interface' (2009) 107 *Michigan Law Review* 1533.

183 Cohen (n 182).

184 *Digital Pulse* (n 152) 353 (Mason P).

185 Edelman (n 3) 5–6, 154.

186 Edelman (n 3) 17.

deserve punishment.[187] The law therefore requires people to act consciously before it finds them to be deserving of punishment. If a person acts unconsciously or without the requisite intention, they are likely to lack responsibility for their actions, or at least (in the case of an instance such as automatism) have a diminished responsibility. This may explain the insistence in case law[188] and commentary[189] that there must be a 'cynical breach' before disgorgement damages are awarded. Conscious wrongdoing is also relevant to deterrence. A person can be deterred from making a conscious choice, but people are incapable of being deterred from an unconscious action.

i The Nature of 'Cynical Breach'

It is not entirely clear what constitutes a 'cynical breach' – whether it means that a breach of contract must be deliberate, or whether it requires something more, such as bad faith or unconscionable conduct. Birks seemed to imply that it requires not only deliberate breach but also *dishonesty.* He insisted courts are able to decide when a breach is 'cynical' because they regularly distinguish between honest and dishonest conduct.[190]

Edelman suggests that disgorgement damages should be available to strip profit where a wrongdoer has acted in the hope of material gain.[191] He explains:

> Cynical breach should be interpreted widely and any conception of material gain should be sufficient. Indeed, once it is shown that a wrong has been deliberately committed, in circumstances in which the defendant profited, it is likely to be very difficult for a defendant to prove that material gain was not the object of the wrong.[192]

Edelman uses *Lumley v Wagner*[193] to illustrate the way in which 'cynical breach' should operate.[194] Ms Wagner had contracted to sing for Mr Lumley and had expressly promised in the contract that she would not sing for anyone else. Ms Wagner then purported to sing for Mr Gye, a competitor. Mr Lumley obtained

[187] Kant (n 126). See also American Law Institute (n 105) § 3, comment e.

[188] The concept seems to have been first introduced in case law in *Hickey & Co Ltd v Roche Stores (Dublin) Ltd* (1975 No 1007P), reported in [1993] *Restitution Law Review* 196 (Irish HC). See also *Hospital Products Ltd v United States Surgical Corporation* (1984) 156 CLR 41 (HCA) [11] (Deane J) and American Law Institute, *Restatement of Restitution* (1937), §§150–59 introductory note: a defendant who is 'consciously tortious in acquiring the benefit' will be deprived of the profit.

[189] See, eg P Birks, 'Restitutionary Damages for Breach of Contract: *Snepp* and the Fusion of Law and Equity' [1987] *Lloyd's Maritime and Commercial Law Quarterly* 421, 429–30; Birks (n 29) 519; D Laycock, 'The Scope and Significance of Restitution' (1989) 67 *Texas Law Review* 1277, 1289; Edelman (n 3) 85, 158–59; Rotherham (n 10) 189–90; A Burrows, *Remedies for Torts and Breach of Contract*, 3rd edn (Oxford, Oxford University Press, 2004) 406–07; Edelman (n 45) 149.

[190] Birks, 'Restitutionary Damages for Breach of Contract' (n 189) 422. Although in a different context, English courts have faced difficulties in applying the 'dishonesty' test proposed by Lord Nicholls in *Royal Brunei Airlines v Tan* [1995] 2 AC 378 (PC) for knowing assistance of breach of fiduciary duty – see *Twinsectra Ltd v Yardley* [2002] UKHL 12, [2002] 2 AC 164 (HL) and *Barlow Clowes International v Eurotrust International* [2005] UKPC 37, [2006] 1 WLR 1476 (PC).

[191] Edelman (n 3) 85.

[192] ibid.

[193] *Lumley v Wagner* (1852) 1 De G M & G 604, 42 ER 687.

[194] Edelman (n 3) 158–59.

an injunction preventing Ms Wagner from singing for Mr Gye. If Ms Wagner had sung for Mr Gye and made a profit, should Mr Lumley be entitled to disgorgement damages? Edelman has suggested that this variation of the facts of the case would fall within the concept of 'cynical breach' and would render compensatory damages inadequate.[195]

ii Reasons Against 'Cynical Breach' as a Criterion

Some argue that the character of a breach should not be relevant to whether disgorgement damages are awarded. For example, Professor Farnsworth says:

> Although opinions in contract cases sometimes lay emphasis on the 'wilful' character of a breach, contract law generally treats unwilling breaches in the same way as knowing breaches committed to realise gain. Indeed, it would be hard to implement a distinction based on the character of the breach. Given the eagerness of contracting parties to find possible legal justifications for non-performance where this is to their advantage, having to decide whether, and perhaps to what extent, a breach was committed knowingly would place a heavy burden on courts. Any extension of the disgorgement principle should be without regard to the character of the breach.[196]

Scholars such as Richard Posner take the more extreme position, and suggest that issues of 'wilfulness' or 'fault' should not be introduced into contract law at all because breach should not be regarded as a wrongful act.[197]

As commentators have noted, in some cases it is difficult to work out when breaches are innocent or cynical (ie did the defendant breach the contract with an intention to make a profit?).[198] In a case like *Blake*, it is obvious that Blake's breach was cynical, but it is easy to imagine a case where the facts are more ambiguous. As Craswell has noted, '[i]n the vast majority of cases, the parties to a contract do not intend to breach at the time they signed it. Instead they hope the contract will be performed as planned, but then something else happens.'[199] It may depend upon which events we focus: the defendant's decisions (which are deliberate) or the events which were not deliberate (an increase in costs, a mistake in performance and so forth).[200]

If cynical breach or advertence were not a requirement, it would be particularly important to confine disgorgement to the actual profit, and not award damages which are effectively punitive and exceed the profit the defendant has made, because this may result in over-deterrence and harsh punishment.[201]

[195] ibid 158. See also Birks, 'Restitutionary Damages for Breach of Contract' (n 189).

[196] Farnsworth (n 110) 1391–92. See also J Dawson, 'Restitution Without Enrichment' (1981) 61 *Boston University Law Review* 563, 614; J McCamus, 'Disgorgement For Breach of Contract: A Comparative Perspective' (2003) 36 *Loyola of Los Angeles Law Review* 943, 961; R Craswell, 'When is a Willful Breach "Willful"? The Link Between Definitions and Damages' (2009) 107 *Michigan Law Review* 1501.

[197] See (n 182).

[198] Jones (n 123) 457; R O'Dair, 'Remedies for Breach of Contract: A Wrong Turn' [1993] *Restitution Law Review* 31, 38–39; Smith (n 85) 364; Craswell (n 196) 1502–07.

[199] Craswell (n 196) 1503.

[200] ibid 1504.

[201] Jaffey, *Nature and Scope of Restitution* (n 121) 387.

Birks argues that to say a court is unable to determine when a breach is cynical is tantamount to arguing that courts cannot distinguish between honesty and dishonesty.[202] Courts *are* able to make judgements about a contractor's honesty or lack thereof, but this will give unwarranted prominence to the moral quality of the defendant's breach. It will make deciding such cases more difficult and uncertain. Judges have declined the invitation to use the concept of 'cynical breach' in practice for this very reason.[203] Consequently I argue that the defendant's honesty, or lack thereof, should not be the focus of the inquiry. Instead the focus should be on the advertence of the breach.

iii Reasons For 'Cynical Breach' as a Criterion

Many have argued that the 'wilfulness' or advertence of a breach should be relevant in contract law more generally.[204] Thel and Siegelman argue that wilfulness of breach is relevant for reasons of deterrence: because it screens for those breaches which should be deterred.[205]

Rotherham argues that our legal system should not allow gain-based remedies in circumstances where the defendant is blameless.[206] He says:

> It is relatively easy to justify punishing cynical wrongdoers by requiring them to disgorge the benefit received as a result of the breach, and such relief will serve to discourage others from acting in this way. We might be especially eager to provide a remedy of this nature against defendants who knowingly infringe and, therefore, are likely to calculate the potential consequences of their actions. Such a remedy is liable to go some way to ensuring that, when weighed against the potential profits and the chances of being caught, conscious wrongdoers are discouraged from engaging in the conduct in question. In addition, regardless of the defendant's conduct, we are more likely to be prepared to tolerate the distributional consequences of providing restitution for wrongs (i.e. the windfall that results for the claimant) if we think that the legal relationship in question demands the protection that would come from such a remedy.[207]

By contrast it is less obvious that we might wish to award gain-based damages in cases where the breach of contract is careless or innocent.[208]

In the *Third Restatement of Restitution and Unjust Enrichment*, the American Law Institute has stipulated that disgorgement damages should only be available

[202] Birks, 'Restitutionary Damages for Breach of Contract' (n 189) 422. See also O'Dair (n 104) 38–39; Smith (n 85) 364.

[203] *Surrey County Council v Bredero* (n 29) 1370 (Steyn LJ); *Blake* (n 149) 457 (Woolf LJ); *Blake* (n 7) 186 (Lord Nicholls).

[204] Cohen (n 182); Eisenberg (n 182); Thel and Siegelman (n 182); Shiffrin (n 182); Grundmann (n 182); Kreitner (n 182).

[205] Thel and Siegleman (n 182) 1518.

[206] Rotherham (n 10) 189. Although Rotherham does not note this, in the area of fiduciary law innocent fiduciaries may be punished by an award of an account of profits: *Keech v Sandford* (1726) 2 Eq Cas Abr 741, 25 ER 223; *Boardman v Phipps* [1966] UKHL 2, [1967] 2 AC 46 (HL); *Regal (Hastings) Ltd v Gulliver* [1967] 2 AC 134 (HL); *Canadian Aero Service v O'Malley* [1974] SCR 592 (SCC). Such awards are very difficult to justify on a retributive basis.

[207] Rotherham (n 10) 190.

[208] ibid 190–91.

where breach is 'opportunistic', in the sense that the promisor *consciously* intended to exploit the fact that damages were an inadequate remedy for the promisee in order to make a profit by breaching his contract.[209] The *Restatement* analogises such a 'conscious advantage taking' to an intentional, profitable tort.[210] Insofar as 'opportunistic' is intended to be synonymous with 'advertent breach', it is suggested that the *Restatement* has the correct approach.

iv Moving from 'Cynical Breach' to 'Advertent Breach'

Some form of wrongful conduct is needed for disgorgement to occur because retention of gains derived from breach of contract is generally perceived as allowable.[211] What is more a requirement of advertence fits with the data provided by the cases, which indicates that courts award disgorgement damages in cases where the breach is advertent and not otherwise. Thus we need to identify some extra quality of the breach which means that the defendant should disgorge his profit.

If one emphasises the retributive rationale of disgorgement damages, then the conduct of the defendant must be intentional. Contrary to Edelman, I argue that the important question is not whether the defendant subjectively intended to make a profit as a result of the breach. The important question is whether the defendant *consciously or advertently disregarded* the rights of the claimant.[212] The deterrent aspect of disgorgement damages also seems more appropriate if wrongful actions are conscious and advertent. The term 'advertent breach' is preferable to 'cynical breach', as it is clearer – it means that the breach was intentional and there was thus an advertent disregard of the rights of the claimant. A claimant who wishes to establish that a breach was advertent must merely show that the defendant intended to breach, and did not breach the contract by accident. The claimant need not show that the defendant knew or ought to have known that she could not procure a substitute performance from elsewhere,[213] nor that the defendant intended to profit. The requirement of substitutability provides a sufficient limitation on liability without the need to prove these other factors.

Friedmann argues that a requirement of conscious wrongdoing is not sufficiently nuanced to distinguish between intermediate possibilities within the extremes of conscious knowledge and innocence. Accordingly, he suggests that the test should be whether or not the defendant was *culpable*.[214] By contrast, I submit it is unnecessary to consider whether or not the defendant's breach was

209 American Law Institute (n 105) § 39, comment c.

210 ibid.

211 Waddams, 'Gains Derived from Breach of Contract' (n 26) 194.

212 In this sense, I draw on Hegel's idea that a person should be punished when they deny the rights of others, which is discussed in Chapman and Trebilcock (n 4) 783. Chapman and Trebilcock use Hegel's theories as expressed in GWF Hegel, *Philosophy of Right* (T Knox trans, 1967) [84]–[85], [95], [220] [trans of: *Grundlinien der philosophie des rechts*]. See generally Chapman and Trebilcock (n 4) 780–83.

213 Compare Jaffey, 'Disgorgement and "Licence Fee Damages" in Contract' (n 121) 7.

214 D Friedmann, 'Restitution for Wrongs: The Measure of Recovery' (2001) 79 *Texas Law Review* 1879, 1888. Friedmann emphasises the punitive nature of disgorgement: see ibid 1887.

'culpable'. Any gradations in the knowledge of the defendant can be taken into account with an equitable allowance, which focuses on whether or not the defendant deserves some kind of acknowledgement of skill and effort, or by the application of one of the relevant equitable defences. If the defendant's breach was not sufficiently advertent, then in the area of breach of contract at least, disgorgement damages should not be awarded.

In any case, substitutability prevents disgorgement damages from being overly harsh. Chapman and Trebilcock have argued that ordinarily, even in jurisdictions where punitive damages can be awarded for breach of contract, punitive damages will not generally be awarded, even if the breach is intentional.[215] This is because the breaching party is not denying the relevance of rights to the dispute; rather the breaching party is prepared to pay damages flowing from that breach if proven.[216]

This changes if a substitute performance cannot be procured. In a 'second sale' type situation, where Boris makes a contract to sell a house to Alice, then breaches his contract by making a more profitable contract with Conrad, damages will no longer be adequate for Alice. Nor can the court award specific relief, for the property has already been conveyed to Conrad. Boris has knowledge of Alice's position, and knows that damages will be inadequate and specific relief will be unavailable. He exploits the lack of substitutability of the subject matter of the contract. Boris' conduct becomes a denial of the relevance of Alice's rights to the dispute. Therefore, the substitutability of the subject matter of the contract can help to establish the blameworthiness of the defendant's conduct, because the defendant's conduct will only become blameworthy if damages are inadequate and specific relief is unavailable.

The case law supports the inclusion of a requirement of advertent breach. It is difficult to find a case where disgorgement damages have been awarded where the breach was inadvertent. However, there is a higher possibility in the 'skimped performance' cases (ie where a defendant saves an expense and makes a profit by his failure to perform) that the breach of contract may be inadvertent.[217] The advertence of the breach (or lack thereof) provides a clue as to why disgorgement damages are less likely to be awarded in skimped performance cases, although as will be discussed in chapter six, disgorgement damages will rarely be an appropriate remedy in most cases of skimped performance.

It must be emphasised that it *does not follow* that disgorgement damages should be available merely because a breach is advertent.[218] This is the danger of introducing 'cynical breach' or advertence as a determinant. Indeed, the Court of Appeal in *Blake* specified that it was not sufficient to establish that the breach was cynical and deliberate, nor the fact that the breach enabled the defendant to enter into a more profitable contract elsewhere.[219] On this point, at least, Posner J is cor-

[215] As discussed earlier, English, American, New Zealand and (arguably) Australian law have not permitted punitive damages for breach of contract. This is in contrast to Canadian law.

[216] Chapman and Trebilcock (n 4) 783.

[217] Thel and Siegelman (n 5) 1216–17.

[218] Edelman (n 45) 150.

[219] *Blake* (n 149). Accepted by Lord Nicholls: *Blake* (n 7) 286.

rect to assert that '[e]ven if the breach is deliberate, it is not necessarily blameworthy.'[220] A breach of a contract may be entirely advertent, but the party who loses out could easily get substitute performance elsewhere.[221] In those circumstances a claimant should only get compensatory damages, so as to enable her to obtain substitute performance. Substitutability leaves open the possibility of efficient breach in some circumstances.

D Retribution, Desert, Mercy and Bars to Relief

Punishment and broader questions of desert are relevant to the availability of bars to relief to a claim for disgorgement damages. As will be outlined in detail in chapter seven, the typical equitable bars to relief should be available to a defendant, namely delay and acquiescence, lack of clean hands and hardship. There should also be allowances for skill and effort. Delay and acquiescence centre on the idea that the claimant does not 'deserve' to have the assistance of the court because of her particular actions in the circumstances, and consequently the defendant does not deserve to be punished by having his gain stripped. Allowances for skill and effort can also be justified according to principles of desert.[222] Desert-based bars to relief, however, cannot be said to be an entitlement on the part of a defendant – desert centres on the notion of 'propriety', not 'right'.[223] A defendant can only argue that it is *proper* that he have the advantage of a bar to relief in the particular circumstances of the case. Desert-based bars to relief and allowances for skill and effort may conflict with the deterrent goal of disgorgement damages, but also with the specific punitive aim of disgorgement damages.

Hardship has another basis, namely 'mercy'. Mercy seeks to ameliorate the excessiveness of punishment in the light of the particular hardships suffered by the defendant.[224] Consequently, it may conflict with both the deterrent and the punitive goals of disgorgement damages. Nonetheless, it will be argued that in some circumstances it is appropriate that the bar to relief be operative, because otherwise the law will potentially be unfair.

V Conclusion

The moral justifications behind disgorgement damages are deterrence and retribution. Despite recurring suggestions to the contrary, disgorgement damages are

[220] *Patton v Mid-Continent Systems* 841 F 2d 742, 750 (7th Cir, 1988) (Posner J).

[221] Jaffey, 'Disgorgement and "Licence Fee Damages" in Contract' (n 121) 7–9.

[222] M Harding, 'Justifying Fiduciary Allowances' in A Robertson and TH Wu (eds), *The Goals of Private Law* (Oxford, Hart Publishing, 2009) 341, 342–44.

[223] J Feinberg, 'Justice and Personal Desert' in J Feinberg, *Doing and Deserving: Essays in the Theory of Responsibility* (Princeton, Princeton University Press, 1970) 56.

[224] J Tasioulas, 'Mercy' (2003) 103 *Proceedings of the Aristotelian Society* 101, 115.

not best explained by a compensatory rationale. Courts should be more transparent about acknowledging the true moral justification behind disgorgement damages. A compensatory analysis does not fit with the cases, and to force disgorgement damages into this framework distorts the concept of compensation and makes it difficult to predict when disgorgement will be ordered. By contrast, if disgorgement damages are seen as a vindication of the infringement of a claimant's right to performance, then the relevant nexus between the defendant's gain and the claimant's injury has been identified.

The deterrent rationale is at the heart of the remedy. It gives primacy to the performance interest in circumstances where it is important that contracts be performed. The retributive rationale explains a criterion for the award of the remedy: a court must be certain that the breach was cynical or advertent so that the defendant must deserve to be punished. In addition, it must consider whether there are any bars to relief which will make the defendant undeserving of punishment. These two rationales create a coherent justification for disgorgement damages, and assist in shaping the award in practice.

3

The Claimant's 'Legitimate Interest' and the Role of Substitutability

I Introduction

In at least some common law countries, courts acknowledge that disgorgement damages may be available for breach of contract.[1] But it remains unclear exactly *when* disgorgement will be available. In *Blake*, Lord Nicholls proposed that courts would award disgorgement damages according to a twofold test: first, the claimant must have a 'legitimate interest' in performance of the contract, and secondly, compensatory damages must be inadequate.[2] Nonetheless, the attempts by courts to apply *Blake* indicate that 'the legitimate interest test remains hopelessly ill-defined and difficult to apply.'[3] This chapter seeks to fit the theory of disgorgement damages to the existing law, and to clarify the way in which the 'legitimate interest' test operates so that the law is more coherent and predictable for courts, lawyers, litigants and contractors. As prefigured in the previous chapter, the criterion according to which disgorgement damages should be awarded for breach of contract is the *substitutability* of the subject matter of the contract.[4] Substitutability is derived from the cases where courts award specific relief, but it should not be limited to that context: it is central to an understanding of remedies for breach of contract, and also informs the measure of expectation damages. The stated aim of contract remedies for breach is to place the claimant in a position as if the con-

[1] In the UK, see *Attorney-General v Blake* (*Blake*) [2000] UKHL 45, [2001] 1 AC 268 (HL); *Esso Petroleum Co Ltd v Niad Ltd* (*Niad*) [2001] EWHC Ch 458, All ER (D) 324 (Ch); *Experience Hendrix LLC v PPX Enterprises Inc* (*Experience Hendrix*) [2003] EWCA Civ 323, [2003] 1 All ER (Comm) 830 (CA). In Canada, see *Bank of America (Canada) v Mutual Trust Co* [2002] 2 SCR 601 (SCC) [25] (Major J); *Amartek Inc v Canadian Commercial Corp* (2003) 229 DLR (4th) 419 (Ontario SC) 467 (O'Driscoll J) (on appeal held there was no collateral contract: (2005) 5 BLR (4th) 199 (Ontario CA)); *Montreal Trust Co v Williston Wildcatters Corp* (2004) 243 DLR (4th) 317(SKQB) 122 (Vancise JA). In the US, see obiter in *Earthinfo Inc v Hydrosphere Resource Consultants*, 900 P (2d) 113 (Colorado SC, 1995) 117–21. The new *Restatement* includes a disgorgement remedy for 'opportunistic' breach of contract: American Law Institute, *Restatement (Third) of Restitution and Unjust Enrichment* (2011) § 39.

[2] *Blake* (n 1) 285.

[3] R Cunnington, 'The Measure and Availability of Gain-based Damages for Breach of Contract' in D Saidov and R Cunnington (eds), *Contract Damages: Domestic and International Perspectives* (Oxford, Hart Publishing, 2008) 207, 235.

[4] Professor Kronman first coined the term 'substitutability' in A Kronman, 'Specific Performance' (1978) 45 *University of Chicago Law Review* 351, 359.

tract had been performed. The contractual context must be emphasised. Substitutability looks to what the claimant hoped to gain from the contract, and therefore what remedy the defendant must give the claimant as a substitute for the performance which was denied as a result of the breach. An effective contractual remedy encourages vindication of the claimant's interest. Although contractual damages may seem at first glance only to be concerned with compensating for loss, in fact the focus of contract damages is generally to vindicate the claimant's performance interest in the best way possible. Generally, courts use the market to ascertain the value of the claimant's expectation, and award expectation damages on that basis, but where that measure would provide an inadequate substitute for performance, courts also use other measures, such as rectification damages (which will be discussed in greater detail in chapter six), reliance damages and damages for loss of a chance.

Before considering the way in which remedies operate in detail, it is first necessary to consider the effect of the parties entering into a contract. I will adopt Professor Stephen Smith's suggestion that there are two effects when parties enter a contract: a tangible effect whereby resources are shifted between parties to the contract, and an intangible effect involving the creation of bonds of trust between the parties.[5] However, cases and commentary tend to favour one effect to the exclusion of the other. The promissory or rights-based analyses emphasise the claimant's right to performance, and argue that the primary obligation arising from a contract is the claimant's right to have the contract performed. On the other hand, others argue that the primary obligation arising from a contract is merely an obligation to compensate the claimant for financial losses suffered as a result of the breach. Primary among those who take this approach are certain law and economics scholars who favour the 'efficient breach' explanation of breach of contract. Neither approach wholly fits with the data which the case law provides. Both theories explain a proportion of the cases, depending on the circumstances of the contract and, pivotally, the nature of the interest contracted for.

My theory recognises the claimant's 'performance interest'.[6] Courts have long suggested that the performance of a contract is central. However, despite general acceptance of the significance of the performance interest, the remedies awarded for breach of contract seem to suggest that the aim of remedies for breach of contract is *not* to ensure performance, but to compensate the claimant for her loss. The cases 'do not speak with one voice.'[7] Some cases emphasise the importance of performance, others say that the only obligation is to pay damages to the claimant for financial losses. Sometimes the same case contains conflicting judgments.

[5] S Smith, 'Performance, Punishment and the Nature of Contractual Obligations' (1997) 60 *MLR* 360, 367.

[6] D Friedmann, 'The Performance Interest in Contract Damages' (1995) 111 *LQR* 628; B Coote, 'Contract Damages, *Ruxley*, and the Performance Interest' (1997) 56 *CLJ* 537, 566; see also B Coote, 'The Performance Interest, *Panatown*, and the Problem of Loss' (2001) 117 *LQR* 81.

[7] E McKendrick, 'The Common Law at Work: The Saga of *Alfred McAlpine Construction Ltd v Panatown Ltd*' (2003) 3 *Oxford University Commonwealth Law Journal* 145, 167.

Consequently, the law has a schizophrenic approach towards contract remedies.[8] This occurs because when courts award 'expectation damages', they simultaneously compensate the claimant for loss *and* satisfy the claimant's performance interest. Compensation for loss is, however, merely one way of satisfying the claimant's performance interest, although it is the most commonly used method. While the primacy of expectation damages might suggest the law is mainly concerned with compensating loss, this is not the case. Courts are concerned to vindicate the claimant's performance interest.[9]

'Vindication' is derived from the Latin *vindicatio*, and has a number of different meanings, including justification of a right and asserting or maintaining a right.[10] In this context, I intend to use it to mean a making good of, and recognition of, a claimant's rights. For a claimant's contractual rights to be recognised, she must have an adequate remedy. In an oft-cited passage, Holt CJ said in *Ashby v White*:

> If the plaintiff has a right, he must of necessity have a means to vindicate and maintain it, and a remedy if he is injured in the exercise or enjoyment to it; and, indeed, it is a vain thing to imagine a right without a remedy; for want of right and want of remedy are reciprocal.[11]

Thus, when a court awards a claimant a contractual remedy, the court vindicates that right by recognising the claimant's assertion of it. The award of the remedy makes the defendant *accountable* for his breach, in the sense that he has to take responsibility for the consequences flowing from his failure to perform his contractual obligation. The law favours expectation damages as the primary remedy which a claimant can assert, because it is a less intrusive way of vindicating the claimant's performance interest, and ordinarily it will be adequate for the purpose.[12] Frequently, the claimant's right to performance may be vindicated by something less than actual performance by the defendant; compensatory damages will be adequate if a substitute performance can be purchased with damages. Thus, sometimes a defendant is 'free' to breach his contract, subject to his obligation to pay damages (as the supporters of 'efficient breach' allege). In addition, there may be situations where we *want* to allow breach, for example, when unforeseen circumstances mean that the defendant breaches to avoid a loss (as opposed to the situation of 'efficient breach' where the defendant breaches to obtain a

[8] Coote, 'Contract Damages, *Ruxley*, and the Performance Interest' (n 6) 540–42; McKendrick (n 7) 167–68; C Webb, 'Performance and Compensation: An Analysis of Contract Damages and Contractual Obligation' (2006) 26 *OJLS* 41, 45–49; D Pearce and R Halson, 'Damages for Breach of Contract: Compensation, Restitution and Vindication' (2008) 28 *OJLS* 73, 79–80.

[9] Pearce and Halson (n 8).

[10] *Oxford English Dictionary*, 'vindication, *n.*', 2nd edn (Clarendon Press, Oxford, 1989) Vol XIX. See also N Witzleb and R Carroll, 'The Role of Vindication in Torts Damages' (2009) 17 *Tort Law Review* 16, 17–19.

[11] *Ashby v White* (1703) 2 Ld Raym 938, 92 ER 126, 136. For a more recent expression of a similar sentiment, see Lord Hope in *Chester v Afshar* [2005] 1 AC 134 (HL) [84], where he states, 'The function of the law is to enable rights to be vindicated and to provide remedies when duties have been breached.'

[12] Witzleb and Carroll (n 10) 20, 32.

gain).[13] However, where damages are inadequate to provide the claimant with a substitute performance, courts are increasingly willing to award specific relief which directly vindicates the claimant's right to performance by awarding her the interest which she contracted for.

It is in this context that the claimant's legitimate interest in the performance of a contract must be assessed. In keeping with the deterrent rationale, the object of disgorgement damages is to encourage future defendants to perform or negotiate out of the obligation rather than merely to breach, at least where certain kinds of contract are concerned. Clearly it is too late to deter the particular defendant in question from breaching: yet the claimant's contractual right should still be vindicated or recognised in some way. The best way to vindicate the claimant's performance interest in the cases where disgorgement damages should be awarded is to strip the defendant of the profit he has made, and put him in a position as if he had performed his contract.

I have explained in the previous chapter that deterrence and punitive rationales shape disgorgement, but I have not yet established the precise limitations on an award of disgorgement damages for breach of contract. 'Substitutability' is an essential limitation: courts must assess whether the claimant is entitled to a substitute performance if the defendant breaches his contract. Generally speaking, disgorgement damages will only be available if compensatory damages are inadequate to recognise the claimant's performance interest, specific relief is no longer available, and if the defendant has made a profit. In these circumstances the 'next best' remedy available to vindicate the claimant's performance interest may be disgorgement damages. Courts have already given extensive thought to questions of substitutability when making awards of specific relief. Thus, disgorgement damages are coherent and consistent with existing principles of contract remedies. Substitutability is also consistent with my 'middle ground' approach to enforcing the claimant's performance interest. That is to say, the claimant is not always entitled to performance, or disgorgement in lieu of performance: it depends upon the subject matter of the contract and the degree of substitutability thereof.

At the end of this chapter, I will introduce the two classes of case where disgorgement damages may be awarded, namely the 'second sale' cases and the 'agency problem'[14] cases. The detailed application of my theory to these categories of case will be found in chapters four and five.

[13] D Campbell, 'The Treatment of *Teacher v Calder* in *AG v Blake*' (2002) 65 *MLR* 256, 269; D Campbell and D Harris, 'In Defence of Breach: A Critique of Restitution and the Performance Interest' (2002) 22 *Journal of Legal Studies* 208, 217–21; D Campbell and P Wylie, 'Ain't No Telling (Which Circumstances Are Exceptional)' (2003) 62 *CLJ* 605, 615–16. See also D Friedmann, 'Economic Aspects of Damages and Specific Performance Compared' in D Saidov and R Cunnington (eds), *Contract Damages: Domestic and International Perspectives* (Oxford, Hart Publishing, 2008) 65, which introduces the concept of 'tolerated breach'.

[14] 'Agency' is used in the *economic sense* to talk about relationships which are difficult to supervise, rather than the legal sense. J Stiglitz, 'principal and agent (ii)', entry in S Durlauf and L Blume (eds), *The New Palgrave Dictionary of Economics*, 2nd edn (Basingstoke and New York, Palgrave Macmillan, 2008).

II The 'Legitimate Interest' Test and Substitutability

Substitutability is not mentioned in the *Blake* decision, which is now the basic English authority supporting an award of disgorgement damages for breach of contract. Lord Nicholls, who delivered the principal speech, said:

> Normally the remedies of damages, specific performance and injunction, coupled with the characterisation of some contractual obligations as fiduciary, will provide an adequate response to a breach of contract. It will be only in exceptional cases, where those remedies are inadequate, that any question of accounting for profits will arise. No fixed rules can be prescribed. The court will have regard to all the circumstances, including the subject matter of the contract, the purpose of the contractual provision which has been breached, the circumstances in which the breach occurred, the consequences of the breach and the circumstances in which relief is sought. A useful general guide, although not exhaustive, is whether the plaintiff had a legitimate interest in preventing the defendant's profit-making activity and, hence, in depriving him of his profit.[15]

This has become known as the 'legitimate interest test'.[16]

Lord Steyn also refused to lay down a general principle. He said:

> I am not at present willing to endorse the broad observations of the Court of Appeal. Exceptions to the general principle that there is no remedy for disgorgement of profits against a contract breaker are best hammered out on the anvil of concrete cases.[17]

Lord Hobhouse, the sole dissentient in *Blake*, concluded with a 'note of warning' about the principles introduced by the majority:

> [I]f some more extensive principle of awarding non-compensatory damages for breach of contract is to be introduced into our commercial law the consequences will be very far reaching and disruptive.[18]

Some commentators share Lord Hobhouse's concern that *Blake* will create commercial uncertainty by allowing 'open slather' for disgorgement damages in commercial contracts.[19] The spectre of unlimited liability can be found in the argument

[15] *Blake* (n 1) 285.

[16] 'Legitimate interest' may have been drawn from Birks' casenote on *Surrey County Council v Bredero Homes Ltd* [1993] EWCA Civ 7, [1993] 1 WLR 1361 (CA): see P Birks, 'Profits of Breach of Contract' (1993) 109 *LQR* 518, 519 and 521.

[17] *Blake* (n 1) 291.

[18] ibid 299.

[19] C Mitchell, 'Remedial Inadequacy in Contract and the Role of Restitutionary Damages' (1999) 15 *Journal of Contract Law* 133 (prior to the House of Lords decision); S Hedley, '"Very Much the Wrong People": The House of Lords and Publication of Spy Memoirs (A-G v Blake)' (2000) *Web Journal of Current Legal Issues*, www.webjcli.ncl.ac.uk/issue4/hedley4#Heading7.html, accessed 31 May 2007; S Erbacher, 'An Account of Profits for a Breach of Contract (Attorney-General v Blake)' (2001) 29 *Australian Business Law Review* 73, 76–77; PW Young, 'Account of Profits For Breach of Contract' (2000) 74 *Australian Law Journal* 817; Campbell (n 13); Campbell and Harris (n 13) 209–10; J O'Sullivan, 'Reflections on the Role of Restitutionary Damages to Protect Contractual Expectations' in D Johnston and R Zimmermann (eds), *Unjustified Enrichment: Key Issues in Comparative Perspective* (Cambridge, Cambridge University Press, 2002) 327; Campbell and Wylie (n 13); D Campbell, 'The

that a promisee has a legitimate interest in preventing the other party from profiting from a breach of contract in almost all circumstances.[20] Other academics have noted the lack of precision in the 'legitimate interest test'.[21] The results of cases which have subsequently applied the 'legitimate interest test' confirm that there is confusion as to how it operates.

Lord Nicholls' test has typically been divided into two stages: first, the claimant must have a 'legitimate interest' in performance of the contract, and secondly, compensatory damages must be inadequate.[22] The two parts of Lord Nicholls' test are really different ways of posing the same intertwined question: is this the kind of bargain where compensatory damages are inadequate to put the claimant in a position as if the contract had been performed, and therefore is it the kind of bargain in which a claimant has a legitimate interest?

Before attempting to answer this question it is necessary to tease out the nature of the rights which a promisee gets under a contract, because to do so assists in identifying when a 'legitimate interest' ought to be found. We must look at the rights of the claimant which courts are seeking to vindicate or recognise when they award remedies for breach of contract.

III Policies behind the Primary Duty to Perform Contracts

We can only fully understand remedies for breach of contract if we understand the policies behind the primary duty to perform contracts.[23] Courts seek to recognise or vindicate the claimant's rights in a way which recognises what people seek

Extinguishing of Contract' (2004) 67 *MLR* 818. See, against M Siems, 'Disgorgement of Profits for Breach of Contract: A Comparative Analysis' (2003) 7 *Edinburgh Law Review* 27, who argues that disgorgement should be allowed for *all* contracts.

[20] R Cunnington, 'Equitable Damages: A Model for Restitutionary Damages' (2001) 17 *Journal of Contract Law* 212, 214; J Beatson, 'Courts, Arbitrators and Restitutionary Liability for Breach of Contract' (2002) 118 *LQR* 377, 378–79; Campbell, 'The Treatment of *Teacher v Calder* in *AG v Blake*' (n 13) 257; Campbell, 'The Extinguishing of Contract' (n 19); Hedley (n 19).

[21] J Anderson, 'Account of Profits for Breach of Contract' [2000] *New Zealand Law Journal* 415; S Doyle and D Wright, 'Restitutionary Damages: The Unnecessary Remedy?' (2001) 25 *Melbourne University Law Review* 1, 7; Cunnington (n 20) 214; Erbacher (n 19) 76; D Ong, 'Non-Financial Loss Resulting from Tort and Breach of Contract: The Availability of a Monetary Remedy that is Non-Compensatory, Non-Restitutionary, Non-Punitive, and Not a Mere Solatium' (2002) 22 *University of Queensland Law Journal* 20, 49; J Gleeson and J Watson, 'Account of Profits, Contracts and Equity' (2005) 79 *Australian Law Journal* 676, 696–97, Hedley (n 19); Cunnington, 'The Measure and Availability' (n 3) 233; A Burrows, *Remedies for Torts and Breach of Contract*, 3rd edn (Oxford, Oxford University Press, 2004) 402–03.

[22] J Edelman, *Gain-Based Damages – Contract, Tort, Equity and Intellectual Property* (Oxford, Hart Publishing, 2002) 152–54; Erbacher (n 19) 76; Cunnington, 'The Measure and Availability' (n 3) 207–42; R Cunnington, 'The Inadequacy of Damages as a Remedy for Breach of Contract' in CEF Rickett (ed), *Justifying Private Law Remedies* (Oxford, Hart Publishing, 2008) 115.

[23] Cunnington, 'Inadequacy of Damages' (n 22) 137.

when they enter into a contract. As I have observed previously, Stephen Smith has argued that performed contracts have two different effects:[24]

1. They have a *tangible* effect because they allow for a shifting of resources between the parties to the contract; and
2. They have an *intangible* effect because they create bonds of trust between contracting parties.

I will now flesh out Smith's analysis further. Breach of contract harms claimants in two different ways. First, it has a tangible effect because it means that resources cannot be shifted between the parties in the manner agreed. Secondly, it has an intangible effect because it erodes the bonds of trust between the parties. Any remedy awarded for breach of contract must recognise and vindicate both harms to be adequate.

Scholars and cases tend to emphasise one kind of harm to the exclusion of the other. One approach, which emphasises performance and the morality of promising, focuses on the second effect of the performed contract, that is, the creation of a relationship of trust between the parties. A primary example of this is Professor Fried's 'promise theory' of contracts, in which he argues that when a contract is breached, the disappointment of the promisee's expectation is an abuse of trust.[25] This analysis fits with the rhetoric of many of the cases mentioned below, where courts strongly insist on the existence of the claimant's performance interest as a matter of principle. Interestingly, given the prominence which he gives to performance of a promise, Fried does not consider why contract law favours expectation damages over specific performance.[26] His analysis does not explain the actual remedies which courts award in practice for breach of contract in many cases, where expectation damages are generally seen as an award of first resort.

The reason why courts award expectation damages for preference in contractual cases is because often, such damages are adequate to vindicate the breach of the bonds of trust between the parties, but it depends very much upon the nature of the subject matter of the contract. An analysis which emphasises the importance of performance should explicitly recognise that the bond of trust has been broken in the remedies which it awards. Indeed, a need to vindicate the breach of the bond of trust on the part of the defendant is one reason why courts may wish

[24] Smith (n 5) 367.

[25] C Fried, *Contract as Promise: A Theory of Contractual Obligation* (Cambridge, Mass., Harvard University Publishing, 1981) 14–17. Compare D Kimel, *From Promise to Contract: Towards a Liberal Theory of Contract* (Oxford, Hart Publishing, 2003) 65–80. Kimel argues that contracts and promises are related, but distinguishable in important ways, in part precisely because contracts involve known remedial sanctions and promises do not. Contracts and promises share an instrumental function whereby they facilitate reliance, coordination and cooperation between people. However, they have diametrically opposed intrinsic functions: contract is designed to enable people to facilitate personal detachment, whereas promise is designed facilitate special bonds. The remedies of contract law assist to assure a party that the other will perform in the absence of a personal relationship with the other.

[26] R Craswell, 'Contract Law, Default Rules and the Philosophy of Promising' (1989) 88 *Michigan Law Review* 489, 517–20; Smith (n 5) 362; Kimel (n 25) 95–96.

to award disgorgement damages; particularly in the category I call the 'agency problem' cases, but also in the category I call 'second sale' cases.

Like Fried, Professor Smith adopts an approach which emphasises the importance of promises to contract law, although he argues that common law contract principles favour expectation damages over specific relief precisely *because* of the importance of promising.[27] According to Smith, ordering specific relief prevents parties from knowing 'whether or not performance has been done for the right reasons', and if it were ordered routinely, contract law would have less opportunity to strengthen bonds between parties.[28] By contrast, following Dori Kimel, I argue that the common law favours expectation damages over specific relief *not* because of the importance of promising, or because of any concern by parties as to the motives for fulfilling obligations, but because the law is concerned to remedy the claimant's performance interest in a way which is least intrusive, via expectation damages.[29] But where expectation damages do not adequately vindicate the breach of the bonds of trust between the parties, and a substitute performance is not available from elsewhere, courts may award specific relief, or – exceptionally – disgorgement damages.

To be contrasted with the promissory theorists, the proponents of 'efficient breach' argue that the only obligation arising from breach of a contract is to pay expectation damages, and that parties should be free to breach their contracts when resources could be allocated more efficiently elsewhere.[30] This analysis focuses only on Smith's first effect of the performed contract, that is, the shifting of resources between the parties and whether this shift is desirable. Thus, under this kind of analysis, the law should favour expectation damages in almost all circumstances because they are more efficient and do not deter parties from breaching their contracts. I argue that this theory does not adequately fit with the case law.[31] Although, as explained above, contract law generally favours expectation damages, there are circumstances where they do not adequately vindicate the performance interest and where courts concentrate not on the shifting of resources, but seek to enforce the promise itself, thus reinforcing the bonds of trust between the parties. Furthermore, courts sometimes require a defendant to disgorge his profit, even if this was not generally explicitly recognised by case law before *Blake*.[32]

Both promissory theory and efficient breach theory can be criticised for taking an unduly individualist approach to contract law which does not fit the way in which contracting parties see their agreements, or the way in which the law operates.

[27] S Smith, *Contract Theory* (Oxford, Oxford University Press, 2004); Smith (n 5). Compare Kimel (n 25) 97–99.

[28] Smith (n 5) 370–71.

[29] Kimel (n 25) 98.

[30] The teleological progression starts with OW Holmes Jnr, 'The Path of the Law' (1897) 10 *Harvard Law Review* 457, 462; OW Holmes Jnr, *The Common Law* (Boston, Little, Brown & Co, 1881) 301 and ends with R Posner, *Economic Analysis of Law,* 8th edn (New York, Aspen Walters Kluwer, 2011) 149.

[31] The specific critiques of efficient breach theory will be discussed in ch 4 in more detail.

[32] Although compare the Israeli case of *Adras Building Material v Harlow & Jones GmbH* 42(1) PD 221, translated in (1995) 3 *Restitution Law Review* 235 (SC of Israel, 1988).

Sometimes the more important aspect of the bargain for parties is the performance of the promise, sometimes the more important aspect of the bargain for the parties is the efficient allocation of resources and they happily accept expectation damages in lieu of performance.

Fried's promise theory adopts an unduly individualist approach to contract law because it insists that all promises should be kept, regardless of context.[33] Contract law has a role in increasing our autonomy and choice; but an overly strict concept of contract as promise may reduce choice rather than increase it.[34] In addition, promise theory does not take into account the subjective nature of a promise, and the different meanings which parties may ascribe to certain terms of the contract.[35]

Efficient breach scholars have also been criticised for taking an overly individualist approach which fails to take into account the broader context and the desirability of cooperative behaviour and trust.[36] A relational analysis of contract law exposes the fallacy that contracts are isolated individual transactions without social context.[37]

It may seem that I am trying to resolve incommensurables here by trying to reconcile these two theories, but I assert that contract law can only really be understood if we seek a *via media* between these two approaches, and acknowledge that the two theoretical approaches to the interest a claimant possesses under a contract only fit *some* contract cases *some* of the time, and that the extent of the fit depends on the subject matter of the contract in question.

Professor Berryman has said in relation to expanded notions of specific performance of contracts:

> Reform which purports to liberalize the availability of specific performance but does not wish to create specific relief as the presumptive remedy for breach of contract, will fail if it is not accompanied by the realization that a single contractual paradigm is not applicable to all circumstances.[38]

[33] J Raz, 'Promises in Morality and Law (Book Review)' (1982) 95 *Harvard Law Review* 916, 931–32.

[34] H Dagan, 'Restitutionary Damages for Breach of Contract: An Exercise in Private Law Theory' (2000) 1 *Theoretical Inquiries in Law* 115, 125.

[35] ibid 118–25.

[36] I Macneil, 'Efficient Breach of Contract: Circles in the Sky' (1982) 68 *Virginia Law Review* 947, 968–69; MA Eisenberg, 'The Disgorgement Interest in Contract Law' (2006) 105 *Michigan Law Review* 559, 573–74. See also J Perillo, 'Misreading Oliver Wendell Holmes on Efficient Breach and Tortious Interference' (2000) 68 *Fordham Law Review* 1085, 1105.

[37] See, eg I Macneil, 'The Many Futures of Contracts' (1974) 47 *Southern California Law Review* 691; I Macneil, 'Contracts: Adjustment of Long-term Economic Relations under Classical, Neo-classical and Relational Contract Law' (1978) 72 *Northwestern University Law Review* 854; I Macneil, *The New Social Contract: An Inquiry into Modern Contractual Relations* (New Haven, Yale University Press, 1980); I Macneil, 'Economic Analysis of Contractual Relations: Its Shortfalls and the Need for a Rich Classificatory Apparatus' (1981) 75 *Northwestern University Law Review* 1018; Macneil (n 36); I Macneil, 'Values in Contract: Internal and External' (1983) 78 *Northwestern University Law Review* 340; I Macneil, 'Relational Contract: What We Do and Do Not Know' [1985] *Wisconsin Law Review* 483; P Gudel, 'Relational Contract Theory and the Concept of Exchange' (1998) 46 *Buffalo Law Review* 763; I Macneil, 'Relational Contract Theory: Challenges and Queries' (2000) 94 *Northwestern University Law Review* 877. See also D Campbell (ed), *The Relational Theory of Contract: Selected Works of Ian Macneil* (London, Sweet & Maxwell, 2001).

[38] J Berryman, 'The Specific Performance Damages Continuum: An Historical Perspective' (1985) 17 *Ottawa Law Review* 295, 323.

Although Berryman is speaking of specific performance of contracts, a similar warning must be sounded in relation to gain-based relief for breach of contract, as the two are akin in many ways. A single contractual paradigm is not applicable to all circumstances, and looking at contract in one way alone does not reflect the cases, nor does it assist in ascertaining when disgorgement relief should be available.

Thus, courts must keep in mind *both* effects of contractual breach when seeking to award remedies which effectively make good the rights of the parties: both the hampering of the ability to shift resources between the parties in the manner agreed and the erosion of the bonds of trust between the parties. It is not advisable to focus on one effect to the exclusion of another. There may be some circumstances in which a contracting party should be entitled to breach his promise, for example, to avoid a loss because of unforeseen circumstances.[39] But by the same token, the effect of allowing parties to breach willy-nilly whenever it is 'efficient' to do so erodes trust in society, and may ultimately erode the concept of contract itself. Both promise theory and 'efficient breach' theory focus on only one effect of breach of contract, and each seeks to exclude contracts from their social context and the reality of the way in which the law operates in different ways. However, if we are to effectively recognise the rights which parties gain when entering contracts, we cannot afford to do this.

Professor Raz argues that the purpose of contract law should not be to enforce promises:

> but to protect both the practice of undertaking voluntary obligations and the individuals who rely on that practice. One enforces a promise by making the promisor perform it, or failing that, by putting the promisee in a position as similar as possible to that he would have occupied had the promisor respected the promise. One protects the practice of undertaking voluntary obligations by preventing its erosion – by making good any harm caused by its use and abuse.[40]

Contract law should be flexible enough to offer parties choice in the obligations which they undertake, but also to put claimants who are injured by breach in a position where their interest in performance is adequately recognised and vindicated by the courts. Contract law must also uphold the institution of contract itself and make it more reliable, otherwise society generally would be harmed by a lack of certainty as to whether obligations are likely to be upheld.[41] To reduce contract law simply to 'upholding promises' or 'promoting economic efficiency' ignores the twofold effect of contractual performance. Contract law is more complex and nuanced than either of these extreme poles of opinion. In many circumstances it results in the upholding of voluntary obligations, but it also has the flexibility to allow parties to breach their contracts at times.

[39] See Campbell (n 13) 269; Campbell and Harris (n 13) 217–21; Campbell and Wylie (n 13) 615–16. See also P Atiyah, 'The Liberal Theory of Contract' in P Atiyah, *Essays on Contract* (Oxford, Oxford University Press, 1986) 121, 126, who argues that liberal theories of contract ought to be able to accommodate a change of mind on the part of the promisor.

[40] Raz (n 33) 933. See also Kimel (n 25) 90.

[41] Raz (n 33) 937.

It is particularly important to keep these considerations in mind when awarding disgorgement damages. We do not want a remedy which preferences one effect of contractual performance over another, and it is important to adequately recognise all rights arising from a contract. The question is then what remedial scheme best achieves this. It will be argued in the next section that we need to have regard not only to compensating a claimant for her losses, but also to recognising the claimant's performance interest by various means (including compensatory damages, specific relief and, exceptionally, disgorgement damages).

IV The Performance Interest

It should be evident from what has been said previously that to understand the role of disgorgement damages more clearly, we must consider what a claimant seeks to gain from a contract. The right the promisee gains as a result of entering into the contract has been described as the 'performance interest'.[42] As Buckland said, 'One does not buy a right to damages, one buys a horse.'[43] A full understanding of the performance interest is essential to understanding when a claimant may have a 'legitimate interest' in the performance of a contract so as to give rise to disgorgement damages.

Courts emphasise the importance of keeping bargains in principle, but in terms of remedies the preference for expectation damages over specific relief could indicate that the law's commitment to performance is less than wholehearted. In this section, I will first canvass the stated attitudes of the courts towards the performance interest. I will then turn to the way in which the performance interest is vindicated – in the sense of being protected or recognised – by contractual remedies (to a lesser or greater degree). The thread that runs through this discussion is substitutability: that is, how courts best ensure that the claimant gets what she bargained for, or an appropriate substitute, in a way that is as non-intrusive as possible.[44]

A The Courts' Attitude towards the Performance Interest: Support in Principle

Much case law on contract emphasises the principle of *pacta sunt servanda* or the notion that agreements must be kept. Courts around the world have adopted

[42] Coote, 'The Performance Interest' (n 6) 82–83.

[43] WW Buckland, 'The Nature of Contractual Obligation' (1944) 8 *CLJ* 247, 249–51.

[44] American Law Institute, *Restatement (Second) of the Law of Contracts* (1981), §360, specifically enumerates 'difficulty in procuring a suitable substitute performance' as a criterion to be taken into account when awarding specific performance. This shows the importance of substitutability to the kind of remedy which is awarded for breach of contract.

a very strict rhetoric in relation to contractual obligations. Roskill LJ famously stated in *The Hansa Nord*, 'contracts are made to be performed and not to be avoided.'[45] It has been stated that upon entry into a contract, each party assumes 'a legal right to the performance of the contract'[46] and, at the same time, each party 'assumes a legally recognised and enforceable obligation to perform'.[47]

The US *Restatement of Contracts* hints at the importance of the performance interest when it defines contract as 'a promise . . . for the breach of which the law gives a remedy, *or the performance of which the law in some way recognises as a duty*'[48] (emphasis added).

Windeyer J's judgment in *Coulls v Bagot's Executor and Trustee Co Ltd* typifies the approach of the Australian High Court:

> The primary obligation of a party to a contract is to perform it, to keep his promise. That is what the law requires of him. If he fails to do so, he incurs a liability to pay damages. That however is the ancillary remedy for his violation of the other party's primary right to have him carry out his promise. It is, I think, a faulty analysis of legal obligations to say that the law treats a promisor as having a right to elect either to perform his promise or to pay damages. Rather, using one sentence from the passage from Lord Erskine's judgment[49] which I have quoted above, the promisee has 'a legal right to the performance of the contract'.[50]

The High Court affirmed Windeyer J's view in *Zhu v The Treasurer of the State of New South Wales*,[51] saying:

> [S]ubject to the established limits on the grant of specific performance and injunctions, in Australian law each contracting party may be said to have a right to the performance of the contract by the other.[52]

The High Court expressly rejected the disjunctive view of contractual obligations: namely that the defendant may elect to either perform or to pay damages.

The Israeli Supreme Court has expressed similar views to the Australian High Court in *Adras*:[53]

[45] *Cehave NV v Bremer Handelgesellschaft mbH ('The Hansa Nord')* [1976] QB 44 (CA) 71.

[46] *Alley v Deschamps* (1806) 13 Ves Jun 225, 228; 33 ER 278, 279 (Lord Erskine).

[47] *In Re T & N Ltd* [2005] EWHC 2870, [2006] 1 WLR 1728 (Ch) [26] (David Richards J).

[48] American Law Institute (n 44) §1.

[49] *Alley v Deschamps* (n 46) 228, 279 (Lord Erskine).

[50] *Coulls v Bagot's Executor and Trustee Co Ltd* (1967) 119 CLR 460 (HCA) 504 (Windeyer J). See also *Placer Development Ltd v Commonwealth of Australia* (1969) 121 CLR 353 (HCA) 373 (Windeyer J) and *Czarnikow Ltd v Koufos* [1966] 2 QB 695 (CA) 730–31 (Diplock LJ) for expressions of similar sentiments.

[51] *Zhu v The Treasurer of the State of New South Wales* [2004] HCA 56, (2004) 218 CLR 530 (HCA).

[52] ibid [129]. See also *Tabcorp Holdings Ltd v Bowen Investments Pty Ltd* (2009) 236 CLR 272 (HCA) [13] where the High Court rejects efficient breach in no uncertain terms.

[53] *Adras* (n 32). See D Friedmann, 'Restitution of Profits Gained by Party in Breach of Contract' (1988) 104 *LQR* 383.

> Contracts are there to be performed, whether or not damages will be payable on breach, an approach by which we encourage people to keep their promises. Promise keeping is a basis of our life, as a society and a nation.[54]

If one takes these decisions at face value, it seems that there will *always* be a legitimate interest in ensuring a promise is kept.

However, in light of the foregoing statements, the remedies for breach of contract present a puzzle for scholars of contract law.

B The Courts' Attitude towards the Performance Interest: Failure to Support Claimants in Practice with Remedies?

In contrast to the sentiments expressed above, there is a strand of thought which suggests that the promisee really gains a right to damages rather than a right to performance upon entry into a contract. Mr Justice Holmes of the US Supreme Court is often held up as the primary advocate of this view. He said:

> The duty to keep a contract at common law means a prediction that you must pay damages if you do not keep it, – and nothing else.[55]

This is supported in some regards by the case law. The traditional approach of the common law towards breach of contract is encapsulated in the well-known statement of Parke B in *Robinson v Harman*:

> [T]he rule of the common law is, that where a party sustains a loss by reason of a breach of contract, he is, so far as money can do it, to be placed in the same situation, with respect to damages, as if the contract had been performed.[56]

The default remedy for breach of contract is 'expectation damages', which seek to make good the expectations of the claimant by means of a monetary award. Generally, this formulation has been interpreted to mean only that the claimant will be placed in a situation as if the contract had been performed from a *financial* point of view. Thus, in *White Arrow Express Ltd v Lamey's Distribution Ltd*,[57] Lord Bingham MR (as he then was) stated that the *Robinson v Harman* formulation assumes 'that the breach has injured [the claimant's] financial position; if he cannot show that it has, he will recover nominal damages only.'[58] This may create an impression that compensation is the only aim of contractual remedies – an

[54] *Adras* (n 32) 272. See Dagan (n 34) fn 12: Dagan notes that similar arguments have been raised by other commentators, eg P Birks, 'Profits of Breach of Contract' (1993) 109 *LQR* 518, 519; D Friedmann, 'Restitution of Benefits Obtained Through the Appropriation of Property or the Commission of a Wrong' (1980) 80 *Columbia Law Review* 504, 515; G Jones, 'The Recovery of Benefits Gained from a Breach of Contract' (1983) 99 *LQR* 443, 454.

[55] Holmes, 'The Path of the Law' (n 30) 462. See also Holmes, *The Common Law* (n 30) 301: 'The only universal consequence of a legally binding promise is, that the law makes the promisor pay damages if the promised event does not come to pass.'

[56] *Robinson v Harman* (1848) 1 Ex 850, 855; 154 ER 363.

[57] *White Arrow Express Ltd v Lamey's Distribution Ltd* (1996) 15 TLR 69 (CA).

[58] ibid 73. See also *Ford v White* [1964] 1 WLR 885 (Ch).

impression which reinforces what Professor Birks called the 'false monopoly of compensation'.[59]

However, as Sir Frederick Pollock responded to Mr Justice Holmes, the proposition that contract only gives rise to an obligation to pay damages is incorrect, and the law recognises the performance interest in a variety of different ways other than awarding expectation damages.[60] First, the most prominent indication that contract law recognises the performance interest comes from the equitable remedies for breach of contract, particularly specific performance and injunctions to restrain breach of negative covenant which promote performance to a greater or lesser degree. Secondly, the doctrine of anticipatory breach indicates that the law ordinarily expects parties to fulfil their performance obligations under a contract. Parties can only excuse themselves from these obligations in exceptional circumstances. Finally, the tort of inducing breach of contract suggests that courts will penalise third parties who induce a party to a contract not to perform.

Nonetheless, as will be discussed in further detail in chapter four, some law and economics scholars have taken Mr Justice Holmes' view of contract to its logical conclusion with the theory of 'efficient breach': promisors should be allowed to breach whenever it is economically efficient to do so, subject to the obligation to pay compensatory damages. Efficient breach continues to have influence because 'whatever its defects, the theory appears to offer the only plausible explanation of the rules regarding specific performance and punishing breach.'[61] However, as I will also discuss in chapter four, there are a number of problems with efficient breach analysis, and it does not produce an accurate fit with the case law, as Pollock foreshadowed.

As the law is currently structured, there is a notional hierarchy of remedies whereby remedies such as specific performance and injunctions are seen as exceptional, and dependent upon 'inadequacy of damages' at law.[62] If compensatory damages are the primary remedy for breach, this suggests that, in practice, courts are not so much concerned with enforcing promises as compensating for losses occasioned by breach.[63] Thus it has been noted that:

[59] P Birks, 'The Law of Restitution at the End of an Epoch' (1999) 28 *University of Western Australia Law Review* 13, 52–54; P Birks, 'Civil Wrongs: A New World' in *Butterworth Lectures 1990–91* (London, Butterworths, 1992) 55, 58.

[60] See Pollock's letter to Holmes dated 17 September 1897, Sir Frederick Pollock, *The Principles of Contracts*, 8th edn (London, Stevens, 1911) 192, fn k and Holmes' subsequent letter to Pollock dated 12 March 1911. The letters are reproduced in M De Wolfe Howe (ed), *The Holmes-Pollock Letters: The Correspondence of Mr Justice Holmes and Sir Frederick Pollock 1874–1932*, Vol I (Cambridge, Mass, Harvard University Press, 1942) 79–80 and 177 respectively.

[61] Smith (n 5) 361.

[62] M Tilbury, *Civil Remedies – Volume I* (Sydney, Butterworths, 1993) [1021]. There have been challenges to the notional hierarchy: see D Laycock, 'The Death of the Irreparable Injury Rule' (1990) 103 *Harvard Law Review* 687.

[63] E McKendrick, 'Breach of Contract and the Meaning of Loss' (1999) 52 *Current Legal Problems* 37, 38; NC Seddon and MP Ellinghaus, *Cheshire and Fifoot's Law of Contract*, 8th Australian edn (Chatswood, NSW, LexisNexis Butterworths, 2002) 1021–22, [24.1]. Although note Berryman (n 38) who points out that prior to the 19th century, courts were vastly more likely to award specific performance for breach of contract, and that the reluctance to award specific relief is (inter alia) a reflection of 19th century legal formalism.

> [t]he fact that the law is not prepared to commit itself to specific performance as the primary remedy does suggest that its commitment to ensuring that performance (rather than the economic end result of performance) is achieved is less than wholehearted.[64]

It is possible to argue that the present regime of contractual remedies does not prioritise the claimant's interest in performance.[65] The claimant's interest in the performance of the contract is an essential precondition for the award of disgorgement damages, so it follows that if contractual remedies indicate that the claimant's performance interest is very weak in most contracts, then disgorgement damages will very rarely, if ever, be awarded.

The common law's preference for expectation damages, however, does not mean that contract law is unconcerned with the performance interest, and merely concerned to compensate for loss. First, the expectation interest involves vindicating the claimant's performance interest by compensating the claimant for her loss, as this is the best substitute for performance in the circumstances. However, although courts usually choose to provide a substitute performance by compensating for loss, it does not follow that courts are only concerned about compensating claimants for loss of a profit, or that contractual damages are only about compensating for loss. They are concerned with providing an adequate substitute performance which properly balances the interests of the parties. The reason why contract law presumes expectation damages are the default remedy is because it is concerned to choose the remedy which is least intrusive for the defendant yet which still recognises the claimant's interests. Courts are increasingly willing to order specific relief when damages are inadequate.

i The Nature of the Expectation Interest

The expectation interest seeks to 'put the claimant in as good a position as if the defendant had performed his promise'.[66] It has been argued that this formulation is ambiguous, because it can mean the defendant's obligation is to ensure that the claimant receives the performance due to her, but it can also mean that the defendant's obligation is simply to make good losses so that the claimant is no worse off.[67] Ordinarily, the difference between the two is not obvious, but it emerges starkly in those cases where the cost of rectifying the performance is far greater than the reduction in value caused by the loss of the stipulated performance.[68]

[64] McKendrick (n 63) 47.

[65] ibid; Seddon and Ellinghaus (n 63) 1021–22, [24.1]; SV Shiffrin, 'The Divergence of Contract and Promise' (2007) 120 *Harvard Law Review* 708, 722–23. Compare Webb (n 8) 52–53, who argues that the 'expectation interest' has simply obscured the two interests being protected by contractual remedies (namely the compensation interest and the performance interest), so that the courts think they are protecting 'the' contractual interest regardless of which remedy they select.

[66] L Fuller and W Purdue, 'The Reliance Interest in Contract Damages: 1' (1936) 46 *Yale Law Journal* 52, 54.

[67] Webb (n 8) 48; Coote, 'Contract Damages, *Ruxley* and the Performance Interest' (n 6) 540.

[68] These cases will be considered in detail in ch 6, which considers the availability of disgorgement damages for skimped performance.

Putting someone in a position as if the contract has been performed should *not* simply involve ascertaining whether a claimant has suffered a loss as a result of breach and compensating her for that loss. Some criticisms of *Blake* and following cases have focussed on the fact that disgorgement damages are said to be awarded when the claimant has suffered a non-compensable loss. Thus it is argued that the trigger for disgorgement cases is not that the defendant has made a wrongful gain, but that the claimant has been under-compensated or uncompensated for loss.[69] It is then said that any deficiencies in contract law could be remedied by a more inclusive conception of loss rather than by disgorgement of gain. However, an under-compensated or uncompensated loss on its own is *not* sufficient to ground a claim for disgorgement damages. Instead, we must separate out the question of whether the claimant suffered a loss from the question of whether the claimant will be put into a position as if the contract had been performed, which will make the analysis clearer. There may be situations where the claimant did not suffer a loss for which expectation damages can be an adequate substitute but she nevertheless has a performance interest which *should* be vindicated in some way such that a promisor is made accountable for his breach.

Charlie Webb argues that the claimant's expectation interest under a contract is a composite of two interests which overlap in part: the performance interest and the compensation interest.[70] The primary interest gained by a claimant from entry into a contract is the performance interest, and loss is *irrelevant* to this category of interest.[71] By contrast, the compensation interest recognises the claimant's right to be compensated for loss suffered as a result of the breach of contract. Compensatory damages seek to compensate the claimant for the loss suffered, but they also affirm the existence of a performance interest, because the breach of the duty to perform creates the obligation to compensate for loss.[72] Ordinarily, expectation damages adequately recognise both the performance interest and the obligation to compensate for loss so that the difference between the two is not obvious to courts.

However, the primary concern of the law with regard to expectation damages is not just to compensate for loss, but to vindicate the performance interest. In this way, contrary to Webb, I argue that it is not so much that there are two separate interests which overlap in part, but that the performance interest is the overarching primary right sought to be vindicated by contract law remedies. Expectation damages are just one way in which courts can vindicate the claimant's performance right. Law and economics writers distinguish between 'the bargain princi-

[69] See, eg Mitchell (n 19) 8; O'Sullivan (n 19) 344; Harris and Campbell (n 13) 224–25; Campbell and Wylie (n 13) 615–17, who argue disgorgement damages will be awarded simply because the claimant has suffered a non-compensable loss, and that they are flawed as a result. The important question is *whether or not the claimant can achieve a substitute performance from elsewhere*, not whether the claimant has suffered a non-compensable loss. This resolves the hypothetical problem proposed by Campbell and Wylie (n 13) 616 – under my analysis, the claimant would not be able to obtain disgorgement damages because she obtained a substitute performance.

[70] Webb (n 8) 41–42, 45–49. See also Pearce and Halson (n 8) and Smith (n 5) 94–95.

[71] Webb (n 8) 56.

[72] ibid 47.

ple' (bargains should be performed according to their terms) and 'the indifference principle' (contractual remedies should be structured so that the claimant should be indifferent between the defendant performing on the one hand and the defendant breaching and paying damages on the other).[73] A promisee enters a contract because she expects to obtain certain benefits from a transaction (or, in economic terms, 'utility') for the thing exchanged.[74] When breach occurs, the law seeks to vindicate the promisee's expectation interest by making her indifferent to the defendant's breach. Compensatory damages calculated according to loss of market value are more likely to be adequate in situations where the claimant seeks to gain a financial advantage.[75] This is because market value provides an adequate measure of the likely value to the claimant, and the claimant is likely to be able to purchase a substitute performance with such damages. However, when the market value of performance does not provide an adequate substitute, courts may choose not to award expectation damages calculated as 'loss of a profit' damages by reference to market value, but instead to calculate expectation damages in a way which more accurately reflects the claimant's interest in performance.[76]

In a situation where the promisee enters into a contract to obtain performance itself, and not the financial equivalent of performance, the law of contract damages struggles to provide an adequate remedy. Contract law extends into many transactions where pursuit of profit is 'not a primary aim for both parties.'[77] This is particularly the case with consumer contracts, where parties enter the contract not to make a profit, but to have certain services performed.[78] Similarly, as will be observed in chapter five, the negative covenant cases often involve contracts which are designed to protect non-financial interests. In cases where monetary awards are inadequate to vindicate the claimant's performance interest, courts prefer to award specific relief for breach of such contracts. However, where specific relief is unavailable as a result of the defendant's breach, I will argue that courts may also award disgorgement damages in some exceptional circumstances.

Thus, when choosing the appropriate remedy for breach of contract, it is important to have regard to the claimant's performance interest, and the objective which the claimant hoped to achieve.[79] The court must pay attention to the claimant's *subjective* interest in the subject matter of the contract,[80] sometimes known

[73] R Craswell, 'Contract Remedies, Renegotiation, and the Theory of Efficient Breach' (1988) 61 *South California Law Review* 629; M Eisenberg, 'Actual and Virtual Specific Performance, the Theory of Efficient Breach, and the Indifference Principle in Contract Law' (2005) 93 *California Law Review* 975, 977–79. See also Friedmann (n 6) 67.

[74] A Loke, 'Cost of Cure or Difference in Market Value? Toward a Sound Choice in the Basis for Quantifying Expectation Damages' (1996) 10 *Journal of Contract Law* 189, 192.

[75] ibid 191–93.

[76] Including by awards of rectification damages, reliance damages and damages for loss of a chance.

[77] McKendrick (n 63) 40. See also McKendrick (n 7) 167–68.

[78] McKendrick (n 63) 40; McKendrick (n 7) 167–68. See also Harris and Campbell (n 13) 232, who are generally critical of the 'performance interest', but concede that consumer contracts for complex services may require an assurance of complete performance.

[79] McKendrick (n 7) 170–71; Friedmann (n 6) 68–71.

[80] Loke (n 74) 190. See also P Linzer, 'On the Amorality of Contract Remedies – Efficiency, Equity, and the *Second Restatement*' (1981) 81 *Columbia Law Review* 111, 131.

as the 'consumer surplus'.[81] Some assessment must be made as to whether the subject matter of the contract has a special value to the claimant, or whether the claimant's interest in the subject matter of the contract is wholly pecuniary, in which case damages are likely to be an adequate remedy.[82] Any remedy is necessarily a 'next best' solution, but some solutions vindicate the claimant's right to performance better than others. Disgorgement damages cannot grant a substitute for performance, and usually in these cases, the very difficulty is that an equivalent to performance is unavailable by the time the case is brought before the court (because damages are inadequate and specific relief is no longer available). Nonetheless, disgorgement damages are a way of vindicating the promisee's performance interest in that the court clearly recognises the promisee's interest, and makes the promisor accountable for the breach of contract by stripping him of his profit.

ii The Primacy of Expectation Damages

The reason for the primacy of expectation damages in the common law is because of the common law's general presumption in favour of liberty: because specific performance is more intrusive to the defendant, damages are preferred in all cases where the claimant will not be made worse off by receiving damages.[83] In a sense, the preference of the common law for expectation damages for breach of contract is an application of JS Mill's 'harm principle', namely that the imposition of legal obligations on individuals is only justified when such obligations are imposed to prevent or redress harm.[84] In choosing a remedy, the common law has chosen the least intrusive remedy to the defendant (in an attempt to balance the interests of the claimant and the defendant). Expectation damages may be less beneficial to the claimant than actual performance,[85] but contract law is nothing if not pragmatic, and as long as damages allow the claimant to purchase a substitute performance, then the common law favours them.

Contract law is nonetheless rightly sensitive to the possibility that damages may be inadequate to recognise the claimant's performance interest. The very concept of inadequacy of damages confirms the importance of the performance interest: '[i]f the primary right of the contract is a right to receive damages, then it is nonsense to speak of damages being inadequate.'[86]

[81] D Harris, A Ogus and J Phillips, 'Contract Remedies and the Consumer Surplus' (1979) 95 *LQR* 581. See also *Ruxley Electronics and Constructions Ltd v Forsyth* [1996] 1 AC 344 (HL) 360 (Lord Mustill, adopting the terminology of Harris, Ogus and Phillips).

[82] Loke (n 74) 192–93.

[83] Kimel (n 25) 102–04.

[84] ibid 103–04.

[85] See Eisenberg (n 73) 989–97 for reasons why compensatory damages may often be undercompensatory in practice.

[86] Cunnington, 'Inadequacy of Damages' (n 22) 136.

Courts are increasingly willing to award specific relief where the claimant's performance interest will not be protected by an award of damages.[87] Professor Laycock has argued that the inadequacy of damages (and the attendant concept that there will be 'irreparable injury to the claimant') creates a misleading impression, and that apart from the loss of non substitutable goods or services in an orderly market, the law does not display even a weak preference for common law damages.[88] He explains:

> Damages are inadequate if the plaintiff cannot use them to replace the specific thing he has lost. This is by far the most important rule in determining the doctrinal relationship among remedies. The emphasis on replaceability turns the alleged preference for damages on its head. Money is an adequate remedy if, and only if, it can be used to replace the specific thing that was lost. That is to say, money is never an adequate remedy in itself. It is either a means to an end or an inadequate substitute that happens to be the best we can do at acceptable cost. But the judicial preference is to give plaintiff specific performance if she wants it – to replace her loss with as identical a substitute as possible.[89]

Indeed, in the context of specific performance and injunctions, it has been suggested that the threshold question of 'are damages inadequate?' has been replaced by a question of 'what is the most *just* remedy in the circumstances?'[90] Courts often start from the position that *unless* damages give rise to identical consequences for a claimant to relief *in specie*, a court should order specific performance (subject to discretionary considerations).[91] In the vast majority of cases, however, damages will suffice for a variety of reasons – because damages and specific relief will be practically indistinguishable, because parties are unable to get specific relief or because the parties do not seek specific relief.[92]

The Scots law of 'specific implement' results in a similar outcome in practice to the common law, even though Scots law starts from the presumption that the pursuer is entitled to specific performance of the contractual obligation.[93] Although it is presumed that specific implement is available as of right, the right is qualified in ways which make the outcome of a Scottish contract case look very

[87] Burrows (n 21) 504. There is a similar trend in the US: Linzer (n 80) 126–30. As Burrows notes, *Co-operative Insurance Society Ltd v Argyll Stores (Holdings) Ltd* [1998] AC 1 (HL) bucks this trend by emphasising the difficulties created by constant supervision.

[88] Laycock (n 62) 695. Note that the new *Restatement* recognises Laycock's criticisms of the 'inadequacy of damages', yet states that it still has utility in a disgorgement context: American Law Institute (n 1) § 39 comment c.

[89] ibid 703.

[90] ICF Spry, *The Principles of Equitable Remedies*, 8th edn (NSW, Law Book Co, 2010) 59–61. See, eg *Beswick v Beswick* [1968] AC 58 (HL) 102 (Lord Upjohn); *Evans Marshall v Bertola SA* [1973] 1 WLR 349 (CA) 379; *The Stena Nautica (No 2)* [1982] 2 Lloyd's Rep 336 (CA); *State Transport Authority v Apex Quarries Ltd* [1988] VR 187 (VSC).

[91] Spry (n 90). See, eg *Sky Petroleum Ltd v VIP Petroleum Ltd* [1974] 1 WLR 576 (Ch) and *Verrall v Great Yarmouth Borough Council* [1981] 1 QB 202 (CA).

[92] Laycock (n 62) 697–99.

[93] E McKendrick, 'Specific Implement and Specific Performance – a Comparison' (1986) *Scots Law Times* 249. See also *Co-operative Insurance Society v Argyll Stores (Holdings) Ltd* [1998] AC 1 (HL) 11–12 (Lord Hoffman). Against *McLaren Murdoch & Hamilton Ltd v The Abercromby Motor Group Ltd* [2002] ScotCS 299, [2003] SCLR 323 (Court of Session, Outer House) [41] (Lord Drummond).

similar to the English common law outcome in practice.[94] Similarly, in French and German law specific performance is the presumptive remedy for breach of contract, but in practice the exceptions to the rule are more important than the rule itself.[95] Ordinarily, parties prefer to claim damages in cases where their losses can be easily assessed.[96] The differences between the common law of specific performance and the approach of civil law systems such as Scots, German and French law is not as dramatic as it seems.[97]

We then return full circle to the question of availability of disgorgement damages. In formulating when such a remedy should be available, we need to consider the circumstances in which we should vindicate the promisee's interest in performance, and protect future promisees from breach by deterring future promisors from breaching their contracts in similar circumstances, but we should leave enough flexibility for promisors to be able to breach in some circumstances. The law needs to protect the practice of contracting, and to protect the parties who enter contracts: both promisee and promisor. Clearly, it is too late to prevent the particular promisor in question from breaching his contract, and only future promisors can be deterred from breaching their contracts, but at the very least, the promisee's performance interest can be vindicated in the case before the court by stripping the promisor of his gain.

V Substitutability and Disgorgement

A Disgorgement should be Available when the Subject Matter of the Contract is Not Substitutable

As noted earlier, various commentators have noted that if specific relief was or ought to have been available to a claimant in a contract claim, but is no longer available, it is likely that the claimant may be able to seek disgorgement damages.[98]

[94] Specific implement is generally unavailable if (a) the obligation is only to pay money, (b) the contract involves a personal or intimate relationship, (c) there is no *pretium affectionis* or subjective special value attaching to the subject matter of the contract, (d) compliance with the decree would be impossible, (e) the decree would be unenforceable, (f) the decree would cause exceptional hardship or be inconvenient or unjust, and (g) the court decides in its discretion that damages are adequate in the circumstances. See McKendrick (n 93).

[95] GH Treitel, *Remedies for Breach of Contract – A Comparative Account* (Oxford, Oxford University Press, 1998) 53.

[96] ibid 71; K Zweigert and H Kötz, *Introduction to Comparative Law*, 3rd edn (Tony Weir tr, Oxford, Oxford University Press, 1998) 484.

[97] Treitel (n 95).

[98] SM Waddams, 'Restitution As Part of Contract Law' in A Burrows (ed), *Essays on the Law of Restitution* (Oxford, Oxford University Press, 1991) 197, 208–09; S Doyle and D Wright, 'Restitutionary Damages – The Unnecessary Remedy?' (2001) 25 *Melbourne University Law Review* 1, 11–13; P Jaffey, *The Nature and Scope of Restitution* (Oxford, Hart Publishing, 2000) 390–94; R Grantham and C Rickett, *Enrichment and Restitution in New Zealand* (Oxford, Hart Publishing, 2000) 480–81; Edelman (n 22) 152–55; P Benson, 'Disgorgement for Breach of Contract and Corrective Justice: An

Mr Beatson (as he then was) described gain-based damages as 'in reality a monetised form of specific performance'.[99] Disgorgement is not a substitute for performance, but it does vindicate the promisee's right to performance where the promisee would have been or had been awarded specific performance before the promisor put the remedy out of the promisee's reach.[100] In this sense, it is related to the relief under *Lord Cairns' Act*,[101] as Lord Nicholls noted in *Attorney-General v Blake*.[102]

It is salutary to illustrate the point with a practical example. Let us say Alice has made a contract with Boris which provides that Boris will supply her with 2000 widgets. In the case of a normal contract for provision of available goods or services, if the contract is not performed, the default position is that the other party will obtain damages to compensate for her loss.[103]

So, in our example, if Boris breaches his contract with Alice, but pays damages to compensate for Alice's loss, Alice can buy widgets from Xenophon instead, using the damages obtained from Boris. A contractor in the position of Boris may choose not to perform, subject to incurring the liability to pay damages.[104] The defendant's conduct is not 'wrongful' because the claimant can take the damages and use them to obtain a substitute performance. She is placed in the position she would have been in if the contract had been performed. Thus, Alice's interest in performance is protected even though Boris is not compelled to perform himself.

However, taking our example above, let us suppose widgets are incredibly rare, and Boris is the only supplier in the world market. Alice will not be able to procure a substitute performance from elsewhere. The lack of substitutability means that she should be entitled to performance of the contract. Compensatory damages will *not* be adequate to put Alice in a position as if the contract had been performed.

Analysis in Outline' in J Neyers, M McInnes and S Pitel (eds), *Understanding Unjust Enrichment* (Oxford, Hart Publishing, 2004) 327–30; P Jaffey, 'Disgorgement and "Licence Fee Damages" in Contract' (2004) 20 *Journal of Contract Law* 57, 61; Eisenberg (n 36) 582; Cunnington, 'The Measure and Availability' (n 3); SM Waddams, 'Gains Derived from Breach of Contract: Historical and Conceptual Perspectives' in R Cunnington and D Saidov (eds), *Contract Damages: Domestic and International Perspectives* (Oxford, Hart Publishing, 2008) 187, 205–06; Cunnington, 'The Inadequacy of Damages' (n 22). See also American Law Institute (n 1) § 39 comment c. Compare however, Burrows, *Remedies for Torts and Breach of Contract* (n 21) 399–400; A Burrows, *The Law of Restitution*, 2nd edn (London, Butterworths, 2002) 485.

99 J Beatson, *The Use and Abuse of Unjust Enrichment – Essays on the Law of Restitution* (Oxford, Oxford University Press, 1991) 17. Compare *Surrey County Council v Bredero Homes Ltd* [1993] 1 WLR 1361 (CA) 1368 (Dillon LJ), 1370 (Steyn LJ). Steyn LJ said at 1370:

> Moreover, so far as the narrower submission restricts the principle to cases where the remedies of specific performance and injunction would have been available, I must confess that it seems to me a bromide formula without any rationale in logic and commonsense.

100 Eisenberg (n 36) 584.

101 See, eg UK: Chancery Amendment Act 1858 (Imp), s 2 (now Supreme Court Act 1981 (UK), s 50). Australia: Supreme Court Act 1970 (NSW), s 68; Judicature Act 1876 (Qld), s 4(7); Supreme Court Act 1935 (SA), s 30; Supreme Court Civil Procedure Act 1932 (Tas), s 11(13); Supreme Court Act 1958 (Vic), s 62(3). New Zealand: Supreme Court Act 1860 (NZ), s 5 and *Ryder v Hall* (1905) 27 NZLR 385 (NZCA).

102 *Blake* (n 1) 281 (Lord Nicholls).

103 *Robinson v Harman* (1848) 1 Ex 850, 154 ER 363; *Photo Production Ltd v Securicor Transport Ltd* [1980] AC 827 (HL).

104 Jaffey, 'Disgorgement and "Licence Fee Damages" in Contract' (n 98) 7.

The first option for Alice is to seek specific performance. Specific performance will ensure that she is put in a position as if the contract had been performed – indeed, she gets exactly what she has bargained for. An award of specific performance is the best way of protecting Alice's interest in performance.[105]

But sometimes Alice may not be able to obtain specific performance of the contract, perhaps because Boris has sold the widgets to Conrad for a profit. It is in these circumstances that she should be entitled to disgorgement of any profits made by Boris. The other remedies which could have put Alice in a position as if the contract had been performed are no longer adequate. Compensatory damages will not enable Alice to purchase a substitute performance, and specific performance is impossible because Boris no longer has the widgets. Boris has taken performance out of Alice's reach by his breach. Disgorgement then becomes the 'next best' option to vindicate Alice's right.

Substitutability is already a familiar principle of contract law because it is central to the decision of courts to award specific performance of contracts in preference to expectation damages.[106] It is also arguably relevant to cases where courts award of cost of cure damages in preference to market value damages for breach of contract.[107] There are two aspects to substitutability:

1. The availability of a substitute performance in the market; and
2. The nature of the claimant's subjective interest in the subject matter of the contract.[108]

Specific relief will be ordered in circumstances where the claimant would be unable (or find it very difficult) to procure a substitute performance in the market.[109] In addition, the court must consider the claimant's subjective interest in the subject matter of the contract, or, in other words, the claimant's aims in entering the contract. If the claimant's interest is non-pecuniary, then it is less likely that compensatory damages will be adequate to protect her performance interest. The necessity to look at the objectives of the claimant extends to situations where courts seek to award disgorgement damages, as Birks hinted:

> A basic commitment to compensatory damages can be maintained and reconciled with exceptional availability of restitutionary damages by adding this restraint on the latter: there should be no recourse to restitutionary damages – not even in the case of cynical breach for the sake of gain – unless on the particular facts compensatory damages are demonstrably an inadequate remedy, *having regard to the objectives which the victim of the breach had hoped to achieve through full performance of the contract.* [Emphasis added][110]

[105] McKendrick (n 63) 47; Webb (n 8) 46.
[106] Kronman (n 4).
[107] Loke (n 74).
[108] ibid 190–92.
[109] *Adderley v Dixon* (1824) 1 Sim & St 607, 610, 57 ER 239, 240.
[110] P Birks, 'Restitutionary Damages for Breach of Contract: *Snepp* and the Fusion of Law and Equity' [1987] *Lloyd's Maritime and Commercial Law Quarterly* 421, 441–42. See also *Attorney-General v Blake* [1997] EWCA Civ 3008, [1998] Ch 439 (CA) 458 (Lord Woolf).

Where there is a lack of substitutability, the law considers that the claimant is justified in compelling the defendant to perform the contract. In the same way, substitutability can help determine whether a claimant is entitled to disgorgement damages.

Contrary to the assertions of dicta in cases such as *Coulls v Bagot's Executor and Trustee Co Ltd*, there is no unequivocal duty to perform a contract. The notion that there is ordinarily no duty to perform a contract seems strange.[111] However, where a benefit under a contract is substitutable, the defendant is merely responsible for ensuring that the claimant does not lose out by proceeding on the basis that the contract will be performed.[112] Damages are an adequate vindication of the claimant's right when the benefit is non-substitutable. The way in which courts choose to recognise the right to performance very much depends upon the context in which it is sought to be protected. A court will not ordinarily force a defendant to perform a contract *in specie* if the claimant can procure an adequate pecuniary substitute for performance.

The same principles can be extended to awards of disgorgement damages. However, it should be emphasised that disgorgement damages cannot be said to be substitutive of the claimant's rights, except in the very broad sense discussed in the previous chapter. The very point of disgorgement damages is that they will only be awarded where no substitute is available, and thus another method has to be found to vindicate the claimant's rights to performance. Nor are disgorgement damages compensatory. While compensatory damages are designed to return the claimant to the position he or she would have been in but for the defendant's breach,[113] disgorgement damages are the 'mirror image'. The primary object of disgorgement damages is to remove the benefit to the defendant so that the *defendant* is put in a position as if the wrongful conduct had never occurred.[114] Thus, the claimant's right is vindicated by seeing the defendant put in the position that he should have been in if he had performed his contract.

Disgorgement damages are a 'tertiary' remedy of last resort. A defendant will only be liable for disgorgement damages if (a) compensatory damages are inadequate, (b) specific performance is no longer available and (c) the defendant has made a profit which can be disgorged.

Because of the punitive rationale behind disgorgement damages, as discussed previously, there must be an *advertent* element to the breach. Furthermore, if there are any reasons why imposition of disgorgement damages would cause undue hardship to the defendant, the court should consider exercising its discre-

[111] Jaffey, 'Disgorgement and "Licence Fee Damages" in Contract' (n 98) 8.

[112] Kimel (n 25) 100–09 recognises that the claimant has an interest in performance, but justifies the law's preference for expectation damages on the basis of Mill's harm principle – ie imposition of legal obligation is justified when it is done to redress harm, but when choosing a remedy for breach of contract, the courts should choose the *less intrusive* remedy.

[113] *Commonwealth v Amann Aviation Pty Ltd* (1991) 174 CLR 64 (HCA) 161.

[114] Eisenberg (n 36) 561; R Cooter and B Freedman, 'The Fiduciary Relationship: Its Economic Character and Legal Consequences' (1991) 66 *New York University Law Review* 1045, 1051; R Cooter and T Ulen, *Law and Economics*, 3rd edn (Reading, Mass, Addison-Wesley, 2000) 234.

tion to disallow disgorgement damages according to one of the traditional equitable bars to relief, as will be discussed in detail in chapter seven.

Disgorgement damages have been analysed as a way of regulating the behaviour of fiduciaries in an efficient manner.[115] In the same way, disgorgement damages for breach of contract can operate as a way of regulating the performance interest in an efficient manner.[116] Stripping defendants of their profit when they breach a contract in certain circumstances encourages future parties to similar contracts to either perform their obligations or negotiate a release from the contract. Ordinarily, expectation damages are the best way to enforce contracts. They provide appropriate incentives to a promisor who is making performance-or-breach decisions, and allow a promisor to decide how much precaution to take to ensure she will be able to perform when the time comes.[117] But this will not be the case in a minority of contracts. In those contracts where the party cannot procure a substitute performance, and where the claimant attaches a special value to performance, the threat of disgorgement damages provides incentives to the promisor to perform or renegotiate.[118]

Disgorgement damages provide an appropriate disincentive against future breaches because they do not prevent breach altogether and in the case of the specific breach at hand, they only place the defendant in the position he would have been in if he had performed his obligations. If the law went further in attempting to discourage breach it would run the risk of over-deterrence, that is, parties may be deterred from entering into socially useful contracts. Or, as with an overly strict promissory analysis, parties may be kept to their bargains where it is unfair or inappropriate. Even where disgorgement damages are available, there is a choice open to the parties other than breaching and disgorging profits or performing and missing out on a profitable opportunity.[119] The promisor can approach the promisee and seek to be released from the contract. If disgorgement damages are payable upon breach, it is likely that a promisor will think carefully before breaching a contract where performance is non-substitutable.

Disgorgement damages and specific performance share a deterrent function. Specific performance compels a defendant to perform by threatening coercive sanctions, but disgorgement damages perform the same function by removing the

[115] Cooter and Freedman (n 114) 1052.

[116] D Fox, 'Restitutionary Damages to Deter Breach of Contract' (2001) 60 *CLJ* 33, 35.

[117] Eisenberg (n 36) 577.

[118] See ibid, Eisenberg identifies six different categories of case:

1. Cases where the promise has bargained for the promisor's breach (including 'second sale' cases);
2. Disgorgement in lieu of performance, where the promise had been awarded specific performance before the promisor put the remedy out of the promisee's reach;
3. Disgorgement as a surrogate for expectation damages;
4. Bargains designed to serve interests other than profit making;
5. Externalities (contracts proscribed in certain ways policy reasons to help society); and
6. Disgorgement of costs saved by breach (skimped performance and diminished value).

[119] Discussed in more detail in ch 4, III.

incentive to breach.[120] Nonetheless, despite their common basis in deterrence, it is important not to confuse disgorgement damages with specific performance. Lord Hobhouse, in his dissent in *Blake*, suggested that disgorgement damages could not be awarded because they were not sought as a substitute for performance.[121] As I have discussed earlier,[122] this mistakes the nature of both specific relief and disgorgement damages. First, what is being protected by an award of specific performance is the right to performance itself, and it is not a substitute for the right.[123] Secondly, although disgorgement will be awarded according to similar criteria as an award of specific relief, and could even be said to be a substitute for specific relief, it differs from specific performance in that it is not awarded in lieu of compensation for the claimant's factual loss. Indeed, whether or not the claimant has suffered a factual loss is utterly irrelevant to disgorgement.[124] As *Blake* shows, the claimant may have suffered no factual loss at all.[125] Nonetheless, there are reasons why the claimant's right should be vindicated in the circumstances.

There is a tension between letting a defendant profit from a wrong on the one hand and giving a claimant a 'windfall' gain on the other.[126] The potential for disgorgement damages to operate harshly and give a claimant a 'windfall gain' is softened by substitutability: a defendant will only be stripped of his profit if the claimant is or was unable to procure a substitute performance elsewhere.

I will now consider whether courts have taken into account principles of substitutability in *Blake* and the cases which followed it.

B Substitutability – *Blake* and Cases Following

i Blake

Blake involves the 'notorious traitor', George Blake, who breached his employment contract with the British Secret Intelligence Service. When he commenced employment in 1944, he signed an undertaking in which he undertook not to divulge any official information gained by him in the course of his employment, either in the press or in book form. The undertaking continued after employment had ceased. As it turned out, Blake had been divulging secret information to the Soviet Union for some years while he was operating in Berlin, until he was exposed by a Polish

[120] Cunnington, 'The Inadequacy of Damages' (n 22) 140–44.

[121] *Blake* (n 1) 297. His Lordship cites *Reid-Newfoundland Co. v Anglo-American Telegraph Co Ltd* [1912] AC 555 (PC) and *Reading v Attorney-General* [1951] AC 827 (HL).

[122] See ch 2, II B ii.

[123] R Stevens, *Torts and Rights* (Oxford, Oxford University Press, 2007) 55; Webb (n 8) 49–50.

[124] Eisenberg (n 36) 561; L Smith, 'Disgorgement of the Profits of Breach of Contract: Property, Contract and "Efficient Breach"' (1994) 24 *Canadian Business Law Journal* 121, 122.

[125] 'Factual loss' looks to the consequential losses suffered as a result of the breach and the actual losses suffered by the claimant. In this way, it differs from substitutive compensation, which seeks to objectively compensate the claimant for the infringement of a right. See Stevens (n 123) 60–61.

[126] Jones (n 54) 451. The validity of the 'windfall' argument as a reason for rejecting gain-based awards has been criticised: see R Cunnington, 'Should Punitive Damages be Part of the Judicial Arsenal in Contract Cases?' (2006) 26 *Legal Studies* 369, 382–83.

defector. In 1961, he was sentenced to 42 years' imprisonment for unlawfully communicating information contrary to section 1(1)(c) of the *Official Secrets Act* 1911 (UK). In 1966, Blake escaped from prison and fled to Moscow, where he still lives. In 1989 Blake wrote his autobiography, *No Other Choice*,[127] and entered into a publishing contract with Jonathan Cape Ltd. Until publication was announced in 1990, the British Government was unaware of the existence of the book. Blake had not sought permission from the British Government or intelligence services before publishing the book. At the time publication was discovered by the British Government, Blake had been paid about £60,000 of the moneys owing to him under the publishing contract. A further amount of about £90,000 remained payable. On 24 May 1991, the British Government instituted proceedings to recover the £90,000. A majority of the House of Lords was prepared to find that Blake was required to disgorge his entire profit remaining in the jurisdiction.[128]

One of the reasons that *Blake* has proved hard to apply in subsequent cases is because substitutability is not the whole reason for the decision. Substitutability helps to explain why courts award specific relief for breach of negative covenant so readily. The rights granted by the negative covenant cannot be bought or sold in any market.[129] Such contracts are not like contracts for beans, where a claimant can go out and purchase beans from a different supplier if the contract is breached. Substitutability also directs us to look at the idiosyncratic value of the promise to the claimant: we need to have regard to the aims which the claimant sought to achieve by entering into the contract.[130] However, I will argue in chapter five that for many of the negative covenant cases, something *more* than a lack of substitutability is required for this category of case. Disgorgement damages should only be available for those negative covenants where the clause was designed to serve interests over and above profit-making.

ii Cases Following Blake

The courts in *Esso Petroleum Co Ltd v Niad Ltd*[131]and *AB Corporation v CD Company (The 'Sine Nomine')*[132] considered the substitutability of the bargains involved. However, *Experience Hendrix*[133] and the *World Wide Fund for Nature v World Wrestling Federation Entertainment Inc* cases[134] show that confusion prevails in cases of breach of negative covenant. Further, if such damages are

[127] G Blake, *No Other Choice* (London, Jonathan Cape, 1990).

[128] Lord Nicholls of Birkenhead, with whom Lord Goff of Chieverley and Lord Browne-Wilkinson agreed, and Lord Steyn in a separate speech. Lord Hobhouse dissented.

[129] Laycock (n 62) 707–08.

[130] P Birks, 'Restitutionary Damages for Breach of Contract: *Snepp* and the Fusion of Law and Equity' [1987] *Lloyds Maritime and Commercial Law Quarterly* 421, 441–42.

[131] *Niad* (n 1).

[132] *AB Corporation v CD Company (The 'Sine Nomine')* [2002] 1 Lloyd's Rep 805 (Arbitration Tribunal).

[133] *Experience Hendrix* (n 1).

[134] *World Wide Fund for Nature v World Wrestling Federation Entertainment Inc* (*WWF – Jacob J*) [2001] EWHC Ch 482 (Ch); *World Wide Fund for Nature v World Wrestling Federation Entertainment Inc* (*WWF – Peter Smith J*) [2006] EWHC 184, [2006] FSR 38 (Ch D); *WWF* (n 1).

available, there is confusion as to which measure should be used (total disgorgement or 'reasonable fee').

The 'Sine Nomine' used substitutability as a criterion for refusing disgorgement damages.[135] The case involved the charter of a ship, the m.v. Sine Nomine by the claimants from the defendants. The defendants withdrew the ship from the claimants before the contract of charter was up and chartered it out to a third party more profitably. The arbitrators' award states:

> It is by no means uncommon for commercial contracts to be broken deliberately because a more profitable opportunity has arisen. Or the contract-breaker takes an over-generous view of his rights, knowing that the law may ultimately be against him. In such a case he may have little or nothing to lose by taking the chance; the downside at worst is that he will have to pay the costs on both sides. International commerce on a large scale is red in tooth and claw. We do not say that the [owners'] action was either deliberate or cynical wrongdoing in this case; they had a reasonable argument on liability, although a commercial judge refused their application for leave to appeal.
>
> *Our solution to the present problem is that there should not be an award of wrongful profits where both parties are dealing with a marketable commodity – the services of a ship in this case – for which a substitute can be found in the market place.* In the ordinary way the damages which the claimant suffers by having to buy in at the market price will be equal to the profit which the wrongdoer makes by having his goods or his ships' services to sell at a higher price. It is in the nature of things unlikely that the wrongdoer will make a greater profit than that. And if he does, it is an adventitious benefit which he can keep. The commercial law of this country should not make moral judgments, or seek to punish contract breakers; we do not, for example, award triple damages, as in the U.S.A. [Emphasis added][136]

The substitutability of the subject matter of the contract was pivotal to the arbitrators' decision not to award disgorgement damages. The claimants could have obtained a substitute performance from elsewhere by chartering a similar ship: there was nothing special about the m.v. Sine Nomine.

In *Niad*,[137] Esso entered into a contract with Niad, providing that Niad was to implement 'Pricewatch', a marketing scheme by which Esso would supply Niad with petroleum at a discount if Niad matched the prices of Esso's competitors in the area. Niad was enriched because it charged pump prices in excess of the recommended price, but received petrol from Esso at discounted prices under the agreement. Morritt V-C held that Esso could elect to take damages, an account of profits for breach of contract or restitutionary damages representing the amount by which Niad had overcharged its customers.

Beatson contrasts the award in *Niad* with the award in *The 'Sine Nomine'*:

> [I]f Esso's interest in the profits was a legitimate interest, it is difficult to see how an account of profits for beach of contract can be said to be available only exceptionally. What principle would prevent an account being ordered in all cases in which it is difficult to prove loss in respect of breach of an important term of a contract?

[135] Beatson (n 20).
[136] *The 'Sine Nomine'* (n 132) 805.
[137] *Niad* (n 1).

> The two decisions are reconcilable because *Niad's* case did not involve parties dealing with a marketable commodity for which a substitute could be found in the market place.[138]

Beatson has hit the nail on the head. The vast majority of commercial cases do not raise disgorgement issues.[139] Nonetheless, *Niad* could be criticised on the basis that substitutability on its own is not enough to ground an award of disgorgement damages in negative covenant cases.[140]

The other two cases following *Blake* are negative covenant cases which both involved breach of settlement agreements. In *WWF*, the dispute was between World Wide Fund for Nature (formerly known as the World Wildlife Fund) ('the Fund'), an organisation and charity which promotes environmental concerns and the preservation of animals, and the World Wrestling Federation ('the Federation'), an organisation which promotes live wrestling. Both parties were generally known by the initials 'WWF'. In the late 1980s, the Fund and the Federation engaged in a global legal battle for the right to use the initials 'WWF'. At the same time, the Federation became the subject of criminal proceedings, and there was adverse publicity about alleged sex scandals, drug use and violence in the wrestling world. In light of these events, the Fund became concerned that a link would be drawn between it and the Federation because both used the initials 'WWF'. A settlement agreement was entered into in 1994 whereby the Federation agreed not to use the initials 'WWF' in certain ways. Initially, the Federation kept to the 1994 agreement, but it began to use the initials 'WWF' in breach of the agreement.

In the wake of *Blake*, the Fund sought to amend its statement of claim to demand that the Federation account for all profits it had made by using the initials 'WWF' in breach the 1994 agreement.[141] Jacobs J applied an extremely narrow test for the award of disgorgement damages, and refused to award them.[142] The Fund later sought to amend its statement of claim to include damages calculated by reference to the hypothetical sum that it would have accepted from the Federation to relax its rights under the 1994 agreement.[143] Leave to amend was denied on the basis that it would be an abuse of process.[144]

Experience Hendrix[145] also involved a settlement agreement – this time, concerning the music of the late great guitar player, Jimi Hendrix. PPX had sued Hendrix pursuant to an agreement made in 1965, alleging that Hendrix had agreed to play music and sing for PPX exclusively. Hendrix died in 1970, and PPX

138 Beatson (n 20) 378–79.

139 Eisenberg (n 36) 561. Compare W Goodhart, 'Restitutionary Damages for Breach of Contract: The Remedy that Dare Not Speak its Name' [1995] *Restitution Law Review* 3; *Adras* (n 32).

140 E McKendrick, 'Breach of Contract, Restitution for Wrongs, and Punishment' in A Burrows and E Peel (eds), *Commercial Remedies – Current Issues and Problems* (Oxford, Oxford University Press, 2003) 93, 112.

141 *WWF – Jacobs J* (n 134).

142 ibid [62].

143 *WWF – Peter Smith J* (n 134) [174].

144 *WWF* (n 1) [73]–[75] (Chadwick LJ).

145 *Experience Hendrix* (n 1) (Mance LJ, Hooper J and Peter Gibson LJ).

then sued his estate. In 1973, PPX and Hendrix's estate settled, and an agreement was reached which provided that Hendrix's estate was entitled to certain royalties in respect of certain recordings, and that other non-listed recordings would not be licensed by PPX to third parties without the consent of Hendrix's estate. PPX breached this settlement agreement twice by selling non-listed recordings to record companies for a profit. The Court of Appeal unanimously held that Experience Hendrix was entitled to a reasonable proportion of the profits arising from the breach of contract.[146] However, the court rejected Experience Hendrix's claim for an account of PPX's entire profit.

Negative covenant cases are difficult. Performance will be intrinsically non-substitutable so that promisees will inevitably have a legitimate interest in the promisor's profit-making activities. Therefore it will be argued in chapter five that something more than substitutability is needed: the claimant must establish that the contract sought to protect some non-financial interest. Despite this, the case law in the negative covenant cases has been unduly cautious. Substitutability is particularly relevant in cases such as *WWF* and *Experience Hendrix*, where disgorgement is awarded as a surrogate for expectation damages.[147] The claimants wanted gain-based relief because the defendants benefited in a measurable way and caused a loss which was speculative or hard-to-quantify.[148] The defendants in these cases deprived the claimants of performance, and the claimants could not obtain a substitute performance, nor could they be adequately compensated for the loss of the performance.

Jacobs J in *WWF* declined to allow the claimant to seek disgorgement damages, saying that the case did not have the exceptional character of *Blake*, and that disgorgement damages should not be awarded just because the facts were 'a bit "trademarkish" or "IPish"'.[149] The Court of Appeal in *Experience Hendrix* criticised Jacobs J's test,[150] but it was not prepared to award full disgorgement damages, even though it found that the claimant had a legitimate interest in the defendant's profit-making opportunity.[151] Substitutability helps to establish why *WWF* and *Experience Hendrix* were wrongly decided, although something more than substitutability is needed to ground relief in these negative covenant cases.

There are also a number of partial disgorgement cases following *Blake* for which reasonable fee awards have been awarded for breach of contract. They involve negative covenants over property,[152] or negative covenants concerning the

[146] R Cunnington, 'Rock, Restitution and Disgorgement' (2004) *Journal of Obligation and Remedies* 46. Against P-W Lee, 'Responses to a Breach of Contract' [2003] *Lloyds Maritime and Commercial Law Quarterly* 301.

[147] Eisenberg (n 36) 587–88.

[148] D Laycock, 'The Scope and Significance of Restitution' (1989) 67 *Texas Law Review* 1277, 1287.

[149] *WWF – Jacobs J* (n 134) [62].

[150] *Experience Hendrix* (n 1) [32] (Mance LJ).

[151] ibid [36], [42] (Mance LJ), [54] (Peter Gibson LJ).

[152] *Amec Developments Limited v Jury's Hotel Management (UK) Limited* [2000] EWHC Ch 454, [2001] 1 EGLR 81 (Ch); *Lane v O'Brien Homes* [2004] EWHC 303, [2004] All ER (D) 61 (Feb) (QB).

keeping of confidences.[153] These cases will be discussed in chapters six and seven, which deal respectively with 'restitutionary damages' and reasons why courts may choose a 'reasonable fee' (ie partial disgorgement) rather than full disgorgement, and bars to relief and allowances.

Finally, as will be discussed in detail in chapter four, in *Luxe Holding Limited v Midland Resources Holding Limited*,[154] a case involving a second sale of shares in a private company, the court obscured its conclusion behind a constructive trust analysis, and rejected the argument that the claimant was entitled to disgorgement damages pursuant to *Blake*. Roth J failed to have recourse to principles of substitutability which would have illuminated the proper approach to the problem. Thus, his Honour concluded that a constructive trust pursuant to a specifically enforceable contract of sale arose, but that disgorgement damages were unavailable because compensatory damages were adequate. These two conclusions were directly contradictory.

Substitutability assists in explaining the results of cases following *Blake*. *The 'Sine Nomine'* was entirely correct to refuse an award of disgorgement damages on the basis of lack of substitutability. *Niad*, *WWF* and *Experience Hendrix* are all more difficult cases because they involve negative covenants. Substitutability was correctly used by the court in *Niad*, although it ought to have taken into account the kind of interest the contract sought to protect. *WWF* and *Experience Hendrix* were incorrectly decided, in part because of a failure to take into account a lack of substitutability. These latter three cases will be analysed in more detail in chapter five. However, even in more straightforward 'second sale' cases such as *Luxe*, confusion still reigns.

Finally, it is necessary to deal with some potential objections to a substitutability analysis.

VI Objections to a Substitutability Analysis

There are a number of objections which could be made to an analysis focussing on substitutability. The principal ones are as follows:

- Objection 1: the availability of specific relief is unsuitable as a peg on which to hang the availability of disgorgement damages.
- Objection 2: it would be simpler to expand the definition of loss in awards of expectation damages than to award disgorgement damages.
- Objection 3: disgorgement damages represent an instance of 'fusion fallacy', where equitable principles are illegitimately imported into common law remedies.

[153] *Pell Frischmann Engineering Limited v Bow Valley Iran Limited* [2009] UKPC 45 (PC); *Vercoe v Rutland Fund Management Limited* [2010] EWHC 424 (Ch).

[154] *Luxe Holding Limited v Midland Resources Holding Limited* (*Luxe*) [2010] EWHC 1908 (Ch).

A Using Availability of Specific Relief as a Peg on which to Hang Availability of Disgorgement Damages

Although many commentators have suggested that the availability of specific relief should be used as guidance for awards of disgorgement damages,[155] this suggestion is not unanimously approved. One criticism of using the availability of specific relief as a peg on which to hang availability of disgorgement damages arises from the way in which specific relief is said to be awarded when damages are 'inadequate'.

Dr Odudu and Professor Virgo have argued that 'inadequacy of damages' is a notoriously slippery concept when awarding specific relief, and it should not then be imported and extended into the law of disgorgement damages. Indeed, as noted earlier, there have been calls for the concept to be scrapped and replaced with a broader concept of what is 'just' in the circumstances.[156] It is true that the concept of 'inadequacy of damages' lacks precision.

The concept of inadequacy of damages as a touchstone for awards of specific relief or disgorgement damages has not been given credence by the case of *Devenish Nutrition Limited v Sanofi-Aventis SA (France)*.[157] *Devenish* was not a breach of contract case, but involved instead breach of statutory duty. The case arose after certain vitamin manufacturers engaged in illegal cartel behaviour in breach of Article 81 of the EC Treaty.[158] The EC imposed substantial fines on the manufacturers. Devenish Nutrition Limited ('Devenish') had purchased vitamins at inflated prices from the cartel members to include in its animal feed. It later sold the products at a reasonable profit to consumers. It alleged that the vitamin manufacturers had committed a breach of statutory duty by contravening the EC Treaty, and that it was entitled to damages as a result. Devenish accepted that compensatory damages were available, but it was concerned that these would be difficult to prove, or that the vitamin manufacturers would argue that it had mitigated its loss by passing on the overcharge to customers. Consequently, Devenish sought an account of profits. The Court of Appeal refused to award any gain-based damages to Devenish for two reasons. First, the Court of Appeal held that *Stoke-on-Trent City Council v W and J Wass Ltd*[159] prevented it from awarding gain-based awards for non-proprietary torts. Secondly, and relevantly for present purposes, it argued that inadequacy of compensatory damages was an essential

[155] See above (n 98).

[156] See, eg E MacDonald, 'The Inadequacy of Adequacy: The Granting of Specific Performance' (1987) 38 *Northern Ireland Legal Quarterly* 244; Laycock (n 62); O Odudu and G Virgo, 'Inadequacy of Compensatory Damages' [2009] *Restitution Law Review* 112.

[157] *Devenish Nutrition Limited v Sanofi-Aventis SA (France)* [2008] EWCA Civ 1086, [2009] Ch 390 (CA). See Odudu and Virgo (n 156); O Odudu and G Virgo, 'Remedies for Breach of Statutory Duty' (2009) 68 *CLJ* 32.

[158] Official Journal C 325, 24/12/2002 P. 0064 – 0065.

[159] *Stoke-on-Trent City Council v W and J Wass Ltd* [1988] 1 WLR 1406 (CA).

precondition to awards of gain-based damages, and that it had not been made out in the circumstances.

Odudu and Virgo say that there are five situations in the context of awards of specific performance where, arguably, damages may be inadequate:

1. Where quantification of damages is difficult. Usually compensatory damages will be adequate, but sometimes they will be inadequate, particularly where damages are impossible to prove;
2. Where damages are too remote. This does *not* render compensatory damages inadequate;[160]
3. Where the type of loss is not recoverable. This *may* render damages inadequate;[161]
4. Where the defendant is unlikely to be able to pay damages. This is likely to render damages inadequate;[162] and
5. Where the claimant is only entitled to nominal damages. This *may* render damages inadequate.[163]

Odudu and Virgo argue that the result in *Devenish* was incorrect, as specific relief will be awarded when loss has not been suffered. Accordingly, they argue that 'inadequacy of damages' is an incoherent and ambiguous concept which should be abandoned in this area of law.[164]

First, I argue that much of the incoherence in the concept of 'inadequacy of damages' can be explained in contract law if one has a proper understanding of the performance interest, and the nature of expectation damages. Contract damages aim not only to compensate the claimant for pecuniary loss, but more broadly to vindicate the claimant's performance interest. The fact that a claimant has not suffered a compensable loss or will only get nominal damages does *not in itself* lead to an award of specific relief or disgorgement damages.[165] Sometimes it is simply appropriate to leave the claimant with nominal damages or no remedy, because a fair vindication of the claimant's right does not require any more than that. It depends upon questions of substitutability and a consideration of what the claimant hoped to get out of the contract, as well as additional considerations as to whether deterrence and punishment are appropriate.

Secondly, as Dr Austen-Baker has argued, much of the confusion about difficulty of calculating damages rendering compensatory damages inadequate can be resolved if one distinguishes between *extrinsic* or *forensic* difficulties in calculating damages and *intrinsic difficulties*.[166] He argues that ordinarily, extrinsic difficulties

160 *The Stena Nautica* (n 90).
161 *Evans Marshall v Bertola SA* (n 90).
162 ibid; *The Oro Chief* [1983] 2 Lloyd's Rep 509.
163 *Beswick v Beswick* (n 90).
164 Odudu and Virgo (n 156) 119.
165 See, eg *Ruxley Electronics and Constructions Ltd v Forsyth* [1996] 1 AC 344 (HL); *Jacob & Youngs, Inc. v Kent* 230 NY 239, 129 NE 889 (1921).
166 R Austen-Baker, 'Difficulties with Damages as a Ground for Specific Performance' (1999) 10 *King's College Law Journal* 1.

in calculating damages will not give rise to inadequacy of damages. *Société des Industries Métallurgiques SA v The Bronx Engineering Co Ltd*[167] is a paradigm case of extrinsic difficulty in calculating damages. The claimants were a Tunisian company which had ordered machinery from the defendant, an English company. There were delays in delivering the machinery as a result of various factors, including delays by the defendant company in producing the machinery, the expiration of the claimant's export licence, and shipping problems. The defendants gave notice that unless the claimants had shipping arrangements in place by 25 December 1974, they would treat the contract as repudiated. On 20 December they informed the claimants that the contract was repudiated and said they were selling the machinery to a Canadian buyer. The claimants sought an interlocutory injunction restraining removal of the machinery and specific performance. The interlocutory injunction was granted at first instance, but refused at the next return date. The claimants appealed to the Court of Appeal. The Court of Appeal refused the interlocutory injunction on the basis that mere difficulty in quantifying damages did not of itself merit specific relief. They recognised that it would be difficult to get evidence from Tunis and translate it:[168] but importantly, it was not *impossible* to do so, it was merely costly and time-consuming. Therefore, compensatory damages were an adequate remedy, because the claimant's losses could be calculated (albeit with some inconvenience and cost). The difficulties were forensic rather than intrinsic to the agreement itself. The only circumstance where a claimant in the position of the Tunisian company might succeed would be if there was an additional factor, such as an inability on the part of the defendant to pay damages.[169]

By contrast, in other cases it is simply *impossible* to calculate what damages will be. Austen-Baker gives the example of specific performance of a contract to purchase a debt proved in bankruptcy, where the buyer of the debt will find it impossible to prove how much she might have received if the seller had performed the agreement, because her calculations are pure speculation.[170] She may have recovered the rest of the debt in full before the end of the bankruptcy; she may have recovered nothing. In that circumstance, the very nature of the agreement means that it is impossible to calculate what damages will be and thus they are inadequate.

Once this division is understood, it can be seen why specific relief is sometimes awarded for difficulty in calculating damages, but in other cases it is not.

However, Burrows has made further objections to the argument that the law should import principles from awards of specific relief into disgorgement damages:

> [O]n closer inspection it is far from clear that one would want to apply principles of specific performance to restitution. For example, would general bars to specific perfor-

[167] *Société des Industries Métallurgiques SA v The Bronx Engineering Co Ltd* [1975] 1 Lloyd's Rep 465.
[168] ibid 468 (Lord Edmund Davies); 470–71 (Buckley LJ).
[169] *Evans Marshall v Bertola SA* (n 90) 380–81 (Sachs LJ).
[170] Austen-Baker (n 166) 4–6.

> mance such as the bar to specific performance in contracts of personal service or the severe hardship bar, apply also to rule out restitution? And how would the theory apply to negative contractual promises where the prohibitory injunction is the primary remedy and damages are generally regarded as inadequate? It would be odd if restitution were widely available for breach of negative but not positive promises.[171]

My theory seeks to deal with each of Burrows' queries and objections.

First, allowances for skill and effort and the general equitable bars to relief apply to disgorgement damages (namely, delay and acquiescence, lack of clean hands and hardship). Bars which are peculiar to specific performance, such as the inability to supervise performance, are irrelevant to disgorgement. The way in which the bars to relief and allowances for skill and effort impact upon disgorgement damages is explained in detail in chapter seven.

Secondly, it will be argued in chapter four that disgorgement damages may provide a better method than an injunction of balancing the competing interests which arise in a contract of personal services in cases where an employee, in breach of contract, seeks employment with the employer's business rival. If a breaching employee is compelled to pay disgorgement damages, the employer's interest in performance of the contract is acknowledged, but on the other hand, the defendant is still free to take up the other job. In addition, the restraint of trade concerns which may arise when an injunction is awarded do not arise for disgorgement damages.

Thirdly, as I will discuss in chapter five, Burrows is right that the benefits under negative covenant are intrinsically non-substitutable, and that, prima facie, disgorgement damages are more likely to be available for breach of negative covenant than for breach of a positive obligation. It is for this reason that substitutability cannot be the only criterion for award of disgorgement damages for breach of negative covenant. There are important additional factors to take into account, already identified in cases involving concurrent breach of fiduciary duty and contract.

B Disgorgement Preferable to an Expanded Definition of Expectation Loss

It has been argued by some that courts should adopt an expanded definition of expectation loss instead of awarding disgorgement damages.[172] In fact, courts sometimes do this, perhaps attempting to make the award of damages appear more in line with orthodox principles.

[171] Burrows, *Remedies for Torts and Breach of Contract* (n 21) 399–400; Burrows, *The Law of Restitution* (n 98) 485.

[172] See, eg Mitchell (n 19); O'Sullivan (n 19); A Phang and P-W Lee, 'Rationalising Restitutionary Damages in Contract Law – An Elusive or Illusory Quest?' (2001) 17 *Journal of Contract Law* 240, 244–51; D Ong, 'Non-Financial Loss Resulting from Tort and Breach of Contract: The Availability of a Monetary Remedy that is Non-Compensatory, Non-Restitutionary, Non-Punitive, and Not a Mere Solatium' (2002) 22 *University of Queensland Law Journal* 20; A Phang and P-W Lee, 'Restitutionary and Exemplary Damages Revisited' (2003) 19 *Journal of Contract Law* 1, 9.

However, this analysis does not represent the best fit with the cases, particularly the total disgorgement cases, because what courts are *actually* doing is causing the promisor to disgorge his gain. Such analyses lack transparency. In addition, as discussed in the previous chapter, it is argued that a compensatory analysis cannot explain the cases without unduly extending the definition of 'loss' and 'gain'.

148 Investment Group, Inc v Elvis Presley Enterprises, Inc[173] illustrates the way in which categorising disgorgement as an extension of expectation loss obfuscates what the court is doing, and makes the law less transparent. The case involved Elvis Presley's gold-leafed Kimball Grand Piano. After Presley's death, Philip Brodnax III ('Brodnax') purchased the piano. When Elvis Presley Enterprises ('EPE') opened Presley's mansion, Graceland, to the public in 1982, Brodnax agreed to lease the piano to EPE for one dollar per month. Pursuant to the terms of the lease, Brodnax retained certain rights to the Piano:

> Lessee [EPE] shall have the right to photograph the Piano and otherwise promote and publicize the exhibition of the Piano without limitation. *However, Lessee shall not sell photographs, souvenirs, miniatures, or any other commercial items with regard to the Piano without the express consent and written agreement of Lessor [Brodnax].* All sales of such commercial items shall be under the sole and exclusive management and control of Lessee. [Emphasis added.][174]

In March 1990, Brodnax learned that Graceland's gift shops had been selling postcards, souvenirs and jewellery depicting the piano without seeking his consent. Brodnax immediately informed EPE that it had breached the lease. Brodnax and EPE agreed that the net profits derived from the unauthorised sales totalled US$109,893.70. Brodnax sold the piano to 148 Investment Group, and assigned any cause of action he had in respect of the unauthorised sales to it.

At trial, Gibbons CJ of the Western District of Tennessee awarded 148 Investment Group the entire profit plus pre-judgment interest. Her Honour stated in her oral ruling:

> What Mr. Brodnax lost here was not the right to negotiate. What he lost was what he had bargained for, which was the right to say no, [he] lost the prohibition he had.
>
> Certainly, he contemplated if permission had been requested, the parties would have negotiated some sort of agreement, and that in all likelihood would have been a royalty agreement. I'm sure that would be what [EPE] would contemplate too, but [EPE] can't fail to ask permission and then come in and expect the Court to craft relief that is based on the agreement it would have gotten if it had negotiated for something it never negotiated for.

EPE appealed, asserting 148 Investment Group was only entitled to a 'reasonable share' of the profits, not the entire profit.

[173] *148 Investment Group, Inc v Elvis Presley Enterprises, Inc*, (*Elvis Presley Enterprises*) 54 F 3d 777 (USCA for 6th Cir, 1995). See K Barnett, 'Comment: The Midas Touch – Profits from the King's Gold Piano' (2010) 18 *Restitution Law Review* 83.

[174] *148 Investment Group, Inc v Elvis Presley Enterprises, Inc*, (*Elvis Presley Enterprises*) 54 F 3d 777 (USCA for 6th Cir, 1995).

The Sixth Circuit of the United States Court of Appeals upheld the trial judge's assessment that 148 Investment Group was entitled to the entire profit. The court noted that Tennessee law established that damages in a breach of contract action should place the claimant in the position that it would have been if the contract had been performed, and that the usual measure of damages for breach of contract was the value of the promised performance. The court stated:

> Pursuant to the lease agreements, EPE had to obtain Brodnax's permission before marketing products depicting the Piano. EPE failed to do so. Though Brodnax admitted that, if EPE had sought his consent, he and EPE would have negotiated an agreement that, in all likelihood would have been a royalty agreement, the district court properly concluded that EPE's conduct deprived Brodnax of his bargained-for right to refuse consent. Accordingly, the district court properly determined the damages attributable to EPE's breach.

The court in effect caused EPE to disgorge its gains arising from the breach by recharacterising the subject matter of the contract.[175] EPE attempted to argue that 148 Investment Group could be put in a position as if the contract had been performed if it was awarded only that proportion of the profits which Brodnax would have gained if EPE had negotiated a royalty agreement with it. The court argued that Brodnax had not just a right to negotiate with EPE, but a right to refuse to negotiate, and that EPE deprived Brodnax of this.

The court appears to have viewed this as an instance of compensatory damages. In other words, EPE had deprived Brodnax of the right to say no, and Brodnax had suffered a 'loss' as a result. Accordingly, the court found that the entire profit was 'attributable' to the breach, and the profit was used to 'compensate' EPE. The court adopted the 'lost opportunity to bargain' theory in order to fit the award into a compensatory rationale (which has been thoroughly questioned in any case).[176] But it then proceeded to ignore the likely consequences of the hypothetical bargain which are essential to the lost opportunity to bargain analysis. If EPE had complied with its obligations under the contract and informed Brodnax of its intention to sell products depicting the piano, Brodnax *admitted* that he would in all likelihood have agreed to enter into a royalty agreement with EPE. Under that royalty agreement Brodnax would only have received a proportion of the profit, not the entire profit. Indeed, the 'lost opportunity to bargain' analysis is used to justify reasonable fee awards rather than disgorgement of the whole profit for this very reason. It is pure fiction to say that Brodnax (or his successor in title) was placed in a position as if the contract had been performed by causing EPE to disgorge the entire profit. The court glosses over this by saying that the profit was 'attributable' to the breach, which is really an argument about causation. The court was not compensating 148 Investment Group for a loss at all, but it required EPE to disgorge its entire gain, motivated by the necessity to punish EPE and by considerations of

[175] S Thel and P Siegelman, 'You Do Have to Keep Your Promises: A Disgorgement Theory of Contract Remedies' (2011) 52 *William and Mary Law Review* 1181, 1212–14.

[176] See discussion of 'lost opportunity to bargain' theory in ch 2, II A.

specific and general deterrence. Accordingly, this award would have been better characterised as an instance of disgorgement damages for breach of contract.

This case illustrates why merely expanding the concept of 'loss' does not work. The result does not hold up under a detailed analysis. By contrast, if the case is analysed as one where the court was forcing EPE to disgorge its gain, the case makes far more sense. It is better to call a spade a spade, and label disgorgement of gain for what it really is.

C Disgorgement Damages are not a Fusion Fallacy

Certain commentators might argue that disgorgement damages for breach of contract are flawed because they represent an instance of 'fusion fallacy'. Fusion fallacy is described as involving:

> the administration of a remedy, for example common law damages for breach of fiduciary duty, not previously available at law or in equity, or in the modification of principles in one branch of the jurisdiction by concepts that are imported from the other and thus are foreign, for example by holding that the existence of a duty in tort may be tested by asking whether the parties concerned were in fiduciary relationships.[177]

There are two limbs to the fusion fallacy. The first limb 'asserts only that remedies from the one jurisdiction cannot go in support of rights in the other jurisdiction where that was impossible before the fusion of the administration of law and equity.'[178] The second limb is more general, and involves the alteration of principles in common law by equity or vice versa. The vice of fusion fallacy is condemned in no uncertain terms by the authors of *Meagher, Gummow and Lehane's Equity*.[179] It comes as no surprise to note that the fourth edition of that text seeks to minimise the impact of the *Blake* case on contract law.[180]

[177] RP Meagher, JD Heydon, MJ Leeming, *Meagher, Gummow and Lehane's Equity – Doctrines and Remedies*, 4th edn (Sydney, Butterworths, 2002) 54.

[178] M Tilbury, 'Fallacy or Furphy? Fusion in a Judicature World' (2003) 26 *University of New South Wales Law Journal* 357, 358–59.

[179] Meagher, Heydon and Leeming (n 177) 54, 57:

> Those who commit the fusion fallacy announce or assume the creation by the Judicature system of a new body of law containing elements of law and equity but in character Equity different from its components. The fallacy is committed explicitly, covertly, and on occasion with apparent indifference. But the state of mind of the culprit cannot lessen the evil of the offence.
>
> . . .
>
> [The fusion fallacy] involves the conclusion that the new system was not devised to administer law and equity concurrently but to 'fuse' them into a new body of principles comprising rules neither of law nor equity but of some new jurisprudence conceived by accident, born by misadventure and nourished by sour but high-minded wet-nurses.

[180] ibid 874–75:

> [A]pparently, an order for an account will be made against persons who make profits from treasonable activities. This was decided recently by the House of Lords in *Attorney-General v Blake* . . .
>
> However, *Blake's* case should be treated with some caution, insofar as it supports the proposition that an account of profits is an appropriate remedy for a mere breach of contract. It is not, at least in Australia: see *Hospitality Group Pty Ltd v Australian Rugby Union Ltd* (2001) 110 FCR 156.

The continuance of the historical distinction between equity and common law in modern law has been criticised by various scholars.[181] Birks noted that the:

> continuing segregation of the account of profits has the effect of reducing the weight of the evidence from the equity side. Something which looks perfectly normal so long as one is wearing an equitable hat disappears as soon as that hat is taken off. Even for those for whom it does not actually disappear, it shrinks and begins to look peculiar.[182]

Perhaps a gradual 'fusion by analogy' will produce a more coherent private law.[183] Interestingly, the American *Restatement of Restitution and Unjust Enrichment* has chosen to stipulate that restitutionary remedies may be legal or equitable or both,[184] and that the division between law and equity in this context is 'artificial'.[185]

Still, while the division between equity and common law remains in countries such as Australia and England and Wales, the barrier can be broken down via equity's auxiliary jurisdiction.[186] Equitable remedies have long entered into the contractual sphere in particular by this method.[187] To borrow Lord Denning's vivid phrase, '[e]quity is not past the age of child-bearing.'[188]

Courts have already been awarding disgorgement remedies under other guises. Disgorgement damages should be seen as another equitable remedy for breach of contract in equity's auxiliary jurisdiction, along with specific performance and injunctions.[189] Equity has always allowed its remedies to support legal rights where the legal remedy is inadequate, and where discretionary factors indicate it is appropriate.[190] Gleeson and Watson argue that equity in its auxiliary jurisdiction *has* been prepared to award accounts of profits for breach of contract on a

[181] See, eg A Burrows, 'We Do This at Common Law But That in Equity' (2002) 22 *OJLS* 1; J Edelman, 'A "fusion fallacy" fallacy?' (2003) 119 *LQR* 375; A Burrows, 'Remedial Coherence and Punitive Damages in Equity' in S Degeling and J Edelman (eds), *Equity in Commercial Law* (Pyrmont, NSW, Lawbook Co, 2005) 381; M Kirby, 'Equity's Australian Isolationism' (2008) 8 *Queensland University of Technology Law Journal* 444. See also United Kingdom and Northern Ireland Law Commission, *Aggravated, Exemplary and Restitutionary Damages*, Report No 247 (1997) para 5.55.

[182] P Birks, 'The Law of Restitution at the End of an Epoch' (1999) 28 *University of Western Australia Law Review* 13, 52.

[183] Edelman (n 181) 377–80.

[184] American Law Institute (n 1) § 4.

[185] ibid comment c.

[186] Doyle and Wright (n 98) 12.

[187] Birks noted that 'contract stands out for having come to terms with the duality of law and equity' better than wrongs and unjust enrichment: P Birks, 'Equity in the Modern Law: An Exercise in Taxonomy' (1996) 26 *University of Western Australian Law Review* 1, 52.

[188] *Eves v Eves* [1975] 1 WLR 1338 (CA) 1341 (Lord Denning MR). Original credit should go to Bagnall J in *Cowcher v Cowcher* [1972] 1 WLR 425, 430: 'This does not mean that equity is past child-bearing; simply that its progeny must be legitimate – by precedent out of principle.' Note the added caveat.

[189] The extent of the auxiliary operation of the account of profits has not been definitively stated: see *North Eastern Railway Company v Martin* (1848) 2 Ph 758, 41 ER 1136, 1138 (Lord Cottenham LC). The categories are not closed: Meagher, Heydon and Leeming (n 177) 875.

[190] Tilbury (n 178) 361.

number of occasions prior to *Blake*.[191] If disgorgement damages are equitable, then it is clear that the equitable bars to relief also apply, as described in chapter seven.[192]

VII Conclusion: a Different Way of Looking at Disgorgement Damages

We need a different way of looking at disgorgement damages and categorising the cases. This assists courts to establish with ease those kinds of breaches of contract where disgorgement is likely to be available. In chapters four and five, I will consider two categories of cases where disgorgement damages are available, namely:

1. **'Second sale' cases.** Alice contracts with Boris for the supply of property, goods or services. Boris sees an opportunity to sell the property, good or service to Conrad for a greater profit. Therefore Boris breaches his contract with Alice and sells to Conrad for a profit. Typically, the contract between Alice and Boris is no longer specifically enforceable but there is a profit for Boris to disgorge.
2. **'Agency problem' cases.**[193] Boris promises Alice he will not do a specific thing which relates to Alice's best interests, but Boris breaches the contract and goes ahead and does the very thing which he has contracted not to do, making a profit as a consequence.

Substitutability has a different role in each context. For the 'second sale' cases, substitutability is the sole answer. However, for the 'agency problem' cases (which encompass breach of negative covenants and concurrent breaches of contract and fiduciary duty) something more is needed in addition to substitutability, although substitutability remains important. There is an important additional factor, which Professors Thel and Siegelman term the 'agency problem'.[194] 'Agency' in this context refers not to the legal concept of agency, but the economic concept of principal–agent which arises whenever one person, the principal (or promisee) seeks to persuade another person, his agent (or promisor), to act in the principal's interests.[195] It will be argued that public policy considerations also have a particularly important role in this category.

[191] Gleeson and Watson (n 21). They cite: *M'Intosh v Great Western Railway Co* (1850) 2 Mac & G 74, 42 ER 29; *Barry v Stevens* (1862) 31 LJ Ch 785; *Shepard v Brown* (1862) 4 Giff 208, 66 ER 681; *Manners v Pearson* [1898] 1 Ch 581; *Davis v Hueber* (1923) 31 CLR 583 (HCA). See also Doyle and Wright (n 98) 9.

[192] See Burrows (n 181) 14–15; Doyle and Wright (n 98) 20–22; *Aggravated, Exemplary and Restitutionary Damages* (n 181) para 3.84.

[193] As noted above at n 14, 'agency' is used in the *economic sense* to talk about relationships which are difficult to supervise, rather than the legal sense.

[194] Thel and Siegelman (n 175) 1208.

[195] Stiglitz (n 14).

4

'Second Sale' Cases

I Introduction

The 'second sale' cases arise when a vendor sells property, goods or services to a purchaser, but the vendor then breaches his contract with the purchaser to sell the item more profitably to a third party.[1] Substitutability assists in ascertaining when disgorgement damages will be available: that is, it depends on where the subject matter of the contract sits on the spectrum: from fungible property, goods or services at one end of the spectrum (which a claimant can easily procure from elsewhere) to unique property, goods or services at the other end of the spectrum (which cannot be procured from elsewhere).[2] However, it will be seen that even if a particular good is fungible in nature and ordinarily easily obtainable courts will order specific performance if there is a particular reason why it would be impossible or difficult for the claimant to procure it from elsewhere. Courts may also order specific performance if damages are impossible to ascertain.

Courts already routinely use principles of substitutability when deciding whether or not to award specific performance or (in some circumstances) an injunction to restrain a breach of negative covenant. In *Adderley v Dixon*, Leach V-C explained the principles of specific performance as follows:

> Courts of Equity decree the specific performance of contracts, not upon any distinction between realty and personalty, but because damages at law may not, in the particular case, afford a complete remedy. Thus a Court of Equity decrees performance of a contract for land, not because of the real nature of the land, but because damages at law, which must be calculated upon the general money value of land, may not be a complete remedy to the purchaser, to whom the land may have a peculiar and special value. So a Court of Equity will not, generally, decree specific performance of a contract for the sale of stock or goods, not because of their personal nature, but because damages at law,

[1] Because disgorgement damages are available *only* for second sale situations where a defendant breaches to obtain a gain, there is no problem with a defendant who breaches to avoid a loss: *cf* D Campbell, 'The Treatment of *Teacher v Calder* in *AG v Blake*' (2002) 65 *MLR* 256, 269; D Campbell and D Harris, 'In Defence of Breach: a Critique of Restitution and the Performance Interest' (2002) 22 *Journal of Legal Studies* 208, 217–21; D Campbell and P Wylie, 'Ain't No Telling (Which Circumstances Are Exceptional)' (2003) 62 *CLJ* 605, 615–16.

[2] H Dagan, 'Restitutionary Damages for Breach of Contract' (2000) 1 *Theoretical Inquiries in Law* 115, 134–36; H Dagan, *The Law and Ethics of Restitution* (Cambridge, Cambridge University Press, 2004) 267–68; S Thel and P Siegelman, 'You *Do* Have to Keep Your Promises: A Disgorgement Theory of Contract Law' (2011) 52 *William and Mary Law Review* 1182, 1201–02.

> calculated upon the market price of the stock or goods, are as complete a remedy to the purchaser as the delivery of the stock or goods contracted for; inasmuch as, with the damages, he may purchase the same quantity of the like stock or goods.[3]

Specific performance will be ordered in circumstances where the claimant is unable (or finds it very difficult) to procure a substitute performance. Because the claimant will not be placed in a position as if the contract had been performed by an award of damages, she is justified in compelling the defendant to perform the contract. The law with regard to disgorgement damages does not require an entirely new way of thinking: it is a logical and coherent extension of principles already tried and tested in awards of specific relief. Thus, in analysing the case law, this chapter will consider the circumstances in which a court is prepared to say that the particular subject matter of a contract is not substitutable. Most of the cases which establish these principles involve awards of specific performance or injunctions to restrain a breach of covenant.

However, in some 'second sale' scenarios, courts have been prepared to award disgorgement damages – most commonly for second sales of land, but also for goods and shares in a limited number of cases. Substitutability explains why courts have chosen to do so. Unfortunately, the courts are not always transparent about what is occurring in these cases. For example, in *Lake v Bayliss*[4] and *Bunny Industries Ltd v FSW Enterprises Pty Ltd*,[5] the courts concealed an award of disgorgement damages for second sale of real property behind a constructive trust analysis. Even in *Luxe Holding Limited v Midland Resources Holding Limited*,[6] a recent case involving a second sale of shares in a private company, the court still found it necessary to obscure its conclusion behind a constructive trust analysis, and rejected the argument that the claimant was entitled to disgorgement damages pursuant to *Attorney-General v Blake*.[7] One of the few 'second sale' cases which is transparent about awarding disgorgement damages for breach of contract is the Israeli Supreme Court Case, *Adras Building Material v Harlow & Jones GmbH*.[8] Unfortunately in *Adras* the court did not make a factual finding as to the substitutability of the subject matter of the contract. If it had done so, the decision might have been justifiable.

Substitutability indicates that the circumstances in which a court will award disgorgement damages for a 'second sale' will be rare. In most commercial contracts, the subject matter of the contract is substitutable, and thus compensatory damages will be adequate. Where compensatory damages are inadequate, and the subject matter of the contract is non-substitutable, the court will award specific performance by preference. It is *only* when specific performance is impossible and the defendant has made a profit from the second sale that disgorgement damages

[3] *Adderley v Dixon* (1824) 1 Sim & St 607, 610; 57 ER 239 (Ch) 240.
[4] *Lake v Bayliss* [1974] 1 WLR 1073 (Ch).
[5] *Bunny Industries Ltd v FSW Enterprises Pty Ltd* [1982] Qd R 712 (QSC).
[6] *Luxe Holding Ltd v Midland Resources Holding Ltd* [2010] EWHC 1908 (Ch).
[7] *Attorney-General v Blake* (*Blake*) [2000] UKHL 45, [2001] 1 AC 268 (HL).
[8] *Adras Building Material v Harlow & Jones GmbH* (1995) 42(1) PD 221, translated in (1995) 3 *Restitution Law Review* 235 (SC of Israel, 1988).

will potentially be available. One area where courts should perhaps have increasing recourse to disgorgement damages is in cases involving the 'second sales' of services. If the services of the defendant are unique, disgorgement damages recognise the claimant's interest in their performance, but do not restrain the liberty of the defendant to provide the services for others. Award of the remedy therefore offers a more balanced approach to the issue than current approaches.

This chapter also discusses the theory of 'efficient breach', and concludes that, despite initial appearances, the theory does not rule out recognition of disgorgement damages for breach of contract as long as substitutability is added to the analysis. Nonetheless, it suffers from certain fatal flaws which mean that it does not fully fit with the reality of contract law, and thus should not be accepted in any event.

The subject matter of the 'second sale' contracts can be broken down into land, chattels and goods, shares and stock, and services. I will consider each category in turn.

II 'Second Sale' Cases

A Contracts for Sale of Land

Land has been 'accorded a unique status as a symbol of the self and as a resource closely linked to personal freedom, rank and power.'[9] It has a 'peculiar and special value',[10] and therefore, it is intrinsically non-substitutable. Specific performance of contracts for sale of land will usually be ordered.

However, a majority of the Canadian Supreme Court has cast doubt in obiter dicta on the presumption that contracts for sale of land are necessarily specifically performable. *Semelhago v Paramadevan*[11] did not raise the issue of specific performance of a contract for sale of land directly. After the contract of sale was breached, the claimant elected to take damages instead of specific performance, and the issue was the way in which those damages were to be calculated. Sopinka J, who delivered the majority judgment, said:

[9] Dagan, 'Restitutionary Damages for Breach of Contract' (n 2) 138; Dagan, *The Law and Ethics of Restitution* (n 2) 267.

[10] *Adderley v Dixon* (n 3) 610; *Dougan v Ley* (1946) 71 CLR 142 (HCA). Of course, an order for specific performance of a contract for sale of land is nevertheless subject to discretionary considerations. See, eg *Patel v Ali* [1984] 1 Ch 283 (Ch); *Summers v Cocks* (1927) 40 CLR 321 (HCA).

[11] *Semelhago v Paramadevan* [1996] 2 SCR 415 (SCC). La Forest J dissented on that issue, saying at [1]:

> However, given the assumption under which the case was argued, I prefer not to deal with the circumstances giving rise to entitlement to specific performance or generally the interpretation that should be given to the legislation authorizing the award of damages in lieu of specific performance. In considering modification to existing law, both these interdependent factors may well require examination, and the arguments in this case were not made in those terms.

> While at one time the common law regarded every piece of real estate to be unique, with the progress of modern real estate development this is no longer the case. Residential, business and industrial properties are all mass-produced much in the same way as other consumer products. If a deal falls through for one property, another is frequently, though not always, readily available.
>
> It is no longer appropriate, therefore, to maintain a distinction in the approach to specific performance as between realty and personalty. It cannot be assumed that damages for breach of contract for the purchase and sale of real estate will be an inadequate remedy in all cases. The common law recognized that the distinction might not be valid when the land had no peculiar or special value . . . [His Honour here cited *Adderley v Dixon* (1824) 1 Sim & St 607, 57 ER 239][12]

His Honour went on to state:

> Specific performance should, therefore, not be granted as a matter of course absent evidence that the property is unique to the extent that its substitute would not be readily available[13]

As Professor Chambers has argued, these dicta misunderstand the reasoning behind specific performance, because '[a]lthough the purchaser might be able to find other land with similar features, it [is] simply not possible to obtain the same land from another vendor.'[14] The availability of specific performance should not hinge on the availability of a substitute performance which is 'good enough' or '90 per cent of what the claimant wanted'. Damages cannot be an adequate response where a claimant is unable to get a full and proper substitute for the benefit for which she bargained. Land is *intrinsically* non-substitutable, as compared to $100 notes or shares or grains of rice. Each plot of land will have its own specific attributes which mean that the plot is not, and can never be identical with another plot, even if it is a part of an apartment block or a development where all the apartments are *similar.*[15]

Chambers highlights the three central problems with *Semelhago*, being a resultant lack of equality in the way in which courts treat claimants,[16] uncertainty created by the new rule,[17] and unintended consequences for the way in which equitable proprietary interests are found to arise from specifically enforceable contracts to create those interests.[18]

[12] ibid [20]–[21].

[13] ibid [22].

[14] R Chambers, 'The Importance of Specific Performance' in S Degeling and J Edelman (eds), *Equity in Commercial Law* (NSW, Lawbook Co, 2004) 431; *cf* W Swadling, 'The Vendor-Purchaser Constructive Trust' in S Degeling and J Edelman (eds), *Equity in Commercial Law* (NSW, Lawbook Co, 2004) 463.

[15] Against T Ulen, 'The Efficiency of Specific Performance: Towards a Unified Theory of Contract Remedies' (1984) 83 *Michigan Law Review* 314, 373: 'The most often cited unique contracts are those for the conveyance of land, and yet, economically speaking, there is nothing unique about parcels of realty. In fact, in most circumstances substitutes abound. Another location at a slightly different price is just as good.'

[16] Chambers (n 14) 437–41.

[17] ibid 441–42.

[18] ibid 442–48.

Semelhago can be contrasted with the Australian case, *Pianta v National Finance & Trustees Ltd.* In that case, Barwick CJ suggested that specific performance will be ordered regardless of whether a property was purchased for the purposes of a real estate development or a personal home.[19] This conclusion must be preferred – there is no possibility of true substitute performance where land is concerned. As Sir Garfield Barwick said in dissent in *Loan Investment Corp of Australasia v Bonner*, 'No two pieces of land can be identically situated on the surface of the earth. When a buyer purchases a parcel, no other piece of land, or the market value of the chosen land can be considered . . . a just substitute for the failure to convey the selected land.'[20]

Therefore, where the subject matter of a contract is land and the vendor has entered into a profitable 'second sale' with a third party, substitutability suggests that the breaching party should disgorge any profit made (subject to discretionary considerations).

In fact, even prior to *Blake*, English and Australian courts were prepared to force a breaching vendor to disgorge his profit to the purchaser. The two examples of this are *Lake v Bayliss*[21] and *Bunny Industries.*[22] In each case the vendor made a contract of sale of certain land with the purchaser, but then, unbeknown to the purchaser, the vendor entered into a more profitable contract of sale with a third party. The land was ultimately conveyed to the third party, and specific performance was no longer available. In *Lake v Bayliss* the matter was further complicated by the fact that the vendor contracted to convey the land to the purchaser in return for the purchaser withdrawing two legal claims against her.

In each case, the vendor was said to be a trustee of the proceeds of sale and had to account for them (subject to the purchaser providing the requisite consideration).[23] Effectively, the vendor was forced to disgorge his or her profits to the purchaser.

Lake v Bayliss and *Bunny Industries* have been explained as cases where profit must be disgorged because of the constructive trust which is said to arise upon execution of the contract of sale (before settlement occurs).[24] The vendor is said to hold the property on constructive trust for the purchaser because the contract is specifically enforceable.[25] But the trust analogy is unsatisfactory, as noted in

[19] *Pianta v National Finance & Trustees Ltd* (1964) 180 CLR 146 (HCA) 151 (Barwick CJ). See also *Sudbrook Trading Estate Ltd v Eggleton* [1983] 1 AC 444 (HL) 478 (Lord Diplock); *cf Loan Investment Corp of Australasia v Bonner* [1970] NZLR 724 (PC) (Sir Garfield Barwick dissenting).

[20] *Loan Investment Corp of Australasia* (n 19) 745 (Sir Garfield Barwick, dissenting on the issue of whether the contract in question was a contract for the sale of land or simply a loan contract).

[21] *Lake v Bayliss* (n 4).

[22] *Bunny Industries* (n 5).

[23] *Lake v Bayliss* (n 4) 1076; *Bunny Industries* (n 5) 717–19.

[24] See, eg S Harder, *Measuring Damages in the Law of Obligations* (Oxford, Hart Publishing, 2010) 228–29. Harder would categorise the contract of sale as giving rise to an exclusive entitlement inter partes between the claimant and the defendant.

[25] See *Englewood Properties Limited v Patel* [2005] EWHC 188, [2005] 3 All ER 307 (Ch) [40]–[43] (Lawrence Collins J) for a useful summary of the law.

Lysaght v Edwards by Sir George Jessel MR.[26] The vendor cannot be considered to be a bare trustee. The vendor is not subject to a fiduciary duty of loyalty to the purchaser, nor does the vendor have any active duties to perform other than to preserve the property and to perform the contract of sale. Indeed, whether a constructive trustee can be said to be a fiduciary at all is controversial. The vendor maintains some beneficial interest in the asset as he is entitled to possession of the property until transfer, and holds a security interest over the property to ensure payment of the purchase price via a vendor's lien. Further, the purchaser's interest corresponds only to the proportion of the purchase price paid. Sir Thomas Plumer MR in *Wall v Bright*[27] described the vendor as 'in progress towards' bare trusteeship. A vendor will only become a bare trustee when the whole of the purchase moneys are paid and the vendor is bound by contract to convey.

The Australian High Court questioned the authority of *Lysaght v Edwards* in *Tanwar Enterprises Pty Ltd v Cauchi.*[28] *Tanwar* said in obiter that where a purchaser had failed to pay the full purchase price by the time specified, there was no equitable interest arising as a result of the entry into a contract for sale of land.[29] Therefore, the purchaser could not found a right to relief against forfeiture on the basis that it had forfeited an equitable interest in the land. Similarly, US courts have rejected the constructive trust analysis.[30]

Chambers has argued that the High Court in *Tanwar* may have been unduly hasty in concluding that a constructive trust does not arise upon entry into a specifically performable contract for sale of land, as the questions then arise – what interest does the purchaser have, and how can she protect her interest if it is not proprietary?[31] Thus it has been argued that it would be too unsettling to the law to conclude a constructive trust does not arise upon entry into a specifically enforceable contract of sale. As Dr Elias has noted, constructive trusts are imposed for a variety of reasons, including the aim of perfecting the parties' intentions.[32] The constructive trust arising pursuant to a specifically enforceable contract of sale could be said to arise from the court's desire to perfect the intention of the parties, as the vendor has indicated he will transfer the property to the claimant, and the court seeks to recognise that commitment in the best way it can.[33]

It is clear that *some kind* of equitable proprietary interest must arise upon entry into specifically enforceable contracts of sale of interests in land, and there are sound reasons for this. *Tanwar* throws the baby out with the bath water by

[26] *Lysaght v Edwards* (1876) 2 Ch D 499 (Ch) 510. See also *Holroyd v Marshall* (1862) 10 HL Cas 191; 11 ER 999.

[27] *Wall v Bright* (1820) 1 Jac & W 494, 503, 37 ER 456 (Ch) 459.

[28] *Tanwar Enterprises Pty Ltd v Cauchi* (2003) 217 CLR 315 (HCA).

[29] *Tanwar* (n 28) 330–55 (Gleeson CJ, McHugh, Gummow, Hayne and Heydon JJ). In casting doubt on the correctness of *Lysaght* (n 26), the High Court cites *Chang v Registrar of Titles* (1976) 137 CLR 177 (HCA) 190 (Jacobs J) and *Kern Corporation Ltd v Walter Reid Trading Pty Ltd* (1987) 163 CLR 164 (HCA) 192 (Deane J).

[30] *Laurin v DeCarolis Construction Co Inc*, 363 NE 2d 675 (Mass SC, 1977).

[31] Chambers (n 14) 448–57.

[32] G Elias, *Explaining Constructive Trusts* (Oxford, Oxford University Press, 1990) 9–16.

[33] ibid 50–56.

jettisoning both the constructive trust analysis *and*, with it, the purchaser's equitable proprietary interest. It may be, however, that the interest which arises is better analysed as some other kind of equitable proprietary interest whereby the vendor becomes obligated to transfer the property to the purchaser, rather than being constrained within a constructive trust analysis because of the well-known difficulties with it.

The constructive trust analysis of contracts for sale of land is particularly problematic in second sale cases. The constructive trust is said to arise from the fact that the contract for sale of land is specifically enforceable. The purchaser can compel the vendor to convey the property to her, and thus she is regarded as having a beneficial interest in the property. In both *Lake v Bayliss* and *Bunny Industries* the contract of sale was no longer actually specifically enforceable, because the land had been conveyed to a third party. Nonetheless, in each case the court was prepared to find that the vendor was liable to account by virtue of the constructive trust. It could be argued that while the vendor no longer holds the land on constructive trust, the claimant has the right to trace the beneficial interest from the land to the money as a result of the breach of the constructive trust. This analysis is attractive, but the difficulty with it is that the vendor is not a bare trustee. The vendor maintains some beneficial interest in the land after the contract of sale has been entered into, being entitled to possession of the property until transfer and a right to the value of the property through the payment of the purchase price via a vendor's lien.[34] It is not clear that full fiduciary obligations arise from the constructive trust arising from a specifically enforceable contract of sale because the vendor is not obliged to act wholly in the purchaser's interests, and thus the basis for tracing in equity may be problematic if the fiduciary requirement is insisted upon.[35] A counter-argument may be that there is at the very least a duty of loyalty in respect of honouring the contract of sale, and that this is enough to satisfy the fiduciary requirement.

In an attempt to bypass the difficulties of the constructive trust analysis American scholars have analysed the remedies arising from these second sale cases as a form of expectation damages rather than disgorgement damages.[36] There is said to be an implied term in contracts for the sale of a commodity that the vendor will not seek out or accept offers from others who wish to pay more, and the buyer pays an implicit premium for that promise. It is argued that where a 'second sale' situation occurs and a vendor is forced to disgorge his profits, this is not disgorgement but a form of expectation damages, because the purchaser has paid

[34] *Lysaght* (n 26) 510.

[35] See *In re Hallett's Estate* (1879) 13 Ch D 696 (Ch); *cf Black v Freeman & Co* (1910) 12 CLR 105 (HCA) (fiduciary requirement ignored where money was stolen) and *Chase Manhattan Bank v Israel-British Bank* [1981] Ch 105 (Ch) (fiduciary requirement arguably distorted – the mere mistaken receipt of money created a fiduciary duty).

[36] EA Farnsworth, 'Your Loss or My Gain? The Dilemma of the Disgorgement Principle in Breach of Contract' (1985) 94 *Yale Law Journal* 1339, 1364–65; MA Eisenberg, 'Actual and Virtual Specific Performance, the Theory of Efficient Breach, and the Indifference Principle in Contract Law' (2005) 93 *California Law Review* 975, 1008–09; MA Eisenberg, 'The Disgorgement Interest in Contract Law' (2006) 105 *Michigan Law Review* 559, 582.

for the right to any profit gained by the vendor pursuant to the implied term. The difficulty with this analysis is that, like the constructive trust analysis, it involves a fiction: namely, that the parties agreed that if the vendor sold to someone else the purchaser would be entitled to the profit made by the vendor. Professor Eisenberg, who advocates the above interpretation, then argues that disgorgement damages should be awarded where the promisee would have been awarded specific performance before the promisor's wrongful action put the remedy beyond reach.[37]

It is better to avoid fictions altogether. In *Blake*, when discussing *Lake v Bayliss*, Lord Nicholls considered the constructive trust analysis was unnecessary where one was attempting to effect disgorgement of profits arising from a second sale; the claimant could merely have relied on the breach of contract and disgorgement damages arising from the breach.[38] This analysis of the basis for disgorgement is preferable to an analysis based on the existence of a constructive trust because it is more transparent and straightforward. These cases award disgorgement for breach of contract because the subject matter of the contract was not substitutable and specific performance was no longer available.

B Contracts for Sale of Goods or Chattels

Where contracts for sale of goods or chattels involve a good or chattel that can easily be obtained elsewhere, the general principle is that damages will be adequate compensation for non-performance.[39] However, a good or chattel may be non-substitutable if it is unique or because the claimant cannot easily procure the chattel or good from elsewhere.[40] Thus, in *Falcke v Gray*, Kindersley V-C said:

> If in a contract for chattels damages will be a sufficient compensation, the party is left to that remedy. Thus if a contract is for the purchase of a certain quantity of coals, stock, &c., this Court will not decree specific performance, *because a person can go into the market and buy similar articles, and get damages for any difference in the price of the articles in a Court of law*. But if damages would not be a sufficient compensation, the

[37] Eisenberg, 'The Disgorgement Interest' (n 36) 584.

[38] *Blake* (n 7) 284. See also J Dawson, 'Restitution or Damages' (1959) 20 *Ohio State Law Journal* 175, 186–87.

[39] *Adderley v Dixon* (n 3) 610; 240.

[40] *Lowther v Lord Lowther* (1806) 13 Ves Jun 95, 33 ER 230 (Ch) (valuable painting); *Lingen v Simpson* (1824) 1 Sim & St 600, 57 ER 236 (Ch) (book of ornamental plates); *Falcke v Gray* (1859) 4 Drew 651, 62 ER 250 (Ch) (unique china vases); *North v Great Northern Railway Co* (1860) 2 Giff 64, 66 ER 28 (Ch) (coal trucks which could not easily be procured elsewhere); *Thorn v The Commissioners of Her Majesty's Works and Public Buildings* (1863) 32 Beav 490, 55 ER 192 (RC) (specially shaped stones from old Westminster bridge, namely arch-stones, spandrel stones (the triangular stone fitting between the arch-stones) and Bramley Fall stones); *Burr v Bloomburg*, 101 NJ Eq 615, 318 A 876 (Ch New Jersey, 1927) (unique diamond ring); *Behnke v Bede Shipping Co Ltd* [1927] 1 KB 649 (KB) 611 (unique ship); *Dougan v Ley* (n 10) (taxi licence of limited availability); *Aristoc Industries Pty Ltd v RA Wenham (Builders) Pty Ltd* [1965] NSWR 581 (NSWSC) (lecture theatre seats specially made to fit a particular hall); *Phillips v Lamdin* [1949] 2 KB 33 (KB) 41 (house with unique Neoclassical door attributed to one of the brothers Adam); *Sky Petroleum Ltd v VIP Petroleum Ltd* [1974] 1 WLR 577 (Ch) (petroleum which could not easily be procured elsewhere); *Howard Perry & Co v British Railways* [1980] 1 WLR 1375 (Ch) (steel which could not be procured elsewhere).

> principle, on which a Court of Equity decrees specific performance, is just as applicable to a contract for the sale and purchase of chattels, as to a contract for the sale and purchase of land.
>
> In the present case the contract is for the purchase of articles of unusual beauty, rarity and distinction, so that damages would not be an adequate compensation for non-performance; and I am of opinion that a contract for articles of such a description is such a contract as this Court will enforce; and, in the absence of all other objection, I should have no hesitation in decreeing specific performance. [Emphasis added][41]

Sometimes a good or chattel may be non-substitutable because the defendant is particularly well situated to meet the claimant's needs, and the claimant could not quickly get a substitute performance.[42] In *North v The Great Northern Railway Company*, where the defendant had contracted to sell 54 coal wagons to the claimant, Stuart V-C said:

> There can be no doubt that, on the statements in the bill, the Plaintiff's trade being such as it is, the coal waggons were of special value to him, in order to carry on his business. The sudden sale of those waggons, without which the trade could not be conducted, must necessarily have inflicted serious injury by the interruption of his trade.
>
> It is not answer to say that it is possible to state a sum of money which would have been sufficient compensation for the injury. The Court looks at the circumstances of the case with reference to the right to the specific thing. *It cannot be pretended that the Plaintiff could have got, on a sudden, fifty-four other coal waggons fit for his business as readily and promptly as he could have purchased fifty-four tons of coal or fifty-four bushels of wheat.* [Emphasis added][43]

In some circumstances, although a good or chattel is generally substitutable, it may be unavailable because of particular circumstances at that time.[44] For example, in *Howard Perry*,[45] members of the National Union of Railwaymen had refused to transport steel in a gesture of solidarity with striking steelworkers. The claimants were steel stockholders, and had consignments of steel waiting to be delivered in two of the defendant's depots. The steel could not be kept for a long period of time because it would harden and become unmalleable and would be

[41] *Falcke v Grey* (n 40) 657–58; 252–53. In the event, Kindersley V-C did not order specific performance because the purchaser knew that the price offered in the contract was grossly inadequate and did not reflect the true value of the chattel.

[42] See, eg *North* (n 40); *Sky Petroleum* (n 40). See against *Société des Industries Métallurgiques SA v Bronx Engineering Co Ltd (Bronx)* [1975] 1 Lloyd's Rep 465 (an interim injunction was not awarded to restrain a breach of contract even though the claimant's business would be substantially disrupted). See also R Austen-Baker, 'Difficulties with Damages as a Ground for Specific Performance' (1999) 10 *King's College Law Journal* 1. Austen-Baker says that *Bronx* can be distinguished from other cases as the difficulties in calculating damages are only extrinsic difficulties, and these do not ordinarily give rise to specific relief without more.

[43] *North* (n 40) 68–69, 30.

[44] *Howard Perry* (n 40); *Sky Petroleum* (n 40) (scarcity of petroleum); *Curtice Bros v Catts*, 72 NJ Eq 831 (Ch New Jersey), 833; 66 A 935, 936 (Ch, 1907) (scarcity of tomatoes for a cannery); *Eastern Air Lines v Gulf Oil Corporation*, 415 F Supp 429, 442–43 (Southern District Florida, 1975); *cf*, however, *Cook v Rodgers* (1946) 46 SR (NSW) 229 (NSWSC) (scarcity of motor cars not enough to ground award of an injunction).

[45] *Howard Perry* (n 40).

unworkable for the claimants' purposes. The defendants would not allow the claimants to collect the steel from the depots themselves. Accordingly, the claimants sought delivery up of the goods pursuant to the contract. Megarry V-C said:

> If a plaintiff can easily replace the goods detained by purchasing their equivalent on the market, then the payment of damages out of which the price of the equivalent may be paid is adequate compensation to the wronged plaintiff, and there is little or no point in making an order for the delivery of the goods. Far better to let the plaintiff fend for himself with the defendant's money.
>
> *In normal times, the steel here in dispute might indeed be in this category; but these times are not normal, and at present steel is obtainable on the market only with great difficulty, if at all. If the equivalent of what is detained is unobtainable, how can it be said that damages are an adequate remedy?* They plainly are not. Mr Irvine observed that at present 'steel is gold,' and one can see what he meant. Yet even that may not do justice to his cause, since as far as I know gold is still available on the open market to those who pay the price. [Emphasis added][46]

Indeed, in the United States, courts have awarded punitive damages for breach of contract where the defendant contracted to supply oil to the claimant, and then breached the contract, knowing that the claimant's business would fail because it would be unable to gain a substitute performance.[47]

In other circumstances, there may be an instalment contract to supply goods and services over a long period of time.[48] This is not substitutable because a complex contract cannot be replaced with an identical deal. For example, in *Eastern Rolling Mill Co v Michlovitz* the defendant had contracted with the claimants to sell them scrap steel for a period of five years. The contract provided that the claimants were to accept delivery of the steel as it accumulated, and the price for both pressed bundled sheet steel and crop end scrap respectively was to be $3 a ton less than the quoted price in 'Iron Age', a publication which contained the Philadelphia market prices for steel. The defendant purported to terminate the contract after the manager of the defendant died some months into the five-year contract. The claimants sought specific performance of the contract. The Court of Appeals of Maryland said:

> The goods which the parties here had bargained for were not procurable in the neighborhood, and, moreover, they possessed a quality and concentrated weight which could not have been secured anywhere within the extensive region covered by the 'Philadelphia Market.' In addition, the delivery of the scrap at Baltimore was one of the valuable

[46] ibid 1383.

[47] *Seaman's Direct Buying Service v Standard Oil*, 686 P 2d 1158 (Cal, 1984) (SC). See also *Freeman & Mills v Belcher*, 900 P 2d 669, 689 (Cal, 1995) (SC) (Mosk J).

[48] *Buxton v Lister* (1746) 3 Atk 383, 26 ER 1020 (Ch); *Adderley* (n 3); *Eastern Rolling Mill v Michlovitz* (*Michlovitz*) (1929) 157 Md 51, 145 A 378 (CA Maryland); *Thomas Borthwick v South Otago Freezing* [1978] 1 NZLR 538 (NZSC); *Sky Petroleum* (n 40). Compare *Fothergill v Rowland* (1873) LR 17 Eq 132, 140; *Laclede Gas Co v Amoco Oil Co*, 522 F 2d 33 (8th Cir, 1975); *Bronx* (n 42). The latter cases have been criticised: see A Burrows, *Remedies for Torts and Breach of Contract*, 3rd edn (Oxford, Oxford University Press, 2004) 467. See also Austen-Baker (n 42) who distinguishes between extrinsic difficulties (involving forensic problems of evidence) and intrinsic difficulties (the damages are simply impossible to calculate for intrinsic reasons).

> incidents of the purchase. It follows that the right to these specific goods is a consideration of great importance, and this and the difficulty of securing scrap of the same commercial utility are factors making for the inadequacy of damages.
>
> The scrap is not to be delivered according to specified tonnage, but as it accumulates, which in the past has been at the rate of one and two, and occasionally three, carloads of scrap a day, so the quantities vary from quarter to quarter. If the plant should cease to operate or suffer an interruption, there would be no scrap accumulating for delivery under the contracts, and its deliveries would end or be lessened. Neither are the prices for the scrap constant during the period of the contracts, but change from quarter to quarter according to the quotations of two specified materials on the Philadelphia market whose quarterly prices are accepted as the standards upon which the contract prices are quarterly computed. The contracts run to September 30, 1932. By what method would a jury determine the future quarterly tonnage, the quarterly contract price, and quarterly market price during these coming years? *How could it possibly arrive at any fair ascertainment of damages? Any estimate would be speculative and conjectural, and not, therefore, compensatory. It follows that the defendant's breach of its contracts is not susceptible of fair and proper compensation by damages; and that to refuse to compel the defendant to do merely what it bound itself to do, and to remit the plaintiffs to their action at law, is to permit the defendant to relieve itself of the contracts and to force the plaintiffs to sell their profits at a conjectural price.* To substitute damages by guess for due performance of contract could only be because 'there's no equity stirring.' [Emphasis added][49]

Indeed, the US Uniform Commercial Code deems certain long-term requirement contracts to be unique.[50] Section 2-716(1) states, inter alia, that '[s]pecific performance may be decreed if the goods are unique or in other proper circumstances.' Comment 2 to §2-716 expands upon this:

> Specific performance is no longer limited to goods which are already specific or ascertained at the time of contracting. The test of uniqueness under this section must be made in terms of the total situation which characterizes the contract. Output and requirements contracts involving a particular or peculiarly available source or market present today the typical commercial specific performance situation, as contrasted with contracts for the sale of heirlooms or priceless works of art which were usually involved in the older cases. However, uniqueness is not the sole basis of the remedy under this section for the relief may also be granted 'in other proper circumstances' and inability to cover is strong evidence of 'other proper circumstances.'

The Israeli Supreme Court has awarded disgorgement damages for a 'second sale' of goods in *Adras.*[51] The defendant, Harlow, a German company, entered into a contract of sale with the claimant, Adras, an Israeli company. The contract provided that the defendant would supply the claimant with 7000 tons of iron at a price of 570 German marks per ton. There was a delay in delivery because of the Yom Kippur war in October 1973, but 5025 tons were eventually shipped to the claimant in early 1974. On 8 April 1974, the defendant told the claimant that it

[49] *Michlovitz* (n 48) 384 (Parke J).

[50] *Uniform Commercial Code* (US), §2-716 (comment 2).

[51] *Adras* (n 8). See D Friedmann, 'Restitution of Profits Gained by Party in Breach of Contract' (1988) 104 *LQR* 383.

had to sell the remaining iron because of high storage costs. In fact the price of iron had spiked, and the defendant proposed to profit by selling the iron to a third party. The claimant demanded that the defendant supply the remaining 1925 tons of iron due under the contract. Instead, the defendant sold the iron in Hamburg for a profitable price of 804.70 German marks per ton. The claimant did not obtain an alternative supply of iron on the market, and sued to recover damages for breach of contract pursuant to the Sale (International Sale of Goods) Law 1971 (Israel)[52] and to recover the profit made by the defendant in respect of the sale of the remaining iron. At a previous hearing the Supreme Court had held that the claimant had never terminated the contract, and therefore the claimant had failed to prove any loss.[53]

A majority of the Supreme Court of Israel[54] found that the claimant was entitled to recover the profit made by the defendant. In his judgment Barak J raised the second sale of land cases where disgorgement is said to arise because of a constructive trust in Anglo-American law. Barak J said:

> The injured party has a right not only to compensation for breach of contract, but also to specific performance . . . Therefore, under Israeli law, a buyer in a contract of sale is entitled to receive the subject-matter of the sale, and an enrichment of the seller which infringes this right is an unjust enrichment at the buyer's expense. . . . When there is a contract for the sale of a horse, the buyer has a right to receive the horse, not damages for non-delivery. If the seller receives a benefit from selling the horse to a third party, he . . . takes from the buyer a right to which the buyer is entitled.[55]

Barak J says that the claimant has a prima facie right to disgorgement damages because the injured party has a right under Israeli law to specific performance which is not subject to the court's discretion.[56] However, where a claimant has a 'substitutable' product, it would presumably not much matter to the claimant whether she gained damages allowing her to purchase the product on the market or specific performance of the contract itself.[57] Because of the non-discretionary

[52] Statute Book No 615, 29 January 1971, 42; authorised English translation, Israeli Ministry of Justice, Laws of the State of Israel, vol 25, 32. This statute implements the Hague Convention Relating to a Uniform Law on the International Sale of Goods 1964 into Israeli law.

[53] *Adras* (n 8). According to s 84(a) of the Sale (International Sale of Goods) Law 1971 (Israel), if a contract is terminated, then, if the goods are available on the market, the claimant can claim the difference between the agreed price and the market price at that time. However, the Supreme Court found the contract was not terminated for the purposes of s 84, and that the claimant could not rely on s 82 of the Sale (International Sale of Goods) Law 1971 (which dealt with losses where a contract was not terminated).

[54] S Levin, Barak and Bach JJ. Ben Porath V-P and D Levin J (diss).

[55] *Adras* (n 8) 271.

[56] ibid, citing *Rabihai v Man Shaket Ltd (in liquidation)* (1977) 33(2) PD 281, 295. See Contract (Remedies) Law 1970 (Israel), s 3.

[57] The difference between systems which recognise specific performance as of right and systems which regard specific performance as exceptional and discretionary is not as great in practice as it might appear. See GH Treitel, *Remedies for Breach of Contract – A Comparative Account* (New York, Clarendon Press, 1988) 71; E McKendrick, 'Specific Implement and Specific Performance – A Comparison' (1986) *Scots Law Times* 249.

specific performance provisions, the court did not consider whether Adras could have procured a substitute performance.[58]

Adras is very reminiscent of *Howard Perry* mentioned above, which also involved a contract for delivery of steel. Megarry V-C was prepared to grant specific performance of the contract. It was pivotal to his Honour's decision that, although ordinarily the claimants would easily be able to purchase equivalent steel on the market, British steelworkers were on strike at that time and so steel was only obtainable with great difficulty (and presumably at great expense).[59]

It has been suggested that *Adras* represents a dangerously broad approach to awarding disgorgement damages.[60] The result of *Adras* was correct, but with respect the decision could not be justified because of the lack of a factual finding as to the substitutability of the iron.[61] The result would have been justifiable if the court had found that the Yom Kippur War had prevented Adras from procuring a substitute performance.[62] Substitutability would have provided a coherent limitation on the *Adras* decision.

If it is merely difficult to procure a substitute performance, and specific relief is no longer available, then disgorgement damages should also be available. For example in *Dougan v Ley*, where the claimant sought to specifically enforce a contract to obtain a taxi licence, it was still possible for the claimant to procure taxi licences which were the subject matter of the breached contract, albeit with some difficulty.[63] The court was prepared to award specific performance. However, if specific performance was unavailable, but the defendant had sold the taxi licence to a third party for an amount exceeding the price payable by the claimant, then disgorgement damages should be available in the absence of relevant bars to relief.

C Contracts for Shares and Stock

Generally, shares in a public company are substitutable since they will usually be available on the open market. A court will not order specific performance for a contract for the sale of shares or stock.[64] But this will not be the case with shares in

[58] The lack of uniqueness of the property was implicitly considered in the two dissenting judgments, but they did not consider substitutability and supply problems in the circumstances. See *Adras* (n 8) 252–53 (Ben Porath V-P, with whom D Levin J agreed).

[59] *Howard Perry* (n 40) 1383.

[60] R O'Dair, 'Restitutionary Damages for Breach of Contract and the Theory of Efficient Breach: Some Reflections' (1993) 46 *Current Legal Problems* 113, 114, 134; H Dagan, 'The Distributive Foundation of Corrective Justice' (1999) 98 *Michigan Law Review* 138; J O'Sullivan, 'Reflections on the Role of Restitutionary Damages to Protect Contractual Expectations' in D Johnston and R Zimmermann (eds), *Unjustified Enrichment: Key Issues in Comparative Perspective* (Cambridge, Cambridge University Press, 2002) 327, 332–33.

[61] See W Goodhart, 'Restitutionary Damages for Breach of Contract – The Remedy that Dare Not Speak Its Name' [1995] *Restitution Law Review* 3, 10.

[62] Against Harder (n 24) 232–33.

[63] *Dougan v Ley* (n 10) 151–52 (Dixon J); 153–54 (Williams J).

[64] *Hyer v Richmond Traction Co*, 168 US 471, 42 L ed. 547 (USSC 1897) 483, 551; *In re Schwabacher* (1907) 98 LT 127, 128; *Chinn v Hochstrasser* [1979] Ch 447, 470.

a private company. Moreover, even in the case of shares in a publicly quoted company, there will not always be an adequate market for a particular share or stock, so that damages will be rendered an inadequate or inappropriate remedy.[65] In *Duncuft v Albrecht*,[66] a case involving a contract of sale for certain shares in a railway company, Shadwell V-C said:

> Then the only question is whether there has been any decision, from whence you can extract a conclusion that the Court will not decree a specific performance of an agreement for the sale of such shares? Now, I agree that it has been long since decided that you cannot have a bill for the specific performance of an agreement to transfer a certain quantity of stock. But, in my opinion, there is not any sort of analogy between a quantity of 3 per cents. or any other stock of that description (*which is always to be had by any person who chooses to apply for it in the market*), and a certain number of railways shares of a particular description; which railway shares are limited in number, and *which, as has been observed, are not always to be had in the market.* [Emphasis added.][67]

In other circumstances, the market price for shares might be uncertain or there may be a risk that requiring the claimant to purchase the shares with damages will prejudice the claimant or a third party. In these circumstances, a court will also order specific performance.[68]

Luxe[69] involves a second sale of shares in a private company. One would expect that the case would be easily resolved upon an application of the principles espoused in *Blake* but unfortunately this was not the case. The case arose when, on 4 May 2010, Midland Resources Holding Limited ('Midland') entered into an agreement with Luxe Holding Limited ('Luxe') to sell shares in 20 companies. However, Midland purported to pull out of the contract because it had found another buyer through a Russian investment bank, Troika Dialog ('Troika'). Luxe proceeded to seek specific performance of the contract of sale and an injunction preventing the sale of the shares to Troika, but Midland sold the shares to Troika on 24 May 2010 before the matter came before Mann J on 26 May 2010. Luxe brought three claims: a proprietary claim under the specifically enforceable contract, a claim for disgorgement of profits made by the second sale to Troika and a claim to compensatory damages between the difference in value of the shares and the contract price.

Roth J first considered the availability of a proprietary claim, and noted that 'it is well established that an agreement for the sale of the shares in a private company, like an agreement for the sale of land, entitles the purchaser to specific

[65] *Cud v Rutter* (1719) 1 P Wms 570, 24 ER 521; *Duncuft v Albrecht* (1841) 12 Sim 189, 59 ER 1104; *Dougan v Ley* (n 10) 151; *General Securities Corporation v Welton*, 223 Ala 299, 135 So 329 (SC Alabama, 1931); *Langen and Wind Ltd v Bell* [1972] Ch 685 (Ch); *Harvela Investments Ltd v Royal Trust Co of Canada* [1986] AC 206 (HL); *Rudder v George Hudson Holdings Ltd* [1972] 1 NSWLR 529 (NSWSC); *Paine v Hutchinson* (1868) LR 3 Ch App 388; *Georges v Wieland* [2009] NSWSC 733 (NSWSC) [17]–[25].

[66] *Duncuft* (n 65).

[67] ibid 198–99; 1107–08.

[68] *In re Schwabacher* (n 65); *General Securities Corporation* (n 65); *ANZ Executors and Trustees Ltd v Humes Ltd* [1990] VR 615 (VSC) 630–31 (Brooking J); *Georges* (n 65) [17]–[25].

[69] *Luxe* (n 6).

performance.'[70] Luxe argued that it had an equitable proprietary interest in the shares pursuant to the specifically enforceable contract of sale.[71] Despite the problems of a constructive trust analysis (particularly in a second sale context) which have been noted above, Roth J concluded that Luxe had a very good arguable case that it had a proprietary interest in the proceeds of sale to Troika, subject to the paying the purchase price under the contract of sale. However, Roth J found that Luxe was *not* entitled to an account of profits pursuant to *Blake* because the contract of sale was not an exceptional case. His Honour stated:

> The [contract for the sale of shares] is an ordinary commercial contract and this is a case of breach of a nature not unfamiliar in business affairs: the seller of goods breaks his contract to deliver because he takes advantage of a more attractive offer available elsewhere. There is no reason in principle why as a matter of contract the ordinary, compensatory measure of damages should not apply.[72]

It is unfortunate that Roth J did not have regard to principles of substitutability when drawing this conclusion. If the shares were such that they were readily available elsewhere, and compensatory damages were adequate to compensate for their loss, then the contract of sale should not have been specifically enforceable, and the constructive trust analysis could not apply in the first place. However, it does not seem that this was the case. Later in the judgment, Roth J noted that counsel for Midland observed that there was no open market value for the shares, and it was difficult to calculate compensatory damages.[73] The conclusion that Luxe had an equitable proprietary interest in the shares directly *contradicts* the later conclusion that compensatory damages are adequate. If the former was the case, Luxe should have been awarded disgorgement damages. Courts are still exceptionally confused about the applicability of principles in *Blake*, as the analysis in *Luxe* shows.

D Contracts of Services

The substitutability of services provided by contract is a difficult area. Courts have traditionally been reluctant to order specific performance of contracts for services.[74] The rationale usually put forward is that it is inappropriate to compel parties to

[70] ibid [28].

[71] It was ultimately immaterial that Russian and Ukrainian law did not recognise the concept of a beneficial interest: ibid [35]–[43].

[72] ibid [53].

[73] ibid [57].

[74] *Rigby v Connol* (1880) 14 Ch D 482, 487 (Jessel MR); *Francis v Municipal Councillors of Kuala Lumpur* [1962] 3 All ER 633; *Hogan v Tumut Shire Council* (1954) 54 SR (NSW) 284 (NSWSC); *J C Williamson Ltd v Lukey and Mulholland* (1931) 45 CLR 282 (HCA) 293 (Starke J); *Sampson v Murray*, 415 US 61, 83 (USSC, 1974); *H W Gossard Co v Crosby*, 132 Iowa 155, 170; 109 NW 483, 488–89 (SC Iowa, 1906); American Law Institute, *Restatement (Second) of the Law of Contracts* (1981) § 367 (personal service contracts not specifically enforced). The US position is further complicated by the 13th Amendment to the Constitution, which says 'neither slavery nor involuntary servitude' shall exist in the US.

maintain a continuous personal relationship with one another where one party is unwilling to do so.[75]

However, in some circumstances a court may order an injunction to restrain a breach of a negative covenant in a contract for services.[76] Although relief in this category of case consists of an injunction to restrain a breach of negative covenant, it will be considered in this section because it 'fits' better with the 'second sale' cases. Frequently, the cases involve what is in effect a 'second sale': the defendant has breached his contract with his employer because a third party has agreed to pay him more money.

This category of cases arises where the defendant has agreed in a negative covenant not to provide those services to any person other than the claimant. Courts are sometimes prepared to award an injunction to prevent a contracting party from providing them to a third party, particularly where the services are unique. However, the cases are controversial. Courts have often been reluctant to award such injunctions because of the prospect of forcing employees to work for an employer for whom they do not wish to work.[77]

Injunctions are frequently ordered where employees possess unique skills, such as opera singers,[78] acrobats,[79] sportsmen,[80] actors and actresses[81] and television presenters.[82] In US cases, because of the way in which *Lumley v Wagner* was interpreted by US textbook writers,[83] there is an explicit consideration of the extent to

[75] *Atlas Steels (Australia) Pty Ltd v Atlas Steels Ltd* (1948) 49 SR (NSW) 157 (NSWSC) 161 (Sugarman J).

[76] *Lumley v Wagner* (1852) 1 De GM & G 604, 42 ER 687.

[77] *Wolverhampton and Walsall Railway Co v London North-Western Railway Co* (1873) LR 16 Eq 433; *Rigby* (n 74) 487 (Jessel MR); *Gossard* (n 74) 170, 488–89; *J C Williamson* (n 74) 293 (Starke J); *Atlas Steels* (n 75) 161 (Sugarman J); *Hogan* (n 74); *Francis* (n 74); *Sampson* (n 74). Note American Law Institute (n 74) § 367. See also RS Stevens 'Involuntary Servitude by Injunction: The Doctrine of *Lumley v Wagner* Considered' (1921) 6 *Cornell Law Quarterly* 235 (injunctions to restrain negative breach of contract constitute 'involuntary servitude', contrary to the 13th Amendment of the US Constitution).

[78] *Lumley* (n 76); *Duff v Russell*, 14 NYS 134, 60 J & S 80 (SC New York, 1891); *Oscar Hammerstein v Marguerite Mann*, 122 NYS 276 (SCCA New York, 1910); *Chapin v Powers*, 73 NYS (2d) 854 (SC New York, 1947).

[79] *Shubert Theatrical Co v Rath*, 271 F 827, 20 ALR 846 (CCA, 2d Cir, 1921) (unique acrobats); *Keith v Kellermann*, 169 F 196 (CCSD New York, 1909) (unique diver); *John Cort v Lassard & Lucifer*, 18 Ore 221; 22 P 1054 (SC Oregon, 1889) (non-unique acrobats).

[80] *Philadelphia Ball Club Limited v Lajoie* (*Lajoie*), 202 Pa 210, 51 A 973 (SC Pennsylvania, 1902); *American Baseball and Athletic Association v Harper* (*Harper*) 54 Central Law Journal 449 (SC Pennsylvania 1902) (baseball players); *Hawthorn Football Club Ltd v Harding* (*Harding*) [1988] VR 49 (VSC); *Buckenara v Hawthorn Football Club Ltd* [1988] VR 39 (VSC) (AFL footballers); *Bulldogs Rugby League Club Ltd v Williams* (*Williams*) [2008] NSWSC 822 (NSWSC) (ARL footballers).

[81] *Montague v Flockton* (1873) 16 LR Eq 189; *Daly v Smith*, 49 How Pr 150 (NY, 1874); *Carter v Ferguson*, 12 NYS 580, 58 Hun 569 (SC New York, 1890); *Grimston v Cuningham* (1894) 1 QB 125; *Warner Brothers Pictures Inc v Nelson* (*Nelson*) [1937] 1 KB 209; *Marco Productions Ltd v Pagola* (*Pagola*) [1945] 1 KB 111; *Warner Brothers Pictures Inc v Ingolia* (*Ingolia*) [1965] NSWR 988 (NSWSC).

[82] *Evening News Association v Peterson*, 477 F Supp 77 (USDC District of Columbia, 1979); *American Broadcasting Company v Wolf*, 52 NY (2d) 394, 420 NE (2d) 363, 438 NYS (2d) 482 (CA New York, 1981); *Curro v Beyond Productions Pty Ltd* (1993) 30 NSWLR 337 (NSWCA).

[83] JN Pomeroy, *Equity Jurisprudence*, vol 4, 4th edn (San Francisco, Bancroft-Whitney & Co, 1919) §1343, 3216–8. See also JN Pomeroy, *Treatise on the Specific Performance of Contracts*, 3rd edn (Albany, Banks & Co, 1926) §24, 75–77. Earlier edition of both texts cited with approval by Supreme Court of Pennsylvania in *Lajoie* (n 80) 216, 973.

which the services provided by the person are unique.[84] So in *Madison Square Garden Corp v Braddock*, the court said:

> enforcement of negative covenants in contracts of personal service is based squarely upon the theory that the defendant's services are unique and extraordinary and therefore cannot be compensated for in money damages.[85]

Courts effectively consider substitutability. If an employee can easily be replaced, damages will suffice, but if an employee possesses special qualities and has agreed not to move to a competitor, they will be restrained by injunction (so long as such restraint is reasonable).

Sometimes it is difficult to predict when an employee will be unique. In two American cases decided within days of one another, both of which involved professional baseball players,[86] the result reached by the respective courts were diametrically opposed, so that it has been said:

> The one has a solemn judicial finding that he is a person of such attainments in his profession that his position cannot possibly be filled. The other is decreed to be simply an ordinary person, whose place can easily be filled, and whose absence from his post can result in no particular or irreparable injury. Lajoie's professional reputation is established and enhanced at the cost of his freedom, while Harper gets his freedom at the expense of his professional reputation.[87]

US courts are less likely to restrain salespersons and managers.[88]

By contrast, for the most part, Australian and English courts do not explicitly consider the unique nature of the service provided,[89] although some Australian cases do acknowledge that the principle in *Lumley v Wagner* applies to contracts for 'special services', inferring that the court is cognisant of the unique nature of

[84] See, eg *Bethlehem Engineering Export Co v Christie*, 105 F (2d) 933, 935 (CA New York, 2d Cir, 1939) (Learned Hand J); *Madison Square Garden Corp v Braddock*, 90 F 2d 924, 926 (CCA 3d Cir, 1937).

[85] *Madison Square Garden Corp* (n 84) 926.

[86] *Lajoie* (n 80) (injunction granted); *Harper* (n 80) (injunction refused).

[87] Note to *Philadelphia Ball Club Limited v Lajoie* (1902) 90 *American State Reports* 627, 649.

[88] *Gossard* (n 74) (saleswoman insufficiently unique); *Clark Paper & Manufacturing Co v Stenacher*, 236 NY 312, 140 NE 708 (CA New York, 1923) (*Stenacher*) (salesman insufficiently unique). The court in *Stenacher*, 711 said:

> Experience, competency and efficiency in selling goods are qualifications which can hardly be so rare as to require the aid of equity to prevent an irreparable loss to an employer who finds himself compelled to substitute one salesman for another.

[89] The exception is Kekewich J's decision at first instance in *Whitwood Chemical Company v Hardman* reproduced at [1891] 2 Ch 416, 419–23. His Honour said at 420:

> There are also cases, of which *Lumley v Wagner* is a well-known example, where the *employé* is an artist, having special knowledge, special powers or special abilities, which he or she has engaged to give up and use for the benefit of the employer. That is the foundation of such cases as *Lumley v Wagner*. It is because the defendant in a case of that kind is an artist who cannot easily be replaced that such an action is brought.

This decision was subsequently overruled by the Court of Appeal in *Whitwood Chemical* [1891] 2 Ch 416. But the correctness of that decision is doubtful, because it was based on the fact that the contract contained only an explicit positive stipulation. See also *Mortimer v Beckett* [1920] 1 Ch 571.

the services involved.[90] Nevertheless, the tendency in Anglo-Australian case law suggests that substitutability has been an operative factor in the reasoning of courts. Actors, footballers, newsreaders and the like will be restrained from breaching a promise not to work for a competitor, so long as the restraint is reasonable and not too long in duration.[91] By contrast, managers,[92] travelling salespersons,[93] porters,[94] or other ordinary employees[95] are *less likely* to be restrained from working for a competitor. However, one must be cautious about overemphasising substitutability in these cases. In recent times in New South Wales in particular, there have been a number of instances where courts have restrained an ordinary employee from working for a competitor for a limited time, so long as the restriction does not prevent the employee from any employment.[96] In those cases, substitutability does not appear to underlie the court's decision to award an injunction. Instead, the essential factor seems to have been whether the employee was privy to confidential information. In *John Fairfax Publications Pty Limited v Birt*, the court was prepared to award an injunction to restrain an advertising manager from moving to a competing firm.[97] The judge granted the injunction because the employee was privy to confidential information.[98] By contrast, in the later case of *Otis Elevator Company Pty Limited v Nolan*, the same judge declined to award an injunction because the employee had only been at the workplace for one day and had not been in receipt of any significant confidential information.[99] In addition, although the employee was working for a competitor, he was in a different field with his new employer. The substitutability of the employee's services in these cases did not enter into the decision. The courts in these cases have been applying a restraint of trade analysis. This analysis requires the court to consider whether the claimant has an interest deserving protection (such as confidential information) and, if so, whether the restraint is reasonable as between the parties and in the public interest.

Thus factors unrelated to substitutability influence a court's decision as to whether to award specific relief. Courts may be convinced to award specific relief to restrain a breach of negative covenant in favour of an employer if the employee is in possession of confidential information.[100]

There are also a number of factors unrelated to substitutability which militate *against* the award of specific relief. First, often courts do not wish to force people

[90] *Atlas Steels* (n 75) 164, 165; *Curro* (n 82) 347; *Williams* (n 80) [53]–[54].

[91] *Grimston* (n 81); *Nelson* (n 81); *Pagola* (n 81); *Ingolia* (n 81); *Harding* (n 80); *Buckenara* (n 80); *Curro* (n 82); *Williams* (n 80).

[92] *Whitwood Chemical* (n 89); *Davis v Foreman* [1894] 3 Ch 654; *Mortimer* (n 89); *Page One Records v Britton* [1968] 1 WLR 157 (Ch); *Warren v Mendy* [1989] 1 WLR 853 (CA).

[93] *Ehrman v Bartholomew* [1898] 1 Ch 671.

[94] *Ryan v Mutual Tontine Westminster Chambers Association* [1893] 1 Ch 116.

[95] *Rely-A-Bell Burglar and Fire Alarm Company Ltd v Eisler* [1926] 1 Ch 609 (Ch); *Heine Bros (Aust) Pty Ltd v Forrest* [1963] VR 383 (VSC).

[96] *William Robinson & Co Ltd v Heuer* [1898] 2 Ch 451; *Chapman v Westerby* [1913] WN 277.

[97] *John Fairfax Publications Pty Ltd v Birt (Birt)* [2006] NSWSC 995 (NSWSC).

[98] ibid [24], [28]–[29].

[99] *Otis Elevator Company Pty Ltd v Nolan* [2007] NSWSC 593 (NSWSC) [32]–[33].

[100] *Birt* (n 97) [24], [28]–[29]; *cf Otis Elevator* (n 99) [32]–[33].

to work in jobs where they are unhappy or where they could obtain a better opportunity elsewhere (although the aforementioned cases in New South Wales may suggest a movement away from this idea in that State).[101]

Secondly, using the facts of *Curro* as an illustration, if a newsreader is prevented from working for another company, there is still a vast range of ordinary professions in which she can work. However, if Ms Curro had been a woman with ordinary skills, she would have found it far more difficult if the court had restrained her from working, for example, as a waitress. She would then have been effectively unemployable. If a restriction contained in a covenant is excessively severe, courts refuse to enforce it or limit its operation.[102] Similarly, if relations between the parties have broken down and it is simply infeasible to require cooperation,[103] courts will not force the parties to work together.

Thirdly, the common law doctrine of restraint of trade may sometimes strengthen the reluctance of the courts to award specific relief.[104] Under this doctrine, contractual obligations restricting someone's ability to trade are void by reason of illegality unless they are reasonable and in the interests of both contracting parties and of the public at large.[105] Courts are generally concerned to safeguard the right of individuals to work in their chosen trade or profession without unjust restriction, and thus they will scrutinise restraints on employment more closely.[106] However, as noted above in relation to the recent New South Wales cases, the doctrine of restraint of trade can also lead courts to be more willing to grant an injunction if it finds that such a restraint is reasonable.

Generally, disgorgement damages have not been thought to be available for a breach of a contract for services, although Edelman suggests in his analysis of *Lumley v Gye* that if Ms Wagner had made a profit, her breach was such that she should be forced to disgorge it.[107]

Professor Wonnell has argued that employees may be disempowered by the lack of availability of such remedies, and that the 'enforced servitude' objection to

[101] *Koops Martin Financial Services Pty Ltd v Reeves* [2006] NSWSC 449 (NSWSC); *Birt* (n 97); *Otis Elevator* (n 99); *Tullett Prebon (Australia) Pty Ltd v Purcell* [2008] NSWSC 852 (NSWSC); *Williams* (n 80).

[102] *Ehrman* (n 93); *Heine Bros* (n 95); *Robinson v Heuer* (n 96); *Whitwood Chemical* (n 89) and *Chapman* (n 96); *cf Rely-a-Bell* (n 95).

[103] *Page One Records* (n 92); *Warren* (n 92).

[104] See also Restraints of Trade Act 1976 (NSW), s 4.

[105] *Bacchus Marsh Concentrated Milk Co Ltd (in liq) v Joseph Nathan & Co Ltd* (1919) 26 CLR 410 (HCA); *Esso Petroleum Co Ltd v Harper's Garage (Stourport) Ltd* [1968] AC 269 (HL); *Amoco Australia Pty Ltd v Rocca Bros Motor Engineering Co Pty Ltd* [1975] AC 561, (1975) 133 CLR 331 (PC).

[106] See, eg *Lindner v Murdock's Garage* (1950) 83 CLR 628 (HCA) 633; *Butt v Long* (1953) 88 CLR 476 (HCA); *Forbes v NSW Trotting Club Ltd* (1979) 143 CLR 242 (HCA); *Minnesota Mining & Manufacturing (Australia) Pty Ltd v Richards* [1963] NSWR 1613 (NSWSC); *Buckley v Tutty* (1971) 125 CLR 353 (HCA); *Geraghty v Minter* (1979) 142 CLR 177 (HCA); *Hughes v Western Australian Cricket Association Inc* (1986) 69 ALR 660 (FCA); *Rentokil Pty Ltd v Lee* (1995) 66 SASR 301 (SASC); *cf Curro* (n 82) 346; *Koops Martin* (n 101); *Birt* (n 97); *Otis Elevator* (n 99); *Tullett Prebon* (n 101); *Williams* (n 80).

[107] J Edelman, *Gain-Based Damages – Contract, Tort, Equity and Intellectual Property* (Oxford, Hart Publishing, 2002) 158. Edelman has suggested disgorgement damages should have been available in a *Lumley v Gye* type situation if Ms Wagner had profited as a result of her breach.

specifically performing contracts for services should be thoroughly questioned.[108] He argues that disgorgement damages could be a way of solving the dilemma:

> To isolate and safeguard only an employee's interest in controlling her human relationships, the law should *refuse an injunction against any employee who is willing to disgorge any economic profit from her breach of contract.* Courts could properly enjoin an employee who could not demonstrate improper conduct by her employer, and who would not disgorge the economic profit from her breach, from working for a competitor.[109]

It is arguable that disgorgement damages should be paid by breaching employees who provide unique services to enable them to leave the service of employers for whom they no longer wish to work.[110] Disgorgement damages better balance the competing interests of the parties than an injunction: on the one hand, they recognise the claimant's interest in the defendant's unique performance but, on the other hand, they allow the defendant to obtain another job.[111] In addition, the restraint of trade concerns which may arise when an injunction is awarded are irrelevant to an award of disgorgement damages.

It is likely in any case that courts would only order a breaching employee to pay partial disgorgement in the form of a 'reasonable fee' rather than the full profit because the court is likely to have declined to order specific relief for discretionary reasons rather than because specific performance is unavailable. As will be discussed in chapter six, when specific relief is declined for discretionary reasons rather than because it is unavailable, partial disgorgement should be preferred.

III 'Efficient Breach' and the 'Second Sale' Cases

Substitutability helps to clarify when a promisor should be allowed to 'efficiently breach' in a second sale scenario. 'Efficient breach' theory argues that a promisor should be able to breach his contract and enter into a more profitable contract with a third party.[112] If one accepts the 'efficient breach' theory without qualification, the second sale cases are prima facie problematic because they involve this

[108] C Wonnell, 'The Contractual Disempowerment of Employees' (1993) 46 *Stanford Law Review* 87.

[109] ibid 136 (emphasis in original).

[110] *cf* Harder (n 24) 235–37.

[111] Note the eventual outcome of *Williams* (n 80), where an Australian Rugby League player, Sonny Bill Williams, sought to play for a French Rugby Union club, Toulon, in breach of his five-year contract to play with the Bulldogs Rugby League Club Ltd ('the Bulldogs'). The Bulldogs successfully obtained an injunction to restrain Williams from playing for Toulon, but they released Williams after Toulon paid a 'transfer fee' of £300,000 – effectively a partial disgorgement of profits by agreement. See R Wildman, 'Sonny Bill Williams set to make Toulon debut against Saracens' *The Telegraph* (18 August 2008) www.telegraph.co.uk/sport/rugbyunion/club/2580942/Sonny-Bill-Williams-set-to-make-Toulon-debut-against-Saracens---Rugby-Union.html.

[112] See, eg R Posner, *Economic Analysis of Law*, 8th edn (New York, Aspen Walters Kluwer, 2011) 149–58.

precise scenario.[113] Disgorgement damages in 'second sale' cases remove the incentive for the promisor to breach his contract.[114] However, it will be argued that substitutability provides a coherent limitation on when promisors should be allowed to breach which is consistent with 'efficient breach' theory.

It is worth noting that, despite the prominence of 'efficient breach' theory in the United States, the new American *Restatement of Restitution and Unjust Enrichment* has chosen to downplay the significance of 'efficient breach', arguing that it will rarely provide a reason to refrain from awarding disgorgement.[115]

A History of 'Efficient Breach' Theory

The 'grandfather' of 'efficient breach' is often said to be Mr Justice Oliver Wendell Holmes of the US Supreme Court, who famously stated that '[t]he duty to keep a contract at common law means a prediction that you must pay damages if you do not keep it, – and nothing else.'[116] This is generally taken to mean that a promisor has a lawful option to choose to perform or not.[117] His theory was based on two principles.[118] First, according to Holmes, the only purpose of the law was to 'induce external conformity to rule' only.[119] Secondly, he was of the opinion that moral blameworthiness should not be considered when ascertaining liability, suggesting that all legal principles should be reduced down to what a 'bad man' would consider the legal duty to mean.[120] Holmes thought that if a promisor were compelled to perform his contract, contract becomes 'a qualified subjection of one will to another, a kind of limited slavery.'[121]

Nonetheless, it has been argued that Holmes' statements have been consistently misunderstood, even by his principal correspondent, Sir Frederick Pollock. Professor Perillo argues that there is no doubt that Holmes saw breach of contract as a wrong.[122] Rather his point of view was that contract was 'an act imposing a liability to damages *nisi*.'[123] Perillo argues that Holmes' real view was that a

[113] American Law Institute, *Restatement (Third) of Restitution and Unjust Enrichment* (2011), § 39 comment h.

[114] See SW De Long, 'The Efficiency of a Disgorgement as a Remedy for Breach of Contract' (1989) 22 *Indiana Law Review* 737, who accepts efficient breach theory at face value, but recognises that disgorgement may be economically efficient in some circumstances. Posner himself is prepared to allow breach where it is 'opportunistic' (n 112) 119.

[115] American Law Institute (n 113) § 39 comment h, particularly Illustration 14.

[116] OW Holmes Jnr, 'The Path of the Law' (1897) 10 *Harvard Law Review* 457, 462. See also OW Holmes Jnr, *The Common Law* (Boston, Little, Brown & Co, 1881) 301.

[117] J Perillo, 'Misreading Oliver Wendell Holmes on Efficient Breach and Tortious Interference' (2000) 68 *Fordham Law Review* 1085, 1085.

[118] R Cunnington, 'Should Punitive Damages Be Part of the Judicial Arsenal in Contract Cases' (2006) 26 *Legal Studies* 369, 384.

[119] Holmes, *The Common Law* (n 116) 42.

[120] Holmes, 'The Path of the Law' (n 116) 461.

[121] Holmes, *The Common Law* (n 116) 235.

[122] Perillo (n 117) 1086–87.

[123] See Holmes' letter to Pollock dated letter of 11 December 1928 in Mark De Wolfe Howe (ed), *The Holmes-Pollock Letters: The Correspondence of Mr Justice Holmes and Sir Frederick Pollock 1874–1932*, Vol I (Cambridge, Mass, Harvard University Press, 1942) 233. *Nisi* means 'unless'.

promisor incurred liability to damages *unless* the stipulated act was performed, and thus that performance was nonetheless seen as an important consequence of a contract. Holmes' real concern was to separate law and morality, not to invent a nascent 'efficient breach'.[124]

B The Theory of 'Efficient Breach'

The law and economics scholars, especially those of the Chicago school, took Holmes' purported views a step further and developed the concept of 'efficient breach'.[125] Judge Richard Posner is the primary exponent of the theory, saying:

> [I]n some cases a party is tempted to break his contract simply because his profit from breach would exceed his profit from completing performance. He will do so if the profit would also exceed the expected profit to the other party from completion of the contract, and hence the damages from breach. So in this case awarding damages will not deter a breach of contract. It should not. It is an efficient breach. Suppose I sign a contract to deliver 100,000 custom-ground widgets at 10¢ apiece to A for use in his boiler factory. After I have delivered 10,000, B comes to me, explains that he desperately needs 25,000 custom-ground widgets at once since otherwise he will be forced to close his pianola factory at great cost, and offers me 15¢ apiece for 25,000 widgets. I sell him the widgets and as a result do not complete timely delivery to A, causing him to lose $1,000 in profits. Having obtained an additional profit of $1,250 on the sale to B, I am better off even after reimbursing A for his loss, and B is also better off. The breach is therefore Pareto superior.[126]

Pareto efficiency is an economic concept which is used to ascertain whether a particular allocation of resources in society is economically efficient. It will be achieved if there is no other allocation in which some other individual is better off and no individual is worse off. It focuses on allocative efficiency, not distributive efficiency or fairness.

'Efficient breach' is more Pareto efficient because the promisor who breaches is financially better off, the initial promisee who does not get the widgets receives compensation which adequately compensates for any loss, and the third party gets the goods he desperately needs. In other words, the subject matter of the contract goes to the 'user who values it the most.'[127]

On this analysis the common law is right to focus on expectation damages as the primary remedy for breach of contract. Posner has argued from the bench that the law of contract should not be developed in a way which deters efficient breach, because 'the law doesn't want to bring about such a result.'[128] Disgorgement for breach of contract is problematic for supporters of efficient breach because it

[124] Perillo (n 117) 1091. According to Perillo, the linking of Holmes with efficient breach has the 'pernicious effect of encouraging the adoption of the efficient breach fallacy into the legal arena.'

[125] Posner (n 112) 151.

[126] ibid.

[127] Ulen (n 15) 345.

[128] *Patton v Mid-Continent System*, 841 F 2d 742, 750 (USCA 7th Cir, 1988) (Posner J).

removes the incentive for the promisor to breach his contract and enter into a more efficient contract.[129] Arguably, the remedy of specific performance is similarly problematic.[130]

One of the difficulties with disgorgement damages from a law and economics perspective is said to be that they force a promisee and promisor to negotiate a promisee's release from the contract. This is said to create a 'bilateral monopoly', where the cost of negotiation between promisor and promisee is prohibitively high because they can only negotiate between one another.[131]

The idea of disgorgement damages providing a disincentive for 'efficient breach' was raised by the English Court of Appeal in *Surrey County Council v Bredero Homes Ltd* as a reason for disallowing partial disgorgement damages.[132] However, other courts have unequivocally rejected the concept of efficient breach, including, most recently, the Australian High Court.[133]

Posner is prepared to prevent efficient breach if it is 'opportunistic', saying, '[i]f a promisor breaks his promise merely to take advantage of the promisee's vulnerability in a setting (the normal contract setting) in which performance is sequential rather than simultaneous, we might as well throw the book at him.'[134] 'Opportunistic breach' according to Posner has a limited definition, applying only to cases where one party invests in assets specifically tailored to the transaction, rendering her vulnerable to exploitation if the other party then breaches.[135]

C Critiques of 'Efficient Breach'

There are a number of critiques of 'efficient breach' which suggest that factual and theoretical premises underlying this theory are wanting. I examine each critique in detail. Perillo sums up the essence of the criticisms in his simple statement that '[t]he theory contains simplifying assumptions that do not hold in the real world.'[136]

129 See De Long (n 114) and Posner (n 112) 149, who both would allow for disgorgement in limited circumstances.

130 A Kronman, 'Specific Performance' (1978) 45 *University of Chicago Law Review* 351; Posner (n 112) 163–64. *cf* A Schwartz, 'The Case for Specific Performance' (1979) 89 *Yale Law Journal* 271 and see especially Ulen (n 15).

131 See O'Dair (n 60) 131; L Smith, 'Disgorgement of the Profits of Breach of Contract: Property, Contract and "Efficient Breach"' (1995) 24 *Canadian Business Law Journal* 121, 134–35; Thel and Siegelman (n 2) 1203.

132 *Surrey County Council v Bredero Homes Ltd* [1993] 1 WLR 1361 (EWCACiv) 1370.

133 See *Butler v Countrywide Finance Ltd* [1993] 3 NZLR 623 (NZHC) 635 (Butler J); *Zhu v Treasurer of the State of New South Wales* (2004) 218 CLR 530 (HCA) 574–75; *Tabcorp Holdings Ltd v Bowen Investments Pty Ltd* (2009) 236 CLR 272 (HCA) 285–86.

134 Posner (n 112) 149.

135 H Dagan, *The Law and Ethics of Restitution* (n 2) 264–65. Consequently Posner's 'opportunistic breach' must be distinguished from the concept of 'opportunistic breach' in the new *Restatement of Restitution and Unjust Enrichment*: *cf* American Law Institute (n 113) § 39 comment b.

136 Perillo (n 117) 1098.

i Third Party Can Acquire Subject Matter of the Contract from Promisee

The natural riposte to the 'efficient breach' scenario is to say that if the law forces the promisor to convey the subject matter of the contract to the promisee, the third party can just then go and buy the subject matter of the contract from the promisee.[137] Professor Friedmann has pointed this out:

> If A performs his contract with B, there will be only one additional transaction, that between B and C. If, however, A is 'allowed' to break his contract with B, there will be two transactions: one between A and C over the sale of the property promised to B, and the other a dispute between A and B regarding the measure of damages. The implied assumption in Posner's analysis is that the payment of damages by A to B entails no transaction costs. This, however, is totally unrealistic. The payment of damages is hardly ever a standard transaction of the type the parties are routinely engaged in. It is likely to follow protracted negotiations, or even litigation, over difficult questions of fact and law. Finally, the breach may lead to an expensive tort action for inducement of breach of contract by the promisee (B) against the third party (C). This claim may breed another transaction between C and A regarding A's liability for losses suffered by C.[138]

However, proponents of efficient breach argue that to require the third party to negotiate with the promisee is unacceptable. Posner says:

> But this would have introduced an additional step, with additional transaction costs – and high ones, because it would be a bilateral-monopoly negotiation.[139]

Posner argues that this will mean that the parties will then try to extract as much as possible from the other, and indeed 'may be so determined to engross the greater part of the potential profits from the transaction that they never succeed in coming to terms.'[140]

Although it is not acknowledged by Posner, the initial negotiation to breach between promisor and the third party would be a bilateral monopoly as well.[141] In addition, it has also been pointed out that when the transaction costs of negotiation are compared with the costs of litigation, negotiation tends to be cheaper.[142] Ulen argues that specific performance is actually *more efficient* than expectation damages because first, applying Guido Calabresi and Douglas Melamed's analysis,[143] it is appropriate to use a 'property rule'[144] when the transaction costs

[137] D Friedmann, 'The Efficient Breach Fallacy' (1989) 18 *Journal of Legal Studies* 1.

[138] ibid 6–7.

[139] Posner (n 112) 151.

[140] ibid 61.

[141] Eisenberg, 'Actual and Virtual Specific Performance' (n 36) 1005–06; Thel and Siegelman (n 2) 1203.

[142] Ulen (n 15) 369–70; W Dodge, 'The Case for Punitive Damages in Contracts' (1999) 48 *Duke Law Journal* 629, 675.

[143] G Calabresi and AD Melamed, 'Property Rules, Liability Rules, and Inalienability: One View of the Cathedral' (1972) 82 *Harvard Law Review* 1089.

[144] Calabresi and Melamed divide legal remedies into 'property rules' (ie injunctions) which they consider to be a mechanism for making parties negotiate voluntarily over the exchange of entitle-

are low, because this forces the parties to negotiate.[145] Negotiation is not problematic because the parties already have a relationship as a result of the contract, they have most likely provided for various contingencies in the contract, and they may have had contact after formation in any case.[146]

ii Lack of Consideration of Transaction Costs

The theory underlying the analysis of efficient breach is the Coase Theorem, which holds that *in the absence of transaction costs*, the same social benefits will accrue regardless of where the law allocates entitlements.[147] 'Transaction costs' have not been satisfactorily defined, but include the energy expended in going to the market to buy a particular thing, the costs expended in finding out information as to the availability and best price available, the costs of making a bargain and the costs of enforcing bargains.[148]

It has been argued that once transaction costs are added into the equation, efficient breach is no longer necessarily efficient.[149] It is impossible to know whether or not breach will be efficient unless one knows the specific circumstances and transaction costs involved in the particular contract in question.[150] Further, Macneil argues that in a real-life situation, there may be 'negative transaction costs' and 'externalities'. Negative transaction costs are consequences of rules which may lessen losses.[151] So, for example, Macneil notes that if the damages rule encourages breach without consultation, but specific performance rules encourage consultation and mutually beneficial agreement, relational costs will be lower under specific performance.[152] Further, the 'externalities' of a rule must be considered (in other words, the costs or benefits that impact society but are not included in the market price of a good or service). Macneil suggests that it may be that an award of damages enables the breaching party to shift the costs of breach to the other party, resulting in inefficient decisions for society more generally.[153] Macneil concludes that the efficient breach theorists favour individual uncooperative behaviour rather than behaviour requiring cooperation between the parties. He says:

ments. This is the preferable approach when transaction costs are low. By contrast, 'liability rules' (ie damages) are considered to be a court-imposed exchange and possible reallocation of entitlements – the court objectively values the entitlement and imposes this on the parties.

145 Ulen (n 15) 364–93.

146 ibid 369.

147 R Coase, 'The Problem of Social Cost' (1960) 3 *Journal of Law and Economics* 1.

148 See O Williamson, 'Transaction-Cost Economics: The Governance of Contractual Relations' (1979) 22 *Journal of Law and Economics* 233; V Goldberg, 'Relational Exchange: Economics and Complex Contracts' in V Goldberg (ed), *Readings in the Economics of Contract Law* (Cambridge, Cambridge University Press, 1989) 21–23.

149 I Macneil, 'Efficient Breach of Contract: Circles in the Sky' (1982) 68 *Virginia Law Review* 947.

150 ibid 954–60.

151 ibid 958–59.

152 ibid 959.

153 ibid.

> The whole thrust of the Posner analysis is breach first, talk afterwards. Indeed, this may be an overstatement of the level of cooperation, since Posner pays singularly little attention to talking afterwards. Although he stresses the transaction costs of negotiations needed to reach efficient results under the specific performance rule, he pays no attention to the transaction costs of talking after a breach. And this is so despite the fact that 'talking after a breach' may be one of the more expensive forms of conversation to be found, involving, as it so often does, engaging high-priced lawyers, and gambits like starting litigation, engaging in discovery, and even trying and appealing cases.
>
> . . .
>
> Cooperative behaviour postulates relations. A model assuming away relations [such as efficient breach theory] slips with the greatest of ease at any stage into favouring uncooperative and – ironically enough – highly inefficient human behaviour.[154]

Because of the theory's failure to consider transaction costs, it remains just a theory. It does not accord with reality, and may lead to inefficient behaviour.

iii Incorrect Factual Predicates

Eisenberg says that the efficient breach theory rests on two basic factual predicates which are incorrect.[155]

First, the theory presumes that the promisee is subjectively indifferent between performance and damages. However, expectation damages rarely provide perfect compensation for loss of performance, for a variety of reasons. Inter alia, expectation damages are based on objective rather than subjective value; the profits a promisee would have earned if performance had occurred may be curtailed by the rule in *Hadley v Baxendale* or certainty rules; expectation damages may not include legal fees and other costs associated with litigation;[156] pre-judgment interest for breach of contract is usually not awarded, and when it is awarded, it is almost invariably less than the time value of the gains the promisee would have made from performance.

Secondly, the theory presumes that at the time when the promisor makes a 'performance-or-breach decision', the promisor knows the value that the promisee places on a contracted-for commodity. However, this is not the case. Eisenberg says that this flaw is thrown into relief by a competing theory of 'efficient termination', in which the promisor *does* know what value the promisee puts on performance. Paul Mahoney argues that 'efficient termination' occurs when:

> the amount of money, *Y*, that [the promisor] would pay to escape performance at a particular point in time is greater than the amount of money, *Z*, that the promisee . . . would accept in lieu of performance. In that situation there is a potential gain of *Y–Z* from terminating the contract.[157]

[154] ibid 968–69.

[155] Eisenberg, 'Actual and Virtual Specific Performance' (n 36) 989–96; Eisenberg, 'The Disgorgement Interest' (n 36) 571–72.

[156] NB: costs rules in the US are different to the rules in the Commonwealth countries. Nonetheless, even if a winning party is granted costs, they will still be significantly out of pocket.

[157] P Mahoney, 'Contract Remedies and Options Pricing' (1995) 24 *Journal of Legal Studies* 139, 141.

This differs from efficient breach because efficient breach contemplates a unilateral breach – that is, one party decides that he no longer wants to perform the contract. The theory of efficient termination contemplates that termination will occur by mutual consent, because the promisor must establish the value the promisee will establish in lieu of performance. Eisenberg concludes:

> In short, as compared with the theory of efficient breach, the theory of efficient termination contemplates that termination of a contract will occur through a process that involves a much richer mix of information; allows the promisee to insist on being paid his actual value for the contracted-for-commodity; and helps ensure that promisees are treated with due respect.[158]

Disgorgement damages provide an incentive for 'efficient termination' instead of 'efficient breach'.

iv 'Efficient Breach' is Inefficient

It is argued that if 'efficient breach' theory were widely followed, it would lead to inefficiency for a number of reasons. The theory would allocate commodities to a third party who lacked the foresight or willingness to invest in ensuring supply of the relevant commodity, and away from a buyer who did have foresight and did invest.[159]

Secondly, the efficiency of the contract law system does not rest solely on legal remedies (as implied by the theory of efficient breach). It also rests on the security of those who contract knowing that they will get what they are promised (which Eisenberg calls 'the moral norm of promise-keeping').[160] It has been noted by various scholars that efficient breach would inefficiently increase the need to resort to litigation.[161] The theory of efficient breach would also remake the parties' contract, implying a term that the promisor was entitled to not perform if a better offer came along. In fact, parties to a contract want to persuade each other of the exact opposite – they seek to reassure each other that they *will* perform.[162] Parties to the contract can then plan future actions and expenditures, and contractors naturally prefer to deal with a party who is reliable.[163] A deterrent measure to prevent breach is needed because the failure of a party to perform a contract not only

[158] Eisenberg, 'The Disgorgement Interest' (n 36) 573. See also Eisenberg, 'Actual and Virtual Specific Performance' (n 36) 1005.

[159] Eisenberg, 'Actual and Virtual Specific Performance' (n 36) 1010–2; Eisenberg, 'The Disgorgement Interest' (n 36) 573.

[160] Eisenberg, 'Actual and Virtual Specific Performance' (n 36) 1012–13; Eisenberg, 'The Disgorgement Interest' (n 36) 573–74. See also Perillo (n 117) 1105; P Linzer, 'On the Amorality of Contract Remedies – Efficiency, Equity and the Second Restatement' (1981) 81 *Columbia Law Review* 111.

[161] Friedmann, 'The Efficient Breach Fallacy' (n 137) 7; Cunnington (n 118) 387; Eisenberg, 'The Disgorgement Interest' (n 36) 573–74.

[162] I Ayres and G Klass, 'Promissory Fraud Without Breach' [2004] *Wisconsin Law Review* 507, 513–14.

[163] Eisenberg, 'The Disgorgement Interest' (n 36) 575–76; SV Shiffrin, 'The Divergence of Contract and Promise' (2007) 120 *Harvard Law Review* 708, 749–51.

harms the promisee but also undermines society's confidence in contracting generally.[164] If parties are not confident that their bargained-for interests will be protected by law, they will be reluctant to contract and the impact upon commercial activity and efficiency will be negative.[165]

It is for this reason Thel and Siegelman argue that disgorgement damages are efficient because they act as a 'bonding device' between the parties:

> Disgorgement remedies are thus best understood as a promisor bonding device. By subjecting himself to promisor expectation, the promisor gives valuable assurance to the promisee – for which he is presumably compensated – and suffers no risk of penalty: he will never be worse off than he would have been if he had performed.[166]

However, the promisor is not only assuring that particular promisee that he will perform. His assurance increases confidence in the mechanism of contracting generally.

v 'Efficient Breach' Does Not Fit with the Law

'Efficient breach' is at odds with the way in which contract law operates in reality. 'Expectation damages' are the primary relief for breach of contract, but it does not follow from this that the law intends to encourage efficient breaches.[167] As I have argued at length in the previous chapter, contract remedies are not simply intended to compensate the claimant for loss, but more broadly to recognise the claimant's performance interest. Further, as Sir Frederick Pollock responded to Mr Justice Holmes, promisors are not always free to breach their contracts, and in reflection of this, the law of contract includes equitable remedies for breach of contract, the doctrine of anticipatory breach, and the development of the tort of inducing breach of contract.[168] Orders for specific relief pose difficulties for supporters of efficient breach, because this suggests that in certain circumstances promisors are not free to breach their contracts. Further, the tort of inducing breach of contract suggests that third parties commit a wrong when they induce a promisor to breach his contract. It comes as no surprise to know that supporters of efficient breach seek to limit the tort of inducing breach of contract.[169] Finally, the established 'second sale' cases mentioned earlier in this chapter (such as *Lake v Bayliss*, *Bunny Industries* and *Adras*) are inconsistent with the theory of efficient breach.

[164] J Raz, 'Promises in Morality and Law' (1982) 95 *Harvard Law Review* 916, 933.

[165] R Cunnington, 'The Measure and Availability of Gain-Based Damages for Breach of Contract' in R Cunnington and D Saidov (eds) *Contract Damages: Domestic and International Perspectives* (Oxford, Hart Publishing, 2008) 205, 240.

[166] Thel and Siegelman (n 2) 1228.

[167] Perillo (n 117) 1094.

[168] See Pollock's letter to Holmes dated 17 September 1897, Sir Frederick Pollock, *The Principles of Contracts*, 8th edn (London, Stevens, 1911) 192, fn k and Holmes' subsequent letter to Pollock dated 12 March 1911. The letters are reproduced in De Wolfe Howe (n 123) at 79–80 and 177 respectively.

[169] See, eg C Remington, 'Intentional Interference with Contract and the Doctrine of Efficient Breach: Fine Tuning the Notion of the Contract Breacher as Wrongdoer' (1999) 47 *Buffalo Law Review* 645.

D Conclusion to 'Efficient Breach'

The scenario proposed by Posner is a typical 'second sale'. The promisee and promisor have a contract, but the promisor becomes aware that a third party will pay a higher price. The promisor then breaches the contract, meaning that he cannot supply the good to the promisee as promised. If 'efficient breach' is adopted wholesale, then the 'second sale' cases must be wrong, subject to Posner's exception of 'opportunistic breaches'.

The factual and theoretical presumptions underlying the efficient breach theory are problematic in some respects (even from the perspective of some law and economics theorists). Further, the law itself does not wholly support the assertions of the efficient breach theorists. Thus we should be wary of placing too much weight on it as a reason for rejecting disgorgement damages.

Nonetheless, there should be some measure of flexibility in contracting; for example, contractors should sometimes be allowed to breach to avoid loss because of unforeseen circumstances.[170] The law should not put incentives in place which cause contracts to be performed in *all circumstances*. By the same token, the law should not (and does not) say that promisors should *always* be free to breach their contracts wherever it is efficient.

Efficient breach theory does not consider the substitutability of the subject matter of the contract.[171] Substitutability establishes when the promisor must disgorge any profit to the promisee in a second sale scenario. There will *only* be a bilateral monopoly where the subject matter of the contract is not available on the market.[172] If Boris wants to breach his contract with Alice, and she can easily procure widgets from elsewhere, there will *not* be a bilateral monopoly, and Boris will be free to breach. However, as Thel and Siegelman observe, 'when widgets are available in the market, the transaction costs of the promisor selling to the promisee and the promisee selling to the third party are likely to be much lower than the cost of negotiating, or litigating, a release from the promisee.'[173] Interestingly, Posner himself is aware of the connection between the availability of specific performance and the likelihood that breach will be wrongful. He contrasts the situation where damages are adequate (in which he says breach will not be wrongful) with the situation where specific relief is available:

> [I]njunctive relief is possible only when the remedy at law – that is, damages – is unavailable. For in such a case the contractual undertaking loses its either-or character; instead of a promise of performance or damages, it is a promise of performance or nothing.[174]

[170] Campbell and Harris (n 1) 217–21; D Friedmann, 'Economic Aspects of Damages and Specific Performance Compared' in D Saidov and R Cunnington (eds), *Contract Damages: Domestic and International Perspectives* (Oxford, Hart Publishing, 2008) 65, 74–83.

[171] Linzer (n 160) 117–18.

[172] Thel and Siegelman (n 2) 1203.

[173] ibid 1203–04.

[174] R Posner, 'Let Us Never Blame A Contract Breaker' (2009) 107 *Michigan Law Review* 1349.

He later says that an award of 'restitution' in a contract case gives rise to a bilateral monopoly, but makes an exception for 'extraordinary situations in which for one reason or another compensatory damages would not compensate the victim of the breach'.[175]

Once substitutability is taken into account, 'efficient breach' is less of a problem for disgorgement damages than it first appears. If a good is substitutable, then the promisor is 'free' to go ahead and breach, selling to the higher bidder. Indeed, the promisor can negotiate a release from the promise if necessary, because there will be no bilateral monopoly in a situation where the subject matter of the contract is freely available in the market.

If, however, the subject matter of the contract is *not* freely available in the market, then, contrary to the supposed preference of the law for expectation damages touted by proponents of the efficient breach theory, the survey of case law in this chapter shows that the court will not award expectation damages, but will award specific performance. The promisor is *not free* to breach his promise, and if specific performance is unavailable, disgorgement damages would be entirely appropriate.

IV Conclusion

This chapter has demonstrated that, as Lord Nicholls argued in *Blake*, prior to *Blake* itself there was already a line of authority (which I name the 'second sale' cases) where courts awarded disgorgement damages for breach of contract. The awards in these cases are disguised under other analyses, such as the constructive trust arising from the specifically enforceable contract of sale analysis, which obscures the true actions of the courts. However, these cases are best analysed as disgorgement damages for breach of contract. Other explanations of these second sale cases, such as the constructive trust analysis, or the 'implied term' argument (which slots the disgorgement into an extended definition of expectation damages), simply do not stand up to rigorous analysis and rely on unconvincing fictions. Consequently, it is disappointing that in *Luxe*,[176] a case which is some 10 years after *Blake*, Roth J adheres to a constructive trust analysis, but then, in direct contradiction to that conclusion, rejects the argument that the claimant was entitled to disgorgement damages.

Instances where courts have awarded disgorgement for breach of contract when there has been a 'second sale' are few and far between. One of the rare cases in which a court has transparently awarded disgorgement damages is *Adras*, the Israeli case. However, that case fails to develop a coherent criterion for awards of disgorgement damages. Substitutability is the criterion which is missing from

[175] ibid 1354.
[176] *Luxe* (n 6).

Adras. Substitutability derives from the law of contract remedies, and thus it is a consistent and familiar principle. Substitutability also helps establish that the theory of 'efficient breach' does not pose a problem for disgorgement damages for breach of contract. If the subject matter of a contract is substitutable, the promisor can breach the contract. The issue of the bilateral monopoly between promisor and promisee will not arise if the subject matter of the contract is readily available. By contrast, if the subject matter of the contract is *not substitutable*, it is likely that a court will award specific performance of the contract rather than expectation damages. If specific relief is no longer available, then it is appropriate that the court award disgorgement damages as a 'next best' solution.

Lord Hobhouse in *Blake* warned:

> [I]f some more extensive principle of awarding non-compensatory damages for breach of contract is to be introduced into our commercial law the consequences will be very far reaching and disruptive.[177]

To the contrary, insofar as commercial contracts for ordinary goods, shares or services are concerned, disgorgement damages will not disrupt the law or create problems if there is a second sale. If the goods, shares or services are substitutable, neither specific relief nor disgorgement is available. The parties will have to be content with compensatory damages. If the goods, shares or services are non-substitutable, the courts will always prefer to award specific relief where possible.[178] Disgorgement damages will *only* be available if (a) specific relief is no longer available, and (b) the promisor has made a profit.[179] There may be some role for disgorgement damages to play in the cases which involve a 'second sale' of services because of the problems with awarding specific relief in those cases, balanced with the need to recognise the employer's performance interest.

However, 'second sale' cases are not the only category of contract the breach of which will give rise to disgorgement damages in some circumstances. The second category of contract is the 'agency problem cases'. It is to this category that I turn in the next chapter.

[177] *Blake* (n 7) 299.

[178] *cf* SM Waddams, 'Gains Derived from Breach of Contract: Historical and Conceptual Perspectives' in D Saidov and R Cunnington (eds), *Contract Damages: Domestic and International Perspectives* (Oxford, Hart Publishing, 2008) 187, 205–06 who argues that if gain-based damages are not available for a particular breach, this may be a reason for refusing specific performance. I argue that specific performance may be available in many circumstances where gain-based damages are not appropriate, and lack of availability of gain-based damages may only be relevant if it goes to the question of substitutability.

[179] In a second sale situation, the promisor is highly likely to have made an actual profit, because he would not have breached the contract otherwise.

5

'Agency Problem' Cases

I Introduction

This chapter places cases involving concurrent breaches of fiduciary duty and breaches of contract and cases involving a breach of a negative covenant within the same category, under the umbrella of 'agency problem cases'. Both involve the same basic scenario. Boris contracts with Alice not to do a specific thing or things which relate to Alice's best interests, but Boris then breaches the contract and goes ahead and does the very thing which he has contracted not to do, and profits thereby. In the case of fiduciary duties Boris is obliged not to conflict with Alice's interests and not to make an unauthorised or secret profit. In the case of a negative covenant, Boris' obligation is not to do the particular thing specified in the negative covenant, but in addition, it will be argued that where trust is conferred on Boris, he also has an obligation not to profit, and if he does profit, that profit should be stripped from him. It should be noted that I do not include those cases which deal with negative covenants providing that the defendant must not provide his services to anyone other than the claimant within the category of 'agency problem cases'.[1]

Both breach of fiduciary duty and breach of negative covenants raise what Professors Thel and Siegelman call 'the agency problem'.[2] 'Agency' in this context does not refer to the legal concept of agency, but the economic concept of 'principal–agent', which attempts to ascertain how a promisee (principal) can design a contract which motivates another individual, the promisor (agent) to act in the promisee's interests.[3] An 'agency problem' arises when the promisee has less information than the promisor about the actions the promisor either has undertaken or should undertake ('information asymmetry'). Agency problems can create a situation of 'moral hazard' because the party that is insulated from risk generally has more information about its actions and intentions than the party paying for the negative consequences of the risk. In both fiduciary duty and

[1] These cases have already been considered in the previous chapter on the 'second sale cases': see ch 4, II D. This chapter will concentrate on negative covenants which *do not* involve preventing the provision of services to third parties.

[2] S Thel and P Siegelman, 'You *Do* Have to Keep Your Promises: A Theory of Disgorgement in Contract Law' (2011) *William and Mary Law Review* 1182, 1208.

[3] J Stiglitz, 'principal and agent (ii)', entry in S Durlauf and L Blume (eds), *The New Palgrave Dictionary of Economics*, 2nd edn (Basingstoke and New York, Palgrave Macmillan, 2008).

negative covenant cases the promisee has particular difficulty in monitoring the promisor's performance as a result of information asymmetry. The promisor can breach before the promisee has a chance to apply for an injunction, and the breach cannot be undone. The promisor is not the one who suffers from the breach; indeed in these cases he profits as a result. The promisee depends upon the good faith of the promisor. Therefore, in order to address the agency problem, the law needs to provide incentives for the promisor (agent) to behave in accordance with the promisee's (principal's) wishes. Otherwise the promisee's performance interest is not adequately vindicated by the available legal remedies.

An agency problem involving a negative covenant would arise if you promised me that you would not write a book detailing my innermost secrets, and I paid you $1000 for this. In breach of your promise, you wrote a book detailing my secrets and received $100,000 from the publishers as an advance.[4] I did not find out about your book until it had been released and it was too late to obtain an injunction to stop you publishing. In such a case, I do not have the relevant information about your intentions in relation to performing the contract. You do not have to bear the negative consequences of breaching the contract; indeed the consequences for you are positive. I cannot prevent the breach which has already occurred, although perhaps I can get an injunction to prevent ongoing breaches. Any compensatory damages for which you are liable will be far outstripped by your profit, and in any case, it is difficult to see any pecuniary loss on my part which can be rectified by monetary compensation. However, if you knew that you might well be legally required to disgorge the profits you had made in breach of contract, you would either perform your obligation not to publish or negotiate a release from the contract, because there would no longer be any incentive to breach unilaterally. Your profit would be stripped from you. Disgorgement damages thus help to rectify my lack of information about your intentions. The deterrent rationale of disgorgement damages operates strongly in this situation because the aim is to deter unilateral breaches and provide incentives for performance or negotiation instead.

The agency problem in breach of fiduciary duty cases has been solved by the availability of profit-stripping remedies which remove the promisor's incentive to breach.[5] It is uncontroversial that disgorgement damages are available for breach of fiduciary duty and for other equitable wrongs such as equitable breach of confidence. By contrast, the law of contract generally does not presently provide incentives for a promisor in a negative covenant situation to perform the promise or, alternatively, to negotiate with the promisee for a release. If compensatory damages are inadequate and specific performance is no longer available, the

[4] I ignore the possibility of breach of confidence for present purposes. Note the similarity between this example and *HRH The Prince of Wales v Associated Newspapers Ltd* [2006] EWCA Civ 1776, [2008] Ch 57 (CA), which involved a concurrent breach of contract and breach of confidence. See also *Vercoe v Rutland Fund Management Ltd* [2010] EWHC 424 (Ch) and the observations of Sales J as to the overlap and differences between breach of confidence and breach of contract at [339]–[343].

[5] R Cooter and BJ Freedman, 'The Fiduciary Relationship: Its Economic Character and Legal Consequences' (1991) 66 *New York University Law Review* 1045, 1047.

promisor has an opportunity to breach which he should not have. The promisee's interest in performance is not adequately vindicated by the courts, and expectation damages do not adequately guard against the breach of trust in such a case. Courts rarely explicitly award disgorgement for breach of a negative covenant. *Attorney-General v Blake* is the watershed case in which disgorgement damages were openly awarded, when – as discussed in chapter three – George Blake, a former spy published a book detailing his double agency for the Soviet Union and profited thereby, breaching a negative covenant in his contract of employment by failing to consult the British Government about his publication even though his employment had long since ceased.[6]

What then of substitutability, which played such a prominent part in the justification of disgorgement damages in the previous chapter? Substitutability remains relevant as to why specific relief and disgorgement damages are awarded for concurrent breach of fiduciary duty and contract and breach of negative covenant. The rights granted by such contracts are intrinsically non-substitutable because they are intangible and cannot be bought or sold in any market.[7] In addition, substitutability requires us to consider the idiosyncratic value of the promise to the claimant. Substitutability is particularly useful in breach of negative covenant cases where disgorgement is awarded as a surrogate for expectation damages.[8] When the defendant has benefited in a measurable way and has caused a loss which is speculative or hard to quantify, it will be in the claimant's interests to obtain disgorgement damages.[9] The kinds of case in which it is typically difficult to measure the losses of the claimant are often intellectual property infringement cases, in which it is very difficult to ascertain what the losses of the claimant are as a result of the infringement, but the sales of the defendant are clear and quantifiable. Nonetheless, substitutability does not provide a complete explanation of the outcome of the negative covenant cases. It is only the first step. If substitutability was the sole criterion, then every breach of negative covenant would give rise to disgorgement damages.[10] Something more is needed to explain why damages are inadequate.

[6] *Attorney General v Blake* [2000] UKHL 45, [2001] 1 AC 268 (HL).

[7] D Laycock, 'The Death of the Irreparable Injury Rule' (1990) 103 *Harvard Law Review* 687, 707–08.

[8] MA Eisenberg, 'The Disgorgement Interest in Contract Law' (2006) 105 *Michigan Law Review* 559, 587–88.

[9] D Laycock, 'The Scope and Significance of Restitution' (1989) 67 *Texas Law Review* 1277, 1287. Although it has been suggested in some cases that mere difficulty in assessing damages does not justify an award of specific relief: see *Fothergill v Rowland* (1873) LR 17 Eq 132, 140; *Laclede Gas Co v Amoco Oil Co*, 522 F 2d 33 (8th Cir, 1975); *Société des Industries Métallurgiques SA v Bronx Engineering Co Ltd* [1975] 1 Lloyd's Rep 465 (CA). Perhaps by extension it could be argued that difficulty in assessing compensatory damages does not justify an award of disgorgement damages. However, the aforementioned cases have been criticised: see A Burrows, *Remedies for Torts and Breach of Contract*, 3rd edn (Oxford, Oxford University Press, 2004) 467. But see *Buxton v Lister* (1746) 3 Atk 383, 26 ER 1020 (Ch); *Adderley v Dixon* (1824) 1 Sim & St 607, 57 ER 239; *Eastern Rolling Mill Co v Michlovitz*, (1929) 157 Md 51, 145 A 378; *Thomas Borthwick v South Otago Freezing* [1978] 1 NZLR 538 (NZCA); *Sky Petroleum Ltd v VIP Petroleum Ltd* [1974] 1 WLR 576 (Ch).

[10] Burrows (n 9) 399–400; A Burrows, *The Law of Restitution*, 2nd edn (London, Butterworths, 2002) 485.

Cases of concurrent breach of fiduciary duty and contract constitute the core of the 'agency problem'. The 'bundle of duties' imposed on a fully-blown fiduciary are typically fourfold, including a duty not to conflict, a duty not to profit, a duty to act in the best interests of the beneficiary and a duty to act in good faith.[11] Some negative covenant cases are on the margins between contract and fiduciary duty, and it is these cases which are most likely to give rise to disgorgement damages even if the relationship between the parties does not give rise to fiduciary obligations. A negative covenantee may have an obligation not to conflict, but it is extremely limited (being merely an obligation not to prefer one's own interests to the obligation contained in the negative covenant). By contrast, this duty not to conflict is potentially very broad in the fiduciary duty cases. Nonetheless, it flows from the duty not to conflict in negative covenant cases that there is also a duty not to profit in certain circumstances. Also, there is the obligation of good faith conferred on the promisor in both kinds of case, usually because some kind of non-financial interest is sought to be protected as well as any financial interest present. However, typically there is no obligation to act in the best interests of the promisee in the case of a negative covenant (absent an express contractual provision), whereas the obligation to act in the best interests of the beneficiary is central to the fiduciary obligation. Nonetheless in Anglo-Australian law courts have not found that there is a *positive* duty to act in the best interests of the principal.[12]

As with the 'second sale' cases, in order for a defendant to be liable for disgorgement damages for breach of negative covenant, the breach must be *advertent.* In breach of fiduciary duty cases, courts are willing to impose liability on parties whose breaches are bona fide, and thus the punitive justification does not sit so well with fiduciary duties. These cases are better justified purely by reference to the deterrent intention.

This chapter will first explore the core uncontroversial cases for disgorgement damages which involve concurrent breach of fiduciary duty and contract. It will then suggest that cases for breach of negative covenant lie on the margins of fiduciary and contract law. Some cases fall within the fiduciary realm (although the justification for their doing so is not always convincing) and others do not. Disgorgement damages are increasingly available not only for those cases which fall within the fiduciary realm, but to those 'quasi-fiduciary' contracts on the margins which suffer from the 'agency problem'. A negative covenant does not necessarily create a fiduciary duty, but it can approach the margins of fiduciary law, particularly when the contract in question is not designed to make a profit, but rather to protect some other kind of interest (including contracts to protect national security, public interest, to resolve a legal dispute or to protect one's family). If the defendant breaches the contract without the claimant knowing, then

[11] See *Bristol & West Building Society v Mothew* [1996] EWCA Civ 533, [1998] Ch 1 (CA) 18 (Millet LJ).

[12] Compare *Breen v Williams* (1996) 186 CLR 71 (HCA) with *McInerney v MacDonald* [1992] CanLII 57 (SCC), [1992] 2 SCR 138. See also comments of the majority of the Australian High Court on *Breen* in *Pilmer v The Duke Group Ltd (in liq)* (2001) 207 CLR 165 (HCA).

there is very little the claimant can do about it. The damage has been done, and the clock cannot be turned back. Therefore it is necessary to have some kind of deterrent remedy to prevent the breach occurring in the first place.

II The 'Agency Problem' and Disgorgement

The core 'agency problem' cases involve concurrent breach of fiduciary duty and contract. In these cases, the principal has difficulty in monitoring the performance of the fiduciary on whom power is conferred. In this section, I will first consider the uncontroversial availability of disgorgement for breach of fiduciary duty and then consider the availability of disgorgement for breach of negative covenant. I will suggest that, where courts have wished to award disgorgement damages because of the 'agency problem', they have used the fiduciary concept in an instrumental fashion which is not wholly convincing.

A Disgorgement, the 'Agency Problem' and Fiduciary Duties

Fiduciary duties are often set apart from other legal duties (including those arising via contract, tort and unjust enrichment). Cardozo J described the duties of a fiduciary in *Meinhard v Salmon*:

> Many forms of conduct permissible in a workaday world for those acting at arm's length, are forbidden to those bound by fiduciary ties. A trustee is held to something stricter than the morals of the market place. Not honesty alone, but the punctilio of an honor the most sensitive is then the standard of behaviour. As to this there has developed a tradition that is unbending and inveterate. Uncompromising rigidity has been the attitude of courts of equity when petitioned to undermine the rule of undivided loyalty by the 'disintegrating erosion' of particular exceptions. *Only thus has the level of conduct for fiduciaries been kept at a level higher than that trodden by the crowd.* It will not consciously be lowered by any judgment of this court. [Emphasis added][13]

Typically, the fiduciary obligation is imposed by reference to the particular relationship between the parties or their status. There are certain relationships which are presumed to be fiduciary (eg trustee and beneficiary, solicitor and client, company and director, agent and principal).

Let us take, for example, one of the 'inner circle' of fiduciary relationships, the relationship between solicitor and client,[14] as an illustration of how the 'agency problem' arises. When the client consults a solicitor, the client is entitled to assume that the solicitor will not give her self-interested advice (or advice which

[13] *Meinhard v Salmon*, 249 NY 458, 465, 164 NE 545, 546 (Ct App, 1928).

[14] *Tyrell v Bank of London* (1862) 10 HLC 26, 44, 11 ER 934, 941 (Lord Westbury LC); *Sims v Craig Bell & Bond* [1991] 3 NZLR 535 (NZCA) 543 (Richardson J).

preferences another client over this client) and that the solicitor will not make a profit by breaching his duty towards her. The client is not well situated to assess whether or not the solicitor is acting in her best interests. The solicitor exercises discretion over the client's affairs, and consequently he may defalcate or make a profit by breaching his duty towards her without her knowledge. However, if any profit made in breach of a fiduciary duty is stripped, then there is no incentive for the solicitor to breach his duty towards the client. Professor Worthington has argued that disgorgement is peculiarly well-suited for preventing breaches of equitable obligations:

> The aim is to exact particular standards of conduct in the protected relationships; to this end, the relevant law is concerned with proscribing certain activities, not with precluding particular outcomes. The appropriate remedial response for breaches of these equitable obligations is disgorgement because this is the remedy which best supports the legal obligation being enforced.[15]

A fiduciary duty may be imposed outside the 'presumptive circle', even in the context of a contractual relationship which is ordinarily self-interested. Usually, courts consider whether the fiduciary has voluntarily undertaken or agreed to act on behalf of another, such as Mason J's 'undertaking test' in *Hospital Products Ltd v United States Surgical Corporation.*[16] Alternatively, it is said that the fiduciary has the exercise of a power or discretion to which the beneficiary is vulnerable.[17]

Commentators have searched for a unifying principle of fiduciary relationships, but again, the cases are notoriously difficult to categorise, so that Sir Anthony Mason has said 'the fiduciary relationship is a concept in search of a principle.'[18]

Justice Easterbrook and Professor Fischel have suggested that the difficulty in discovering a unifying principle of fiduciary relationships arises because scholars are mistakenly looking for something unique or special about fiduciary relationships.[19] They argue that, in fact, fiduciary relationships are just an extreme variety of contractual relationship,[20] and that fiduciary relationships tend to arise when a transaction is very complex, and one party wishes to impart a discretion on the

[15] S Worthington, 'Reconsidering Disgorgement for Wrongs' (1999) 62 *MLR* 218, 237.

[16] *Hospital Products Ltd v United States Surgical Corporation* (1984) 156 CLR 41 (HCA) [68] (Mason J).

[17] There are also clear parallels with Dawson J's 'vulnerability' test from *Hospital Products* (n 16), [55]:

> There is, however, the notion underlying all the cases of fiduciary obligation that inherent in the nature of the relationship itself is a position of disadvantage or vulnerability on the part of one of the parties which causes him to place reliance upon the other and requires the protection of equity acting upon the conscience of that other.

Dawson J's test was preferred by the Canadian Supreme Court in *Lac Minerals Ltd v International Corona Resources Ltd* [1989] 2 SCR 574, (1989) 61 DLR (4th) 14.

[18] A Mason, 'Themes and Prospects' in PD Finn (ed), *Essays in Equity* (NSW, Lawbook Co, 1985) 246.

[19] F Easterbrook and D Fischel, 'Contract and Fiduciary Duty' (1993) 36 *Journal of Law and Economics* 425, 438. See also M McInnes, 'Account of Profits for Common Law Wrongs' in S Degeling and J Edelman (eds), *Equity in Commercial Law* (NSW, Lawbook Co, 2005) 405, 426.

[20] Easterbrook and Fischel (n 19) 425–38.

other, but it is too difficult to specifically enumerate each and every undertaking.[21] Edelman, too, has argued that fiduciary obligations are just another species of voluntary undertaking, and it is for this reason that the scope of the fiduciary duty depends upon the circumstances and scope of the undertaking involved.[22]

Worthington has argued that accounts of profit are appropriate for fiduciary duties because the aim of the remedy is to ensure that the imposed obligation is not breached. This is in contrast to compensatory damages, which are typically the default remedy for non-equitable private law duties such as tort and contract, and simply seek to ensure that a breach does no harm.[23] Where equitable duties are concerned, as previously mentioned, she argues that the law is concerned to prevent certain activities, not with preventing certain outcomes.[24] I will argue that the same can hold true for some breaches of negative covenant, and thus disgorgement damages may be an appropriate remedy.

B Disgorgement, the 'Agency Problem' and Negative Covenants

While disgorgement damages are an uncontroversial remedy for breach of fiduciary duty, until *Blake* at least, they were not awarded for breach of negative covenant in the absence of a fiduciary duty. Generally speaking courts are far more willing to award disgorgement for breaches of equitable obligations than for breaches of common law obligations.[25]

By contrast, courts are prepared to award an injunction to restrain a breach of negative covenant where specific performance of the contract as a whole would not be ordered (known as an injunction pursuant to the rule in *Lumley v Wagner*).[26] As with specific performance, the basis for the injunction is that 'damages are inadequate' or that it is 'necessary to do justice'. It has sometimes been said that injunctions for a breach of negative covenant in a contract will be granted as a matter of course, drawing on the following statement of Lord Cairns in *Doherty v Allman*:[27]

> My Lords, if there had been a negative covenant, I apprehend, according to well-settled practice, a Court of Equity would have had no discretion to exercise. If parties, for valuable consideration, with their eyes open, contract that a particular thing shall not be done, all that a Court of Equity has to do is to say, by way of injunction, that which the parties have already said by way of covenant, that the thing shall not be done; and in such case the injunction does nothing more than give the sanction of the process of the Court to that which already is the contract between the parties. It is not then a question of the balance of convenience or inconvenience, or of the amount of damage or of

[21] ibid 426–27; Thel and Siegelman (n 2) 24.

[22] J Edelman, 'When Do Fiduciary Duties Arise?' (2010) 126 *LQR* 302.

[23] Although as discussed in ch 3 contractual remedies do not merely compensate for loss.

[24] Worthington (n 15) 237.

[25] ibid 235.

[26] *Lumley v Wagner* (1852) 1 De GM & G 604, 42 ER 687.

[27] *Doherty v Allman* (1878) 3 App Cas 709.

> injury – it is the specific performance, by the Court, of that negative bargain which parties have made, with their eyes open, between themselves.[28]

However, despite the apparent adoption of this dictum in some cases,[29] the bulk of the case law suggests that the usual equitable discretions remain relevant.[30] Nonetheless, courts are far more ready to award injunctions restraining the breach of a negative covenant than they are to enforce a positive obligation. It has been speculated that this is because injunctions do not contradict the claimant's duty to mitigate, they do not infringe individual liberty to the same extent as a positive order, they do not have the problem of constant supervision, and damages are often less easy to assess for breach of a negative covenant compared to a positive obligation.[31]

Many of these cases involve a covenant that property will not be used for certain purposes or in certain ways.[32] Or there may be a clause in a contract to the effect that the defendant will only supply products to the claimant[33] or use products supplied by the claimant.[34] Although it was an employment contract, the contract in *Blake* falls into this category, because the clause did not seek to restrict the provision of George Blake's services. Instead, Blake promised not to publish any information obtained in the course of his employment without seeking the consent of his employer first.

As noted previously, the reason why specific relief is granted is partially as a result of lack of substitutability. The rights granted by the negative covenant cannot be bought or sold in the marketplace.[35]

However, in order to fully understand why specific relief is readily awarded for breach of negative covenant, we should also revisit Birks' suggestion to have 'regard to the objectives which the victim of the breach had hoped to achieve

[28] ibid 719–20.

[29] eg *McEacharn v Colton* [1902] AC 104 (PC); *Macintosh v Bebarfalds Ltd* (1922) 22 SR (NSW) 371 (NSWSC) and *Ampol Petroleum Ltd v Mutton* (1952) 53 SR (NSW) 1 (NSWSC).

[30] *Dalgety Wine Estates Pty Ltd v Rizzon* (1979) 141 CLR 552 (HCA) 560 (Gibbs CJ), 573–74 (Mason J); *J C Williamson Ltd v Lukey and Mulholland* (1931) 45 CLR 282 (HCA) 298–300 (Dixon J); *Curro v Beyond Productions Pty Ltd* (1993) 30 NSWLR 337 (NSWCA) 346–47. See also *Bowes v Law* (1870) LR 9 Eq 636; *Harrison v Good* (1871) LR 11 Eq 338; *Leader v Moody* (1875) LR 20 Eq 145; *Sharp v Harrison* [1922] 1 Ch 502 (Ch); *Shaw v Applegate* [1977] 1 WLR 970 (CA).

[31] Burrows, *The Law of Restitution* (n 10) 528.

[32] eg *Bowe v Law* (n 30) (agreement not to erect building on road across from claimant); *Harrison v Good* (n 30) (agreement not to do anything which would be a nuisance to adjoining property owners); *Wolverhampton & Walsall Railway Company v London and North-Western Railway Company* (1873) LR 16 Eq 433 (agreement to use only claimant's railway line for purposes of travel between Wolverhampton and Walsall); *Leader v Moody* (n 30) (agreement not to use theatre for any purpose except for performing of plays and operas); *Macintosh v Bebarfalds Ltd* (1922) 22 SR (NSW) 371 (NSWSC) (agreement not to alter leased premises without consent of landlord); *Ampol Petroleum Ltd v Mutton* (1953) 53 SR (NSW) 1 (NSWSC) (agreement that defendants would not sell their service station without consent of claimant).

[33] eg *Wood v Corrigan* (1928) 28 SR (NSW) 492 (NSWSC) (defendants would only sell logs to claimants).

[34] eg *Metropolitan Electric Supply Co Ltd v Ginder* [1901] 2 Ch 799 (Ch) (defendant agreed to use only electricity supplied by claimant).

[35] Laycock (n 7) 707–08.

through performance of the contract.'[36] This is the aspect of substitutability which looks to the idiosyncratic value of performance to the claimant. The courts look at what the claimant hoped to gain through performance of the contract, and ascertain whether compensatory damages would put the claimant in a position as if the contract had been performed. An injunction is readily awarded because once the negative covenant has been broken, it cannot be undone, or as Pomeroy puts it:

> Judges have been brought to see and to acknowledge . . . that a remedy which *prevents* a threatened wrong is in its essential nature better than a remedy which permits the wrong to be done, and then attempts to pay for it[37]

An injunction is intended to prevent future wrongdoing or to ameliorate future consequences of a past wrong.[38] Without the security provided by an injunction, the defendant's bargain will be valueless to the claimant. The claimant is at the mercy of the defendant, and cannot rely on anyone else to perform that agreement. Nevertheless, there may be circumstances where an injunction is not granted for discretionary reasons (hardship, lack of clean hands and the like).

Breaches of negative covenant usually involve a specific promise *not to do* a particular thing. Unlike a fiduciary, a contractor who is subject to a negative covenant does not have discretion. The choice is to perform the obligation, or to fail to perform the obligation. There is no obligation on the part of a promisor to act in the best interests of the promisee.

Courts *do* award disgorgement damages for breach of negative covenant, but, at least until *Blake*, they seldom do so openly. The tendency before *Blake* was to characterise the contract containing the negative covenant as 'fiduciary' in an instrumental fashion, purely in order to obtain the disgorgement remedy. Courts did this because they instinctively sensed that the claimant's right to performance should be protected and that the defendant should be deterred from breaching the negative covenant because of the 'agency problem'.

It is trite to say that the fiduciary concept has often been misused in order to achieve a just result.[39] The label 'fiduciary' is notoriously flexible, and has been dubbed the 'accordion term' because of its ability to be stretched or contracted.[40] There is a risk that the term will be rendered meaningless if it is stretched too far merely because a court wishes to award a particular remedy. Some of the cases cited by Lord Nicholls in *Blake* as examples of cases where disgorgement damages

[36] P Birks, 'Restitutionary Damages for Breach of Contract: *Snepp* and the Fusion of Law and Equity' [1987] *Lloyd's Maritime and Commercial Law Quarterly* 421, 441–42.

[37] JN Pomeroy, *Equity Jurisprudence*, 1st edn (San Francisco, Bancroft-Whitney, 1887) vol 3, §1357, 389 (emphasis in original).

[38] Laycock (n 9).

[39] Birks (n 36). Birks cites the infamous example of *Chase Manhattan Bank v Israel-British Bank* [1981] 1 Ch 105 (Ch) in which a fiduciary obligation was imputed to Israel-British Bank to ensure that Chase Manhattan could recover a mistaken payment of £2m. See also P Birks, 'Profits of Breach of Contract' (1993) 109 *LQR* 518, 520; P Birks, 'Equity in the Modern Law: An Exercise in Taxonomy' (1996) 26 *University of Western Australian Law Review* 1, 18, 55–56.

[40] F Kessler and E Fine, 'Culpa in Contrahendo, Bargaining in Good Faith and Freedom of Contract: A Comparative Study' (1964) 77 *Harvard Law Review* 401, 444.

have been awarded for breach of fiduciary duty concurrent with breach of contract involve instrumental applications of the fiduciary concept.[41] An instrumental use of the fiduciary concept means the judicial determinations lack transparency; the real reason for the decision is concealed.

One of the cases relied upon by the House of Lords in *Blake* was *Snepp*. There, the US Supreme Court found that Snepp, a former employee of the Central Intelligence Agency ('CIA') was liable to disgorge profits made after he released an unauthorised book about the activities of the US Government and the CIA in Vietnam. Snepp was found to owe concurrent contractual and fiduciary obligations to the CIA, and the CIA was awarded a constructive trust over the profits. The US Supreme Court subjected Snepp to a fiduciary obligation because of the 'extremely high degree of trust' involved in his relationship with the CIA and the US Government.[42] However, as noted by the English Court of Appeal in *Blake*, it seems extraordinary to subject Snepp to the full brunt of fiduciary obligations even after his employment had finished.

Easterbrook and Fischel observe that negative covenants are often included in contracts where one party seeks to govern the future conduct of the other, but cannot specify exactly which obligations will arise in advance without costly and inconvenient negotiation.[43] They regard the negative covenant in *Snepp* as initiating a process for making decisions in the future as to what Snepp could and could not write. Snepp should have tried to negotiate a second contract to ascertain exactly which parts of his manuscript could be published:

> The first contract established the employment relation and the submission requirement. The second contract would establish the terms of publication. Just as restitution plus an additional penalty induces the would-be thief to enter into market transactions instead, the profits remedy induces the parties to contract explicitly. It is a contract inducing, not a contract-frustrating, approach.[44]

The threat of a disgorgement remedy removes the incentive for the promisor to breach, and instead gives the promisor incentive to negotiate with the promisee or to perform the contract. The rationale behind this is deterrence; otherwise negative covenants become ineffectual. Where negative covenants have been breached, it is too late to deter the promisor in relation to the breach which has already occurred, but the promisee's right is vindicated by stripping the profit from the promisor. In those cases where disgorgement has been ordered, the concern of the courts is more to exact adherence to the specific obligation rather than to ensure that the breach does no harm. In most cases, compensatory damages are wholly inadequate to recognise the claimant's performance interest, and the law ought to attempt to prevent potential defendants from breaching in the first place rather than compensate for harm once the breach has occurred. Once the breach has

[41] *Snepp v United States*, 444 US 507 (1980) (USSC); *Reading v Attorney General* [1951] UKHL 1, [1951] AC 507 (HL); *Reid-Newfoundland Co v Anglo-American Telegraph Co Ltd* [1912] AC 555 (PC).

[42] *Snepp* (n 41) 510.

[43] Easterbrook and Fischel (n 19) 444–45.

[44] ibid 444.

occurred, the promisor's profit is stripped in order to vindicate the promisee's right to performance and in order to punish the promisor.

In analysing the overlap between the breach of fiduciary duty cases and the breach of negative covenant cases, I propose that fully-blown fiduciary duties have a special 'bundle of obligations' attached to them. These obligations can be limited or shaped by contract. Some of the negative covenant contracts have a modified, less demanding version of the fiduciary 'bundle of obligations' implied into them. Crucially, the negative covenant cases include a duty to act in good faith which distinguishes them from ordinary commercial contracts, in part because of the 'agency problem' which also bedevils fiduciary law. This explains why breach of negative covenant sits on the margins of fiduciary law, and why disgorgement damages are available for some breaches of negative covenant. They could be said to be 'quasi-fiduciary' cases, falling between fully-blown fiduciary obligations and purely self interested contract law.

III The Fiduciary 'Bundle of Obligations'

Fiduciary relationships generally have a special 'bundle of obligations' attached to them. Fiduciary obligations can be limited and shaped by the terms of a contract,[45] and accordingly, the line between contract and fiduciary obligation is not sharp. The breach of negative covenant cases are on the margins of fiduciary law because they also raise the 'agency problem' and thus they may also be candidates for awards of disgorgement damages, even if no fiduciary relationship is found. Courts do not always require a fiduciary relationship when imposing remedies which are usually an incident of a fiduciary relationship.[46] For example, in *White City Tennis Club* a limited fiduciary duty was found on the facts, but Macfarlan JA would still have awarded a constructive trust even if one had not been established.[47] A fiduciary relationship was not a necessary precondition for an award of a constructive trust.[48] Indeed, the line of authority represented by *Muschinski v Dodds*[49] and *Baumgartner v Baumgartner*[50] involves imposing a constructive trust in situations where no fiduciary relationship exists.

[45] *Hospital Products* (n 16) 97 (Mason J). In addition, both *Armitage v Nurse* [1997] EWCA Civ 1279, [1998] Ch 241 (CA) and *ASIC v Citigroup Global Markets Australia Pty Ltd (No 4)* (*Citigroup*) (2007) 160 FCR 35 (FCA) allowed for exclusion of liability for negligence on the part of trustees; *cf Reader v Fried* [2001] VSC 495.

[46] See J Gleeson and J Watson, 'Account of Profits, Contracts and Equity' (2005) 79 *Australian Law Journal* 676, 704–05.

[47] *White City Tennis Club Ltd v John Alexander's Clubs Pty Ltd (No 2)* [2009] NSWCA 114, [64], [83]–[91] (Macfarlan JA), (2009) 261 ALR 112 (NSWCA) (overturned on other grounds: *John Alexander's Clubs Pty Ltd v White City Tennis Club Ltd* (2010) 241 CLR 1 (HCA).

[48] *White City Tennis Club* (n 47) [64], [78]–[82] (Macfarlan JA) (overturned on other grounds: *John Alexander* (n 47)). See also *Avondale Printers & Stationers Ltd v Haggie* [1979] 2 NZLR 124 (NZSC) 159 (Mahon J).

[49] *Muschinski v Dodds* (1985) 160 CLR 583 (HCA).

[50] *Baumgartner v Baumgartner* (1987) 164 CLR 137 (HCA).

There is a particular group of duties which are typically characterised as fiduciary:

1. The fiduciary must not place himself in a **position of conflict** between his own interests and those of the beneficiary without consent, nor must a fiduciary allow his duty towards two different beneficiaries to conflict.
2. The fiduciary must not make an unauthorised or secret **profit** from his fiduciary position.
3. The fiduciary must act in the **best interests** of the beneficiary, that is, an obligation to act for the proper purposes for which the fiduciary has agreed to act.
4. The fiduciary must act in **good faith**, that is, act in a manner which is candid, honest, reasonable and forthright.[51]

I call these obligations the 'fiduciary bundle of obligations'. It will be suggested that different voluntary undertakings may have all, some or none of the 'fiduciary bundle of obligations' attached to them.

A party who is subject to a 'fully-blown' fiduciary obligation will be subject to all four of the fiduciary bundle of obligations. But there are other voluntary obligations to which only some of the fiduciary bundle of obligations may attach or, most frequently, none will attach. It is worth noting that some of the specific fiduciary obligations can be excluded by an appropriately drafted clause in a contract.[52] The only obligation which *cannot* be excluded by contract is the duty of good faith.[53] In addition, even in a fiduciary context, the full 'fiduciary bundle of obligations' may not be present depending upon the circumstances. In *Kelly v Cooper*[54] the Privy Council suggested that fiduciary obligations may be limited by the nature of the activities pursued by the fiduciary. The estate agent in that case owed fiduciary duties to his clients, but the nature of these obligations was modified by the fact that he worked for multiple principals. Thus, the estate agent did not have to disclose confidential information about other clients to the claimant.

If we take the 'fiduciary bundle of obligations' above and see how they apply to the negative covenant cases, including those cases which are arguably masquerading as fiduciary, it is hard to see that there is a fiduciary-type obligation to act in the best interests of the other party. An obligation to act in the best interests of another party suggests that the promisor has discretion to use a particular power for proper purposes. However, many of the negative covenant cases do not involve discretion at all. The obligation is unequivocal: the promisor *is not to do* the stipulated thing. The only discretion on the part of the promisor is whether the promisor chooses to breach.

Similarly, the duty not to conflict is extremely limited in some of the cases involving negative covenants and concurrent fiduciary duties. By contrast, the

[51] See *Bristol & West Building Society* (n 11) 18 (Millet LJ). As to the first two obligations, see *Chan v Zacharia* (1984) 154 CLR 178 (HCA) 199 (Deane J). See also Edelman (n 22) 316.

[52] *Armitage* (n 45); *Citigroup* (n 45); *cf Reader* (n 45).

[53] *Armitage* (n 45) 253–54 (Millett LJ).

[54] *Kelly v Cooper* [1993] AC 205 (PC) 215 (Lord Browne-Wilkinson).

notion of conflict of interest is extremely broad in many 'proper fiduciary' cases. So the majority in *Boardman v Phipps* found that there was no need for an actual conflict of interest: 'even if the possibility of conflict is present between personal interest and the fiduciary position the rule of equity must be applied.'[55]

One of the suggestions made by the Court of Appeal in *Blake* was that disgorgement damages should be awarded where the defendant had done 'the very thing which he agreed not to do'.[56] This was rejected by Lord Nicholls in *Blake*.[57] However, a conflict of interest arises in these negative covenant cases in a very limited sense, and it arises *precisely* because the defendant has done the very thing which he agreed not to do. The defendant agreed to do something for the benefit of the claimant, and if the defendant had kept his obligations, he would have foregone a potential profit. By doing the very thing he had agreed not to do, and making a profit thereby, the defendant should be obliged to disgorge that profit. There will be a conflict of interest in these cases.

To summarise, the primary obligations in negative covenant cases are a modified and less stringent version of the 'fiduciary bundle of obligations'. The obligations typically include the following:

1. An obligation not to conflict, limited to the terms of the relevant negative covenant – that is, the defendant is not to prefer his own interests over the obligation contained in the covenant.
2. Flowing from the first, an obligation on the part of the promisor not to profit by putting his own interests over the obligation contained in the covenant.
3. An obligation to act in good faith because of the particular circumstances of the contract – that is to say, the contract is designed to protect non-financial interests.

Worthington argues that there may be circumstances where it would be appropriate to import a duty of good faith into particular relationships (including some contractual relationships).[58] She notes:

> The standard [of good faith] being mooted is not one which demands self-denial (ie a fiduciary standard) in all relationships; that would be inappropriate. It probably does not even go so far as to require positive regard for the legitimate interests of others (ie a conventional good faith standard). What it seems to demand is avoidance of activities which display cynical *disregard* for the legitimate interests of others – true, this is not as

[55] *Boardman v Phipps* [1966] UKHL 2, [1967] 2 AC 46 (HL) 111 (Lord Hodson); *cf* Lord Upjohn (dissenting) 124:

> The phrase 'possibly may conflict' requires consideration. In my view it means that the reasonable man looking at the relevant facts and circumstances of the particular case would think that there was a real sensible possibility of conflict; not that you could imagine some situation arising which might, in some conceivable possibility in events not contemplated as real sensible possibilities by any reasonable person, result in conflict.

[56] *Attorney General v Blake* [1998] Ch 439 (CA) 458.

[57] *Blake* (n 6) 286.

[58] Worthington (n 15) 238–39. See also H Dagan, *The Law and Ethics of Restitution* (Cambridge, Cambridge University Press, 2004) 278–82.

> demanding as a strict obligation of good faith; it is perhaps more correctly styled as an obligation not to act with contumelious bad faith.[59]

This is exactly what I propose should be done for the negative covenant cases. The promisor is required to refrain from acting with contumelious disregard for his obligations to the promisee under the negative covenant, and this obligation is imposed because of the particular nature of the relationship between the parties.

Thus, it is argued that *Snepp*[60] and *Reading*[61] should be considered as cases involving negative covenants in contracts designed to serve national security or the national interest. The latter case will be discussed in more detail shortly. Alternatively, they could be considered to be 'quasi-fiduciary'. In *Blake*, two members of the majority noted that Blake was in a quasi-fiduciary position.[62]

Reid-Newfoundland is cited in *Blake* as another example of concurrent breach of fiduciary duty and contract.[63] A railway company had contracted with the telegraph company for the installation of a 'special wire', and promised not to use the wire to transmit any commercial messages save those 'for the benefit and account of the telegraph company.'[64] Later successors of the railway company had notice of the contract,[65] but proceeded to use the telegraph wire for their own purposes. The Privy Council held that the successor in title to the railway company should disgorge any profits made through the unauthorised use of the wire. Lord Robson seems to infer that the terms of the contract imposed fiduciary duties on the recipients of funds on behalf of the telegraph company.[66] The negative covenant itself gave rise to the specific fiduciary duty in question. The true reason for the award is not that a fiduciary duty had been broken,[67] but because of the non-substitutable nature of the benefit under the contract, and the necessity of protecting the claimant's property rights in the wire. The Privy Council also reached this conclusion because there was a clause in the contract which provided for any profits to be handed over to the claimant.[68]

The question is then what criteria should be used to decide whether disgorgement damages should be available for the breach of a negative covenant. Substitutability remains relevant, but in many cases, it is *not* the whole answer. A claimant must also identify a non-financial interest which the contract is designed to protect.

[59] Worthington (n 15) 238.

[60] *Snepp* (n 41).

[61] *Reading* (n 41).

[62] *Blake* (n 6) 287 (Lord Nicholls), 291–92 (Lord Steyn).

[63] *Reid-Newfoundland* (n 41).

[64] ibid 558.

[65] Edelman notes that in *Blake*, Lord Nicholls assumed that the defendants were the original railway company: J Edelman, *Gain-Based Damages – Contract, Tort, Equity and Intellectual Property* (Oxford, Hart Publishing, 2002) 156.

[66] *Reid-Newfoundland* (n 41) 559.

[67] See J McCamus, 'Disgorgement for Breach of Contract: A Comparative Perspective' (2003) 36 *Loyola of Los Angeles Law Review* 943, 957–58. McCamus agrees this is an instrumental use of fiduciary duty to obtain disgorgement.

[68] G Virgo, *The Principles of the Law of Restitution*, 2nd edn (Oxford, Oxford University Press, 2006) 505.

IV Criteria for the Award of Disgorgement Damages for Breach of Negative Covenant

In this section I will first consider the role of substitutability as a criterion for the award of disgorgement damages for breach of a negative covenant. I will then suggest that a claimant must also identify a non-financial interest which the contract is designed to protect, and will draw four categories of non-financial interest from the existing case law.

A Criterion 1: Substitutability

Substitutability is particularly relevant where disgorgement is awarded as a surrogate for expectation damages.[69] Claimants will wish to claim gain-based damages in circumstances where the defendant has benefited in a measurable way and has caused a loss which is speculative or hard to quantify.[70] In many cases disgorgement of profits is available even when it bears no relationship to the claimant's losses.[71] The kinds of case in which it is typically difficult to measure the losses of the claimant are intellectual property infringement cases in which it is very difficult to ascertain what the losses of the claimant are as a result of the infringement, but the sales of the defendant are clear and quantifiable. Two of the post-*Blake* cases fit precisely within this scenario: *World Wide Fund for Nature v World Wrestling Federation Entertainment Inc*[72] and *Experience Hendrix LLC v PPX Enterprises Inc.*[73] By reason of the very nature of the breach of negative covenant we will never know what would have happened had the defendant not breached the covenant. The defendant has not only put specific relief out of the claimant's reach; he has also made it very difficult for her to calculate her losses. The defendant has deprived the claimant of performance, and the claimant can obtain neither substitute performance nor adequate compensation for the loss of performance. As with the instalment contracts to supply goods and services over a long period of time discussed in the previous chapter,[74] a complex contract cannot be replaced with an identical deal. The situation is analogous to *Eastern*

[69] Eisenberg (n 8) 587–88.

[70] Laycock (n 9) 1287.

[71] ibid.

[72] *World Wide Fund for Nature v World Wrestling Federation Entertainment Inc* (*WWF – Jacobs J*) [2001] EWHC Ch 482, [2002] FSR 32 (Ch); *World Wide Fund for Nature v World Wrestling Federation Entertainment Inc* [2006] EWHC 184 (Ch), [2006] FSR 38 (Ch D) (*WWF – Peter Smith J*); *WWF – World Wide Fund for Nature v World Wrestling Federation Entertainment Inc* [2007] EWCA Civ 286, [2008] 1 WLR 445.

[73] *Experience Hendrix LLC v PPX Enterprises Inc* [2003] EWCA Civ 323, [2003] 1 All ER (Comm) 830 (CA).

[74] See ch 4, II B.

Rolling Mill Co v Michlovitz, where the estimate of the claimant's loss was speculative and conjectural, and accordingly the court was prepared to award specific performance because of the lack of substitutability.[75] In addition, courts must consider the idiosyncratic value of the promise to the claimant, and what the claimant sought to achieve by entering into the contract.

Similarly, the grant of relief in *Esso Petroleum Company Limited v Niad Limited*[76] can be explained at least partially because of the lack of substitutability. There, a service station owner, Niad Limited ('Niad'), breached a marketing scheme it had entered into with Esso, the supplier of petrol to the service station at that time. Esso would 'recommend' a price reduction in order to keep the fuel price competitive with surrounding stations, and in return, participating retailers paid less for their fuel than other non-participating retailers. There were four occasions where Niad did not charge the recommended price, but charged a higher price. This resulted in a considerable profit for Niad and its director.

This was a commercial contract designed to create mutual profit for the parties. But by failing to apply the recommended prices and still taking fuel at discounted prices, Niad acted in bad faith. Mr Beatson argues that substitutability helps to establish that this is indeed a case in which an account of profits is appropriate.[77]

Morritt V-C held that Niad had breached its contract with Esso and that Esso could elect to take damages, an account of profits for breach of contract or restitutionary damages representing the amount by which Niad had overcharged its customers. In finding that an account of profits was available pursuant to the principles expressed in *Blake*, Morritt V-C said:

> In my judgment the remedy of an account of profits should be available for breaches of contract such as these. First, damages is an inadequate remedy. It is almost impossible to attribute lost sales to a breach by one out of several hundred dealers who operated Pricewatch. Second, the obligation to implement and maintain the recommended pump prices was fundamental to Pricewatch. Failure to observe it gives the lie to the advertising campaign by which it was publicised and therefore undermines the benefits intended for both Esso and all its dealers within Pricewatch. Third, complaint was made of Niad on four occasions. On all of them Niad appeared to comply without demur. It now appears that the breaches of its obligation were much more extensive than Esso at first thought. Fourth, Esso undoubtedly has a legitimate interest in preventing Niad from profiting from its breach of obligation.[78]

Nevertheless, the Vice Chancellor said that an account of profits was 'unlikely to yield by way of recompense the amount of additional price support obtained by Niad from Pricewatch which it did not pass on',[79] and found that restitution of the

[75] *Michlovitz* (n 9) 384 (Parke J).

[76] *Esso Petroleum Company Limited v Niad Limited* (*Niad*) [2001] EWHC 458 (Ch), [2001] All ER (D) 324 (Ch).

[77] J Beatson, 'Courts, Arbitrators and Restitutionary Liability for Breach of Contract' (2002) 118 *LQR* 377, 378–79.

[78] *Niad* (n 76) [63].

[79] ibid [57].

amounts by which customers were overcharged would be a more appropriate remedy.[80] It must be queried whether this is correct.

However, substitutability is not the sole reason for awarding disgorgement damages for breach of negative covenant. The difficulty with *Niad* is that it is hard to identify an interest other than profit-making in the contract. If substitutability alone is the criterion for the award of disgorgement damages for breach of negative covenant, then every breach of negative covenant which results in a profit will give rise to disgorgement damages. It would be strange if disgorgement damages were more readily available for breach of negative covenants than for breach of positive obligations.[81]

Professor McKendrick has suggested the result in *Niad* is incorrect 'because it adopts too liberal an approach of the concept of remedial inadequacy and it fails to recognize the exceptional, subsidiary nature of the claim for an account of profits.'[82] The only relevant interest which the contract could potentially serve would be the public interest insofar as the agreement could be said to result in more competitive fuel prices for consumers. However, this is drawing a long bow.

B Criterion 2: a Contract Designed to Serve Interests Other than Profit-making

Disgorgement is awarded for breach of negative covenant not only for reasons of substitutability, but because the contract is designed to serve interests other than profit-making. Sometimes courts will order specific relief of such contracts, as in *Beswick v Beswick*,[83] but if specific relief is unavailable (as is frequently the case in breach of negative covenant cases) the court should consider whether an award of disgorgement damages is appropriate.

Most of the cases where disgorgement damages have been awarded for breach of contract fall into this category. These kinds of contracts involve a conferral of trust on the promisor by the promisee, and therefore courts are particularly willing to say for public policy reasons that the claimant's performance interest in the contract should be protected.[84] Sometimes the promisee may suffer losses from the promisor's breach which are difficult to measure, and therefore expectation damages will be speculative. In these circumstances disgorgement damages will often be the only way to recognise the claimant's performance interest. In addition, the deterrent rationale is strong because disgorgement damages give promisors efficient incentives to perform.[85] Accordingly, it will be argued that it is

[80] ibid [64].

[81] Burrows (n 9) 400.

[82] E McKendrick, 'Breach of Contract, Restitution for Wrongs, and Punishment' in A Burrows and E Peel (eds), *Commercial Remedies – Current Issues and Problems* (Oxford, Oxford University Press, 2003) 93, 112.

[83] *Beswick v Beswick* [1967] UKHL 2, [1968] AC 58 (HL).

[84] Eisenberg (n 8) 588–92.

[85] ibid 592.

appropriate for courts to imply obligations on promisors not to place themselves in a position of conflict with the interest protected by the negative covenant, and to behave in good faith.

There are five different categories of contracts involving non-financial interests which typically lead to awards of disgorgement damages:

1. Contracts involving a proprietary or quasi-proprietary interest;
2. Contracts involving national security or the national interest;
3. Contracts involving resolution of a legal dispute;
4. Contracts involving the protection of third party family members; and
5. Contracts involving the public interest that do not fall under one of the preceding heads.

These categories are not mutually exclusive, and some cases fall within more than one category. Each will now be examined in turn.

i Contracts Involving a Proprietary or Quasi-proprietary Interest

It has been long established that courts will order partial disgorgement for breach of a negative covenant in a contract which involves a proprietary interest.[86] The landmark case in this area is *Wrotham Park Estate Co Ltd v Parkside Homes Ltd*[87] which Lord Nicholls in *Blake* described as shining 'rather as a solitary beacon'[88] because of its recognition of the possibility of partial disgorgement of profit for breach of contract. There are a number of other cases which now fall into this category.[89] These cases will be considered in greater detail in chapter six which considers partial disgorgement.

Both partial and full disgorgement may be available for breach of confidence as a matter of course, depending on the level of confidentiality of the information.[90] However, following *Blake*, disgorgement may be available for breach of contract just as it would be for the concurrent action in breach of confidence, bringing coherence and consistency to the law of remedies.[91] Some argue that disgorgement

[86] See Virgo (n 68) 506–07; R Grantham and C Rickett, *Enrichment and Restitution in New Zealand* (Oxford, Hart Publishing, 2000) 477–78. See also S Harder, *Measuring Damages in the Law of Obligations* (Oxford, Hart Publishing, 2010) 218–22, who would classify these cases as exclusive entitlements *erga omnes*.

[87] *Wrotham Park Estate Co Ltd v Parkside Homes Ltd* [1974] 1 WLR 798 (Ch).

[88] *Blake* (n 6) 283.

[89] *Shaw* (n 30); *Jaggard v Sawyer* [1994] EWCA Civ 1, [1995] 1 WLR 269 (CA); *Gafford v Graham* [1998] EWCA Civ 666, [1999] 3 EGLR 75 (CA); *Amec Developments Limited v Jury's Hotel Management (UK) Limited* [2000] EWHC Ch 454, [2001] EGLR 81 (Ch); *Lane v O'Brien Homes* [2004] EWHC 303 (QB), [2004] All ER (D) 61 (QB).

[90] Although difficulties in calculation mean an account of profit is sought less often than might be supposed: see M Gronow, 'Restitution for Breach of Confidence' (1996) 10 *Intellectual Property Journal* 219.

[91] See, eg *Pell Frischmann Engineering Ltd v Bow Valley Iran Ltd* [2009] UKPC 45, [2010] BLR 73 (PC); *Vercoe* (n 4) (partial disgorgement).

may be available because the confidence protected by the contract has a quasi-proprietary nature in the eyes of the law.[92]

ii Contracts Involving National Security or the National Interest

Blake and *Snepp* are both cases where the courts ordered disgorgement of gains made in breach of contract. Each case involved a bargain which was designed to serve an interest other than profit-making, namely the interest of national security.[93]

As already mentioned, *Blake* involved a breach of contract by Blake, a British spy and double agent for the Soviets. The British Government instituted proceedings to recover the £90,000 paid to Blake for his unauthorised autobiography. A majority of the House of Lords found that Blake was required to disgorge his profit made in breach of contract.[94]

The House of Lords in *Blake* relied on *Snepp*, as both cases involved former government agents who released unauthorised books about their activities. The US Supreme Court held that Snepp owed concurrent contractual and fiduciary obligations to the CIA, and awarded a constructive trust in favour of the CIA over the profits from Snepp's book. Snepp was subjected to fiduciary obligations because of the trust involved in his relationship with the CIA and the US Government.[95]

The similarity between *Blake* and *Snepp* highlights the kinship between breach of fiduciary duty cases and breach of negative covenant cases generally. In both *Snepp* and *Blake*, there was an implied obligation not to conflict, but this was limited to the terms of the relevant negative covenant. Each defendant was not permitted to prefer his own interests over the obligations towards the promisee specified in the negative covenant. The defendant therefore had an obligation not to profit by placing his own interests ahead of the obligation contained in the covenant. By contrast, there was no obligation to act in the best interests of a beneficiary, and indeed, it is difficult to see how such a broad obligation to act would subsist after the termination of the employment contract. There was no discretion which the defendants in each case were bound to exercise for proper purposes. The main obligation was rather that each defendant should not publish material with regard to their former employment without consent. There is no discretion whatsoever contained in that undertaking.

However, it is possible to argue that there was an implied and continuing obligation imposed on both Blake and Snepp to act in good faith because of the

[92] M Richardson, 'Breach of Confidence' in P Parkinson (ed), *The Principles of Equity*, 2nd edn (Sydney, Lawbook Co, 2003) 436; *Smith Kline & French Laboratories (Aust) Ltd v Secretary, Department of Community Services & Health* (1990) 22 FCR 73 (FCA) 120–21 (Gummow J). While confidential information can be recognised as proprietary in certain senses (eg it can be assigned), it is controversial whether or not it is really a proprietary interest.

[93] Eisenberg (n 8) 588.

[94] Lord Nicholls, with whom Lord Goff and Lord Browne-Wilkinson agreed, and Lord Steyn in a separate speech. Lord Hobhouse dissented.

[95] *Snepp* (n 41) 510.

circumstances of the original contract. Neither defendant had acted in good faith in publishing their memoirs without the consent of the employer. Thus, Eisenberg argues that:

> *Snepp* and *Blake* were correctly decided. The contractual purpose of each government in these cases was the management of potentially sensitive information. That purpose could not be readily served by protecting the expectation interest, because the information had no market value and the Governments suffered no economic loss by its publication. . . . [C]ourts should protect the disgorgement interest in the case of bargain contracts that are not designed for profit-making purposes, so as to give the promisor in such contracts efficient incentive to perform, and effectuate contracts of this type.[96]

In any event, the interest being protected by these contracts was not financial. It was control over sensitive information.[97] The interest was also one of national security. Apparently a number of British agents had died as a result of George Blake's disclosures to the Soviets. In contracts of this type, therefore, it is appropriate to imply a duty not to conflict with the terms of the negative covenant, and to imply an obligation of good faith.

In both contracts, the 'agency problem' lies at the base of the claimant's legitimate interest in the profits arising from the breach of contract. The claimants had no realistic opportunity to control or monitor the performance of the obligation, and compensatory damages would be inadequate. Deterrent and punitive goals are both evident in the reasoning of the courts in these cases. The courts wished to deter others from behaving as Blake and Snepp behaved. They also wished to ensure that Blake and Snepp did not profit undeservedly from their breach of contract – the contracts involved a special level of trust and confidence between the parties, the promisors advertently breached their contracts, and accordingly it was appropriate that they be stripped of their profits.

Reading is cited by the majority in *Blake* as a further example of disgorgement for breach of fiduciary duty and of contract.[98] However, it could also be characterised as a case of breach of a negative covenant in which the government had a national interest. Reading was a sergeant in the British Army on active service in Egypt. He dressed in military uniform and accompanied trucks containing illicit imports of alcohol to prevent them from being inspected by police. He received bribes worth about £20,000 sterling for his services, which were confiscated by military officials. After he was released from prison he applied to have the bribe money returned to him. The House of Lords found that Reading owed fiduciary obligations to the Crown and ordered him to disgorge his profits.[99] Lord Porter expressed agreement with the Court of Appeal judgment below,[100] saying:

96 Eisenberg (n 8) 591.

97 There was no breach of confidence in *Blake.* At first instance the claimants conceded (and the trial judge agreed) that Blake did not owe a continuing a duty of confidence in relation to the information in the book because it was no longer confidential: *Attorney-General v Blake* [1997] Ch 84 (Ch) 91–94.

98 *Reading* (n 41).

99 Viscount Jowitt, LC, Lord Porter and Lord Normand all agreed that Reading was subject to a fiduciary duty.

100 *Reading v The King* [1949] 2 KB 232 (CA) 236 (Asquith LJ).

> the words 'fiduciary relationship' in this setting are used in a wide and loose sense and include, inter alia, a case where the servant gains from his employment a position of authority which enables him to obtain the sum which he receives.[101]

This use of the fiduciary concept is unconvincing. At first instance Denning J said:

> This man Reading was not acting in the course of his employment: and there was no fiduciary relationship in respect of these long journeys nor, indeed, in respect of his uniform. In my opinion, however, these are not essential ingredients of the cause of action. The uniform of the Crown, and the position of the man as a servant of the Crown were the sole reasons why he was able to get this money, and that is sufficient to make him liable to hand it over to the Crown. The case is to be distinguished from cases where the service merely gives the opportunity of making money. A servant may, during his master's time, in breach of his contract, do other things, to make money for himself, such as gambling, but he is entitled to keep that money himself. The master has a claim for damages for breach of contract, but he has no claim to the money.[102]

Although the House of Lords ultimately held that Reading had to account as a fiduciary for the bribes Denning J's judgment correctly identifies why this conclusion is problematic. Reading's misuse of his authority caused his conduct to be wrongful, and there was a causal link between his employment and the illicit profit. The case could be seen as one where a negative covenant was implied that army officers should not misuse their position of authority to make an illicit profit at the Crown's expense. By breaching the covenant Reading placed himself in a position of conflict between his financial self-interest and his duty to promote the security objectives of his army employment. As with *Blake* and *Snepp*, a fiduciary analysis does not provide the most convincing explanation of this decision. As Denning J noted, on this analysis if Reading had gambled in his spare time, he could have kept his winnings; the Crown would have had no right to them.

Attorney-General for Hong Kong v Reid[103] could also be characterised as a case involving the national interest. Reid, a policeman, was employed by the Hong Kong Government to stamp out corruption. Instead, Reid accepted illicit bribes, and used the bribes to buy real estate in New Zealand which subsequently rose in value. The Privy Council unanimously found that the Hong Kong Government was entitled to trace the bribes into the real estate in New Zealand, and awarded a constructive trust in favour of the Hong Kong Government over the New Zealand property.[104] Lord Templeman justified the imposition of a constructive trust by saying:

> But if the bribe consists of property which increases in value or if a cash bribe is invested advantageously, the false fiduciary will receive a benefit from his breach of duty unless he is accountable not only for the original amount or value of the bribe but also for the increased value of the property representing the bribe. As soon as the bribe was received it should have been paid or transferred instanter to the person who suffered from the

[101] *Reading* (n 41) 516.
[102] *Reading v The King* [1948] 2 KB 268, 276 (Denning LJ).
[103] *Attorney-General for Hong Kong v Reid (Reid)* [1993] UKPC 2, [1994] 1 AC 324 (PC).
[104] ibid 336–39 (Lord Templeman). Against *Lister & Co v Stubbs* (1890) 45 Ch D 1 (CA).

> breach of duty. Equity considers as done that which ought to have been done. As soon as the bribe was received, whether in cash or in kind, the false fiduciary held the bribe on a constructive trust for the person injured.[105]

The case therefore effected disgorgement of gains by the imposition of a constructive trust. It has been criticised for its potential impact where fiduciaries are insolvent.[106] Its correctness has now been doubted by the Court of Appeal in *Sinclair Investments (UK) Ltd v Versailles Trade Finance Ltd*,[107] which preferred to apply *Lister v Stubbs* in deciding that the preferred remedy for bribe cases is a non-proprietary equitable account.[108] Still, it may be that a constructive trust will be appropriate in some limited cases.[109] In any case, even if a constructive trust is inappropriate, the award of a disgorgement remedy is nonetheless justified.

iii Contracts Involving Resolution of a Legal Dispute

A number of the breach of negative covenant cases involve contracts which have been entered into to settle a legal dispute or to prevent continuing breaches of the law.

For example, in *British Motor Trade Association v Gilbert*,[110] a case cited with approval by Lord Nicholls in *Blake*, the defendant breached an undertaking given when an injunction was awarded against him. The injunction had been issued because the defendant was in breach of legislation preventing the unauthorised sale of second-hand cars. The defendant undertook that he would not sell a car in breach of the legislation. The policy of the post-Second World War legislation was to regulate and limit the sale of cars to prevent an inflationary black market in cars. However, the defendant subsequently breached the undertaking. The defendant was ordered to pay an account of profits made by breaching the injunction.[111]

WWF involved a dispute between the World Wide Fund for Nature ('the Fund') and the World Wrestling Federation ('the Federation') over the right to use the initials 'WWF'. As described earlier in the book, in 1994, after a long running legal battle, the parties entered into a settlement agreement in which the Federation agreed not to use the initials 'WWF' in certain ways. The Federation kept to the 1994 agreement for a while, but then began to use the initials 'WWF' in breach of the agreement.

The Fund sought security by entering into the settlement contract. It also sought to protect its reputation. These were non-financial interests. The Fund therefore took legal action against the Federation for its breach of contract. In the

[105] *Reid* (n 103) 331–32.

[106] P Birks, 'Property in the Profits of Wrongdoing' (1994) 24 *University of Western Australia Law Review* 8, 16; D Cowan, R Edmunds and J Lowry, '*Lister & Co v Stubbs*: Who Profits?' [1996] *Journal of Business Law* 22, 38; Burrows (n 10) 461.

[107] *Sinclair Investments (UK) Ltd v Versailles Trade Finance Ltd* [2011] EWCA Civ 347 [80]–[88] (Lord Neuberger MR, with whom Richards LJ and Hughes LJ agreed).

[108] ibid [88].

[109] McCamus (n 67) 972–73.

[110] *British Motor Trade Association v Gilbert* [1951] 2 All ER 641 (Ch).

[111] ibid 645.

wake of the *Blake* case it sought to amend its statement of claim to demand that the Federation account for all profits it had made by using the initials 'WWF' in breach the 1994 agreement.[112] Almost as a postscript to the judgment, Jacobs J rejected that application. He said:

> I can see nothing which makes this case of the exceptional character called for by the decision in *Blake*. All one really has here is a negative covenant. The fact that it relates to the use of initials and so is a bit 'trademarkish' or 'IPish' does not mean the common law should provide what Parliament provides by state for an infringement of a registered mark or intellectual property right. It would indeed be odd if breach of an ordinary full restraint of trade clause (eg, not to work in a defined area at a defined job for a defined period of time) did not attract an account, whereas breach of a lesser restraint (not to use a mark in a trade otherwise permitted) did. I conclude that the proposed amendment should not be allowed.[113]

The Fund later sought to amend its statement of claim to include damages calculated by reference to the hypothetical sum that it would have accepted from the Federation to relax its rights under the 1994 agreement.[114] Leave to amend was refused on the basis that it would be an abuse of process if the Fund were allowed to claim damages on the *Wrotham Park* basis.[115] The judgment of the Court of Appeal has added further confusion to the area of gain-based damages generally as Chadwick LJ seemed to suggest that the justification for both *Wrotham Park* style damages and disgorgement damages was *compensatory*.[116] With respect, this conclusion seems wrong, particularly in the case of disgorgement damages.[117]

The contract was not designed to serve a profit-making purpose, and therefore compensatory damages were unlikely to be adequate to place the claimant in a position as if the contract had been performed. The Fund sought to end a protracted and unpleasant legal battle. Presumably, it had thought the matter had come to an end when the 1994 settlement agreement was entered into, but instead it found itself embroiled in a further legal battle. The other purpose of the agreement was for the Fund to distinguish itself from the Federation, and protect its reputation. It was impossible for the breach to be reversed: performance had been put out of the reach of the Fund. Furthermore, the losses to the Fund as a result of the breach would be difficult, if not impossible, to quantify, but the profits made by the Federation would be more easily quantifiable.

In these circumstances there was an obligation on the Federation not to put its own interests ahead of its obligations under the negative covenant, and there was

112 *WWF – Jacobs J* (n 72).

113 ibid [62].

114 *WWF – Peter Smith J* (n 72) [174].

115 *WWF* (n 72) [73]–[75] (Chadwick LJ).

116 *WWF* (n 72) [58] (Chadwick LJ).

117 See R Cunnington, 'A Lost Opportunity to Clarify' (2007) 122 *LQR* 47; R Cunnington, 'Changing Conceptions of Compensation' (2007) *CLJ* 507; R Cunnington, 'The Measure and Availability of Gain-Based Damages for Breach of Contract' in R Cunnington and D Saidov (eds), *Contract Damages: Domestic and International Perspectives* (Oxford, Hart Publishing, 2008) 221; C Rotherham, '"*Wrotham Park* Damages" and Accounts of Profits' [2008] *Lloyd's Maritime and Commerical Law Quarterly* 25, 36–55.

also an obligation not to profit by putting its own interests first. Given the context of the agreement, which was to resolve a legal dispute, it is appropriate that a duty of good faith be implied into the agreement. The Federation breached this duty of good faith.

It is unfortunate that the court did not allow the Fund to seek disgorgement damages as it is arguable that they should have been available on these facts. Not only was the benefit under the contract non-substitutable, but also the promisee sought by contract to protect itself from the very thing that happened. It was a contract with a deterrent purpose. Further, it appeared that the court *could not* award specific relief in relation to past breaches of contract, which suggests that a greater measure of profit should be disgorged. Nonetheless, as will be discussed in the next chapter, there may be some reason for awarding the claimant a 'reasonable fee' because the Fund delayed in bringing proceedings for some three or four years.[118] Counsel for the Fund suggested that the Fund was reluctant to become embroiled in legal proceedings because of its charitable status.[119] Delay is a recognised bar to specific performance, and it would be appropriate to recognise similar limitations on disgorgement of damages for breach of contract. In that case, the court could have awarded specific relief if proceedings had been brought in a more timely fashion, and thus a lower measure of profit should be disgorged.

Another post-*Blake* case, *Experience Hendrix LLC v PPX Enterprises Inc*,[120] also discussed previously in chapter three, involved a settlement of litigation concerning the right to licence recordings of Jimi Hendrix before he was famous. PPX had commenced legal proceedings against Hendrix before his death for breach of an agreement to play exclusively for them. In 1973, PPX and Hendrix's estate entered into a settlement which provided that Hendrix's estate was entitled to certain royalties in respect of certain recordings, and that other non-listed recordings would not be licensed by PPX to third parties without the consent of Hendrix's estate. PPX breached this settlement agreement twice. In 1995 it granted licences to CBH Records GmbH for an advance of $350,000 (although PPX claimed to have been paid only $250,000 of that amount). Over half of the recordings were not listed in the settlement agreement. In 1999 PPX granted a licence to Nippon Crown Co Ltd for an advance of $35,000. There was no indication of the sales resulting from these licences or the royalties PPX earned from them. The Hendrix estate was primarily concerned to control the quality of the recordings of Hendrix which were released, and would never have granted PPX consent to breach the agreement.

The Court of Appeal unanimously held that Experience Hendrix was entitled to a *Wrotham Park* award: a reasonable proportion of the profits arising from the breach of contract.[121] However, the court rejected Experience Hendrix's claim for an account of PPX's entire profit.

[118] *WWF – Jacobs J* (n 72) [13].

[119] ibid [14].

[120] *Experience Hendrix* (n 73) (Mance LJ, Hooper J and Peter Gibson LJ).

[121] R Cunnington, 'Rock, Restitution and Disgorgement' (2004) *Journal of Obligation and Remedies* 46; *cf* PW Lee, 'Responses to a Breach of Contract' [2003] *Lloyd's Maritime and Commercial Law Quarterly* 301. Lee concludes the damages were compensatory.

With respect, the court was incorrect to decide that PPX did not have to pay the full measure of its profits, particularly as the court was prepared to find Experience Hendrix had a 'legitimate interest' in the performance of the contract.[122] Mance LJ distinguished the case from *Blake*, saying that the case did not involve special or sensitive information and questions of national security, nor did PPX's breach of contract contribute to its notoriety and therefore the profit which it had made.[123] As Professor Campbell and Mr Wylie have said, 'almost every case that will ever be heard will be distinguishable from *Blake* on this basis'.[124] Finally, Mance LJ said that there was no analogy between PPX's position and that of a fiduciary.[125]

It may be that the Court of Appeal was attempting to restrict the availability of disgorgement damages to the exceptional facts of *Blake* but, if so, this is hardly consistent with the court's approval of *Niad* and its criticism of Jacobs J's narrow test in *WWF*.[126] Cunnington rightly concludes that after *WWF* and *Experience Hendrix* 'the legitimate interest test remains hopelessly ill-defined and difficult to apply.'[127]

As in *WWF*, the contract in *Experience Hendrix* was designed to serve interests other than profit-making. The aim of the contract was partly to end a protracted and unpleasant legal battle.[128] It was also intended to enable Experience Hendrix to control the quality of releases of Jimi Hendrix's music. Hendrix had been unhappy with the quality of the PPX recordings which had been made before he was famous. Experience Hendrix and its predecessor were reliant on PPX to keep its side of the bargain, and neither Experience Hendrix nor its predecessor could seek substitute performance. The losses suffered by Experience Hendrix as a result of the breach would be difficult to quantify but the profits made by PPX would be more easily quantifiable. Specific relief with respect to past breaches could not be awarded by the court; PPX's actions had put it out of Experience Hendrix's reach.

There was an obligation on PPX not to put its own interests ahead of its obligations under the negative covenant, and there was an obligation not to profit thereby. Again, given that the purpose of the agreement was to resolve a legal dispute, it is appropriate that a duty of good faith be implied into the agreement. The 'agency problem' is particularly stark in this case. Mance LJ notes that from 1993 to 1995 the administrators of Hendrix's estate were attempting to wrest control of various parts of the estate from the former US administrators. Thus, it would have been difficult for Experience Hendrix to supervise the performance of PPX's obligations at this time.

[122] Cunnington (n 121) 52.
[123] *Experience Hendrix* (n 73) [29] (Mance LJ), [55] (Peter Gibson LJ).
[124] D Campbell and P Wylie, 'Ain't No Telling (Which Circumstances Are Exceptional)' (2003) 62 *CLJ* 605, 618.
[125] *Experience Hendrix* (n 73).
[126] ibid [32] (Mance LJ); Cunnington, 'The Measure and Availability of Gain-Based Damages' (n 117) 235.
[127] Cunnington (n 117).
[128] Campbell and Wylie note that Hendrix wilfully breached his contract with PPX and was not blameless in the initial dispute: Campbell and Wylie (n 124) 620–23.

Any unfairness created by the award of a full disgorgement of profit could be mitigated by an allowance for skill and effort. Mance LJ conceded that PPX was entitled to an allowance for skill and effort when awarding a 'reasonable fee'.[129]

iv Contracts Involving the Protection of Third Party Family Members

Courts have been prepared to award specific performance of agreements which have been entered into to protect third party family members.[130] I suggest that if an analogous case arose where a contract was designed to reinforce familial relations and to increase trust, but instead one party made a profit by breaching, disgorgement damages should be available.

In *Beswick*[131] the court specifically enforced an agreement which was entered into to benefit a third party family member who was not privy to the contract. Mr Beswick, an elderly man, entered into an agreement with his nephew in which he agreed to transfer his business to his nephew in return (inter alia) for the nephew promising to pay a weekly annuity to Mr Beswick's widow when he died. The business was transferred to the nephew, but when Mr Beswick died the nephew refused to pay the annuity to the widow. The widow sued the nephew for specific performance of the agreement in her capacity as personal representative of Mr Beswick's estate. The nephew argued that Mr Beswick's estate had suffered no loss as a result of his breach, and was only entitled to nominal damages.[132] Lord Reid described such a conclusion as 'grossly unjust'.[133] Lord Upjohn said:

> [I]t is said nominal damages are adequate and the remedy of specific performance ought not to be granted. That is, with all respect, wholly to misunderstand that principle. Equity will grant specific performance when damages are inadequate to meet the justice of the case.[134]

Notions of 'justice' do not explain the reason why the court awarded specific performance in this case. Looking at the objectives which the claimant hoped to gain through performance of the contract provides more illumination. This contract was intended to provide peace of mind for Mr Beswick and financial security for his widow. However, Mr Beswick's estate did not suffer any loss, and only nominal damages would be available for breach.[135] It was *Mrs Beswick* who suffered the loss. Accordingly, the court was prepared to specifically enforce the contract because otherwise the wife's interest in performance would not be recognised. In this way, it is analogous to the cases involving settlement of legal actions: a

[129] *Experience Hendrix* (n 73) [44] (Mance LJ).

[130] R Cunnington, 'The Inadequacy of Damages as a Remedy for Breach of Contract' in CEF Rickett (ed), *Justifying Private Law Remedies* (Oxford, Hart Publishing, 2008) 114, 119, 131–32.

[131] *Beswick* (n 83). See also *Coulls v Bagot's Executor and Trustee Co Ltd* (1967) 119 CLR 460 (HCA).

[132] See now Contracts (Rights of Third Parties) Act 1999 (UK) enacted partly to solve this problem.

[133] *Beswick* (n 83) 73.

[134] ibid 102.

[135] For suggestions that Mr Beswick's estate should have been able to obtain substantial damages for loss, see B Coote, 'Contract Damages, *Ruxley*, and the Performance Interest' (1997) 56 *CLJ* 537, 547. See also E McKendrick, 'The Common Law at Work: The Saga of *Alfred McAlpine Construction Ltd v Panatown Ltd* (2003) 3 *Oxford University Commonwealth Law Journal* 145, 164–66.

contract which was intended to provide peace of mind provided the very opposite. The contract was intended to reinforce familial bonds of trust. The nephew had received his benefit under the contract, and thus in order to achieve the objectives which Mr Beswick had intended to achieve through the contract, the court was prepared to specifically enforce the agreement, even though the wife was a third party to the contract.

Extrapolating from *Beswick*, Cunnington has argued that courts will be prepared to find that damages are inadequate when 'only nominal damages are available'.[136] But this nomenclature provides a misleading impression; it may seem to suggest that specific relief and disgorgement damages are available in *all* cases where only nominal damages are available. Campbell and Wylie have cogently argued that using the availability of nominal damages as a criterion for an award of disgorgement damages provides unworkable results.[137] The important question is not whether nominal damages are available, but: *if* the only damages which are available are nominal damages, are such damages adequate to put the claimant in a position as if the contract had been performed? In some circumstances nominal damages are entirely appropriate. However, in other cases nominal damages are not adequate – and these cases, like *Beswick*, tend to be cases where the bargain is designed to serve interests other than profit-making, or cases where there is some kind of public interest in seeing the contract performed.

No cases involving familial relations and disgorgement damages have yet arisen. However, *Beswick* indicates that courts may hold damages are inadequate where there is an attempt to buttress familial obligations with contractual obligations. In *Beswick*, specific relief was still available. Suppose Mr Beswick's nephew had an obligation to pay Mr Beswick's widow an annuity from shares invested by him. Instead, he took the shares and made a profit by his breach. It is suggested that on these facts a court would award an injunction to restrain any further breach, but that the nephew would also be asked to disgorge any profits he had made by breaching the contract. And, as with the other categories of case, the contract between uncle and nephew would include implied obligations imposed on the nephew not to prefer his financial interests to the obligations owed under the contract to the widow, and not to make an unauthorised profit from the contract. Also, because of the familial context of the agreement, an obligation of good faith would be implied into the contract.

v Other Contracts Involving the Public Interest

Many of these cases involve not only the interests of the parties, but also the interests of the broader public. *Blake* and *Snepp* involve the public interest because they impinge upon matters of national security. The contract in *Gilbert* was another contract intended to benefit the public rather than the contracting par-

[136] Cunnington (n 130) 130–32.
[137] Campbell and Wylie (n 124) 615–16.

ties.[138] In these kinds of cases, disgorgement damages will be the best or only way to deter promisors from breaching their contracts because the public may not have standing to sue. Similarly in *Niad*, it could be argued that the contract had a public benefit aspect in that it was designed to result in more competitive fuel prices for consumers. However, this should not be overstated; presumably it was also in Esso's interest to reduce prices so as to force smaller operators out of the market.

The cases of 'skimped performance', which involve contracts designed to avoid risk, could also be said to be fall within the public interest head.[139] These will be discussed in detail in chapter six. Similarly, consumer contracts may involve public policy considerations because such contracts are entered into with a view to having certain services performed rather than with a view to making profit.[140]

V Conclusion

The negative covenant cases present an agency problem – there is no adequate incentive for a promisor to keep his bargain to the promisee. Compensatory damages will typically be inadequate to recognise the performance interest, particularly where contracts involve non-financial interests. Ordinarily, too, specific relief is impossible because the obligation has already been breached. Because of the broad kinship with the fiduciary cases, it is appropriate that disgorgement damages be awarded in these cases. The damages have a deterrent object: the promisor makes the decision about whether to breach or not in the knowledge that the financial benefits derived from the breach may be stripped from him. Thus, there is an incentive for the promisor to negotiate with the promisee for release from the covenant rather than breach the covenant, rendering it impossible for the promisee gain specific relief.

[138] Eisenberg (n 8) 592.

[139] *City of New Orleans v Firemen's Charitable Association*, 9 So 486 (Lou SC, 1891) (SC) and possibly *Teacher v Calder* [1899] UKHL 1, [1899] AC 451 (HL).

[140] McKendrick (n 135) 167–68. See also D Campbell and D Harris, 'In Defence of Breach: A Critique of Restitution and the Performance Interest' (2002) 22 *Journal of Legal Studies* 208, 232, who concede that consumer contracts for complex services may require an assurance of complete performance.

6

The Role of 'Restitutionary Damages'

I Introduction

'Restitutionary damages' do not have a settled definition. At the least, they are said to encompass instances of subtractive unjust enrichment, and at the highest, they are said to encompass all forms of gain-based award. I suggest that 'restitutionary damages' for breach of contract should be subsumed into the category of disgorgement damages, because under my analysis, they are simply a mechanism for achieving partial disgorgement of gain. Rather than distinguishing between restitutionary damages and disgorgement damages for breach of contract, I argue that the scale of disgorgement ranges from a proportion of the profit at the lower end to disgorgement of full profit at the upper end. Typically courts assess the proportion of profit at the lower end of the scale by using the 'reasonable fee' measure, representing the amount which the claimant would have accepted for release from the contractual term. This is no more than a convenient fiction by which to assess the appropriate level of partial disgorgement.

The court's choice between partial disgorgement at the lower end of the scale (ie a 'reasonable fee' representing a proportion of the profit) and full disgorgement (ie the entire profit) depends upon the reason why the specific relief was no longer available. There are two possibilities:

1. The court 'will not' order specific relief (eg because of delay on the part of the claimant, hardship to the defendant or broader public policy considerations).
2. The court 'cannot' order specific relief (eg impossibility or the need for constant supervision).[1]

In the second circumstance, the defendant has put specific performance out of the claimant's reach by his conduct. Accordingly, it is appropriate that the defendant disgorge all or most of his profits because of the enhanced need for deterrence in such a situation. By contrast, in the first category specific relief is still available but the court has chosen not to award it for discretionary reasons. Thus, the defendant need only disgorge a 'reasonable fee' because the deterrent and punitive considerations are not as strong. And there are also reasons to deter

[1] R Cunnington, 'The Measure and Availability of Gain-Based Damages for Breach of Contract' in D Saidov and R Cunnington (eds), *Contract Damages: Domestic and International Perspectives* (Oxford, Hart Publishing, 2008) 207, 236.

claimants from excessive and inexcusable delays by reducing the award to a reasonable fee.

The position of damages for 'skimped performance' must also be considered. 'Skimped performance' involves a contract where the defendant saves an expense by not delivering full performance. There is an overlap between some 'reasonable fee' cases and skimped performance, in that the defendant could be said to have saved himself the expense of paying a fee to the claimant for release from his obligation, and the award of a 'reasonable fee' might reflect this. The Court of Appeal in *Blake* considered that skimped performance was a situation in which a court should award 'restitutionary damages', because such an award would be 'simpler and more open'.[2]

Instead I will argue that in most cases of skimped performance, it will *not* be simpler or indeed necessary to award disgorgement damages, or 'restitutionary damages' for that matter.[3] In many cases, damages will still be adequate to put the claimant in the position she would have been in if the contract had been performed, and thus this is the 'next best' remedy in the circumstances. The primary question in these cases is how the damages should be measured: according to the decrease in value or according to cost of rectification.[4] In rare cases, it may be necessary to award disgorgement damages for skimped performance where damages are inadequate and performance is impossible. The main example of this is the case of a contract designed to avoid risk where the defendant skimped on performance and no harm occurred, but the claimant was exposed to risk as a result.

At the outset, however, I will analyse the concept of 'restitutionary damages'.

II What are 'Restitutionary Damages'?

'Restitutionary damages' do not have a settled definition. It was for this reason that Lord Nicholls preferred not to use the term in his judgment in *Blake*, calling it an 'unhappy expression'.[5]

The confusion stems in part from the two mutually exclusive meanings of the word 'restitution'. Restitution may mean a 'giving back' of a benefit unjustly received, but it may also be a 'giving up' of a benefit made at the expense of a claimant, because a wrong has been committed against her.[6] Commentators began to suggest that defendants who profited from their breach of contract

[2] *Attorney-General v Blake* [1997] EWCA Civ 3008, [1998] Ch 439 (CA) 458 (Lord Woolf).

[3] See also J O'Sullivan, 'Reflections on the Role of Restitutionary Damages to Protect Contractual Expectations' in D Johnston and R Zimmermann (eds), *Unjustified Enrichment: Key Issues in Comparative Perspective* (Cambridge, Cambridge University Press, 2002) 327, 337–42.

[4] See A Loke, 'Cost of Cure or Difference in Market Value? Toward a Sound Choice in the Basis for Quantifying Expectation Damages' (1996) 10 *Journal of Contract Law* 189 for an excellent summation of the issues.

[5] *Attorney-General v Blake* [2000] UKHL 45, [2001] 1 AC 268 (HL) 284.

[6] P Birks, *An Introduction to the Law of Restitution*, 2nd edn (Oxford, Clarendon Press, 1989) 12.

should disgorge their gains, and called such damages 'restitutionary damages' in the second sense of the term above.[7] However, restitutionary damages for breach of contract may also encompass other forms of remedy. This has caused difficulties for courts.

Section 344 of the US *Restatement (Second) of Contracts* provides a prime example of the confusion that is produced by a non-specific use of the word 'restitution'. It states that contract law remedies have the purpose, among other things, of protecting a claimant's '"restitution interest," which is his interest in having restored to him any benefit that he has conferred on the other party'. Professor Kull has argued that in the *Restatement (First) of Contracts*, the restitution interest was intended to restore parties to the status quo because there was no 'reliance interest'.[8] By contrast, in the *Second Restatement* the comments on the section say that the court may 'grant relief to prevent unjust enrichment.' The examples cited in the comments suggest that in the United States, 'restitutionary damages' are intended to cover subtractive unjust enrichment or a 'giving back' of a benefit which has been conferred on the defendant by the contract and which it would be unjust for the defendant to retain. However, as Kull explains, because of the ambiguity of the word 'restitution' the section has also been used to justify a 'giving up' of a gain (ie disgorgement damages for wrongs).[9]

Scholars have also tried to fit the 'reasonable fee' cases into a subtractive unjust enrichment analysis. Beatson argues that restitutionary damages are awarded in cases involving unauthorised sale or use of property because there has been a substraction from the claimant's *dominium* or his right to exclusive enjoyment of the property.[10] The damages in these cases, whether awarded in contract or tort, are said to be restitutionary. Taking Beatson's analysis a step further, Edelman has distinguished between restitutionary damages (an award based on unjust enrichment) and disgorgement damages (an award based on 'giving up' of a gain).[11] He

[7] See, eg D Friedmann, 'Restitution of Benefits Obtained Through the Appropriation of Property or the Commission of a Wrong' (1980) 80 *Columbia Law Review* 504, 515; G Jones, 'The Recovery of Benefits Gained from a Breach of Contract' (1983) 99 *LQR* 443; P Birks, 'Restitutionary Damages for Breach of Contract: *Snepp* and the Fusion of Law and Equity' [1987] *Lloyd's Maritime and Commercial Law Quarterly* 421.

[8] A Kull, 'Disgorgement for Breach, the "Restitution Interest" and the Restatement of Contracts' (2001) 79 *Texas Law Review* 2021, 2029. The new *Restatement* drafted by Kull includes a disgorgement remedy for 'opportunistic' breach of contract: American Law Institute, *Restatement (Third) of Restitution and Unjust Enrichment* (2011) § 39.

[9] See, eg *Earthinfo Inc v Hydrosphere Resource Consultants Inc* 900 P2d 113 (Colo SC, 1995).

[10] J Beatson, 'The Nature of Waver of Tort' in J Beatson (ed), *The Use and Abuse of Unjust Enrichment* (Oxford, Clarendon Press, 1991) 232. *cf* Professor McInnes who has argued that 'reasonable fee damages' are compensatory, providing compensation for the lost right of *dominium*: M McInnes, 'Account of Profits for Common Law Wrongs' in S Degeling and J Edelman (eds), *Equity in Commercial Law* (NSW, Lawbook Co, 2004) 416–18; M McInnes, 'Gain, Loss and the User Principle' (2006) 14 *Restitution Law Review* 76, 84–86. See also F Giglio, *The Foundations of Restitution for Wrongs* (Oxford, Hart Publishing, 2007).

[11] J Edelman, 'Gain-based Remedies for Wrongdoing' (2000) 74 *Australian Law Journal* 231; J Edelman, 'Restitutionary Damages and Disgorgement Damages for Breach of Contract' [2000] *Restitution Law Review* 129; J Edelman, *Gain-Based Damages – Contract, Tort, Equity and Intellectual Property* (Oxford, Hart Publishing, 2002) 65–78.

argues that restitutionary damages give back to the claimant an illegitimate transfer of value as a result of the defendant's wrong, as measured by the objective receipt by the defendant. The cases where the claimant is awarded a 'reasonable fee' are said to be instances of restitutionary damages under this formulation: the reasonable fee represents the use value of a property or quasi-property right.[12] By contrast, disgorgement damages are said to be damages which strip a defendant of a profit made at the claimant's expense. This is not measured by what has been transferred (indeed, there need be nothing transferred from the claimant at all) but is purely measured by the subjective value of the gain to the defendant.[13] Edelman sees awards of restitutionary damages and disgorgement damages as available throughout tort, equity, intellectual property and contract.

Thus far in this book, I have concentrated on disgorgement damages. The premise of disgorgement damages is clear enough. The claimant identifies a subjective actual profit made by the defendant as a result of the breach of contract, and the defendant must disgorge it to the claimant. The essence of disgorgement is deterrence.[14]

'Restitutionary damages' are more difficult. Edelman argues that the defendant has been unjustly enriched when he has appropriated the claimant's rights, property or money, and that this unjust enrichment must be reversed. He uses the example of a tenant wrongfully remaining on the landlord's land, committing trespass as a result.[15] He explains:

> Value, in the form of the use of the landlord's premises, has been transferred to the trespassing tenant. Restitutionary damages could be sought by the landlord to reverse that wrongful transfer of value, measured in the form of the fair market value for the wrongful use of the land gained by the defendant during the appropriate period.[16]

According to Edelman, this does not mean that the claimant must have suffered a financial loss to match the 'transfer of value'. In the landlord case, there is a subtraction from the claimant's *dominium* rather than from his financial wealth. He goes on to say:

> It might be objected that where the transfer is of the *use* of money or the *use* of property there is only a transfer from the claimant in the metaphysical sense that the defendant has utilised the valuable opportunity inherent in the claimant's asset. But the word 'transfer' is still used . . . as it directs attention to the fact that the objective value received by the defendant must come *from* the claimant.[17]

[12] See also S Worthington, 'Reconsidering Disgorgement for Wrongs' (1999) 62 *MLR* 218, 219–35. Worthington has argued that subtractive unjust enrichment is the *only* appropriate explanation for cases which involve a defendant's unauthorised use of the plaintiff's property.

[13] See above (n 11).

[14] Edelman, *Gain Based Damages* (n 11) 83–86; J Edelman, 'Gain-Based Damages and Compensation' in A Burrows and Lord Rodger of Earlsferry (eds), *Mapping the Law – Essays in Honour of Peter Birks* (Oxford, Oxford University Press, 2006) 141, 149.

[15] Edelman, *Gain Based Damages* (n 11) 67. See *Swordheath Properties Ltd v Tabet* [1979] 1 WLR 285 (CA), cited by Edelman.

[16] ibid.

[17] ibid.

Edelman argues that, in contrast to disgorgement damages, the goal of 'restitutionary damages' is not deterrence, but Aristotelian corrective justice (ie restoring something belonging to the claimant to her).[18] He groups a large number of disparate awards under the umbrella of 'restitutionary damages'.

By contrast, in this book, I will concentrate on the cases involving breach of contract. It has been noted that Edelman's thesis is particularly difficult to reconcile with the law on restitution for breach of contract.[19]

It should also be observed that it is difficult to separate out breach of contract cases definitively from cases involving other private law wrongs. In many of these cases there may also be a tort or an infringement of intellectual property rights concurrent with the breach of contract.[20] Further, it is important to consider some of the wayleave cases, mesne profit cases and damages under *Lord Cairns' Act* because these cases formed an essential plank of Lord Nicholls' reasoning in *Blake*.[21] Lord Nicholls drew from a variety of areas in common law and equity to show that gain-based damages (of one sort or another) had long been awarded in many areas of private law, and that there was no reason not to extend this into contract law. Nonetheless, the cases in tort and contract should not be elided: the two forms of action give rise to different considerations.[22] Central to contract is the idea that the claimant has an interest in performance as a result of a voluntary obligation entered into by the parties. By contrast, in tort law the courts impose obligations absent a voluntary undertaking. Compensation in contract law is different to compensation in tort. Indeed, some have argued that 'expectation damages' for breach of contract are not really compensatory at all because, at least in some circumstances, the focus is on restoring the claimant to the position she would have been in if the contract had been performed, not on recompensing loss.[23]

In any case, it is suggested in the next section that the distinction between disgorgement damages and restitutionary damages is unsustainable.

[18] ibid 80; Edelman, 'Gain-Based Damages and Compensation' (n 14) 150.

[19] A Burrows, *The Law of Restitution*, 2nd edn (Oxford, Oxford University Press, 2002) 462.

[20] See, eg *Penarth Dock Engineering Co Ltd v Pounds* [1963] 1 Lloyd's Rep 359 (trepass); *Pell Frischmann Engineering v Bow Valley Iran Limited* [2009] UKPC 45; *Vercoe v Rutland Fund Management Limited* [2010] EWHC 424 (Ch) (breach of confidence).

[21] *Blake* (n 5) 278–81 (citing, inter alia: *Whitwham v Westminster Brymbo Coal and Coke Co* [1896] 2 Ch 538 (CA); *Martin v Porter* (1839) 5 M & W 351, 151 ER 149; *Jegon v Vivian* (1871) LR 6 Ch App 742 (CA); *Penarth Dock* (n 20); *Strand Electric and Engineering Co Ltd v Brisford Entertainments Ltd* [1952] 2 QB 246 (QB); *The Mediana* [1900] AC 113 (HL); *Watson, Laidlaw & Co v Pott, Cassels and Williamson* (1914) 31 RPC 104 (HL); *Ministry of Defence v Ashman* [1993] 2 EGLR 102 (CA); *Ministry of Defence v Thompson* [1993] 2 EGLR 107 (CA); *Hogg v Kirby* (1803) 8 Ves Jun 215, 32 ER 336; *Lever v Goodwin* (1887) 36 ChD 1 (CA); *United Australia Ltd v Barclays Bank Ltd* [1941] AC 1 (HL); *Lamine v Dorrell* (1790) 2 Ld Raym 1216, 92 ER 303; *Johnson v Agnew* [1980] AC 367 (HL); *Bracewell v Appleby* [1975] Ch 408 (ChD); *Jaggard v Sawyer* [1994] EWCA Civ 1, [1995] 1 WLR 268 (CA).

[22] B Coote, 'Contract Damages, *Ruxley*, and the Performance Interest' (1997) 56 *CLJ* 537, 545.

[23] MA Eisenberg, 'Actual and Virtual Specific Performance, the Theory of Efficient Breach, and the Indifference Principle in Contract Law' (2005) 93 *California Law Review* 975, 979; S Smith, 'Substitutionary Damages' in CEF Rickett (ed), *Justifying Private Law Remedies* (Oxford, Hart Publishing, 2008) 93, 96–97.

III Restitutionary Damages – Still Unhappy

While Edelman's distinction between disgorgement damages and restitutionary damages is beguiling, it should be rejected. The primary reason is that it is very difficult to identify the transfer of value from claimant to defendant in many cases, and this renders the analysis problematic for litigants, lawyers and judges to apply. One only need witness the confusion of cases following *Blake* described in the previous chapter to see how problematic the distinction may be. As Edelman has correctly intuited, my criticism is essentially that the notions contained in his analysis are too metaphysical. First, there is often no transfer of value in any concrete sense and, secondly, in many cases the benefit is not really *taken* from the claimant. It is for these reasons that the analysis has been described as 'fundamentally misconceived', as it 'elides an important analytical distinction between subtractive transfers or "takings" and non-appropriative interferences with rights.'[24] Secondly, different obligations give rise to rights of different strengths, and the restitutionary damages analysis risks obscuring the difference between them.

There are numerous 'reasonable fee' cases which involve no subtraction or transfer from the claimant, including breaches of restrictive covenant, breaches of intellectual property rights and breaches of contract. All these cases concerned intangible rather than tangible property, and in these cases it is particularly difficult to argue that the defendant has appropriated anything from the claimant. Taking *Wrotham Park* as an example, the servient tenement holder made more extensive use of its own property than was permitted, but it is hard to say that anything is actually *transferred* from the owner of the dominant tenement. In fact, the defendant obtained a benefit which the claimant could never have had; the covenant merely entitled the claimant to deny the benefit in question to the defendant.[25] Rotherham argues:

> One problem with the analysis that interferences with rights amount to subtractions from the right holder's dominium is that it proves too much: it is true whether or not the defendant really obtains a benefit from the wrong in question. . . . Such an analysis would miss the rather obvious point that the mere fact that an owner's rights are breached does not mean that the defendant has obtained a benefit in the process.[26]

In those 'reasonable fee' cases where the defendant acquires possession of the claimant's property, it is also difficult to see how value is transferred from the claimant to the defendant. Beatson has argued that the defendant acquires the claimant's right to exclusive enjoyment of her property.[27] However, this cannot be

[24] C Rotherham, 'The Conceptual Structure of Restitution for Wrongs' (2007) 66 *CLJ* 172, 173. See also C Rotherham, '"*Wrotham Park* damages" and accounts of profits: compensation or restitution' [2008] *Lloyd's Maritime and Commercial Law Quarterly* 25.

[25] Rotherham, 'The Conceptual Structure of Restitution for Wrongs' (n 24) 177.

[26] ibid 180–81.

[27] Beatson (n 10) 232.

correct because the claimant continues to have a right to exclusive enjoyment, and it is this very right which allows her to sue.

By contrast, Edelman argues that the defendant acquires 'value' from the claimant by infringing her proprietary rights, in that the defendant utilises the valuable opportunity inherent in the claimant's asset. However, this does not stand up on close analysis. First, it is difficult to see where there is a transfer from the claimant to the defendant if the defendant receives something which is apparently different from the thing owned by the claimant in the first place. In the case of a contract, the right to performance has not been 'gained' by the defendant, and it remains vested in the plaintiff.[28] Secondly, Edelman's account of restitutionary damages is founded on the idea that the claimant need not suffer any concrete loss, so it is not obvious that something has been transferred from the claimant to the defendant.

In cases where a defendant makes use of the claimant's property, there may well be a subtraction from the claimant's proprietary rights. However, the defendant simply obtains possession and use of the claimant's property, and it is difficult to see how this is a transfer in value from claimant to defendant.[29]

Rotherham has identified at least three ways in which a defendant could derive value by infringing the claimant's rights:

1. A defendant may be 'negatively enriched' by saving the expense that would be incurred in paying a reasonable fee for the relaxation of the right infringed;
2. A defendant might sell an asset belonging to the claimant without authorisation, thereby realising its exchange value; and
3. A defendant might exploit an asset belonging to the claimant in a way which generates revenue.[30]

There are difficulties in analysing any of these situations involving an exchange of value from the claimant to the defendant. In the second and third situations, the defendant receives value, but that value is not derived from the claimant; rather it is derived from a third party or parties.[31] In any case, the second and third situations are more likely to arise in relation to proprietary torts than in breach of contract cases.

The distinction between 'restitutionary damages' and disgorgement damages is ultimately unworkable because it does not distinguish between different types of rights adequately, but assumes all interests are equally important and should be protected in the same way. A particular focus of this book is the way in which the rights arising from contract are different to rights arising from torts or property. There is a danger if scholars lump together all 'wrongs' and apply an over-arching analysis. This will unintentionally eliminate important distinctions and ignore differences between juridical rights. The specific aim of contract law is to protect

[28] R Stevens, 'Damages and the Right to Performance: A *Golden Victory* or Not?' in J Neyers, R Bronagh and S Pitel (eds), *Exploring Contract Law* (Oxford, Hart Publishing, 2009) 171, 193.

[29] Rotherham, 'The Conceptual Structure of Restitution for Wrongs' (n 24) 182.

[30] ibid 183.

[31] ibid.

the claimant's interest in performance, and thus breach of contract should not be elided with breach of tortious obligations: they do not share precisely the same aims, although some of the aims overlap.

A taxonomical criticism of Edelman's analysis has been made by Professor Burrows who has noted that for every case of restitutionary damages for a wrong there also appears to be a case of subtractive unjust enrichment. This raises the question of the significance of the wrong to the relief. He notes, '[i]n contrast, the wrong is normatively crucial if the claimant seeks compensation or a gain-based measure that goes beyond compensation (or beyond reversing a transfer of value).'[32] Therefore, it may even render the wrongs analysis otiose.

My fundamental difficulty with Edelman's account is that it does not provide a set of criteria which indicate *when* a defendant has appropriated value from the claimant. It is hard to see how a court would apply his analysis in practice. Let us take, for example, the case of *Experience Hendrix LLC v PPX Enterprises Inc*,[33] and apply his analysis to it. Using Edelman's schema, there are two ways in which it could be analysed: first as a case of disgorgement damages for breach of contract, and secondly as a case where 'restitutionary damages' are available because there has been a 'transfer of value' from the claimant to the defendant. Analysing the case as one of full disgorgement damages is relatively easy. One looks at the actual profits made by PPX which it made as a result of breaching its agreement with Experience Hendrix not to publish certain songs, and one strips PPX of the profits attributable to the release of those songs.

How then would we analyse the case as one of restitutionary damages? It could perhaps be argued that there was a transfer of value from Experience Hendrix to PPX when PPX sold the rights to the songs to third parties in breach of its contract with Experience Hendrix. Using Edelman's analysis, we might say that Experience Hendrix had the right to control the use of those songs (much as a landlord has a right to control the use of his property when a tenant wrongfully occupies it) and by letting another use the songs, PPX has transferred value from Experience Hendrix. However, PPX did not really receive value from Experience Hendrix; rather it received value from the third parties to whom it sold the recordings in breach of contract cases. There was never really any transfer. Moreover, Edelman would see that PPX utilised the valuable opportunity inherent in Experience Hendrix's property; but Experience Hendrix never wanted to exploit that opportunity – its concern was rather to protect the quality of released recordings.[34] The analysis looks rather forced and seems to rely on a very diffuse and imprecise notion of 'transfer' and 'value' which is unworkable in practice. In addition, a reasonable fee award could be regarded as an 'expense saved', which looks more like a disgorgement analysis than a restitutionary analysis. There is then a question of whether we choose a 'restitutionary damages' analysis or a

[32] Burrows (n 19) 461.

[33] *Experience Hendrix LLC v PPX Enterprises Inc* [2003] EWCA Civ 1804, [2003] 1 All ER (Comm) 830 (Mance LJ, Hooper J and Peter Gibson LJ).

[34] See criticisms of 'lost opportunity to bargain' analysis in ch 2 II A.

disgorgement damages analysis. Given that the case can at least notionally be analysed as both, it is not clear which analysis should be preferred in the circumstances. Clearly the courts have had difficulties in establishing which analysis should be preferred.

Many of the problems which beset a restitutionary damages analysis fall away in the context of breach of contract if we see the 'reasonable fee' cases as instances of partial disgorgement. I will suggest in the next section that we ought to 'collapse the categories' of disgorgement damages and restitutionary damages into a single category of disgorgement damages designed to strip profit, albeit to a lesser or a greater degree.[35] I do not seek to resolve the more fiercely debated controversy concerning the award of restitutionary damages for proprietary torts, as that is beyond the scope of this book. Nonetheless, I argue that my analysis is to be preferred in the context of contract law because, by the end of this book, it should be clear to lawyers, academics and litigants when and why a court may choose a 'full disgorgement' analysis over a 'partial disgorgement' analysis in some circumstances, and there is no need to resort to metaphysical 'transfers' or diffuse concepts of 'loss' and 'gain'. Thus my theory is coherent and practical.

IV A Collapsing of Categories

Lord Nicholls himself seems to have envisaged the 'reasonable fee' and account of profits cases as being varieties of the same remedy for breach of contract. In *Blake* he said:

> In a suitable case damages for breach of contract may be measured by the benefit gained by the wrongdoer from the breach. The defendant must make a reasonable payment in respect of the benefit he has gained.[36]

Lord Nicholls has since confirmed in extra-judicial comments[37] that he envisaged a continuum of profits being stripped. Other commentators have also analysed the cases in this way.[38] Certainly, in the cases under *Lord Cairns' Act* upon which Lord Nicholls relied in *Blake*, the damages represent a form of monetised specific

[35] Against J Edelman, 'Gain-Based Damages and Compensation' in A Burrows and Lord Rodger of Earlsferry (eds), *Mapping the Law – Essays in Memory of Peter Birks* (Oxford, Oxford University Press, 2006) 141, 152.

[36] *Blake* (n 5) 283–84.

[37] A Burrows, 'Are "Damages on the *Wrotham Park* Basis" Compensatory, Restitutionary or Neither?' in D Saidov and R Cunnington (eds), *Contract Damages: Domestic and International Perspectives* (Oxford, Hart Publishing, 2008) 165, 178; E McKendrick, 'Breach of Contract, Restitution for Wrongs and Punishment' in A Burrows and E Peel (eds), *Commercial Remedies – Current Issues and Problems* (Oxford, Oxford University Press, 2003) 129.

[38] M Graham, 'Restitutionary Damages: The Anvil Struck' (2004) 120 *LQR* 26, 28; D Campbell and P Wylie, 'Ain't No Telling (Which Circumstances Are Exceptional)' (2003) 62 *CLJ* 605, 605–06; Rotherham, 'The Conceptual Structure of Restitution for Wrongs' (n 24) 188.

relief, awarded on principles previously discussed in the chapters on disgorgement damages.[39]

It is simpler and cleaner to reduce the two categories of award to one category of disgorgement damages, encompassing partial to full disgorgement. A sharp-line distinction between restitutionary damages and disgorgement damages is very difficult to make in practice, as Burrows has argued:

> While one admires James Edelman's sophisticated attempt to draw a principled distinction between restitutionary damages on the one hand and disgorgement damages on the other, it seems more accurate to accept that, putting to one side an account of profits, both negative and positive gains can be, and are, removed by an award of restitutionary damages. The measure of restitutionary damages may therefore be the 'expense saved' by the wrong or, more commonly, a 'fair proportion of profits made' by the wrong, taking into account a number of discretionary factors.[40]

By contrast, a division between partial and full disgorgement better accommodates the 'expense saved' cases.

An account of profits is at the top of the scale (maximum profit), but if the account of profits is reduced by an allowance for skill and effort[41] then it will only represent a certain proportion of the profit (albeit probably a higher proportion than a 'reasonable fee'). The 'reasonable fee' cases are generally lower in amount than the full account of profit but, depending upon what kind of a 'reasonable fee' the court thinks is appropriate, they may edge up towards the quantum of an account of profits reduced by an allowance. Indeed, the American *Restatement of Restitution and Unjust Enrichment* sees the market value of a benefit as the lower limit of restitution available, saying at § 51(2):

> The value for restitution purposes of benefits obtained by the misconduct of the defendant, culpable or otherwise, is not less than their market value. Market value may be identified, where appropriate, with the reasonable cost of a licence.[42]

This is contrasted with what is effectively 'full disgorgement' in § 51(4).[43]

To add further complexity, there is an overlap between cases of 'skimped performance' (where damages are assessed according to the expense saved) and the 'reasonable fee' measure in some cases. The two are often one and the same because the failure to pay a licence fee is a notional expense which the defendant has saved. For example, both *Strand Electric*[44] and *Penarth Dock*[45] can be seen as cases where the 'reasonable fee' award also reflects the defendant's saving in failing to pay a licence fee. *Strand Electric* was not a contract case, and the reasonable

[39] *Johnson* (n 21); *Bracewell* (n 21); *Jaggard* (n 21); *Wrotham Park Estate Co Ltd v Parkside Homes Ltd* [1974] 1 WLR 798 (Ch).

[40] Burrows (n 37) 176–77. See also Burrows (n 19) 461–62; A Burrows, *Remedies for Torts and Breach of Contract*, 3rd edn (Oxford, Oxford University Press, 2004) 405.

[41] The criteria for the award of an allowance for skill and effort will be discussed in ch 7.

[42] American Law Institute (n 8) § 51(2); see also comment d to that section.

[43] ibid § 51(4).

[44] *Strand Electric* (n 21).

[45] *Penarth Dock* (n 20).

fee in that case was awarded for the tort of detinue, but *Penarth Dock* concerned concurrent contractual and tortious liability. In *Penarth Dock*, the defendant bought a pontoon from the claimant dock company. The written contract between the parties provided that '[a]lthough it [was] desirous to remove the Pontoon as speedily as possible, no time limit [was] to be imposed.' However, express oral terms provided that the pontoon was to be removed within three months at the latest. Both parties knew the dock was to be closed and that this was why the claimant wanted the pontoon to be removed as speedily as possible. Notwithstanding this, the defendant did not remove the pontoon, despite requests from the claimant. The claimants alleged that the defendant became a trespasser on the docks once he had failed to remove the pontoon within three months and should pay a 'reasonable fee' representing what he would have had to pay to have the pontoon stored.[46] Although *Penarth Dock* has generally been analysed as a case where a reasonable fee was awarded because the defendant had committed the tort of trespass, the court also found a breach of contract (including a breach of the collateral oral term). Thus, it could equally well be analysed as a case where a reasonable fee was awarded because the defendant breached his contract, and the 'reasonable fee' represented the amount he would have had to pay to have the pontoon stored at the dock (ie an 'expense saved' award).[47]

The Canadian case of *Arbutus Park Estates v Fuller*[48] is another which could be analysed as either a 'reasonable fee' case or an 'expense saved' case. The defendant breached a restrictive covenant in favour of the claimant which prohibited the building of a 'detached garage' until the plans and specifications were approved by the claimant. The court refused to award an injunction, but the claimant was allowed to recover 'reasonable fee' damages, calculated according to the amount which the defendant had saved by failing to hire an architect to prepare the required plans.

It is difficult to fit cases like *Penarth Dock* or *Arbutus Park* into the prism of subtractive unjust enrichment, particularly if one chooses to analyse them as a case of an 'expense saved' under a contract. Expenses saved do not fit into a subtractive unjust enrichment analysis. Instead, they fit better into a disgorgement analysis because there has been an 'effective profit', a saving of costs which would otherwise have been incurred, and these represent the 'flip side' or the 'mirror' of profits earned by breach.[49] Consequently, it has been argued that expenses saved should be treated as a relevant gain for the purpose of the operation of gain-based relief.[50]

[46] Following *Strand Electric* (n 21) and *Whitwham* (n 21).

[47] Against D Campbell and D Harris, 'In Defence of Breach: A Critique of Restitution and the Performance Interest' (2002) 22 *Legal Studies* 208, 224–25, who argue the case cannot be analysed on a contractual basis.

[48] *Arbutus Park Estates v Fuller* (1976) DLR (3d) 257 (BCSC).

[49] S Thel and P Siegelman, 'You Do Have to Keep Your Promises: A Disgorgement Theory of Contract Remedies' (2011) 52 *William and Mary Law Review* 1181, 1216; Edelman, *Gain-Based Damages* (n 11) 74.

[50] *Blake* (n 2) 458; G Virgo, 'Restitutionary Remedies for Wrongs: Causation and Remoteness' in CEF Rickett (ed), *Justifying Private Law Remedies* (Oxford, Hart Publishing, 2008) 301, 302–03; American Law Institute (n 8) § 39 (3).

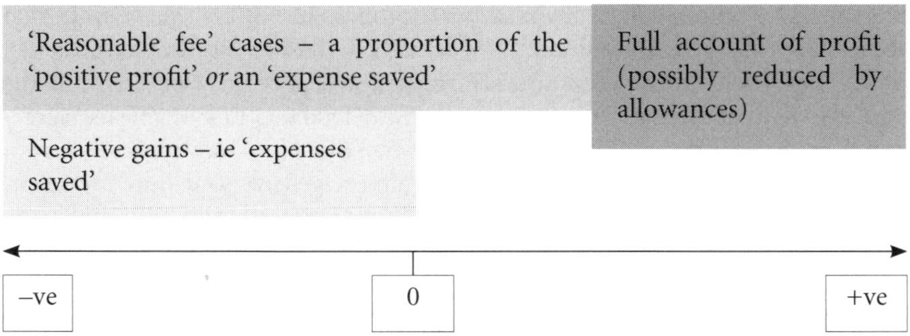

Full disgorgement strips the defendant of the actual gain, whereas partial disgorgement of a reasonable fee or an 'expense saved' only strips the defendant of a proportion of his profit, limited to a reasonable fee or market value of relaxation of the right.[51] As Rotherham notes:

> Much has been made of the distinction between two approaches to determining relief for restitution for wrongs: the award of a reasonable sum for the relaxation of the right in question and the account of profits. The suggestion is sometimes made that two such different remedies must reflect entirely different substantive rights. This is somewhat overstated. Both are measures of relief for enrichment by wrongs. Where the right breached has a market value, a choice has to be made between the remedies. The market value for relaxation of the right in question represents the immediate benefit made from the breach and reflects an objective or abstract measure. In contrast, profits subsequently made from exploiting the claimant's property are less directly connected to the breach and, as the defendant's actual gain, represent a more subjective measure.[52]

Expanding on this point, full disgorgement reflects the actual full gain made, and the 'reasonable fee cases' reflect a proportion of the gain (that is to say, the market price of gaining a release from the contract).[53] Compelling a defendant to disgorge his actual profit ordinarily has a greater deterrent power than awarding a lesser 'reasonable fee'.

Cunnington has argued that 'reasonable fee' awards cannot be the same as an account of profit because the former deals with *anticipated profit* whereas the latter deals with *actual profit*.[54] According to Cunnington, the defendant's actual profit is only used as a yardstick for what the anticipated profit would have been if

[51] Full disgorgement includes disgorgement of gain subject to an allowance which will be discussed in ch 7. My notion of 'full disgorgement' is equivalent to what some commentators have termed 'subjective gain' (ie disgorgement of actual gain) as opposed to 'objective gain' (ie disgorgement of a reasonable fee). See, eg D Friedmann, 'Restitution for Wrongs: The Measure of Recovery' (2001) 79 *Texas Law Review* 1879, 1880–83; R Cunnington, 'The Assessment of Gain-Based Damages for Breach of Contract' (2008) 71 *MLR* 559, 563, 573. I have avoided the subjective/objective terminology because of possible ambiguity and confusion.

[52] Rotherham, 'The Conceptual Structure of Restitution for Wrongs' (n 24) 188.

[53] Friedmann (n 51) 1880–83.

[54] Cunnington (n 51) 573. Supported by the analysis in *Lunn Poly Ltd v Liverpool & Lancashire Properties Ltd* [2006] EWCA Civ 430, [2006] 2 EGLR 29 (CA); *Pell Frischmann* (n 20).

the parties had entered into a hypothetical negotiation.[55] By contrast, I argue that the actual profit is highly relevant to the remedy in these cases.[56] In fact, an actual profit *must* be identified. The courts are imposing a licence fee ex post facto on the parties in light of the actual profits made by the defendant. 'Reasonable fee' agreements are frequently made between parties when one party wants to make use of another's valuable resource or right. This is a more generous measure for defendants, because it is only a proportion of the actual gain, not the full actual gain. There is no special magic in Brightman J's reference in *Wrotham Park* to 'anticipated profit'.[57] Brightman J simply causes the defendant to disgorge a proportion of the profit, and in working out the hypothetical licence fee, he presumes the actual profit is reflected in the hypothetical licence agreement the parties would have entered into. However, one must not be too dazzled by the hypothetical licence agreement: it is merely a convenient fiction to enable courts to calculate a lesser proportion of the profit.[58]

It is said that 'reasonable fee' awards may be made even when there is no actual profit made by the defendant. The case often used to illustrate this principle is *Inverugie Investments Ltd v Hackett*.[59] In that case, the defendants owned a large hotel complex. The claimants occupied 30 apartments under a long term lease, but the defendants wrongfully ejected them and proceeded to use the apartments for their own benefit. Because of the low occupancy rates (35–40 per cent), the defendants did not make any profit from the trespass, but the Privy Council still awarded the claimant substantial 'user damages' calculated by reference to a reasonable rental value for *all* the apartments during the period the defendants had wrongfully occupied them.[60] Under my scheme it could be said that the defendants still made a profit because they saved an expense by failing to pay fair rent for the hotel.

Mance LJ in *Experience Hendrix LLC v PPX Enterprises Inc* seemed to accept that 'reasonable fee' damages for breach of contract could be awarded regardless of whether any actual profit was made, saying:

> In such a context it is natural to pay regard to any profit made by the wrongdoer (although a wrongdoer surely cannot always rely on avoiding having to make reasonable recompense by showing that despite his wrong he failed, perhaps simply due to his own incompetence, to make any profit). The law can in such cases act either by ordering payment over of a percentage of any profit or, in some cases, by taking the cost

[55] Against Stevens (n 28) 193: 'The actual profits or expenses saved do not form the basis of the award, save in so far as they evidence the value of the right.'

[56] Against Stevens (n 28) 193–94.

[57] *Wrotham Park* (n 39) 815.

[58] Note that McInnes makes a similar argument that one should not be sidetracked by the hypothetical award, but sees it simply as a yardstick for compensating for loss: M McInnes,'Gain, Loss and the User Principle' (2006) 14 *Restitution Law Review* 76, 85. See also Stites J in *Edwards v Lee's Administrator*, 96 So W 2d 1028 (1936) (Kentucky CA), 1030: 'it is apparent that rental value has been adopted, either consciously or unconsciously, as a convenient yardstick by which to measure the proportion of profit derived by the trespasser directly from the use of the land itself. . . . In other words, rental value ordinarily indicates the amount of profit realised directly from the land as land'.

[59] *Inverugie Investments Ltd v Hackett* [1995] 1 WLR 713 (PC).

[60] ibid 718.

> which the wrongdoer would have had to incur to obtain (if feasible) equivalent benefit from another source.[61]

Again, this could simply be seen as an award of a reasonable fee to reflect the expense saved by the defendant. However, one must be careful in measuring the reasonable fee, as the court may end up awarding what Friedmann has called 'attributed gain'.[62] That is to say, the court 'attributes' a gain to the defendant although this bears very little resemblance to what did occur, or what was likely to occur. This is *not the same* as partial disgorgement because it does not depend on the specific actual gains made by the defendant, but on certain assumptions the court is willing to make in the claimant's favour.[63]

Where torts such as trespass, detinue and the like are concerned, courts are more likely to award 'attributed gains' to a claimant. The question is whether we should allow this in breach of contract as well. In *Pell Frischmann* the court effectively awarded an 'attributed gain' for breach of contract.[64] The claimant, Pell Frischmann Engineering Limited, entered into a joint venture agreement with the defendants to develop an oilfield in Iran. The Iranian government agency with which the parties were dealing became frustrated with the claimant's behaviour over the course of negotiations. Eventually, the defendants commenced negotiations with the Iranian government agency to develop the oil field without the claimant's involvement. This was in breach of the joint venture contract between the claimant and the defendants, which provided that the defendants were to work exclusively with the claimant, and that the defendants were not to approach the Iranian government agency without the consent of the claimant. The Privy Council found that the claimant was entitled to a 'reasonable fee' representing the amount it would have accepted to be released from its contract. The 'reasonable fee' was calculated according to the *anticipated* profit rather than actual profit. The proportion of the anticipated profit awarded by the Privy Council (US$2.5 million) was vastly greater than the actual profit made by the defendants (at the greatest estimate, US$1 million to US$1.8 million). The generosity of the Privy Council's award was particularly surprising because it found that the claimant showed 'extraordinary and unexplained delay in bringing proceedings', and the claim would have been statute-barred in most jurisdictions.[65] Contrary to *Pell Frischmann*, I submit that partial disgorgement damages for breach of contract should be based on a proportion of *actual gains*. Perhaps some would argue that the claimant should not lose out merely because the venture was less profitable than expected.[66] But when the court stripped the defendants of *more* than the actual gain made, it effectively awarded punitive damages. As discussed in chapter

[61] *Experience Hendrix* (n 33) [26] (Mance LJ). See also *Sempra Metals Ltd (formerly Metallgesellschaft Ltd) v Inland Revenue Commissioners* [2007] UKHL 34, 3 WLR 354, [230] (Lord Mance).
[62] Friedmann (n 51) 1883–84.
[63] ibid 1884.
[64] *Pell Frischmann* (n 20).
[65] ibid [54] (Lord Walker).
[66] *Lunn Poly* (n 54) [27]–[29].

two,[67] punitive damages for breach of contract are generally unavailable in most common law countries, and when they are available, as in Canada, the behaviour in question tends to involve an abuse of contractual power which is morally repugnant.[68] The parties in *Pell Frischmann* were commercial entities who were evenly matched. While the conduct in question may have been sharp, it appears that the claimant also flirted with other joint venture partners and engaged in hard-nosed commercial conduct. Consequently it is not a case where it was appropriate to punish the defendants.

Thus, although Lord Nicholls said in *Blake* that there was no reason that contract rights should be treated differently to proprietary rights,[69] in this regard, the law should proceed cautiously. A precondition of any relief is that the defendant must have made an *actual profit*. This profit may be a 'negative gain' in the sense that it may be an expense saved. Further, the actual profit should be the yardstick of the award.

In assessing the 'reasonable fee', courts should utilise evidence of real bargains wherever possible.[70] It has been noted that 'reasonable fee' awards tend to be arbitrary, and that in some cases, there is no evidence of whether there was an actual profit, let alone what an appropriate proportion of that profit would be in the circumstances.[71] Although it may increase the cost of litigation,[72] claimants should produce evidence as to the actual profit, and where appropriate, evidence of similar bargains. This is preferable to arbitrary awards based on unknown profits.

Finally, as with full disgorgement damages, I argue that the breach of contract must be advertent for partial disgorgement damages to be awarded.[73] It has been argued that such awards do not possess deterrent characteristics.[74] Rather, I would say that the strength of the deterrent and punitive effect of partial disgorgement damages correlates directly to the proportion of the gain disgorged, and thus they certainly tend to be weaker in this regard than full disgorgement damages. Nonetheless, it is appropriate that the advertence requirement be maintained.

[67] Ch 2, IV B.

[68] See, eg *Vorvis v Insurance Corporation of British Columbia* [1989] 1 SCR 1085 (SCC); *Whiten v Pilot Insurance Co* [2002] 1 SCR 595 (SCC).

[69] *Blake* (n 5) 283 (Lord Nicholls).

[70] See D Campbell, 'The Extinguishing of Contract' (2004) 67 *MLR* 818, 820–21; *Marine and General Mutual Life Assurance Society v St James Real Estate Co* [1991] 2 EGLR 178, in which evidence of a real settlement made by the defendant in very similar circumstances was led to assist in quantification of the reasonable fee. See also discussion of this point in *Vercoe* (n 20) [298]–[299]. At [299], Sales J observed:

> The relevance of expert evidence [to assessing a reasonable fee] is likely to be greatest where the notional agreement on a fair price is closely analogous to normal commercial bargains on an established market; it may be much less helpful, or not relevant at all, in unusual one-off cases where there is nothing equivalent to a going rate for the type of notional transaction under consideration.

[71] See Campbell and Wylie (n 38) 623–24; Campbell (n 70) 820–22.

[72] Campbell (n 70) 828–29.

[73] Against Edelman, 'Gain-Based Damages and Compensation' (n 14) 151.

[74] ibid 150.

V When Should 'Reasonable Fee' Awards be Granted?

If one is to distinguish between 'reasonable fee' awards and full accounts of profit it is necessary to establish criteria according to which a claimant will be awarded a lesser or a greater measure. The measure which is awarded depends upon *why* specific relief could not be awarded in a particular case. There are two reasons why specific relief may be declined:

1. The court 'will not' order specific relief (eg because of delay on the part of the claimant, hardship to the defendant or broader public policy considerations).
2. The court 'cannot' order specific relief (eg impossibility or the need for constant supervision).[75]

Where a court *could* order specific relief for breach of contract but 'will not', a court will order a 'reasonable fee' award. *Wrotham Park* itself is just such a case. The defendants in that case were aware of a restrictive covenant preventing them from building more than a specified number of houses, but received advice that the covenant would be unenforceable, and so proceeded to build more houses than were allowed in breach of the covenant. The court *could* have ordered that the terms of the restrictive covenant be obeyed by ordering the houses, which were built in breach of it, to be pulled down, but Brightman J refused to order an injunction, saying:

> The erection of the houses, whether one likes it or not, is a fait accompli and the houses are now the homes of people. I accept that this particular fait accompli is reversible and could be undone. But I cannot close my eyes to the fact that the houses now exist. It would, in my opinion, be an unpardonable waste of much needed houses to direct that they now be pulled down and I have never had a moment's doubt during the hearing of this case that such an order ought to be refused.[76]

Therefore, his Honour declined to award specific relief for public policy reasons, on the basis that to pull down perfectly good housing would be a waste. Instead, his Honour awarded 5 per cent of the anticipated gain from the development.[77]

Other recent cases where a 'reasonable fee' has been awarded for breach of contract include *Amec Developments Ltd v Jury's Hotel Management (UK) Ltd*[78] and

[75] R Cunnington, 'The Measure and Availability of Gain-Based Damages for Breach of Contract' in D Saidov and R Cunnington (eds), *Contract Damages: Domestic and International Perspectives* (Oxford, Hart Publishing, 2008) 207, 236.

[76] *Wrotham Park* (n 39) 811.

[77] As Friedmann has noted, this award is rather ungenerous: Friedmann (n 51) 1901. Also, it is hard to argue that the deterrent and punitive motives were paramount in the mind of the court because of the small quantum of the award: C Mitchell, 'Remedial Inadequacy in Contract and the Role of Restitutionary Damages' (1999) 15 *Journal of Contract Law* 1, 10. Accordingly, I argue that the proportion of the profit should have been far greater.

[78] *Amec Developments Ltd v Jury's Hotel Management (UK) Ltd* [2000] EWHC 454 (Ch), (2001) 82 P & CR 22.

Lane v O'Brien Homes.[79] As with *Wrotham Park*, each case involved a negative covenant over land.

In *Amec*, the negative covenant was in favour of land owned by Amec. It provided that any building on Jury's land would not be nearer than a certain specified distance. Jury breached this covenant by constructing a hotel which was closer to Amec's land than the specified distance. Amec became aware of the breach once foundations were laid. It initially sought a mandatory injunction to demolish the premises. Both parties seemed to have delayed resolving the issue during which time the hotel was erected. By the time the matter came before Mann QC, the claimant merely sought damages in lieu of an injunction. Mann QC held that a proportion of Jury's profit from building in breach of the covenant should be paid to Amec. He faced substantial difficulty in calculating the profit Jury had gained by building in breach of the covenant. It was clear that Jury could not have fitted the same number of rooms in a smaller footprint, and that they profited to some extent. Jury argued that the profit was very small (half of £281,000), and Amec argued that the profit was enormous (half of £3 million). In the event, Mann QC applied *Wrotham Park* and used hypothetical negotiations as a basis for calculation and arrived at a 'reasonable fee' of £375,000.[80]

Lane concerned a contract of sale of certain land in Sussex. The claimant sold the land to the defendant but retained another neighbouring piece of land. The claimant's house was on the land which she sold to the defendant. The trial judge found that there was no relevant restrictive covenant in the contract for the sale of land, but that a collateral contract was formed whereby the defendant promised not to build more than three new houses on the land.[81] The defendant obtained planning permission which allowed it to build *four* new houses on the land. The claimant obtained an interlocutory injunction restraining the defendant from building any further. The trial judge found that the claimant had lost an opportunity to bargain with the defendant for the building of four houses, and that the claimant would have considered such a bargain. He awarded the claimant over 50 per cent of the profit, which he calculated according to the profit the defendant made by building an extra house (£150,000 damages derived from an expected profit of £280,000). The trial judge's decision was upheld by David Clarke J. The damages in *Lane* represented an unprecedentedly large proportion of the profit. This shows that the dividing line between an account of profit and a 'reasonable fee' is not clear. *Lane* looks almost like an account of profit reduced by an allowance for skill and effort rather than a 'reasonable fee'.

By contrast, where a court *cannot* order specific relief, because it is impossible to do so or because the performance must be constantly supervised, Cunnington argues that a court will order full disgorgement (subject perhaps to an allowance).

[79] *Lane v O'Brien Homes* [2004] EWHC 303, [2004] All ER (D) 61(QB).

[80] It has been noted that no real justification was offered for this quantification: Campbell (n 70) 821.

[81] Campbell has trenchantly criticised the finding of a collateral contract in this case, because the court failed to consider s 2 of the Law of Property (Miscellaneous Provisions) Act 1989 (UK) which holds that the all agreed terms should be part of the main written contract: Campbell (n 70) 825–27.

Blake was a case where specific relief was impossible: George Blake had breached his contract irredeemably, and it was impossible to rectify. Accordingly, the House of Lords was correct to award full disgorgement for breach of contract. In the circumstances of the case, too, it is not surprising that the House of Lords declined to award an allowance for skill and effort.

This analysis shows further why *WWF* and *Experience Hendrix* were both incorrectly decided. In each of these cases, specific relief *could not* be awarded. The World Wrestling Federation had already breached the terms of its settlement agreement with the World Wildlife Fund by using the initials 'WWF' repeatedly. PPX had already given third parties access to certain recordings of Jimi Hendrix's guitar music in breach of its settlement agreement, in which it had agreed not to allow access to those recordings without the prior consent of Hendrix's estate. There was no way in these cases that the judge could reverse the breaches which had already occurred. The defendant had, in each case, put specific relief out of the reach of the claimant by its advertent actions. Accordingly, the appropriate measure of relief was full disgorgement damages. Such damages could have been reduced appropriately by an allowance for skill and effort, or the court could have considered any equitable bars which might have militated against such an award.

However, one can envisage cases similar to *WWF* and *Experience Hendrix* where it *would* be appropriate to award a 'reasonable fee'. Suppose the claimants in each case had become aware that the defendants had commenced breaching the contract but had not sought an interlocutory injunction. It is arguable that the claimant *could have* sought specific relief but chose not to do so. Because the claimant let slip the opportunity of obtaining specific relief only a reasonable fee should be awarded. There is some hint of this in *WWF*.[82] Apparently, the Fund delayed in bringing proceedings, and the breaches of the 1994 agreement had been occurring since at least 1997.[83] Counsel for the Fund suggested that the Fund was reluctant to become embroiled in legal proceedings seeking to enforce the agreement again because it was a charity.[84] If a 'reasonable fee' award was made, it should have been made *on this basis* explicitly. Indeed, courts have previously awarded 'reasonable fee' awards in cases in lieu of an injunction where the claimant delayed in seeking an interlocutory injunction.[85] However, it is impossible to say without

[82] Note that Peter Smith J appeared to accept that this would affect the quantum of the award in *World Wide Fund for Nature v World Wrestling Federation Entertainment Inc* (*WWF*) [2006] EWHC 184 (Ch) [174] at point 6:

> The decision whether or not to award damages on this basis can take into account factors such as delay in intimating the claim and prosecuting the action, if appropriate. Those factors could also be taken into account at a later stage in quantifying the claim. Thus it may be possible to argue that where a wrongdoer was led to believe that no claim would be forthcoming on this head and acted to its detriment in reliance upon that that may bar the claim completely. Equally part of a claim may be disallowed by reason of delay if the delay caused prejudice: see the *Shaw v Applegate* and *Gafford* cases referred to above.

[83] *World Wide Fund for Nature v World Wrestling Foundation* [2001] EWHC 482 (Ch) [13] (Jacobs J).

[84] ibid [14].

[85] *Gafford v Graham* [1998] EWCA Civ 666, (1999) 77 P & CR 73 (CA); *Shaw v Applegate* [1977] 1 WLR 970 (CA).

more information what the result in *WWF* should have been. The mere effluxion of time is not an a priori basis for finding delay: the relative positions of the parties and their actions during the interval in question would need to be carefully considered.[86]

Cunnington argues that acquiescence cannot reduce the quantum of disgorgement damages because the delay took place after the date of the hypothetical negotiations.[87] This problem does not arise with partial disgorgement damages analysis because the hypothetical negotiations are nothing more than a way of quantifying the appropriate percentage of the profit to be disgorged.

The measure in full disgorgement damages cases differs from that of the 'reasonable fee' cases because of the difference in the defendant's conduct in each type of case. In the first case, where a court awards a 'reasonable fee', the defendant has not deprived the claimant of specific relief. In cases involving hardship or policy considerations, specific relief is still available, but for other discretionary reasons the court will not award it. In cases involving delay, specific relief *was* in the grasp of the claimant, but because of the claimant's delay in taking action, specific relief is no longer available. Thus it is appropriate to effect partial disgorgement represented by a market value of the right rather than requiring disgorgement of the full measure of the defendant's gain. The former tends to operate rather less harshly. In the second case, where a court awards full disgorgement damages, specific relief is *impossible*. Therefore, the defendant has deprived the claimant of specific relief. The deterrent and retributive considerations in the second scenario are more serious, and thus the penalty is more serious – it has a greater deterrent and punitive operation. In a sense this is a way of apportioning profit between the two parties.[88]

Finally, before concluding this section, it may be asked why I have positioned the 'reasonable fee' cases in the 'gain-based' category. As I noted in chapter two, it is rather easier to argue that the 'reasonable fee' cases are compensatory than it is to argue the same for the 'full disgorgement' cases, as it could convincingly be argued that *Wrotham Park* damages are a form of compensation for the loss of the right to performance, because (where contracts are concerned at least) the objective value of the right infringed will always be the same as the objective value of the benefit received.[89] Some have argued that such awards can be both compensatory and 'restitutionary' at the same time.[90] However, for the sake of clarity, a disgorgement analysis should be preferred because one of the preconditions for an award of *Wrotham Park* damages is that compensatory damages must be inadequate, and if *Wrotham Park* damages are themselves compensatory, then one of

[86] *Lindsay Petroleum Co v Hurd* (1874) LR 5 PC 221, 239–40.

[87] Cunnington (n 51) 572–73.

[88] See the suggestion in H Dagan, *The Law and Ethics of Restitution* (Cambridge, Cambridge University Press, 2004) 278–82.

[89] Cunnington (n 51) 565–67.

[90] SM Waddams, 'Gains Derived from Breach of Contract: Historical and Conceptual Perspectives' in D Saidov and R Cunnington (eds), *Contract Damages: Domestic and International Perspectives* (Oxford, Hart Publishing, 2008) 187, 192; *Inverugie Investments* (n 59) 718 (Lord Lloyd).

the preconditions for their award has not been met.[91] Arguing that partial disgorgement is compensatory produces incoherent results. In addition, if one sees the reasonable fee cases as representing an 'expense saved', the expense saved looks like an effective profit which can be disgorged.

Fundamentally, the cases in this area come down to the idea that the claimant has been deprived of performance in some way, and thus it is necessary to look at the reasons why performance has been rendered impossible, and what kind of remedy is appropriate in the circumstances. These remedies seek to recognise and protect the claimant's performance interest, but are also tailored to reflect the defendant's role in depriving the claimant of performance. This links into questions of desert which will be considered in chapter seven on bars to relief.

However, before moving to the topic of bars to relief, the implications of recognition of disgorgement for 'expenses saved' by breach of contract will be considered.

VI Scope of Disgorgement for 'Skimped Performance'

The Court of Appeal in *Blake* thought that 'restitutionary damages' were the remedy of choice in situations of 'skimped performance'.[92] Skimped performance was defined as 'where the defendant fails to provide the full extent of the services which he has charged the plaintiff'.[93] Lord Woolf cited *City of New Orleans v Firemen's Charitable Association*,[94] and said:

> Justice surely demands an award of substantial damages in such a case, and the amount of expenditure which the defendant has saved by the breach provides an appropriate measure of damages. This could be achieved by presuming that the plaintiff has suffered a loss of an amount corresponding to the amount by which he has been overcharged for the service actually provided; and the presumption could be justified by invoking the notion of 'the consumer surplus.' *But it would surely be preferable, as well as simpler and more open, to award restitutionary damages.* [Emphasis added.][95]

As Mindy Chen-Wishart commented in relation to the Court of Appeal judgment in *Blake*, the approval of an award of disgorgement damages for skimped performance in that case raises many questions. She asks:

[91] Cunnington (n 51) 567; O Odudu and G Virgo, 'Inadequacy of Compensatory Damages' [2009] *Restitution Law Review* 112, 118.

[92] *Blake* (n 2) 458. See also EA Farnsworth, 'Your Loss or My Gain? The Dilemma of the Disgorgement Principle in Breach of Contract' (1985) 94 *Yale Law Journal* 1339, 1382–92.

[93] *Blake* (n 2) 458.

[94] 9 So. 486 (Lou SC, 1891).

[95] *Blake* (n 2) 458.

> But what is the precise scope of 'skimped performance'? How is it distinguishable from defective performance? How would *Ruxley Electronics & Construction Ltd v Forsyth* . . . be viewed?[96]

This section will attempt to answer those questions. It will be argued that 'skimped performance' is analogous to cases of 'defective performance'. However, in most cases of skimped performance it will *not* be necessary to award disgorgement damages. An award of disgorgement may be somewhat arbitrary as a deterrent for breach of contract because disgorgement will only be awarded if the defendant has been efficient enough (or dishonest enough) to save an expense as a result of the breach. Courts are concerned to recognise the performance interest *regardless of* whether the defendant made a profit by skimping, but putting too much emphasis on disgorgement or restitutionary damages will only deter *some* kinds of breaches.[97]

In many, if not most, cases of skimped performance, some form of compensatory damages will still be adequate to put the claimant in the position she would have been in if the contract had been performed, or alternatively specific relief may be awarded. The primary question in these cases is how the compensatory damages should be measured: according to the decrease in value or according to cost of rectification.[98] There is some kinship between the award of both compensatory damages awarded on the rectification measure and disgorgement damages for an 'expense saved' because both seek to vindicate the claimant's performance interest and both require the defendant's breach to be advertent. Substitutability is relevant to awards of rectification damages.[99]

In rare cases it may be necessary to award disgorgement damages for skimped performance.[100] This will arise where damages on *any* measure are inadequate and performance is impossible.[101] The primary situation where this might arise is a case like *City of New Orleans*,[102] involving a contract designed to avoid risk where the defendant skimped on performance and no harm occurred, but the claimant was exposed to risk as a result of the breach.

Lord Nicholls in *Blake* would not have awarded an account of profits for 'skimped performance'. His Lordship said:

[96] M Chen-Wishart, 'Restitutionary Damages for Breach of Contract' (1998) 114 *LQR* 363, 365 (citations omitted).

[97] O'Sullivan (n 3) 338–39.

[98] Edelman has recently argued that the default position in both common law and equity should be that damages are calculated according to cost of rectification: J Edelman, 'Money Awards of the Cost of Performance' (2010) 4 *Journal of Equity* 122, 137.

[99] Loke (n 4) 190–94.

[100] See also American Law Institute (n 8) § 39, comment g, which says that 'saved expenditure' may be a measure of damages for *unintentional* breach. By contrast I argue that breach must be advertent, regardless of whether the profit is 'negative' or 'positive'.

[101] *cf* Edelman (n 98) 128. I agree with Edelman that where no performance is possible it may be appropriate to award a reasonable fee award, but say that the reasonable fee award is partial disgorgement of an expense saved.

[102] *City of New Orleans* (n 94).

> But a part refund of the price agreed for services would not fall within the scope of an account of profits as ordinarily understood. Nor does an account of profits seem to be needed in this context. The resolution of the problem of the cases of skimped performance, where the plaintiff does not get what was agreed, may best be found elsewhere. If a shopkeeper supplies inferior and cheaper goods than those ordered and paid for, he has to refund the difference in price. That would be the outcome of a claim for damages for breach of contract. That would be so, irrespective of whether the goods in fact served the intended purpose. There must be scope for a similar approach, without any straining of principle, in cases where the defendant provided inferior and cheaper services than those contracted for. [103]

Edelman contends that Lord Nicholls means that damages for skimped performance are probably best seen as a remedy based upon 'perfection' or 'performance damages'.[104] In fact, Lord Nicholls' comments seem to suggest that the measure of damages for skimped performance should be the reduction in value between the stipulated performance and the provided performance (the typical measure for compensatory damages for loss). While Lord Nicholls' statement is consistent with the law relating to sale of goods,[105] it is not consistent with the approach of the law towards building contracts in particular, which tend to award rectification damages where performance is defective.[106]

Lord Nicholls' view that an account of profits cannot be awarded for an 'expense saved' is supported by *Celanese International Corporation v BP Chemicals*

[103] *Blake* (n 5) 286.

[104] Edelman, *Gain-Based Damages* (n 11) 176.

[105] UK: Sale of Goods Act 1979, ss 50(3), 51(3), 53(3).
US: Uniform Commercial Code §§ 2-708(1), 2-713(1), 2-714(2).

Australia: Sale of Goods Act 1954 (ACT), ss 53(3), 54(3), 56(3); Sale of Goods Act 1923 (NSW), ss 52(3), 53(3), 54(3); Sale of Goods Act (NT), ss 51(3), 53(3), 54(3); Sale of Goods Act 1896 (Qld), ss 52(3), 53(3), 54(3); Sale of Goods Act 1895 (SA), ss 49(3), 50(3) and 52(3); Sale of Goods Act 1896 (Tas), ss 54(3), 55(3), 57(3); Goods Act 1958 (Vic), ss 56(3), 57(3), 59(3); Sale of Goods Act 1895 (WA), ss 49(3), 50(3), 52(3);

New Zealand: Sale of Goods Act 1903 (NZ), ss 51(3), 52(3), 54(3).

Canada: Sale of Goods Act, RSA 2000, c S-2, ss 49(3), 50(3), 52(3) (Alberta); Sale of Goods Act, RSBC 1996, c 410, ss 53(3), 54(4), 56(3) (British Columbia); Sale of Goods Act, CCSM c S10, ss 51(3), 52(3), 54(3) (Manitoba); Sale of Goods Act, RSNB 1973, c S-1, ss 47(3), 48(3), 50(3) (New Brunswick); Sale of Goods Act, RSNL 1990, c S-6, ss 51(3), 52(3), 54(3) (Newfoundland and Labrador); Sale of Goods Act, RSNWT 1988, c S-2, ss 57(3), 58(3), 60(3) (Northwest Territories); Sale of Goods Act, RSNS 1989, c 408, ss 51(3), 52(3), 54(3) (Nova Scotia); Sale of Goods Act, RSNWT (Nu) 1988, c S-2, ss 57(3), 58(3), 60(3) (Nunavut); Sale of Goods Act, RSO 1990, c S1, ss 48(3), 49(3), 51(3) (Ontario); Sale of Goods Act, RSPEI 1988, c S-1, ss 50(3), 51(3), 54(3) (Prince Edward Island); Sale of Goods Act, RSS 1978, c S-1, ss 49(3), 50(3), 52(3) (Saskatchewan); Sale of Goods Act, RSY 2002, c 198, ss 47(3), 48(3), 50(3) (Yukon Territory).

See also *DRC Distribution Ltd v Ulva Ltd* [2007] EWHC 1716 (QB) [70], [2007] All ER (D) 337; *cf* Edelman (n 98) 135.

[106] Loke (n 4) 189–90; M Bell, 'After *Tabcorp*, for Whom Does the *Bellgrove* Toll? Cementing the Expectation Measure as the Ruling Principle for Calculation of Contract Damages' (2009) 33 *Melbourne University Law Review* 684. See, eg *Groves v John Wunder Company*, 286 NW 235 (Minn 1939); *Bellgrove v Eldridge* (1954) 90 CLR 613 (HCA); *Radford v De Froberville* [1977] 1 WLR 1262 (ChD); *Dean v Ainley* [1987] 1 WLR 1729 (CA); *Tabcorp Holdings Ltd v Bowen Investments Pty Ltd* (2009) 236 CLR 272 (HCA) for examples of cases where rectification damages have been awarded in preference to loss of value damages.

Ltd[107] where there were two measures of profit which could be disgorged: either the actual profit made by the defendant or the expense saved. The defendant had infringed the claimant's patent in two separate processes when manufacturing acetic acid. The two processes were effectively separate businesses.

One business made an actual profit, and Laddie J ordered disgorgement of the profit. His Honour rejected the defendant's submission that it could have made the same profit using another non-infringing method of production and that therefore disgorgement damages should be nominal, because little expense had been saved by using the method.

The other business made a large loss, although the losses were significantly reduced by reason of the infringement, and therefore it could be said that the defendant had saved an expense by failure to seek the claimant's permission to use the patented method. However, Laddie J concluded no account of profits could be awarded for expenses saved.

The rejection of the 'expense saved' measure of profit had quite different results for each business. His Honour said that the expense saved method of calculation could prove difficult to make, and could depend upon fortuitous happenstance. He gave as an example the following scenario:

> Now imagine that, quite independently and at the same time, some other inventor invents another new process for making the same product but does not patent it so that the infringer could have made the same product in a non-infringing way. The fact is that he did not do so. The profits he made were made by use of the patented invention and he should account for them.[108]

His Honour also said that the claimant could not argue that the award should be increased by arguing that the defendant could or should have generated higher profits. The corollary of this is that the defendant should not be able to argue that the profits could have been made in a non-infringing way so that no expense was saved. These policy considerations are only really likely to occur in the specific context of patent infringement but not in contract law. The policy in patent law is to grant an artificial statutory monopoly whereby an infringer must pay for the use of a patented process, and it is enforceable against the rest of the world. By contrast, the policy behind contract law is to enforce voluntary undertakings, but still to leave some freedom to breach in some circumstances, and the contract is generally not intended to be enforceable against third parties or the rest of the world. It is difficult to think of a way in which profits could have been made by breach of contract in a 'non-infringing way' which still flowed from the parties' relationship.

Edelman argues a third reason for denying awards based on expense saved which is 'the enormous difficulty in estimating the expense saved if the alternative method of making the profit were adopted.'[109] However, the same could be said

[107] *Celanese International Corporation v BP Chemicals Ltd* [1999] RPC 203 (ChD).
[108] ibid 220.
[109] Edelman, *Gain-Based Damages* (n 11) 76.

for 'reasonable fee' awards and accounts of profit, and indeed, *Amec* shows the difficulty of working out actual or projected profits or proportions thereof. The Australian High Court has recognised the difficulties in calculating profit derived from wrongdoing, and noted that '"mathematical exactitude" is generally impossible'.[110] In *Blake*, Lord Nicholls said:

> Despite the niceties and formalities once associated with taking an account, the amount payable under an account of profits need not be any more elaborately and precisely calculated than damages.[111]

Indeed, Lord Nicholls has recently cast doubt on the correctness of the *Celanese* decision in extra-judicial comments, suggesting it imposed an unprincipled and unnecessary restriction on awards.[112]

Nonetheless, it can be difficult to measure expenses saved, and it is important to use a reasonable alternative as a basis for calculating the expense saved.[113] Friedmann gives an example of a defendant who uses another's tractor to plough his land: the expense saved is not the cost of manual labour but of the reasonable rent for this type of machine.[114]

Before moving on, it is necessary to clear up a taxonomical issue. American commentators such as Eisenberg and Thel and Siegelman have characterised awards for rectification damages as an instance of disgorgement of the effective profit arising from breach in that the defendant profited by failing to render the full performance.[115] On this view, rectification damages are just a species of disgorgement damages representing the expense saved by the defendant in failing to provide the specified performance. However, this view cannot be accepted. In some cases awards for rectification *may* be equivalent to the expense saved, but there is no necessary correlation between the two.[116] Burrows give the example of where a contractor saves an expense by using substandard building material.[117] The cost of replacing the material is likely to be far greater than the expense saved.

[110] *Dart Industries Inc v Décor Corporation Pty Ltd* (1993) 179 CLR 101 (HCA) 111. See also *Warman International Ltd v Dwyer* (1995) 182 CLR 544 (HCA) 556–58; *Colbeam Palmer Ltd v Stock Affiliates Pty Ltd* (1968) 122 CLR 25 (HCA) 37 (Windeyer J).

[111] *Blake* (n 5) 288.

[112] 'Breach of Contract, Restitution for Wrongs, and Punishment: Review of Discussion' in A Burrows and E Peel (eds), *Commercial Remedies – Current Issues and Problems* (Oxford, Oxford University Press, 2003) 129.

[113] Friedmann (n 51) 1894. He cites *Olwell v Nye & Nissen Co*, 173 P 2d 652 (Wash SC, 1946), in which the defendant wrongfully used the plaintiff's egg-washing machine for a period of three years, during which time the plaintiff had no use for it. The trial judge calculated the expense saved on the basis of what it would have cost the defendant to hire people to hand-wash the eggs, rather than by reference to the cost of hiring a similar machine. As to reasonableness, see *Pell Frischmann* (n 20) [49]; *Vercoe* (n 20) [291].

[114] Friedmann (n 51).

[115] M Eisenberg, 'The Disgorgement Interest in Contract Law' (2006) 105 *Michigan Law Review* 559, 592–97; Siegelman and Thel (n 49) 1216–20.

[116] Burrows, *Remedies for Torts and Breach of Contract* (n 40) 397: 'In a nutshell, cost of cure damages are indisputably compensatory not restitutionary.'

[117] ibid.

The question of where exactly rectification damages fit in private law is vexed. Edelman argues that rectification damages are *not* disgorgement damages, but what he terms 'performance damages'.[118] In a similar vein, Webb argues that the 'expectation interest' that parties gain under a contract is a composite of two interests which do not overlap entirely: the performance interest and the compensation interest.[119] He argues that the primary interest for breach of contract is the performance interest, and loss is irrelevant to this category of interest.[120] By contrast, the compensation interest concerns losses suffered. Webb argues that damages for rectification protect the performance interest, as they effectively provide the claimant with a means of obtaining the promised performance.[121] Similarly, Stephen Smith argues that damages for rectification are 'substitutionary damages'. Damages for rectification cannot be compensatory because they 'do not compensate for losses, but instead eliminate or prevent them (at least, as much as they can be eliminated or prevented).'[122] Thus, he argues that 'substitutionary damages' are closer to specific relief than to compensatory damages: they seek to undo the wrong done to the claimant, but through a monetary award rather than by specific relief.[123] Rectification damages represent another attempt to vindicate the claimant's performance right and to offer the 'next best' alternative to performance in the circumstances. They should be ordered in preference to disgorgement damages where possible and appropriate, because they are a better way of recognising the claimant's performance interest. They 'fit' with the expectation which the claimant had in the first place from the contract, as they allow her to obtain complete performance from elsewhere.

In this regard, at least, it is agreed that courts should focus on deficiencies in compensatory damages for breach of contract rather than restitutionary damages (contrary to the suggestion of the Court of Appeal in *Blake*).[124] Recognition of the claimant's 'performance interest'[125] has been recognised as a possibility by the House of Lords in *Ruxley Electronics and Constructions Ltd v Forsyth*[126] and *Alfred McAlpine Construction Ltd v Panatown*.[127] It has also been argued that the Australian High Court has recognised the 'performance interest' in *Tabcorp*.[128]

[118] Edelman, *Gain-Based Damages* (n 11) 182–85; Edelman (n 98).

[119] C Webb, 'Performance and Compensation: An Analysis of Contract, Damages and Contractual Obligation' (2006) 26 *OJLS* 41, 41–42, 45–49. See also D Pearce and R Halson, 'Damages for Breach of Contract: Compensation, Restitution and Vindication' (2008) 28 *OJLS* 73.

[120] Webb (n 119) 56.

[121] ibid 60.

[122] Smith (n 23) 95.

[123] ibid 94–95.

[124] O'Sullivan (n 3) 337–42.

[125] Coote (n 22) 566; see also B Coote, 'The Performance Interest, *Panatown*, and the Problem of Loss' (2001) 117 *LQR* 81.

[126] *Ruxley Electronics and Constructions Ltd v Forsyth* [1996] AC 344 (HL).

[127] *Alfred McAlpine Construction Ltd v Panatown* [2000] UKHL 43, [2001] 1 AC 518 (HL) 548 (Lord Goff), 587 (Lord Millett), 577 (Lord Browne-Wilkinson).

[128] D Saidov, 'A Further Step Towards Protecting the Performance Interest' [2009] *Lloyd's Maritime and Commercial Law Quarterly* 295; Bell (n 106) 717; S Rowan, 'Protecting Contractual Expectations: An Australian Perspective' (2009) 68 *CLJ* 276, 278; Edelman (n 98) 136.

There are two different categories of cases where skimped performance may be relevant. The first category is populated by what are termed 'restoration cases' and the second category involves contracts designed to reduce risk. The considerations in the restoration cases are different to those in contracts designed to reduce risk. First, the deterrent considerations are generally stronger for contracts designed to reduce risk (particularly contracts designed to promote public safety). Secondly, in the contracts designed to reduce risk, typically, specific relief *cannot* be awarded – thus it is too late to remedy the defects in performance.

I will first consider the 'restoration cases'. The choice for the court in such cases is typically between different measures of damages, that is, for rectification or reduction in value. The difficulty for a court is to decide which measure is most appropriate in the circumstances. However, in rare cases it may be necessary to award disgorgement for 'skimped performance' because compensatory damages on any measure are inadequate and specific relief is no longer available. To date, however, most restoration cases have not been appropriate for an award of disgorgement damages because (a) compensatory damages representing the reduction in value have been adequate; (b) specific relief or damages for rectification have been awarded or (c) while specific relief is no longer available and compensatory damages are not adequate, the requisite requirement of advertence is not present. The possible exception to this is *Tito v Waddell (No 2)*[129] where, if not for the procedural difficulty that some affected landowners were not before the court, the court should have awarded partial disgorgement of an expense saved by means of a 'reasonable fee' award.

A Skimped Performance and the 'Restoration Cases'

There are two broad sub-categories of restoration cases. The first typically involves a construction project where performance of the contract is substandard to a greater or lesser degree. The second sub-category typically involves the restoration of land after materials have been mined or taken from it.

In these 'restoration cases' it *is* often still possible for the court to award performance of the contract as stipulated, or, at the least, to order rectification damages so that the claimant can get the stipulated performance from a third party. However, in these cases, the rectification damages are vastly greater than the diminution in value of the land or property in question. The response of the courts to these disputes varies widely depending upon the nature and extent of the breach, the cost of rectification as compared to the cost of the original contract, the cost of rectification as compared to the value of the land or structure and the advertence or inadvertence of the breach.

Substitutability can assist in assessing the measure of damages because it goes to the heart of the contractual obligation – what is needed to provide the claimant with the performance she was promised? If the defective performance is not an

[129] *Tito v Waddell (No 2)* [1977] Ch 106 (Ch).

effective substitute, it is more likely that cost of rectification will be ordered. By contrast, if the defective performance *is* for all intents and purposes an effective substitute, courts will be far more likely to award reduction in value damages, loss of amenity damages, or indeed, nominal damages or no damages at all.

Where it is possible to fulfil the claimant's expectation in one way or another, this should generally be awarded in preference to disgorgement damages, because it provides a better fit with the interest the claimant is intended to get under the contract.

i Construction Contracts and Other Cases Involving Building

If a performance in a construction contract is seriously defective and the breach was advertent a court will generally award damages calculated according to full rectification costs. In these cases the loss of value is vastly exceeded by the cost of rectification, but in the interests of recognising the claimant's performance interest, courts have tended to order rectification damages. English and Australian courts have ordered rectification damages, with a view to allowing the claimant to purchase a substitute performance from elsewhere, in cases including *Bellgrove v Eldridge*,[130] *Radford v De Froberville*,[131] *Dean v Ainley*[132] and *Tabcorp*.[133] The approach of the courts in these construction law cases has been to presume that rectification damages are the most appropriate remedy, and only to decline rectification if the damages would be 'unreasonable', or, in the United Kingdom at least, if the damages would not be used to effect the repairs.[134]

These cases where full rectification damages were awarded can be compared with *Ruxley*.[135] In *Ruxley* the performance was defective in a way that did not affect the value of the contracted-for item. The defendant had contracted for a swimming pool to be built in his garden. The contract had been varied to specify that the pool should have a diving area which was 7' 6" deep. On completion, the

[130] *Bellgrove* (n 106). Cited with approval by the House of Lords in *Ruxley* (n 126) 357 (Lord Jauncey of Tullichettle), 367–68 (Lord Lloyd of Berwick) and recently by the High Court in *Tabcorp* (n 106). For earlier cases with similar holdings, see *Thornton v Place* (1832) 1 Moo & R 218, 174 ER 74 (HC); *H Dakin & Co Ltd v Lee* [1916] KB 566 (CA); *Pearson-Burleigh Ltd v Pioneer Grain Co* (1933) 1 DLR 714 (CA).

[131] *Radford* (n 106); *cf Wigsell v Corporation of the School for Indigent Blind* (1882) 8 QBD 357.

[132] *Dean* (n 106).

[133] *Tabcorp* (n 106). See Saidov (n 128) 297–98. Unfortunately, as Saidov notes, the High Court did not resolve the question of the application and relevance of the rule in *Joyner v Weeks* [1891] 2 QB 31 (QB) which suggests that landlords can get cost of repair damages *only* if the claim is brought at or near the end of the lease. The rule has been abolished by statutory provisions in some jurisdictions: Landlord and Tenant Act 1929 (UK), s 18(1); Conveyancing Act 1919 (NSW), s 133A; Property Law Act 1974 (Qld), s 112 which restrict damages to diminution of value of the reversion of the lease. In jurisdictions where the rule in *Joyner v Weeks* has not been abolished, it has arguably been weakened by *Conquest v Ebbetts* [1896] AC 490 (HL) which held that such damages could not be recovered during the term of the lease although *cf* Coote (n 22) 553–54, noting *Conquest v Ebbetts* [1895] 2 Ch 377 (CA).

[134] See Edelman (n 98) 135 for trenchant criticism of the 'reasonableness requirement'. He notes, 'Reasonableness, without more, obscures more than it illuminates.'

[135] *Ruxley* (n 126).

pool was suitable for diving, but the diving area was only 6' 9" deep. The contract price was £17,797.40. The defendant refused to pay for the pool, and therefore the claimant bought a claim for debt. The defendant counterclaimed that the performance was defective and that he was entitled to rectification damages. The estimated cost of rectifying performance was £21,560. At trial, the defendant was awarded £2,500 representing the loss of amenity. On appeal, a majority of the Court of Appeal found that the defendant should be awarded rectification damages.[136] The House of Lords reinstated the judgment of the trial judge, holding that it was unreasonable to award damages representing the full cost of rectifying the defect.[137] Lord Mustill emphasised that damages reflecting reinstatement and depreciation in value were not the only two measures of recovery in such a case. He said the loss suffered by the defendant was the 'consumer surplus', that is, where the subjective value of the promise to the promisee exceeds the financial value of the promise in objective terms.[138] Lord Lloyd said that the damages reflected the defendant's 'loss of amenity'.[139]

This case could instead be considered to be a case of skimped performance, in which the claimants profited by reason of the lesser depth of the pool. Presumably it took less 'man hours' to dig a pool of 6' 9" in depth than it did to dig a pool of 7'6". The surface area of the pool would be less, and less material would be needed to line the inside of the pool. Such cost savings may be minimal, but disgorgement damages would arguably provide a more principled basis for recovery than damages for 'loss of amenity', for which the figures are plucked out of the air. The nature of the breach would have to be considered. It is unclear whether the breach in *Ruxley* was advertent. Most cases of skimped performance are inadvertent, and thus disgorgement damages are not available.[140]

Alternatively, because the facts in *Ruxley* were not analysed in such as way as to reflect any gain on the part of Ruxley, it has been argued that *Ruxley* is best recognised as an example of 'vindicatory damages' – that is, damages which are not loss-based or gain-based, but simply seek to vindicate the promisee's rights.[141]

Another analysis is that *Ruxley* was a case where the court refused to award full rectification damages because of the disproportionate effect on the claimant in that case, and thus it was in effect a recognition of the hardship defence.[142] It is certainly true that a court may refuse to specifically perform a contract on the basis that the cost of performance far exceeds its value to the claimant,[143] and there seems no reason why this kind of bar to relief should not extend to

[136] *Forsyth v Ruxley Electronics and Construction Ltd* [1994] 1 WLR 650 (CA) (Staughton LJ and Mann LJ, Dillon LJ dissenting).

[137] *Ruxley* (n 126) 353 (Lord Bridge), 358–59 (Lord Jauncey), 359–60 (Lord Mustill), 367–71 (Lord Lloyd). Lord Keith concurred with Lord Jauncey, Lord Mustill and Lord Lloyd.

[138] ibid 360, citing D Harris, A Ogus and J Phillips, 'Contract Remedies and the Consumer Surplus' (1979) 95 *LQR* 581.

[139] *Ruxley* (n 126) 374.

[140] Thel and Siegelman (n 49) 34.

[141] Pearce and Halson (n 119) 74, 95.

[142] Smith (n 23) 104.

[143] *Tito* (n 129); *Morris v Redland Bricks Ltd* [1970] AC 652 (HL).

rectification damages. Similarly, Edelman has argued that the defendant in *Ruxley* did not receive rectification damages because there was a five-year delay before the defendant even raised his complaint about the depth of the swimming pool. Thus it could be argued that rectification damages were not awarded because of the inordinate delay in raising the complaint and the defendant's apparent acquiescence to the performance.[144] Perhaps hardship and delay and acquiescence worked together to provide the claimant builder in that case with a defence against the defendant's counter-claim for rectification damages.

A US version of *Ruxley* occurred in *Jacob & Youngs, Inc v Kent*.[145] The claimant was a builder who built a country house for the defendant. The contract specified that the plumbing pipe had to be standard 'Reading' brand pipe. Once the house was completed, the defendant learned that some of the pipe was not 'Reading' brand, but 'Cohoes' brand pipe. The breach of contract was an inadvertent oversight by one of the claimant's subcontractors. The Cohoes pipe was the same in quality, appearance, market value and cost as Reading pipe. A majority of the New York Court of Appeals found:

> Reading pipe is distinguished from Cohoes pipe and other brands only by the name of the manufacturer stamped upon it at intervals of between six and seven feet. Even the defendant's architect, though he inspected the pipe upon arrival, failed to notice the discrepancy.[146]

The defendant demanded that the pipe be replaced, and refused to pay the final payment to the builder. In order to replace the pipe, the claimant would have needed to tear down substantial parts of the completed building and then rebuild it, at a massive expense. The majority held that the measure of damages was not the cost of replacement but the difference in value (ie nominal or nil). Thus, the defendant was required to make the claimant's final payment.

Importantly, Cohoes brand pipe was entirely substitutable with Reading brand pipe. Substitutability confirms that the defendant should be awarded nominal damages, because the performance which the defendant received was indistinguishable from the performance he had contracted for.[147] But, as Eisenberg points out, the conclusion might be different if the claimant had profited at the defendant's expense by using an inferior grade pipe. The performance would not be substitutable, because the defendant would not have received the performance he expected. In such circumstances, Eisenberg suggests it would be appropriate at the very least to require a builder to disgorge profits made through skimping on performance.[148] Disgorgement damages could represent a 'middle ground' option

[144] Edelman (n 98) 135.

[145] *Jacob & Youngs, Inc v Kent*, 230 NY 239, 129 NE 889 (NYCA, 1921).

[146] ibid 241, 890 (Cardozo J, with whom Hiscock Ch J, Hogan and Crane JJ agreed. McLaughlin J dissented and Pound and Andrews JJ concurred in the dissent).

[147] *cf* S Thel and P Siegelman, 'Willfulness Versus Expectation: A Promisor-Based Defense of Willful Breach Doctrine' (2009) 107 *Michigan Law Review* 1517, 1527–28, who argue that if a builder substitutes a cheaper yet otherwise entirely substitutable brand of pipe, he should still be liable.

[148] Eisenberg (n 115) 594.

for courts; a recognition of the claimant's performance interest where full rectification damages were inappropriate.[149]

However, there is another issue which might affect recovery of disgorgement damages in a case like *Jacob & Youngs*. In the case itself, the breach was inadvertent. The defendant's own architect did not even notice that the pipe was the wrong kind. Thus, it is unlikely that disgorgement damages would be appropriate. Advertence has an increased significance where skimped performance is concerned. In the 'second sale cases' and 'agency problem cases', by the very nature of the cases concerned, it is highly probable that the breach was advertent. By contrast, it is more likely that skimped performance will be inadvertent. There is a punitive aspect to disgorgement damages, and it is only appropriate to impose them on a defendant who has breached the contract advertently.

Samson & Samson Ltd v Proctor[150] is the only case in which a court has awarded damages representing an 'expense saved' for work done under a building contract. The case arose in the usual fashion, with the claimant claiming moneys owing under a building contract, whereupon the defendant alleged that the performance was defective in certain aspects, including that there was insufficient steel reinforcing. The defendant had sold the house at the same price for which he would have sold it had the claimant fully performed the building contract. Consequently, the claimant argued that the defendant suffered no loss as a result of the breach of contract. Macarthur J said:

> In my opinion the proper measure of the defendant's damages, on the facts of the present case, is the difference in cost to the plaintiff of the actual work done and the work specified. *I should add that the plaintiff should also give credit for any element of profit that would have been exclusively referable to the performance of the work as specified. I do not think that the adoption of that measure of damages is a departure from the fundamental principle of compensation. As I see the matter the plaintiff is suing for the balance of the contract price but concedes that he has not fully performed his contract; the defendant, I think, is entitled to deduct from the contract price that which the builder saved by not carrying out his contract.* The fact that the defendant sold the property advantageously is irrelevant to the dispute between plaintiff and defendant. [Emphasis added.][151]

Unfortunately, the judge's discussion is brief and does not give any guidance as to the particular circumstances which would give rise to disgorgement damages representing expenses saved in this case. It cannot serve as principled authority in this area.

ii Contracts for Restoration of Land

The other typical restoration case arises when parties enter into a contract in which a landowner agrees that the other party is allowed to take something of value from the land, but there is also term of the contract that the land must be

[149] ibid 595.
[150] *Samson & Samson Ltd v Proctor* [1975] 1 NZLR 655 (NZSC).
[151] ibid 656.

restored to its previous condition after the valuable commodity has been removed. Once the valuable commodity has been removed, the other party refuses to restore the land, usually because the cost of doing so is prohibitive and vastly disproportionate to the actual value of the land. Again, the primary choice for a court is between rectification damages and damages for diminution of value.

Two American cases can be compared and contrasted. In *Groves v Wunder*,[152] rectification damages were awarded. Groves, the claimant, leased its property to John Wunder, the defendant, for seven years, with a clause allowing the defendant to remove the sand and gravel on the property. At the end of the lease the defendant was required to restore the property to a specified condition. The court found that the defendant breached the contract deliberately, taking only the richest and the best of the gravel, and did not restore the property to the specified condition.[153] The majority ordered the defendant to fix the property at a cost of $60,000, despite the fact that had the property been repaired according to the contract, it would have only been worth $12,160.[154] It is suggested that this result was appropriate in the circumstances.[155]

In the second case, *Peeveyhouse v Garland Coal & Mining Company*,[156] the court refused to order rectification damages and merely awarded damages for the diminution in value of the property. Willie and Lucille Peeveyhouse leased their farm to Garland Coal & Mining Company ('Garland Coal'). Garland Coal was permitted to 'strip-mine' the farm for coal. The contract specifically provided that the defendant would restore the property to its former condition at the end of the lease period, but the defendant did not comply.[157] In order to restore the property as specified by the contract the defendants would have had to move thousands of cubic yards of dirt at a cost of approximately $29,000, but the value of the farm property itself was less than $5000, and the restoration work would add only marginally to its value.[158] A majority of the court refused to order the defendants to restore the property to its former condition,[159] because it was a case of 'economic waste' (ie the costs of remedying the defects were disproportionate to the results obtained).[160] It was considered that an order of rectification damages would be contrary to substantial justice.[161]

[152] *Groves* (n 106).
[153] ibid 165, 236.
[154] ibid 165–71, 236–39.
[155] *cf* R Posner, *Economic Analysis of Law*, 8th edn (New York, Aspen Walters Kluwer, 2011) 152. Apparently the plaintiff did not use the damages to restore the property: see P Linzer, 'On the Amorality of Contract Remedies – Efficiency, Equity, and the *Second Restatement*' (1981) 81 *Columbia Law Review* 111, 135. Linzer suggests an award of specific performance might have been more appropriate to prevent a 'windfall'.
[156] *Peeveyhouse v Garland Coal & Mining Company*, 382 P (2d) 109 (Okla SC, 1962).
[157] ibid 114.
[158] ibid 111.
[159] The primary judgment was delivered by Jackson J, with whom Welch, Davison, Halley and Johnson JJ concurred.
[160] *Peeveyhouse* (n 156) 113. See also American Law Institute, *Restatement of Contracts* (1932), §346(1), comment (b), subsequently amended in *Restatement (Second) of Contracts* (1981).
[161] *Peeveyhouse* (n 156).

There was a strong dissent by Irwin J (with whom Williams CJ, Blackbird VCJ and Berry J concurred). As the dissenting judges point out in *Peeveyhouse*, it could be inferred that the breach of the defendant was advertent.[162] The inclusion of the clause was essential to the claimant entering into the bargain in the first place. The preferable result would therefore have been for the court to order the defendants to pay rectification damages.[163]

In some ways, *Groves v Wunder* and *Peeveyhouse* are the mirror image of the negative covenant cases – the defendants in these two cases failed to do the very thing they said they would do. It is submitted that if rectification damages were inappropriate, another option for the courts in both cases would have been to award the entire profit derived from the mining leases, particularly in view of the advertent nature of the breaches. Alternatively, the court could calculate a 'reasonable fee' award according to the expense saved (ie the sum the claimants would have demanded that defendants pay to be released from their obligation to restore the land). The choice of remedy would depend upon the reason why the court declined to award specific relief or rectification damages (ie whether it could not or would not award specific relief or an equivalent).

Tito v Waddell[164] involved phosphate mining on the Pacific island of Ocean Island (called 'Banaba' by the locals), and is a case where a reasonable fee award of some kind would have been appropriate. Phosphate was discovered there in 1900 and the island became a British settlement. The British Crown then granted a British company exclusive licences to occupy the island and mine for phosphate. Certain royalty payments had to be made to the Crown. In 1913 an agreement was made with the Banaban locals requiring the company to pay royalties to the Crown which were then to be applied for the benefit of the Banaban people. The company also agreed that it should return all 'worked out' land to the original owners and should 'replant such lands – whenever possible – with coconuts and other food-bearing trees, both in the lands already worked out and in those to be worked out.' In 1916 Ocean Island became part of the Gilbert and Ellice Islands Colony. In 1920 the Australian, New Zealand and United Kingdom governments purchased the undertakings of the company in Ocean Island and Nauru. Each country appointed a British Phosphate Commissioner to oversee the business. In 1940 Ocean Island had been mined to such an extent that the Banabans petitioned the Secretary of State to acquire an island in the Fiji group which would serve as a second home for them. In 1942, Rabi, an island in the Fiji group, was bought for the Banabans out of their royalty funds. In 1942, during the Second World War, the Japanese occupied Ocean Island and killed the inhabitants or deported them to other islands. The island was totally devastated. After the war ended in 1945 Ocean Island was uninhabitable. The High Commissioner collected the Banabans

[162] Against R Craswell, 'When is a Willful Breach "Willful"? The Link Between Definitions and Damages' (2009) 107 *Michigan Law Review* 1501, 1503.

[163] Eisenberg (n 115) 595–96.

[164] *Tito* (n 129).

together and moved them to Rabi. In 1947 the British Phosphate Commissioners negotiated for the acquisition of the remaining phosphate land.

The Banabans sued the British Phosphate Commissioners and the UK Attorney General on a variety of bases, one of which involved seeking specific performance of the obligation to replant.

Megarry V-C declined to specifically enforce the obligation to replant. His Honour found that the obligation was certain enough to be specifically enforced, but there were other practical difficulties which meant that it could not be undertaken. First, some of the plots of land to which the replanting obligation attached were owned by multiple parties, but some of the co-owners were not parties to the action and did not seek specific performance. Secondly, not all owners of plots of land to which the obligation to replant attached were before the court, and thus only some patches of land would be the subject of the order. Thirdly, the cost of replanting was exorbitant and would take years to complete, with little chance that the coconut trees would bear fruit.[165]

The Banabans also sought to gain a sum representing the cost of rectification, or alternatively a 'suitable proportion' of the cost of rectification, representing what the British Phosphate Commissioners would have paid to be released from their obligation to replant.[166] Megarry V-C rejected the analogies with cases such as *Wrotham Park* and *Bracewell v Appleby*, saying 'the two authorities in question seem to me to be a long way away from a case where the issue is not one of invading the property rights of another without consent, but of breach of a contract to replant his land.'[167]

Megarry V-C held that there was no longer an enforceable obligation on the part of the British Phosphate Commissioners, so there was no obligation from which they could seek release.[168] However, the impossibility of specifically enforcing the contract should have meant that the court gave thought to the 'next best' solution. If all interested parties had been before the court, it could be said that the court refused to award specific performance on public policy grounds (ie that replanting would be 'futile' and unlikely to achieve much benefit). Therefore, in the absence of the procedural difficulties mentioned above, a 'reasonable fee' award was appropriate in lieu of specific performance, representing the expense saved by failing to negotiate a release from the obligation to replant. It does not matter that the British Phosphate Commissioners would never have agreed to such a release; nor would many of the defendants in 'reasonable fee' cases.[169] It is simply an appropriate way of calculating a proportion of the profits to be disgorged by the British Phosphate Commissioners. The Banabans had an interest in performance which was not adequately recognised by the court.[170]

[165] ibid 321–28.
[166] ibid 334–36.
[167] ibid 336.
[168] ibid.
[169] eg *Wrotham Park* (n 39) 815.
[170] See also on this point Burrows (n 40) 404.

Edelman initially defended the result in *Tito v Waddell* on the basis that the Islanders no longer had a legitimate interest,[171] although he has later argued that it is unlikely that *Tito v Waddell* would survive the House of Lords' emphasis of the importance of performance interest in *Ruxley*.[172]

From restoration cases we now turn to contracts designed to reduce risk, the other category of cases in which skimped performance is problematic. These cases are distinguishable from the restoration cases on the ground that specific relief is no longer available to the claimant and damages are inadequate on any measure. Therefore, these cases are ones where disgorgement may be appropriate, particularly given the deterrent considerations involved.

B Skimped Performance and Contracts Designed to Reduce Risk

Contracts designed to reduce risk where the defendant skimps on performance resemble negative covenant cases in that both involve an 'agency problem'. The defendant has control over performance, and the claimant has difficulty monitoring whether he has performed the promised act. The claimant is generally the one who suffers the adverse consequences if performance is skimped. No specific relief is available; no measure of damages is adequate to compensate the claimant because she has suffered no easily quantifiable financial loss. It is likely that the defendants in these cases would have difficulty arguing the breach was inadvertent. Consequently, disgorgement damages should be available for such contracts.

City of New Orleans is the paradigmatic case of skimped performance involving a contract designed to reduce risk.[173] The Fireman's Charitable Association was paid to maintain certain specified levels of staff and fire fighting equipment for New Orleans. However, the claimant alleged that the defendant 'skimped' on its performance. First, rather than hiring the specified 124 employees, the Association instead hired no more than 70 men, resulting in a saving of $25,920. Secondly, the defendant did not keep the specified number of horses and carriages at Milnerberg, resulting in a saving of $8,800. Finally, the defendant did not keep the stipulated length of hose (10,000 feet). There was a deficiency of 4,750 feet which resulted in a saving of $4,275. The total saving to the Association was $38,995. During the currency of the contract the court found that New Orleans did not suffer any losses as a result of the skimped performance, and all fires were successfully extinguished.[174] Professor Jaffey has suggested that the purpose of contracts such as these is in part to reduce the risk of any loss occurring to the promisee.[175] In the instant case the purpose of the contract was not only to ensure that New Orleans was compensated for any loss which it suffered by a failure of the Fireman's

[171] Edelman, *Gain-Based Damages* (n 11) 173.
[172] Edelman (n 98) 133–34.
[173] *City of New Orleans* (n 94).
[174] ibid 488.
[175] P Jaffey, *The Nature and Scope of Restitution* (Oxford, Hart Publishing, 2000) 393–94; P Jaffey, 'Disgorgement and "Licence Fee Damages" in Contract' (2004) 20 *Journal of Contract Law* 1, 10.

Charitable Association to fight a fire adequately. It was also designed to reduce the risk of any loss occurring to the City and its citizens. In these circumstances the deterrent justification behind disgorgement is very strong. Organisations such as the Fireman's Charitable Association, which provide a public benefit, should be deterred from skimping on performance and putting the public at risk.[176] At the very least the Fireman's Charitable Association should have been made to disgorge any profits it made from skimping on performance.[177]

Jaffey argues that *Teacher v Calder*[178] could be analysed as a case of skimped performance.[179] There, the claimant advanced £15,000 to the defendant for use in the defendant's timber business, for which the claimant expected to receive an interest in the business, as well as a share of the profits. The defendant did not use the money for the timber business, but instead used it to set up a distillery, from which he made a significant profit. The claimant argued that he could trace his money into the profits made from the distillery business. The House of Lords rejected this argument, and the claimant could not recover his profit. The Court of Appeal in *Blake* affirmed *Teacher v Calder*, saying that the breach of contract in *Teacher* provided the defendant with an opportunity to profit, but did not render it incapable of performing its contractual duties to the claimant,[180] and that the profits did not arise directly from the breach of contract.[181] Lord Nicholls approved the Court of Appeal's conclusion on this point.[182]

However, if one analyses the case as one of skimped performance, the claimant should have been able to recover at least *some* of the profit.[183] The House of Lords assumes that because the claimant's loan was repaid in full and he suffered no loss, he was not entitled to a share of the profits. But the provision that the defendant was not to withdraw the money was designed to reduce the risk of default and to safeguard the claimant's investment. There was a clear agency problem in the circumstances, as well as a situation of moral hazard, because the claimant was the one whose money was exposed to risk. Once the money had been withdrawn, although the claimant suffered no loss, he incurred an additional risk for which he did not bargain.

[176] M McInnes, 'Restitutionary Damages for Breach of Contract: *Bank of America Canada v Mutual Trust Co*' (2002) 37 *Canadian Business Law Journal* 125, 132.

[177] Edelman suggests under his analysis that the City of New Orleans would have recourse to other gain-based remedies which may have been greater in amount. See Edelman, 'Gain-Based Remedies for Wrongdoing' (n 11) 241–43. *cf* O'Sullivan (n 3) 338–39, suggesting the court should have awarded compensatory damages but did not because it took an unduly narrow view of loss.

[178] *Teacher v Calder* [1899] UKHL 1, [1899] AC 451 (HL).

[179] Jaffey, 'Disgorgement and "Licence Fee Damages" in Contract' (n 175) 10–11.

[180] *Blake* (n 2) 458.

[181] Edelman notes that Lord Denning applied a similar test at first instance in *Reading v R* [1948] 2 KB 268 (KB) 275 – the breach must play a predominant part in obtaining the profit, not just a mere opportunity for profit.

[182] *Blake* (n 5) 285.

[183] See also D Campbell, 'The Treatment of *Teacher v Calder* in *AG v Blake*' (2002) 65 *MLR* 256, 260 who argues that the court in *Blake* could not simultaneously allow disgorgement in that case, but say that disgorgement was correctly denied in *Teacher v Calder*. Note that I do not agree with Campbell's argument that *Teacher v Calder* supports 'efficient breach'.

Arguably, a modern version of *Calder* occurred in *Smith v Landstar Properties Inc.*[184] The defendant, an investment advice company, invited the claimant, a retired school teacher, to invest in the company for an 8 per cent return. The president of the defendant, McCutcheon, promised the claimant that her investment funds would be secured by a mortgage over the properties being developed by the defendants. Accordingly, on 8 November 2005, the claimant loaned the defendant $100,000, evidenced by the issuance of a non-convertible debenture, in which it was covenanted that the claimant would obtain securities over the defendant's properties in second position to bank securities over the land. The claimant's loan was for two years, callable after one year, with full price and accrued interest at 8 per cent per annum payable quarterly. On 14 July 2006, the claimant wrote to McCutcheon seeking copies of the security documents in which her interest appeared, together with details of any prior charges. In fact, there was no security on the claimant's loan, and the defendant had never intended to give her any security. Thus, the claimant again wrote to McCutcheon, giving the defendant 15 days to secure the debenture against the title, and giving notice of default. When the claimant failed to receive an unconditional offer to redeem the debenture, she lodged a caveat over the defendant's land. The defendant applied to cancel the caveat, but lost its claim, and was ordered by the court to pay the claimant $100,000 plus interest at 8 per cent up to 7 November 2006. The claimant then commenced an action for damages on the basis of negligent misrepresentation and breach of contract. The trial judge ordered the defendant to pay the claimant the difference between the interest it actually paid to the claimant and the interest a reasonable person would demand for an unsecured loan. The evidence was that the market interest rate for an unsecured loan was at least three times higher than the rate contained in the claimant's contract.[185] The trial judge held that the defendant had made negligent misrepresentations and breached its contract such that 'restitutionary damages' ought to be paid, representing the use value of the money. It was immaterial that the claimant did not suffer any loss. The defendant appealed to the British Columbia Court of Appeal.

Finch CJ delivered a judgment with which Kirkpatrick and Groberman JJ agreed. The court found that there had been negligent misrepresentation, or even fraudulent and deliberate misrepresentation on the part of the defendant. Rather confusingly, this was an operating factor in the court's decision to uphold the claimant's *contractual* damages award. Finch CJ said:

> Tort is usually concerned with reliance damages, that is putting the plaintiff in their original position, and contract is usually concerned with expectation damages, that is giving the plaintiff the fruits of their bargain. However, this case does not fit neatly within either category. While these categories are helpful, the guiding principle is that damages are compensatory.
>
> . . .

[184] *Smith v Landstar Properties Inc* (2011) BCCA 44 (BCCA).
[185] ibid [40] (Finch CJ).

> In the unique circumstances of this case such damages compensate the plaintiff for the effect of the defendant's wrongdoing. There is no circumstance or policy present that would require a different measure of damages for tort from that for contract.[186]

Although the trial judge's award was upheld, the court refused to use the expression 'restitutionary damages' and it was further emphasised that the case did not concern an 'account of profits or damages measured by the defendant's gain.'[187] However, the court then went on to say that the case was very similar to *Experience Hendrix*, where 'restitutionary damages' or a reasonable fee was awarded in the claimant's favour pursuant to *Attorney-General v Blake*. Finch CJ then said:

> [T]he law should give effect, as it did in *Hendrix*, to the notion that the wrongdoer should not profit for free and should make some reasonable recompense.
>
> Damages on the basis of an interest rate differential merely compensate the plaintiff for the way in which the contract was actually performed, which resulted from the defendant's breach. The interest rate differential between secured and unsecured loans was an appropriate measure of damages in this case. It is based on the commercial value of the right infringed and assesses the sum payable by reference to the interest rate that might have been payable between willing parties.[188]

It should be clear from my analysis thus far that I regard the result in this case as correct, but contrary to the Court of Appeal, I would analyse this as an award of disgorgement damages. By failing to pay the claimant the going rate of interest for an unsecured loan, the defendant saved an expense which is a form of 'negative profit'. Thus, the court is really ordering the defendant to disgorge its profit in the form of the money it saved by breaching its contract. As with *City of New Orleans* and *Teacher v Calder* this is a contract designed to avoid risk, and the claimant had been exposed to a risk for which she did not bargain when the defendant failed to obtain security for her loan. Disgorgement should be awarded in order to recognise the claimant's performance interest because compensatory damages are inadequate and specific relief is no longer available. And in cases such as these, the deterrent rationale of disgorgement damages is strong.

Now that the picture of disgorgement damages has been painted more fully, I will go on to outline how the courts should choose a remedy.

VII Conclusion: Choice of Remedy

The first step is to establish whether or not compensatory damages are adequate by reference to concepts of substitutability. Substitutability goes to the heart of the contractual obligation because it seeks to ascertain to what extent the remedy awarded vindicates the claimant's performance interest. In cases of skimped per-

[186] ibid [36], [38] (Finch CJ).
[187] ibid [39] (Finch CJ).
[188] ibid [43]–[44] (Finch CJ).

formance, where perfection of the contractual obligation is still possible, it is likely that the court's primary choice will be between the two measures of damages: rectification damages and diminution of value damages. Ordinarily, damages for loss of value operate to recognise the claimant's performance interest because the value of performance is reflected in the value of the subject matter of the contract matter on the market, and thus in compensating for loss the court also operates to recognise the performance interest. All that needs to be protected in most contracts is the value of the bargain, and thus damages for loss of value are the most convenient remedy.[189]

As a result courts do not always adequately explore the nature of the interest to which contracts give rise, and tend to assume that loss of value is the sole measure used to vindicate the claimant's expectation. However, this breaks down in contracts where the cost of rectification is likely to be vastly greater than the loss of value. It is for this reason courts prefer to award rectification damages in building cases. Rectification damages operate to perfect the claimant's performance interest more accurately than damages for loss of value. Courts should always be aware that the claimant's interest is *not* simply to be compensated for loss, but it is also to gain the promised performance.

If compensatory damages are not adequate, the next question is whether specific relief is available. If specific relief is available, this should be the remedy of choice for the court. This is the method which best perfects the claimant's performance interest. However, common law courts prefer to award compensatory damages as a remedy of first resort as they are generally less intrusive than specific relief, and where damages are sufficient to either redress the harm caused as a result of breach or to place the claimant in a position as if the contract had been performed, the court presumes in favour of liberty.[190] In choosing to impose legal obligations, the legal system should choose the remedy which is least intrusive to the parties in the circumstances.

Disgorgement damages only become relevant if compensatory damages are inadequate, specific relief is no longer available, and the defendant has made an *actual* profit (whether by a positive gain or by an expense saved). The breach must also be advertent for disgorgement damages to be awarded.

Disgorgement damages should be available regardless of whether the gain is an 'expense saved' or a 'positive gain'.[191] However, in most cases of skimped performance disgorgement damages will be inappropriate because compensatory damages will be adequate, whether to rectify performance or simply to compensate for loss. The exception to this is the contract designed to avoid risk.

It is likely that disgorgement damages for positive gain will be easier to establish because of the advertence requirement. It is harder to establish that a breach caused by an 'expense saved' is advertent.[192]

[189] D Kimel, *From Promise to Contract: Towards a Liberal Theory of Contract* (Oxford, Hart Publishing, 2003) 101.

[190] ibid 100–04.

[191] Note that a breach of contract to avoid a loss is *not* a relevant gain.

[192] Thel and Siegelman (n 49) 1216–17.

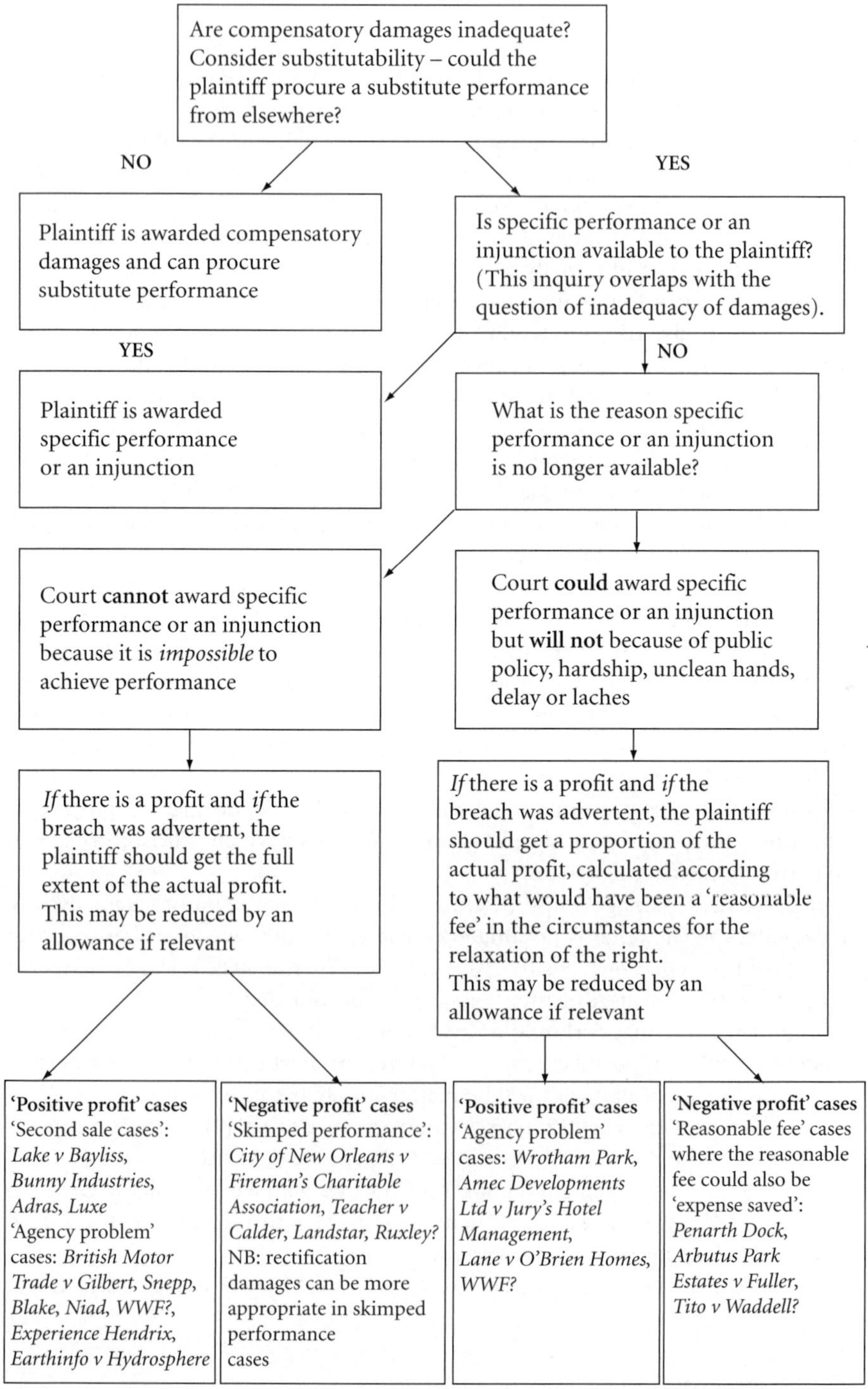
Are compensatory damages inadequate? Consider substitutability – could the plaintiff procure a substitute performance from elsewhere?
NO
YES
Plaintiff is awarded compensatory damages and can procure substitute performance
Is specific performance or an injunction available to the plaintiff? (This inquiry overlaps with the question of inadequacy of damages).
YES
NO
Plaintiff is awarded specific performance or an injunction
What is the reason specific performance or an injunction is no longer available?
Court cannot award specific performance or an injunction because it is impossible to achieve performance
Court could award specific performance or an injunction but will not because of public policy, hardship, unclean hands, delay or laches
If there is a profit and if the breach was advertent, the plaintiff should get the full extent of the actual profit. This may be reduced by an allowance if relevant
If there is a profit and if the breach was advertent, the plaintiff should get a proportion of the actual profit, calculated according to what would have been a 'reasonable fee' in the circumstances for the relaxation of the right. This may be reduced by an allowance if relevant
'Positive profit' cases 'Second sale cases': Lake v Bayliss, Bunny Industries, Adras, Luxe 'Agency problem' cases: British Motor Trade v Gilbert, Snepp, Blake, Niad, WWF?, Experience Hendrix, Earthinfo v Hydrosphere
'Negative profit' cases 'Skimped performance': City of New Orleans v Fireman's Charitable Association, Teacher v Calder, Landstar, Ruxley? NB: rectification damages can be more appropriate in skimped performance cases
'Positive profit' cases 'Agency problem' cases: Wrotham Park, Amec Developments Ltd v Jury's Hotel Management, Lane v O'Brien Homes, WWF?
'Negative profit' cases 'Reasonable fee' cases where the reasonable fee could also be 'expense saved': Penarth Dock, Arbutus Park Estates v Fuller, Tito v Waddell?

The measure of disgorgement depends upon whether or not specific relief *could not* be awarded, or the court simply *would not* award it for discretionary reasons. If specific relief is impossible to award the court should award 'full disgorgement damages'. This represents a full measure of the actual gain and has a greater deterrent and punitive effect. By contrast, if specific relief was not awarded for discretionary reasons, then the appropriate award is a 'reasonable fee', representing a partial measure of the defendant's actual gain. Partial disgorgement is ordered because the defendant has not made specific relief impossible: rather, it has been rendered impossible for some other reason. Thus the deterrent and punitive considerations are less strong. It can be said to be an apportionment of a kind.

My scheme has been reduced to a one-page flowchart on the facing page. Bars to relief are not yet present on the scheme, except insofar as they are relevant to 'reasonable fee' awards, and will be discussed in the next chapter.

7

Allowances and Bars to Relief

I Introduction

Once liability for disgorgement damages is established, it becomes necessary to establish how the quantum of the profit should be calculated, as well as whether any allowances for skill and effort should be made in the defendant's favour and whether there are any bars to relief. It is suggested that allowances for skill and effort should be allowed in some circumstances on the basis that the defendant deserves recognition of the skill and effort that contributed to the profits derived from the breach. This position is consistent with the principles applied to the account of profits remedy for breach of fiduciary duty. In addition, it is also suggested that some of the equitable bars to relief should be applicable to awards of disgorgement damages for breach of contract. This would ensure that disgorgement damages for breach of contract are not too 'claimant-focused', and that the interests of both parties are adequately recognised. The bars to relief are similar to those already developed for other equitable remedies such as specific performance, and thus disgorgement damages are consistent with existing law. The availability of allowances and bars to relief ensure that disgorgement damages are not over-deterrent. Further, they allow for recognition of circumstances where the claimant does not deserve relief, where the defendant's efforts deserve recognition, or where the defendant either should not be punished at all or should be punished to a lesser degree (whether because he does not deserve it, or for reasons of mercy). In this way, disgorgement damages are nuanced according to the circumstances.

This chapter will first consider how profit is to be calculated, including issues of causation and apportionment. The method by which the court chooses to calculate the net profit also raises the issue of allowances for skill and effort. *Attorney-General v Blake*[1] was not an appropriate case for an allowance for skill and effort given the nature of Blake's breach, but in other cases lack of good faith will not be a sufficient reason for denying a defendant an allowance.[2] Allowances can also

[1] [2000] UKHL 45, [2001] 1 AC 268 (HL).

[2] R Cunnington, 'The Assessment of Gain-Based Damages for Breach of Contract' (2008) 71 *MLR* 559, 576–77. Cunnington notes that the fact that Blake was liable to pay over the entire profit did not necessarily indicate that the law of allowances did not apply. First, it could be argued that the costs incurred by Blake were personal (time, skill and effort), and the courts are very reluctant to make an allowance for time, skill and effort on the part of the defendant when he has been dishonest. Secondly,

accommodate different shades of advertence in the conduct of the defendant. A defendant who breached his contract advertently, but genuinely thought he was entitled to break his contract, is more likely to obtain a generous allowance than a defendant whose breach is cynical and wilful.

Once the net profit has been quantified, the court must assess whether there are any bars to relief. The appropriate bars to relief are the recognised equitable discretionary factors: delay and acquiescence, hardship and lack of clean hands.

The availability of equitable allowances and the operation of the bars to relief are premised on the concept of desert. There may be reasons why the defendant does not deserve to be punished (to a greater or lesser degree). Or there may be reasons why the claimant does not deserve to have the benefit of disgorgement damages. In addition, principles of mercy may be relevant to ascertaining whether or not hardship can be established. Hardship, like mercy, implies that even when a defendant deserves to be punished, extenuating circumstances exist which mean that the court should be lenient.

As discussed in chapter two, the primary aim of disgorgement damages is deterrence. Perfect disgorgement strips the defendant of his profit and puts him in the position he would have been in if the breach had not been committed.[3] Because the defendant receives no gain from breach, disgorgement damages effectively remove any incentive for potential contract breakers to breach and make a profit thereby. Considerations of desert and punishment do not necessarily conflict with deterrence. For example, in *Blake* the two aims of deterrence and punishment were working in tandem. George Blake *deserved* to be punished by being stripped of his profit because of the advertent nature of the breach of negative covenant. For the same reason, it was important that Blake and other potential defendants be deterred from committing a similar wrong in the future. However, in other cases considerations of desert may conflict with considerations of deterrence to such an extent that total disgorgement is not appropriate.

It follows that if the law allows bars to relief or makes allowances which reduce the amount of disgorgement damages awarded to the claimant, the corollary is that the deterrent effect of disgorgement damages is reduced. As Associate Professor Harding has argued in the context of equitable allowances for breach of fiduciary duty, the deterrent effect of disgorgement damages is lessened to the extent that the quantum of damages is reduced.[4] If disgorgement damages are not awarded at all for some discretionary reason the deterrent effect of disgorgement damages is non-existent. It must be noted, however, that in circumstances where the bars to relief operate to prevent an award of disgorgement damages, an award of common law damages remains possible.

Blake had in fact already received £60,000 as an advance before publication, and this sum could not be recovered. Thus, the profits disgorged were only the remaining £90,000 remaining in the jurisdiction.

[3] R Cooter and T Ulen, *Law and Economics*, 3rd edn (Harlow, Addison-Wesley, 2000) 234.

[4] M Harding, 'Justifying Fiduciary Allowances' in A Robertson and TH Wu (eds), *The Goals of Private Law* (Oxford, Hart Publishing, 2009) 341, 342–44; *cf Guinness plc v Saunders* [1989] UKHL 2, [1990] 2 AC 663 (HL) 700 (Lord Goff).

I will first look at causation, remoteness and apportionment, which have an impact on how the actual gain is assessed. I will then move to consider allowances for skill and effort and bars to relief, which may lead to a reduction of the profit disgorged (or even, in some circumstances, no disgorgement being ordered at all).

II Calculating the Account – Causation, Remoteness and Apportionment

A The Nature of the Account

The account has its origins in the common law writ of *praecipe quod reddat*, but the common law account was ultimately overtaken by the more efficient equitable account.[5] The account of profits was particularly well suited to ensuring compliance with equitable obligations as it ensured that breach was less likely by deterring potential defendants.[6] Thus, over time, the account of profits became synonymous with breach of equitable obligations.

The immediate function of an account is merely to provide an account to the claimant of the defendant's financial affairs insofar as they relate to the claimant's claim.[7] However, once a profit has been identified, it can then be disgorged. The purpose of the account of profits is 'neither compensatory nor restitutionary: rather it is designed to strip the [defendant] of the unauthorised profits he has made'.[8] Importantly, the profits are the defendant's *net* profits, rather than the defendant's gross receipts.[9]

In assessing net profit, courts have traditionally made allowance for certain expenses incurred by the defendant in two ways.[10] First, they have sometimes allowed specific disbursements, such as expenditures of money and other capital, as well as skilled labour by the defendant (perhaps a form of quantum meruit calculated according to an hourly rate of pay).[11] Secondly, courts have credited

[5] M McInnes, 'Account of Profits for Common Law Wrongs' in S Degeling and J Edelman (eds), *Equity in Commercial Law* (Pyrmont, Lawbook Co, 2005) 405, 406–07; G Jones, 'The Role of Equity in the English Law of Restitution' in EJH Schrage (ed), *Unjust Enrichment: The Comparative History of the Law of Restitution* (Berlin, Dunker & Humblot, 1995) 147, 168–69.

[6] S Worthington, 'Reconsidering Disgorgement for Wrongs' (1999) 62 *MLR* 218, 236.

[7] S Doyle and D Wright, 'Restitutionary Damages – The Unnecessary Remedy?' (2001) 25 *Melbourne University Law Review* 1, 10.

[8] *Murad v Al-Saraj* [2005] EWCA Civ 959, [2005] All ER (D) 503 [108] (Jonathan Parker LJ).

[9] *Patel v London Borough of Brent* [2003] EWHC 3081 (Ch) [29] (Morritt V-C); *Regal (Hastings) Ltd v Gulliver and Others* [1967] AC 134 (HL) 154 (Lord Wright); *O'Sullivan v Management Agencies & Music Ltd* [1985] QB 428 (CA) 458, [1984] 3 WLR 448, 466 (Dunn LJ).

[10] Harding (n 4) 346–47.

[11] *Brown v Litton* (1711) 1 PWms 140, 24 ER 329; *Yates v Finn* (1880) 13 Ch D 839; *Chirnside v Fay* [2007] 1 NZLR 433, [2006] NZSC 68 (NZSC) [153] (Tipping J).

the defendant with an allowance which is not specifically itemised, but more of an 'all things considered' allowance.[12]

B Causation and Remoteness

Commentary suggests that the test of causation for an award of an account of profits for breach of contract is whether the claimant can show that the defendant would not have made the profit 'but for' the breach in question.[13] Similarly, the Court of Appeal in *Blake* required that recovery should be limited to profits 'occasioned directly by the breach.'[14] As will be discussed when considering apportionment below, the courts should distinguish between profits which arise directly as a result of the breach and profits which do not.[15] This should not be confused with allowances, which involve making some recognition of the defendant's skill and effort *despite* the fact that his acts were legally responsible for causing the gain.

The 'but for' causation rule for accounting for profits for breach of contract is less harsh on defendants than the more 'claimant-friendly' rule which is applied to fiduciaries. In breach of fiduciary duty cases, the breach need only be 'a cause' of the gain, and need not be a predominant cause.[16] This reflects the greater need for deterrence in such cases. By contrast, the rule in disgorgement for breach of contract cases should be less stringent than that for fiduciaries.[17]

Disgorgement damages for breach of contract have also been limited by notions of remoteness.[18] Edelman has argued that the Court of Appeal in *Blake*'s approval[19] of *Teacher v Calder*[20] imposes a remoteness requirement on disgorgement damages.[21] In *Teacher v Calder* the claimant advanced money to the defendant for the purpose of investing in the defendant's timber business. The defendant did not

[12] *Brown v De Tastet* (1821) Jac 284, 37 ER 858; *Featherstonhaugh v Turner* (1858) 25 Beav 382, 53 ER 683; *Lord Provost of Edinburgh v Lord Advocate* (1879) 4 App Cas 823; *Phipps v Boardman* [1964] 1 WLR 993 (Ch); *O'Sullivan* (n 9).

[13] EA Farnsworth, 'Your Loss or My Gain? The Dilemma of the Disgorgement Principle in Breach of Contract' (1985) 94 *Yale Law Journal* 1339, 1343; Cunnington (n 2) 579; G Virgo, 'Restitutionary Remedies for Wrongs: Causation and Remoteness' in CEF Rickett (ed), *Justifying Private Law Remedies* (Oxford, Hart Publishing, 2008) 301, 304. See also American Law Institute, *Restatement (Third) of Restitution and Unjust Enrichment* (2011) § 51(5)(a) and comment f.

[14] *Attorney General v Blake* [1997] EWCA Civ 3008, [1998] Ch 439 (CA) 458 (Lord Woolf MR).

[15] Cunnington (n 2) 584. Cunnington notes that the distinction can be difficult to apply in practice.

[16] C Mitchell, 'Causation, Remoteness, and Fiduciary Gains' (2006) 17 *King's College Law Journal* 325, 332; *Fexuto Pty Ltd v Bosnjak Holdings Pty Ltd (No 2)* (1998) 29 ACSR 290, 297 (Young J). Compare *Chirnside* (n 11) [36] (Elias CJ) and [54] (Gault J), where the 'but for' test was applied in a fiduciary context, but this is explained by the antecedent profit sharing agreement – see also *Murad* (n 8) [160] (Clarke LJ, dissenting).

[17] R Grantham and CEF Rickett, *Enrichment and Restitution in New Zealand* (Oxford, Hart Publishing, 2000) 487.

[18] *Regal (Hastings) Ltd* (n 9) 143 (Lord Russell); *Warman International Ltd v Dwyer* (1995) 182 CLR 544, 565; Mitchell (n 16) 336–39. See also American Law Institute (n 13) § 51(5)(a).

[19] *Blake* (n 14) 458. Adopted in *Blake* (n 1) 285 (Lord Nicholls).

[20] *Teacher v Calder* [1899] UKHL 1, [1899] AC 451.

[21] J Edelman, *Gain-Based Damages – Contract, Tort, Equity and Intellectual Property* (Oxford, Hart Publishing, 2002) 160–61.

use the money for this purpose, but instead invested the money in a distillery business and made significant profits. The House of Lords declined to award the claimant any interest in the profits.[22] The Court of Appeal in *Blake* said of *Teacher v Calder*:

> The mere fact that the defendant's breach of his contract with the plaintiff has enabled him to enter into a more profitable contract with someone else should also not be sufficient. *Teacher v. Calder* . . . is sound law. Nor should it suffice that, by entering into the later and more profitable contract, the defendant has put it out of his power to perform his contract with the plaintiff: the distinction between the two cases is not one of substance.[23]

As will be evident from the previous chapter, I disagree with the Court of Appeal's conclusion that *Teacher v Calder* is sound law, but I agree that it is important to have a test of remoteness where disgorgement damages for breach of contract is concerned. A test of remoteness asks whether it would be *fair* to hold the defendant responsible for gain which has arisen as a result of his wrongful act, but which was a distant or unusual consequence of that act, or which was more immediately caused by the defendant's non-wrongful acts, the acts of a third party or a natural event.[24] It is appropriate to apply such a test in these cases.

Remoteness can be used by courts to moderate the severity of the effect of an award of disgorgement damages on a defendant.[25] Remoteness could also be used to solve some of the difficulties which occur with the 'reasonable fee' cases, for example, when unanticipated events occur after the date upon which a 'hypothetical negotiation' would have taken place.[26]

C Apportionment

The principle of apportionment allows a defendant to argue that some portion of the profits should not be disgorged because these profits were not occasioned directly by the breach.[27] In *Warman International Ltd v Dwyer*, the High Court left open the possibility that it may be appropriate to apportion profits where some profit resulted as a result of the breach and other profit did not, although the 'general rule' is that courts will not order apportionment in breach of fiduciary duty cases without a prior agreement for profit-sharing.[28] Apportionment is frequently adopted in accounts of profits awarded for breach of copyright and patent cases, so

[22] *Teacher* (n 20) 468 (Lord Davey).

[23] *Blake* (n 14) 458 (Lord Woolf) (citations omitted).

[24] Mitchell (n 16) 337. Remoteness is also sometimes known as 'scope of liability'.

[25] ibid 328.

[26] See, eg *Lunn Poly Ltd v Liverpool & Lancashire Properties Ltd* [2006] EWCA Civ 430, [2006] 2 EGLR 29 (where it became evident that the plaintiff was liable to forfeiture of the lease after the date hypothetical negotiations would have taken place).

[27] See, eg *Docker v Somes* (1834) 2 MY & K 656 (Ch), 39 ER 1095; *Scott v Scott* (1963) 109 CLR 649 (note, both cases involve tracing profits through exchange-substitutes). See also American Law Institute (n 13) § 51(5), comment g.

[28] *Warman* (n 18) 562.

that the profit is split between that resulting directly from the infringement and that resulting from other sources.[29] Similarly, it is appropriate that in other cases, such as breach of contract, there should be apportionment between profits made as a direct result of the breach and profits which are attributable to other reasons.[30] However, apportionment is less likely to be appropriate in breach of fiduciary duty cases where infringing and non-infringing acts cannot be separated because of the broad scope of the duties infringed.[31] The only cases in which apportionment has been made have involved antecedent profit sharing arrangements, in regards to which courts have taken a 'but for' approach to causation.[32] Nonetheless, it is argued that apportionment may provide a solution to those cases where an allowance for skill and effort is difficult to justify according to principles of desert.[33]

An interesting alternative to apportionment has been proposed by Professor Dagan where commercial contracts are concerned. He argues the parties should divide the profit between themselves.[34] He rejects the idea that the defendant should be allowed to retain the entire profit because 'it implicitly sanctions the promisor's unilateral pursuit of [his] own interests, irrespective of the relationship [he] has already established with [his] contractual partner.'[35] On the other hand, he also argues that the claimant should not be entitled to the net profits from the breach as a matter of course.[36] Thus, he argues that the parties should divide the difference between the promisor's gain from the breach and the promisee's expectation between themselves.[37] Still, this is not entirely straightforward. Dagan notes that there are arguments either way as to whether the parties should always divide the profit equally, or whether the court should have discretion to apportion the profit.[38]

An agreed apportionment occurred in *Vercoe v Rutland Fund Management Limited*.[39] The claimants developed a management buy-in proposal for a chain of pawn broking stores and put it to the defendants, who were associated with a venture capital business. The defendants ultimately purchased the pawn broking

[29] See, eg *Potton Ltd v Yorkclose Ltd* [1990] FSR 11 (Ch) 16 (Millet J); *Sheldon v Metro-Goldwyn Pictures Corp*, 309 US 390, 404 (1940) (Hughes CJ).

[30] D Friedmann, 'Restitution for Wrongs: The Measure of Recovery' (2000) 79 *Texas Law Review* 1879, 1898–99; J McCamus, 'Disgorgement For Breach of Contract: A Comparative Perspective' (2003) 36 *Loyola of Los Angeles Law Review* 943, 971; Cunnington (n 2) 579–80.

[31] Cunnington (n 2) 580; Friedmann (n 30) 1904–17 notes the different approaches of the law to tracing into property contributed to by a fiduciary (where apportionment is common) compared to accounts of profit for breach of fiduciary duty.

[32] Harding (n 4) 345; *Warman* (n 18) 562; *Murad* (n 8) [160] (Clarke LJ, dissenting); *Chirnside* (n 11) [36] (Elias CJ), [54] (Gault J).

[33] Charles Mitchell has argued that in some circumstances courts should limit accounts of profits for breach of fiduciary duty according to principles of remoteness: Mitchell (n 16) 328.

[34] H Dagan, *The Law and Ethics of Restitution* (Cambridge, Cambridge University Press, 2004) 278–82.

[35] ibid 279.

[36] ibid.

[37] ibid 280. See also W Goodhart, 'Restitutionary Damages for Breach of Contract: The Remedy that Dare Not Speak its Name' [1995] *Restitution Law Review* 3, 12–13.

[38] Dagan (n 34) 281.

[39] *Vercoe v Rutland Fund Management Limited* [2010] EWHC 424 (Ch).

business, developed it and sold it at a profit. However, they cut the claimants out of any involvement with the business prior to purchasing it, in breach of a contract between the parties which provided that the defendants would not use the confidential information provided in the claimant's buy-in proposal without involving and consulting them. Roth J calculated damages according to a hypothetical 'reasonable fee' which the claimants would have accepted from the defendants to be released from their contractual obligations. The parties *agreed* that a reasonable fee award was an appropriate measure,[40] although they disagreed as to precise quantum. It would not have been fair in the circumstances to strip the entire gain from the defendants when they had expended a good deal of risk, money and effort.

In some senses, the analysis described in the previous chapter, where the court declines to award specific relief even though it could do so, and instead awards a 'reasonable fee', represents a form of judicial apportionment, where the claimant takes only a proportion of the profit.

Thus, 'but for' causation, remoteness and apportionment are all principles which have been adopted in awards of disgorgement damages for breach of contract. In the next section, I will first consider the nature of desert and mercy before looking at how these concepts impact and inform allowances and bars to relief. These concepts provide the moral justification for courts to make such defences available.

III Desert and Mercy

A The Nature of 'Desert'

Professor Feinberg has argued, '[t]o say that a person deserves something is to say that there is a certain sort of propriety in his having it'.[41] Desert is based on 'propriety', not entitlement. Someone who deserves a thing cannot say that they have a *right* to it; rather they can only argue that it is proper that they be given an interest in the thing.[42]

The question is then when it will be proper for a person to be given an interest in a thing on the basis of desert. Desert looks to a person's qualities, actions and status.[43] As with the punitive rationale generally, desert is always backward-looking;[44] it looks at what a person has done in the past. This can be contrasted

[40] ibid [289].

[41] J Feinberg, 'Justice and Personal Desert' in J Feinberg, *Doing and Deserving: Essays in the Theory of Responsibility* (Princeton, Princeton University Press, 1970) 56.

[42] ibid 86; SR Munzer, *A Theory of Property* (Cambridge, Cambridge University Press, 1990) 260.

[43] Harding (n 4) 352; J Kleinig, 'The Concept of Desert' (1971) 8 *American Philosophical Quarterly* 71, 73; D Miller, *Social Justice* (Oxford, Clarendon Press, 1976) 85; L Becker, *Property Rights: Philosophic Foundations* (London, Routledge & Paul, 1977) 50; Munzer (n 42) 257; JW Harris, *Property And Justice* (Oxford, Clarendon Press, 1996) 205.

[44] Kleinig (n 43) 73.

with specific and general deterrence, which are always forward-looking.[45] Further, desert is personal;[46] it links to the specific conduct of the people involved, not to the conduct of third parties. In this way it is also different to general deterrence, which looks to prevent other people from committing the same conduct in the future.

Despite its personal nature, convention plays an important part in desert.[47] Convention is important not because of any principle particular to desert itself, but because of the moral principles which shape the rule of law. That is, in order to be treated justly, a person deserves the same or similar treatment to that which is given to a person whose qualities and actions are the same as theirs. Someone can only be said to have received his '*just* deserts' if there is parity between the treatment of that particular person and the treatment of other people who have done the same kind of thing. In other words, like cases should be treated alike.

Desert also links to the notion that when a person expends labour, he deserves remuneration in some way. This must be qualified according to circumstance. As Becker argues, 'we must hold the principle of desert to be totally inapplicable to cases in which gains are gotten by violating moral prohibitions – e.g. by unjustifiably overriding the rights of others.'[48] Thus, expending labour on a bank robbery is not deserving of remuneration. Nonetheless, our society has a general concept that labour should be rewarded when it benefits other people.[49]

Desert plays an important role in the operation of allowances for skill and effort, and in the availability of delay and acquiescence and lack of clean hands as bars to relief. However, before turning to this, I will first outline the nature of mercy.

B The Nature of 'Mercy'

The nature of mercy is that, although the defendant deserves to be punished, he ought not to be punished because of his difficult personal circumstances. Rainbolt argues that mercy has three features. First, it is thought to be a virtue, secondly, it is thought to temper justice,[50] and thirdly, no one has a right to mercy.[51] Like desert, therefore, mercy is based on propriety, not entitlement. A person can only

[45] J Berryman, 'The Case For Restitutionary Damages Over Punitive Damages: Teaching the Wrongdoer that Tort does not Pay' (1994) 73 *Canadian Bar Review* 320, 322.

[46] Harding (n 4) 352–53.

[47] ibid 353. See also Harris (n 43) 207–8; Feinberg (n 41) 82; Miller (n 43) 91.

[48] Becker (n 43) 51.

[49] Harding (n 4) 355–56.

[50] Some have argued that the fact that mercy 'tempers' justice means that it creates an unjust result: see, eg A Smart, 'Mercy' (1968) 43 *Philosophy* 345; C Card, 'On Mercy' (1972) 81 *Philosophical Review* 182; HS Hestevold, 'Justice to Mercy' (1985) 46 *Philosophy and Phenomenological Research* 281; J Murphy, 'Mercy and Legal Justice' in J Murphy and J Hampton (eds), *Forgiveness and Mercy* (Cambridge, Cambridge University Press, 1988) 162, 167; GW Rainbolt, 'Mercy: An Independent, Imperfect Virtue' (1990) 27 *American Philosophical Quarterly* 169.

[51] Rainbolt (n 50); *cf* J Tasioulas, 'Mercy' (2003) 103 *Proceedings of the Aristotelian Society* 101, 125–28.

argue that it is proper in the circumstances that an exception ought to be made with regard to the imposition of a deserved punishment.

John Tasioulas says that in contrast to other manifestations of charity, mercy alleviates suffering which is in some sense *deserved*.[52] Mercy highlights the potential inappropriateness of an otherwise just punishment once other considerations of the defendant's life or circumstances are taken into account.[53] Mercy has most often been linked with the imposition of punishment for wrongdoing. Most accounts of mercy focus on the imposition of criminal punishment.[54] However, mercy has also been extended more broadly to the civil law, where a person has a right to enforce a certain remedy against another person, but does not do so.[55] I argue that some private law remedies, such as disgorgement damages, have punitive aspects, and thus it is appropriate that mercy has a role to play, albeit in very limited circumstances. Even an award of compensatory damages can sometimes involve censure of wrongdoing.[56] Nonetheless, when a claimant seeks fulfilment of an existing obligation, this does not ordinarily constitute punishment, and if mercy is shown by failing to impose an existing obligation, the claimant's rights will not be vindicated fully. Therefore it is important that if courts do show mercy, they must do so after full consideration of any negative effects on the claimant.

This highlights a difficulty with the judicial exercise of mercy. It has been said that 'judges have no right to be merciful because it is not *to them* that any obligation is due. And they have an obligation to impose the sentence the law prescribes.'[57] Therefore, under this rubric the only person who has any right to extend mercy is the claimant herself; the judge has no standing to exercise mercy on her behalf. Like desert, there is a strongly *personal* aspect to mercy, and it must be queried why the court will deny the claimant full relief if the claimant does not benefit from the defendant's conduct in any way or if the claimant does not choose to extend mercy. These criticisms have some force, and it is suggested that if judges exercise mercy in the stead of the claimant, they must be particularly careful to ensure that the claimant's rights are not unduly prejudiced, and that there is still adequate vindication of the claimant's rights.

In addition, judicial mercy has been criticised because it is said to violate the rule of law and the precept that like cases should be treated alike.[58] However, other commentators have argued that mercy is an essential component of a just legal system and that it is an important facet of equity in particular.[59] In Aristotelian

[52] Tasioulas (n 51) 104.

[53] ibid 115.

[54] See, eg ibid; Smart (n 50); Card (n 50).

[55] P Twambley, 'Mercy and Forgiveness' (1976) 36 *Analysis* 84, 85–86; A Brien, 'Mercy Within Legal Justice' (1998) 24 *Social Theory and Practice* 83, 84. The paradigm case here is Portia's speech to Shylock in Shakespeare's *The Merchant of Venice* to show mercy and not take his 'pound of flesh'.

[56] As Tasioulas acknowledges: Tasioulas (n 51) 106.

[57] Twambley (n 55) 87.

[58] R Harrison, 'The Equality of Mercy' in H Gross and R Harrison (eds), *Jurisprudence: Cambridge Essays* (Oxford, Clarendon Press, 1992) 107, 107–08.

[59] MC Nussbaum, 'Equity and Mercy' (1993) 22 *Philosophy and Public Affairs* 83; *cf* C Bennett, 'The Limits of Mercy' (2004) 17 *Ratio* 1. However, a number of authors have argued that mercy may be

terms, equity is 'a rectification of law where the law falls short by reason of its universality.'[60] Thus, it is necessary to have some method whereby the general harshness of the law is mitigated by consideration of individual circumstances, and in a sense, mercy is a sub-species of equity.

Where a judge has discretion to choose which level of liability to impose, or where there is discretion as to the appropriate penalty, it follows that there may be room for mercy. Some scholars have therefore argued that mercy is a species of 'disjunctive desert', where a judge is merciful if she chooses the lesser of the available ranges of liability or penalty.[61] If desert does enter into mercy, then it is in a broader sense than discussed above. That is, the court takes into account more than just the facts of the dispute before them and considers desert in a global sense given the defendant's specific circumstances.

Tasioulas argues that there are four paradigm cases of mercy:[62]

1. Where the offender's history and upbringing may have presented obstacles to forming a decent and law-abiding character;
2. Where wrongdoing has occurred in a context which generates reasons for leniency because there were obstacles to law-abiding behaviour (eg where a woman kills her abusive spouse);
3. Where 'the offender is already suffering some grave misfortune which will be cruelly exacerbated by the infliction in full measure of his just deserts';[63]
4. Where the offender has sincerely repented of wrongdoing and made apologies and reparation to those he wronged.

The bar to relief based on hardship is informed by mercy rather than desert – although the defendant deserves to be punished, because of the exigencies of his circumstances, the court extends mercy to him. The extent of the mercy in this context is limited because a defendant will still be liable for common law damages.

I will now consider the operation of allowances for skill and effort in detail, and will then consider bars to relief.

unjust because it involves a departure from justice. See, eg Murphy (n 50) 167: 'If mercy requires a tempering of justice, then there is a sense in which mercy may require a departure from justice . . . Thus to be merciful is perhaps to be unjust. But it is a vice, not a virtue, to manifest injustice. Thus mercy must be, not a virtue but a vice – a product of morally dangerous sentimentality.'

[60] P Loughlan and P Parkinson, 'The History and Nature of Equity' in *The Laws of Australia: Equity* (Sydney, Butterworths, 1993) vol 15 para 15.1.160; Aristotle, *Nichomachean Ethics*, 2nd edn (T Irwin tr, Indiana, Hackett Publishing, 1999) Book V, Ch 10.

[61] Hestevold (n 50) 363.

[62] ibid 116–18.

[63] ibid 117.

IV Allowances and Disgorgement Damages

An allowance for skill and effort should be made for disgorgement damages in some circumstances.[64] Indeed, allowances have been made in some cases to date. In *Earthinfo Inc v Hydrosphere Resource Consultants Inc*,[65] Hydrosphere had made a series of contracts with EarthInfo's predecessor, whereby Hydrosphere would develop hydrological and meteorological software and EarthInfo's predecessor would package, market and sell the software. EarthInfo had an obligation to pay Hydrosphere royalties for the products it developed, but it ceased paying the royalties in breach of the contract. The court inter alia ordered EarthInfo to disgorge the profits it had made by selling Hydrosphere's product since the breach of contract.[66] However, the court also found that the efforts of EarthInfo in packaging, marketing and promoting the products should be recognised.[67]

Similarly, in *Experience Hendrix* the English Court of Appeal was prepared to make an allowance for skill and effort when awarding a 'reasonable fee' award,[68] although it could reasonably be asked what exactly PPX did to deserve such an allowance.

Allowances deal in some measure with the concern of law and economics scholars that 'efficient' breaches of contract would be prevented by an award of disgorgement damages.

Nonetheless, I suggest that desert provides the best justification for an allowance for skill and effort because allowances reflect the notion that people deserve remuneration for their labour, a desert-based concern.[69] However, as will be explored below, the desert justification runs into difficulties in cases where the defendant's labour has *not* benefited the claimant. The case law regarding allowances for breaching fiduciaries has been inconsistent. Sometimes allowances have been withheld where the defendant's labour has not benefited the claimant,[70] but in other circumstances allowances have been made regardless. There are also particular problems with justifying an allowance when a fiduciary is dishonest,[71] and this may also prove a problem in breach of contact cases.

[64] Cunnington (n 2) 600–1. See also American Law Institute (n 27) § 51(5) and comment h.
[65] 900 P 2d 113 (Colo SC, 1995).
[66] ibid 120.
[67] ibid 121.
[68] *Experience Hendrix LLC v PPX Enterprises Inc* [2003] EWCA Civ 1804, [2003] All ER (D) 328 (CA) [44].
[69] Harding (n 4) 356–67.
[70] *Blake* (n 1).
[71] Harding (n 4) 361–62.

A Justifications for Allowances

Courts and commentators have sometimes suggested that allowances are made because the profit made by the defendant is not sufficiently causally connected to the breach.[72] So, for example, the Australian High Court has said:

> [I]t may be appropriate to allow the fiduciary a proportion of the profits, depending on the particular circumstances. That may well be the case when it appears that a significant proportion of an increase in profits has been generated by the skills, efforts, property and resources of the fiduciary, so long as they are not risks to which the principal's property has been exposed. Then it may be said that the relevant proportion of the increased profits is not the product or consequence of the plaintiff's property, but the product of the fiduciary's skills, efforts, property and resources.[73]

However, this justification does not accord with the practice of courts in making allowances. The court does not divide up expenses in order to work out which ones were causally related to the breach and which ones were not.[74] Nor does the justification accord with the law regarding breach of fiduciary obligations: the defendant's conduct after the breach has never been taken into account in determining whether the defendant has breached; courts do not say that some conduct was 'not a cause' but other conduct 'was a cause'.[75] It is suggested that these courts and commentators are confusing apportionment with allowances.

Secondly, some courts and commentators have suggested that profit can be 'too remote' from the breach of fiduciary obligation and, therefore, need not be disgorged, and that this is a justification for awarding allowances.[76] However, remoteness 'tells us nothing meaningful about how allowances may be justified.'[77]

There needs therefore to be some other justification for the allowance for skill and effort.[78] The most convincing justification is desert: namely, that the defendant expended time and skilled labour and deserves some recognition of this. Because desert gives rise to a claim of propriety, not to an entitlement, desert seems eminently suitable as an explanation for a discretionary allowance.

A defendant who wants to make a logically consistent claim for a reduction in the claimant's award should point to some benefit he conferred upon the claimant by his skill and effort.[79] Although the defendant's labour may have benefited other people, this does not seem to be a justification for an allowance *against* the

[72] *Regal (Hastings) Ltd* (n 9) 144–45 (Lord Russell), 153 (Lord Macmillan); *Chan v Zacharia* (1984) 154 CLR 178 (HCA) 199 (Deane J); *Warman* (n 8) 561; *Murad* (n 9) [72]–[79] (Arden LJ). See also Edelman (n 21) 104–05, 171–72; G Virgo, *The Principles of the Law of Restitution*, 2nd edn (Oxford, Oxford University Press, 2006) 516–19; Virgo (n 13) 309–10, 325–26.

[73] *Warman* (n 8) 561.

[74] Harding (n 4) 346–47.

[75] ibid 347–48.

[76] *Warman* (n 8). See also A Burrows, *The Law of Restitution*, 2nd edn (Oxford, Oxford University Press, 2002) 500–01; Grantham and Rickett (n 17) 486–87.

[77] Harding (n 4) 349.

[78] ibid.

[79] ibid 359.

claimant specifically. Because of the personal and specific nature of desert it seems appropriate that the defendant must justify to the claimant why he properly deserves an allowance against her.

Nonetheless, a desert-based analysis does not sit well with the more utilitarian concerns of law and economics scholars. Easterbrook and Fischel exemplify this approach:

> Recompense of some kind is necessary to spur the fiduciary to discover and exploit opportunities; the alternative is a structure of compensation such as a flat fee or a percentage of the managed assets that promotes idleness.[80]

Further, desert does not sit well with some of the fiduciary duty cases where the defendant's profits have not benefited the claimant in any way, such as *Warman*.[81]

In *Warman* the Australian High Court awarded an account of profits for a concurrent breach of fiduciary duty and contract by the defendant. Warman International Ltd ('Warman') was the Australian distributor of Bonfiglioli, an Italian company which manufactured gearboxes. The local manager of Warman in Queensland was Dwyer. Bonfiglioli was unhappy with Warman's performance as a distributor. Dwyer was also unhappy, and flew to Italy to discuss the possibility of setting up his own distribution company as the Australian distributor of Bonfiglioli. Bonfiglioli gladly agreed, and Dwyer's new company became the Australian distributor of Bonfiglioli. Warman then sued Dwyer for breach of fiduciary duty because Dwyer breached his duty to Warman by redirecting his employer's business to a personal enterprise. The trial judge had held that Bonfiglioli would have terminated the distributorship contract with Warman anyway, regardless of the actions of Dwyer.

It was clear that there was a breach of Dwyer's employment contract with Warman, as well as a breach of fiduciary duty. The High Court found that Warman was entitled to elect between an account of profits or equitable compensation. The trial judge had calculated Dwyer's profits over the four years since the breach, but the High Court found that because Bonfiglioli would have terminated the contract within two years anyway, Warman should only be entitled to two years of profit if it elected to take an account of profit. For present purposes, the critical point is that the High Court was prepared to award Dwyer an equitable allowance representing the time and effort which he spent in building up the competing business, even though his breach was deliberate and cynical.[82]

Warman is a troubling case, for if Dwyer's breach did not benefit Warman in any way, what justification had the court for reducing the profit Warman could receive as a result of Dwyer's breach? Certainly, as Easterbrook and Fischel might argue, the award of an allowance rewards Dwyer's entrepreneurial skill and effort and ensures that fiduciary law is not overly deterrent, but there seems no reason

[80] F Easterbrook and D Fischel, 'Contract and Fiduciary Duty' (1993) 36 *Journal of Law and Economics* 425, 442.

[81] *Warman* (n 8).

[82] Compare *Boardman v Phipps* [1967] 2 AC 46 (HL).

why Warman should bear the brunt of that particular policy consideration because Dwyer's skill and effort did not specifically benefit it. Considerations of desert should be personal and relate directly to the parties involved. Perhaps the court formed a view that Warman did not deserve to have the full profit because it was not an efficient company, but this scarcely seems principled. Apportionment may perhaps provide some justification for *Warman*: namely, that some of the profits were not caused directly by the breach.

By contrast, *Boardman v Phipps* is entirely explicable under a desert-based analysis: Mr Boardman deserved an allowance for skill and effort because he was a good faith fiduciary whose hard work and effort benefited not only him, but also the beneficiaries of the trust he administered.[83] It may be that the allowance in *Warman* should rather have been dealt with by the application of principles of apportionment instead: that is to say, Dwyer did not have to disgorge that proportion of the profit which did not arise from his breach.

B Advertence and Allowances

Warman does not sit well with those cases which suggest only *honest* breaches of duty will give rise to allowances.[84] This difficulty arises in part from the clash between the utilitarian concern of deterrence and the personal nature of the desert justification. Deterrence is forward-looking, and seeks to prevent other people from doing the same thing in the future. Eisenberg has said that if an award for skill and effort would nullify the deterrent effect of the disgorgement damages or unduly reward the defendant for the very wrong he committed, the allowance should be very much reduced or non-existent.[85] By contrast, desert is backward-looking and seeks to identify exactly why this particular defendant deserves an allowance and why this particular claimant deserves to have that allowance carved out of the profits awarded to her. It is not in the least concerned with the impact of a rule on the future behaviour of the parties.

The allowance in *Warman* is difficult to justify on the basis of desert because the defendant's breach was advertent and not in good faith. Nor was the claimant in that case benefited in any way by the defendant's labour and skills, and it is therefore unfair that the claimant should have the account of profits reduced by the award of an allowance.

This may present a problem, too, for allowances for disgorgement damages for breach of contract because, as canvassed earlier, the remedy will usually only be awarded where the breach is advertent.[86] If the defendant knew that he had an

[83] Of course, Boardman owed his fiduciary duties to the trustees, but in substance he was acting for the beneficiaries.

[84] *Phipps v Boardman* [1965] Ch 992 (CA) 1020 (Lord Denning MR); *United States Surgical Corp v Hospital Products International* [1983] 2 NSWLR 157 (NSWCA) 243.

[85] MA Eisenberg, 'The Disgorgement Interest in Contract Law' (2006) 105 *Michigan Law Review* 559, 599–601.

[86] Cunnington (n 2) 581.

obligation under a contract and breached it nonetheless there is a strong argument that the breach was in bad faith.

However, it has been noted that '[b]etween the two extreme situations – conscious wrongdoing and innocent action – there is a whole gamut of possibilities.'[87] Friedmann raises a number of possibilities, including a defendant who advertently breached but was labouring under a mistake that he was entitled to do so, and a defendant who breached consciously but under pressure or necessity.[88] Thus, he argues that the court should assess the degree of the defendant's culpability, rather than merely requiring the defendant's wrong to be advertent or conscious.[89] By contrast, I argue that advertence should remain the relevant criterion rather than any notion of culpability. Although punitive considerations have some place in private law, they should not be overstated, and it is not appropriate for courts to make fine judgments as to moral culpability. It is more appropriate to deal with any extenuating circumstances by means of an allowance. Again, however, the justification for an allowance of this type presents difficulty. Why should a claimant be burdened with an allowance if she did not benefit from the defendant's actions? I do not think an allowance of this kind can be justified by desert because of the personal nature of desert considerations, but it may be justifiable according to principles of mercy. That is to say, the defendant deserves to have the profit stripped, but because of extenuating circumstances the court makes some allowance for his situation. The relevant situations which may invite mercy are likely to fall into Tasioulas' second and third paradigm cases[90] (ie where there were obstacles to law-abiding behaviour which generate reasons for leniency or where the offender is suffering from a grave misfortune which would be exacerbated if some allowance were not made). So if the defendant were mistaken as to his legal rights, or breached his contract because he was under some sort of duress, the court may make an allowance for reasons of mercy. Alternatively, as discussed later, the court may choose to extend mercy by applying the hardship bar to relief.

V Operation of Bars to Relief

Not all equitable bars to relief applicable to an award of specific performance will be relevant to disgorgement damages for breach of contract. The following bars to relief, which may preclude an award of specific performance, are not relevant to disgorgement damages:

[87] Friedmann (n 30) 1888.
[88] ibid.
[89] ibid.
[90] Tasioulas (n 51) 116–18.

- The bar of 'constant supervision'.[91] This will not be relevant because unlike an order for specific relief, there is no need for the court to supervise performance.
- The bar of 'want of mutuality'. This will also be irrelevant (and there are questions about the extent to which the stricter form of this bar remains relevant to specific performance in any case).[92]
- The bar of 'uncertainty'.[93] This will be irrelevant because it is only problematic when the defendant is required to perform and the obligations are too uncertain.
- The bar of 'impossibility'. While this is a bar to specific relief it is in fact a *prerequisite* to an award of disgorgement damages. If specific relief is still possible, it should be awarded in preference to disgorgement damages.

The relevant bars to relief are thus delay and acquiescence, lack of clean hands and hardship.

Desert figures in the justification for delay, acquiescence and lack of clean hands. The focus of the court is on some conduct of the claimant which means that she does not deserve a judicial exercise of discretion in her favour. If a person has violated moral prohibitions by overriding the rights of others, they may not be deserving of relief.[94] The specific ways in which the rights of the defendant may be unjustifiably overridden are if there is delay and acquiescence on the part of the claimant, or if the claimant does not come to court with clean hands. By contrast, mercy provides the justification for hardship. There is a notion that, although the defendant would ordinarily deserve to have a remedy awarded against him, there are some extenuating circumstances which mean that the court should extend mercy in this instance.

A Delay and Acquiescence

Delay and acquiescence are difficult to categorically define, in part because acquiescence is often used in a way which overlaps with delay.[95]

[91] See *JC Williamson Ltd v Lukey and Mulholland* (1931) 45 CLR 282 (HCA) 297–98 (Dixon J); *Co-operative Insurance Society Ltd v Argyll Stores (Holdings) Ltd* [1997] UKHL 17, [1998] AC 1 (HL) 12 (Lord Hoffmann).

[92] *Price v Strange* [1978] Ch 337 (CA); *Rainbow Estates Ltd v Tokenhold Ltd* [1999] Ch 64 (Ch).

[93] See, eg *Joseph v National Magazine Co Ltd* [1959] Ch 14, [1958] 3 WLR 366 (Ch); *South Wales Railway Co v Wythes* (1854) 1 K & J 186, 68 ER 422; *Greenhill v Isle of Wight (Newport Junction) Railway Co* (1871) 23 LT 887; *cf Sudbrook Trading Estate Ltd v Eggleton* [1983] 1 AC 444 (HL).

[94] Becker (n 43) 51.

[95] RP Meagher, JD Heydon and MJ Leeming, *Meagher, Gummow and Lehane's Equity Doctrines and Remedies*, 4th edn (Sydney, Butterworths, 2002) 1031, 1043–44; M Cope, *Equitable Obligations – Duties, Defences and Remedies* (Pyrmont, Lawbook Co, 2007) 287; *Orr v Ford* (1989) 167 CLR 316, 338 (Deane J). Note that Meagher, Heydon and Leeming would not be likely to approve of efforts to extend delay and acquiescence to common law actions (see Meagher, Heydon and Leeming, ibid 1036–37 where they describe cases which do so as 'heresy') but James Edelman has argued that once one sees acquiescence as a form of waiver, this objection falls away, as this kind of defence spans across common law and equity: J Edelman, 'Money Awards of the Cost of Performance' (2010) 4 *Journal of Equity* 122, 129–30.

In *No 68 Ltd v Eastern Services Ltd*, McGrath J said:

> Situations giving rise to laches are never closed, but the vast majority of cases fall into one of two categories: first, a party inappropriately refrains for an excessive period from seeking redress once he or she knows his or her rights have been violated, giving rise to the inference of acquiescence; and secondly, because of a party's unreasonable delay, significant prejudice is caused to the other party.[96]

In the case of delay, therefore, the claimant does not deserve a remedy because she delayed in bringing an action, and the defendant does not deserve to have a remedy ordered against him because he assumed he was 'in the clear'.[97] In the case of acquiescence, the claimant does not deserve a remedy because her unreasonable delays have caused prejudice to the defendant, in the sense that the defendant will now find it difficult to defend the claim because of the effluxion of time since the events occurred.[98]

The courts constantly emphasise, however, that the mere fact of delay is not enough in itself to militate against the grant of a remedy.[99] It depends upon the specific facts of each case. This indicates the desert basis of delay and acquiescence: the bar to relief focuses on the specific actions of the claimant in question and is highly personal. There is no entitlement to the bar to relief, but a court may choose to extend the bar to relief if it is 'proper' to do so, depending upon the facts of the case. Nonetheless, one can deduce some guidelines from the cases as to the sorts of delay or acquiescence which courts will deem constitute a bar to relief. To ensure a claimant gains her 'just deserts' courts must be careful to ensure that like cases are treated alike, by ensuring that similar kinds of delay are treated in the same way.

Queensland Mines Ltd v Hudson[100] provides a good example of how laches and acquiescence could work in the context of breach of contract and breach of fiduciary duty, although the Privy Council did not expressly consider the issue. The first defendant had been managing director of the claimant company. In this role he became aware of a potentially profitable iron ore mine, and he personally negotiated with the Tasmanian Government in the hope that Queensland Mines would be granted a mining licence. However, by the time that the mining licence was awarded, Queensland Mines had liquidity problems and could not exploit the opportunity. Hudson therefore resigned as managing director, informed the Tasmanian Government that Queensland Mines was no longer part of the venture, and formed his own company for the purpose of exploiting the mine. He provided the capital for the company and took the development risks. In the event, the mine was very successful and Hudson formed a partnership with an

[96] *No 68 Ltd v Eastern Services Ltd* [2006] 2 NZLR 43 (NZCA) [56].

[97] Edelman argues that this should be known as 'waiver': see Edelman (n 95) 129–30.

[98] ibid. Edelman argues that this could be partially subsumed within a change of position defence.

[99] *Lindsay Petroleum Co v Hurd* (1874) LR 5 PC 221, 239–40. Edelman ibid, fn 39 notes two cases where mere delay was not enough: *Burroughes v Abbott* [1922] Ch 86 (12-year delay not sufficient) and *Weld v Petre* [1929] 1 Ch 33 (26-year delay not sufficient).

[100] *Queensland Mines Ltd v Hudson* (1978) 18 ALR 1 (PC).

American firm in order to exploit its commercial potential. Eleven years later, Queensland Mines sued Hudson, claiming an account of the profits he had made in breach of fiduciary duty.

The Privy Council analysed the issue as one of consent. It found that Queensland Mines had forgone the opportunity to exploit the iron ore mines, and that therefore Hudson no longer owed a fiduciary duty in respect of that opportunity. In the alternative, it found that Hudson had acted with the implied consent of the board of Queensland Mines, thereby stopping the company from alleging a breach of fiduciary duty.[101]

This case is not entirely satisfactory. The evident aim of the Privy Council opinion is to prevent Queensland Mines from taking the profit when Hudson took all the commercial risks that the company was unable to assume. Although the result is sound, the reasoning of the opinion is problematic. It suggests that consent of co-directors to what would otherwise be a breach of fiduciary duty exonerates the director from liability, and that consent of the shareholders is not necessary for this purpose. The directors were majority shareholders in this case, but there will often be situations where they are not. Furthermore, the case does not sit comfortably with *Cook v Deeks*,[102] which holds that fiduciaries cannot prescribe their own duties.

The case is better rationalised as one of delay and acquiescence. First, in waiting 11 years until it was clearly established that the mine was profitable before suing Hudson, Queensland Mines unduly delayed enforcing its rights, giving rise to an inference of acquiescence. Secondly, Queensland Mines' unreasonable delay caused Hudson significant prejudice. As the Privy Council noted, the trial judge had commented that the facts 'have proved to be complex and voluminous, and have been made more difficult to unravel by reason of the long lapse of time.'[103] On this view *Queensland Mines* is really a decision on the bars of delay and acquiescence, and an account of profits was refused in part because Hudson could establish delay and acquiescence.

By analogy, the same principles should apply to disgorgement damages for breach of contract.[104] In *Blake*, if the Crown had delayed for 10 years before suing George Blake for the profits of his book, disgorgement damages should have been denied.[105]

[101] ibid 9–10.

[102] *Cook v Deeks* [1916] 1 AC 554.

[103] *Queensland Mines Ltd* (n 100) 3.

[104] Although see S Worthington, *Equity*, 2nd edn (Oxford, Oxford University Press, 2006) 37, who says that it would be difficult to import equitable notions of delay to actions for disgorgement damages for breach of contract because, she argues, the limitation periods will be decided under the common law statutory regime. By contrast, I do not see why it is necessary that disgorgement damages are treated any differently to, eg, specific performance, an auxiliary equitable remedy. However, note that the US *Restatement* has included such a provision where a remedy originates in equity: American Law Institute (n 27) § 71(2)(b).

[105] If 10 years had elapsed, the profits would obviously no longer have been in the jurisdiction, so the point is somewhat moot. The facts of *United States v Snepp*, 444 US 507 (USSC, 1980) can be adapted more realistically.

In the previous chapter, it was said that a court must look at the reason why specific relief cannot be awarded when ascertaining whether the claimant is entitled to full disgorgement damages or a 'reasonable fee'.[106] Delay in seeking specific relief is a bar, to a lesser or greater degree, to a claim of full disgorgement damages. This may be because the claimant has conducted herself in such a way that indicates she has forgone insisting upon strict performance of contractual obligations. If the defendant has put performance out of the claimant's reach because he believed that she had acquiesced in his action, the claimant does not *deserve* full disgorgement. She deserves a lesser amount represented by a 'reasonable fee' award.[107] Alternatively, delay may be relevant because the defendant is now in a disadvantageous position because of the claimant's delay. Again, the claimant cannot be said to deserve full disgorgement.

The continuing application of the acquiescence and delay bars to disgorgement damages is part of the law's broader commitment to the doctrine of mitigation (ie the claimant must avoid the consequences of the breach). Cunnington argues:

> [I]t is suggested that mitigation, and in particular the policy in favour of the avoidance of waste, may justify the continuing existence of the bar. It is clearly undesirable, both commercially and socially, for a claimant to be permitted to stand by and watch the contract breaker accumulate gains with the intention of obtaining those gains for herself through an action for breach of contract. Such conduct is wasteful and likely to result in undue hardship for the defendant.[108]

This also goes to the question of *desert* – the claimant cannot fairly be said to deserve the full profit if she has stood by and watched the defendant make a profit. Further, the defendant can be said to deserve some portion of the profit if he has put in skill and effort (in the same way that desert informs the allowance for skill and effort).

Judicial decisions are mostly consistent with this analysis. In *Gafford v Graham*[109] restrictive covenants in favour of the claimant's land were breached by the defendant of a neighbouring property.[110] The claimant sought damages in lieu of an injunction in relation to an unauthorised extension of a bungalow and a

[106] See ch 6, V.

[107] Note that Cunnington suggests acquiescence should *not* apply to '*Wrotham Park* damages': see Cunnington (n 2) 572–73:

> As a parenthesis, it should be noted that Peter Smith J also suggested that the claimant's delay in intimating the claim could be taken into account in quantifying damages. With respect, this must be wrong. Delay may constitute a bar to the claim, but since the delay took place after the date of the hypothetical negotiations, it cannot be taken into account in assessing the quantum of damages under the *Wrotham Park* approach.

To the contrary, I argue that the reason why *Wrotham Park* damages are on the lower end of the scale is precisely *because* acquiescence and delay have been taken into account.

[108] ibid 578.

[109] [1998] EWCA Civ 666, [1999] 3 EGLR 75 (CA).

[110] See also *Sayers v Collyer* (1884) 28 Ch D 103; *Habib Bank Ltd v Habib Bank AG Zurich* [1981] 1 WLR 1265 (CA) (passing off case); *cf Shaw v Applegate* [1977] 1 WLR 970 (CA) where no injunction was made in the plaintiff's favour for a breach of covenant because of the plaintiff's acquiescence, but the court still awarded 'reasonable fee' damages in lieu of an injunction.

barn, and the unauthorised building of an indoor riding school and carrying on a full-scale riding school business. Nourse LJ, with whom Pill LJ and Thorpe LJ agreed, found that the claimant was not entitled to damages in lieu of an injunction in respect of the unauthorised extension of the bungalow and barn. The extensions occurred in 1985, but the claimant did not complain about them until 1989, when the defendant also built an indoor riding school and carried on a riding school business. The claimant was therefore not entitled to damages in lieu of an injunction in respect of the extension of the bungalow and barn because of his acquiescence. However, when the defendant commenced building an indoor riding school and carrying on a full-scale riding school business the claimant immediately commenced legal proceedings against the defendant. Nonetheless, the claimant did not seek an interlocutory injunction at this stage, despite the fact that he would have almost certainly have been entitled to relief for breach of the restrictive covenant. The trial judge had refused to grant a mandatory injunction requiring the defendant to demolish the riding school, but granted an injunction requiring the defendant to cease operating the business of a riding school and livery stable. The Court of Appeal held that no mandatory injunctions ought to be granted because of the claimant's failure to seek an interlocutory injunction at an early stage. However, the court awarded a 'reasonable fee' sum of £25,000 (plus interest), representing an amount which the claimant might reasonably have asked for a relaxation of the covenant. Peter Smith J adopted *Gafford* in *WWF*, specifying that delay and acquiescence could reduce the amount of damages awarded, or even disallow a claim entirely if it caused prejudice to the defendant.[111]

Many of the 'reasonable fee' cases involve a failure to seek an interlocutory injunction soon after the wrong has been committed, and thus an argument can be made that the court in these cases is effectively reducing the disgorgement of profit because of the claimant's acquiescence or delay.[112] Acquiescence and delay provides a better explanation for the outcome of *Surrey County Council v Bredero Homes Ltd*,[113] a case that was notoriously similar to *Wrotham Park*,[114] but in which the Court of Appeal declined to award a 'reasonable fee'. The defendant bought land from the claimant councils. The contract of sale contained a covenant that the defendant would develop the land in accordance with the first planning permission, which permitted the building of only 72 houses. The defendant then obtained a second planning permission from the second claimant that permitted it to build 77 houses, but the covenant still only provided for the building of 72

[111] *World Wide Fund for Nature v World Wrestling Federation Entertainment Inc* [2006] EWHC 184 (Ch) [174] at point 6.

[112] See, eg *Wrotham Park Estate Co Ltd v Parkside Homes Ltd* [1974] 1 WLR 798 (Ch); *Amec Developments Limited v Jury's Hotel Management (UK) Limited* [2000] EWHC Ch 454, [2001] EGLR 81 and *World Wide Fund for Nature* (n 111).

[113] *Surrey County Council v Bredero Homes Ltd* (*Bredero*) [1993] EWCA Civ 7, [1993] 1 WLR 1361.

[114] For examples of spirited criticism of *Bredero*, see P Birks, 'Profits of Breach of Contract' (1993) 109 *LQR* 518; A Burrows, 'No Restitutionary Damages for Breach of Contract' [1993] *Lloyd's Maritime and Commercial Law Quarterly* 453.

houses. The defendant built 77 houses in breach of covenant. The claimants never sought an injunction to prevent the defendant from developing the land, and conceded that the sole purpose of the covenant was to force the defendant to pay for a relaxation of the terms if it wanted to build more than 72 houses. The Court of Appeal declined to award damages to the claimants. Dillon LJ refused an award on the basis that the claimants had not suffered a loss, and thus only nominal damages were appropriate.[115] Steyn LJ acknowledged the possibility of 'restitutionary damages' for breach of contract, but held that this was not an appropriate case for such an award because it did not involve a breach of fiduciary duty or an invasion of the claimants' property interests.[116] Rose LJ said simply:

> In the *Wrotham Park* case the plaintiffs objected to building works in breach of covenant as soon as they learnt of them and, within a month, issued a writ seeking restraining and mandatory injunctions. . . . From first to last they objected to what the defendants did. . . .
>
> In the present case, from first to last the plaintiffs have neither objected nor wished to object to what the defendant has done.[117]

The claimants stood by and let the defendant accumulate a profit with the intention of obtaining those gains for themselves through an action for breach of contract. While at first blush the case resembled *Wrotham Park*, disgorgement damages were not awarded because the claimant's delay and apparent acquiescence barred relief. The judgment of Rose LJ provides a far better explanation for the result than the analyses of Dillon LJ and Steyn LJ.

By contrast, in *Lane*, where the claimant acted promptly and obtained an interlocutory injunction preventing erection of the houses in breach of covenant, the claimant received over 50 per cent of the defendant's profit, closer to full disgorgement.[118]

Although the cases generally accord with the principles I suggest, *Pell Frischmann Engineering v Bow Valley Iran Limited*[119] is an exception. As discussed in the previous chapter, the case involved a joint venture contract for the exploitation of an Iranian oilfield which provided, inter alia, that the defendants were to work exclusively with the claimant and that the defendants were not to approach the Iranian government agency without the consent of the claimant. The defendants breached this contract. The Privy Council found that the claimant was entitled to a 'reasonable fee' representing the amount it would have accepted to be released from its contract. The US$2.5million 'reasonable fee' outstripped the actual profit made by the defendants (at most, US$1million to US$1.8million). This was despite the claimant's 'extraordinary and unexplained delay in bringing

[115] *Bredero* (n 113) 1364–68.

[116] ibid 1368–71.

[117] ibid 1371.

[118] *Lane v O'Brien Homes* [2004] EWHC 303 (QB), [2004] All ER (D) 61. This case can be criticised on other grounds, including the court's finding of a collateral contract: see D Campbell, 'The Extinguishing of Contract' (2004) 67 *MLR* 818.

[119] *Pell Frischmann Engineering v Bow Valley Iran Ltd* [2009] UKPC 45, [2010] BLR 73.

proceedings.'[120] Stripping the defendants of an amount greater than their actual gain is overly punitive. In addition, the claimant's inordinate delay should have resulted in a substantial reduction of the award.

B Lack of Clean Hands

In the case of the 'lack of clean hands' bar to relief, the claimant's behavior disentitles her to equitable relief. Like delay and acquiescence, 'lack of clean hands' has a desert basis, in that relief is refused because the claimant has overridden the rights of others. 'Lack of clean hands' does not mean general impropriety, but that the claimant deceived the court, the other party or the public.[121] The bar will not be made out merely because the claimant has committed some impropriety.[122] It was held in *Moody v Cox* that 'the depravity, the dirt in question on the hand, [must have] . . . an immediate and necessary relation to the equity sued for.'[123] Consequently, the lack of clean hands must relate to the relief which is sought.[124] Its most common applications are when the court has been deceived by one of the parties or one party has failed to disclose material facts.[125] The court effectively declares, 'Since you have deceived others, you should not get the benefit of our justice, and we will exercise our discretion so as to refuse to order a remedy in your favour.'

In *Summers v Cocks*,[126] the Australian High Court refused to order specific performance because the claimant lacked 'clean hands'. Summers, the claimant, contracted to sell a hotel to Cocks. At the time of contracting, Summers was aware that licensing authorities were considering revoking the liquor licence for the premises. After the contract was signed, the liquor licence was revoked. Cocks became aware of this, and refused to go ahead with the sale. Summers sought specific performance of the contract of sale. A majority of the High Court refused specific performance because Summers had not come to equity with clean hands in view of his failure to disclose material facts.[127]

The 'clean hands' doctrine reflects the view that claimants should not be allowed to abuse the judicial process.[128] Because equitable remedies are

[120] ibid [54] (Lord Walker).

[121] Meagher, Heydon and Leeming (n 95) [3]–[115].

[122] *Attorney-General (UK) v Heinemann Publishers Australia Pty Ltd* (1987) 8 NSWLR 341 (NSWSC) 383 (Powell J).

[123] *Moody v Cox* [1917] 2 Ch 71 (CA), 87–88. See also *Dering v Earl of Winchelsea* (1787) 1 Cox Eq Cas 318, 319–20, 29 ER 1184, 1185 (Eyre CB).

[124] *Duchess of Argyll v Duke of Argyll* [1967] Ch 302 (Ch) 331–32 (Ungoed-Thomas J).

[125] See, eg *Armstrong v Sheppard & Short Ltd* [1959] 2 QB 384 (CA), 397; *Kettles & Gas Appliances Ltd v Anthony Hordern & Sons Ltd* (1934) 35 SR (NSW) 108 (NSWSC); *Walters v Morgan* (1861) 3 De GF & J 718, 45 ER 1056; *Webster v Cecil* (1861) 30 Beav 62, 54 ER 812; *Lamare v Dixon* (1873) LR 6 HL 414 (HL); *Quadrant Visual Communications Ltd v Hutchison Telephone (UK) Ltd* [1993] BCLC 442 (CA). However, a unilateral mistake on the part of the defendant which is neither known to nor induced by the plaintiff will not be a bar: see *Tamplin v James* (1880) 15 Ch D 215 (CA).

[126] *Summers v Cocks* (1927) 40 CLR 321 (HCA).

[127] ibid 324 (Isaacs ACJ), 331–32 (Starke J) (Higgins J diss).

[128] Worthington (n 104) 40.

discretionary, the claimant does not deserve to have discretion exercised in her favour if she has deceived the court, the other party, or the public.

Lack of clean hands should also be a bar to an award of disgorgement damages. So, for example, if the British Government had said that any British citizen could kill George Blake for his treachery and claim a reward, the Government should not be allowed to recover disgorgement damages. Such an example may bear little relation to reality, until one considers *Hubbard v Vosper*.[129] The defendant, Vosper, a former Minister of the Church of Scientology, alleged in a book that the Church authorised extreme actions against persons in a state of 'enemy' with the Church (even killing). The Church sought to restrain publication of this information on the basis that it was confidential. Insofar as it was alleged that the breach of confidence concerned the sanctions of the Church against its 'enemies', it was not permitted to protect its confidential information.[130] The Church did not come to court with clean hands because of the very nature of the confidential information concerned. If the Church had tried to gain disgorgement of any profits made by Vosper from the disclosure, it is suggested that it would also have been unsuccessful.

Because the claimant in a disgorgement case could be said to obtain what some might regard as a 'windfall', it is appropriate that the 'clean hands' limitation should apply. A claimant who has deceived, or attempted to deceive, the defendant, the court, or the public does not deserve to strip the defendant of his profit, and does not deserve to have their right vindicated by the court, as they have failed to respect the rights of others.

Even where a bar applies, a claimant may still be able to claim compensatory damages for breach of contract. Nonetheless, there may be circumstances where a contract that is too unfair to warrant a discretionary remedy, is also too unfair to permit a compensatory damages award.[131] Chafee argues that at the very least the court should 'take the facts which bar specific performance and ask whether they do not also render damages unjust.'[132]

C Hardship

A court can refuse relief where to do so would cause undue hardship to the defendant.[133] As with unclean hands, the hardship must relate directly to the relief sought.

The hardship bar to relief looks like a desert claim, but is probably what Feinberg would call an '"ought" judgment'.[134] Feinberg argues that a claim of this

[129] [1972] 2 QB 84 (CA).

[130] ibid 100–01 (Megaw LJ).

[131] Z Chafee Jr, 'Coming Into Equity With Clean Hands' (1949) 47 *Michigan Law Review* 877, 895–96.

[132] ibid.

[133] Again, note that the US *Restatement* has included a hardship defence where a remedy originates in equity: American Law Institute (n 27) § 71(2)(b).

[134] Feinberg (n 41) 60. See also Kleinig (n 43) 76.

kind is not really a desert claim. 'Ought judgments' sound final, but are not. We say that someone 'ought' to get a particular thing but then there is the implied disclaimer that the person will only deserve to get the thing 'insofar as things presently stand' or 'if all other things are equal'. Thus, desert is not a conclusive reason for giving the person that thing but merely informs the 'ought judgment'. It is mercy that informs the court's decision.

An example of hardship is *Patel v Ali*,[135] where the defendants, the Alis, had entered into a contract of sale with the claimants, the Patels. After the contract was signed but before settlement could occur, the defendants suffered various terrible misfortunes. Mr Ali became bankrupt, and for a time the property was subject to an injunction awarded to Mr Ali's trustee in bankruptcy which prevented the sale from going ahead as planned. Mr Ali was eventually sent to prison for a year. Mrs Ali was diagnosed with cancer and underwent treatment (involving amputation of her leg). At the time of application for relief the couple had three children. Mrs Ali was of Pakistani background, and spoke very little English. She did not want the contract to be enforced because she was reliant on the support of her local community.

Goulding J refused to order specific performance of a contract of sale because it would cause undue hardship to the defendants. His Honour said that there had already been unforeseen delays to completion of the contract which meant that compensatory damages would be an adequate remedy for the claimants.[136] By contrast, the defendant could suffer great hardship if the contract was specifically enforced.[137]

Patel v Ali is a case where mercy was extended to Mrs Ali because she was already suffering grave misfortunes which would have been exacerbated if she had been forced to specifically perform the contract. It is as if the court said, 'The defendant ought to specifically perform, and, absent the context, she would be ordered to do so, but in this case, once all other things are taken into consideration, we have decided she should not be forced to perform because of her terrible circumstances.' The case would fall within Tasioulas' third category, namely where the defendant is already suffering from grave misfortune which would be cruelly exacerbated by the full measure of his just deserts being exacted upon him.[138] In such a case, the need for mercy towards the individual defendant outweighs the need for general and specific deterrence *and* the need for the defendant to receive his just deserts. This is consistent with equity's principles of fairness.

It should be noted that the mercy extended by equity is limited – even if a defendant is not liable for disgorgement damages he may still be liable for compensatory damages, just as Mrs Ali remained liable for compensatory damages for breach of contract in *Patel v Ali*.

[135] *Patel v Ali* [1984] 1 Ch 283 (Ch).
[136] ibid 288.
[137] ibid.
[138] Tasioulas (n 51) 117.

Hardship will not exist merely because a contract is 'risky' or the defendant has been unwise.[139] Hardship may be established where the terms of the original contract to which the defendant was bound were unconscionable, and in such circumstances the defendant should not be penalised for breaching the contract and making a profit thereby. Let us take the facts of *Dowsett v Reid* and tweak them a little.[140] There, the defendant entered into an agreement to lease his property for 10 years with an option to purchase. Griffith CJ found that the terms of the lease were unconscionable, and that the court should not specifically enforce the lease.[141] What if the defendant had made a profit by breaching the lease and making a more profitable lease arrangement with a third party? The claimant may then have sought disgorgement of the defendant's profit. The defendant should not be stripped of his profit because of the unconscionable nature of the original bargain. Disgorgement damages will be unavailable in part because the claimant is not a deserving recipient of the defendant's profit. But in addition the court will also extend mercy to a defendant whose wrong has been committed in a context which generates reasons for leniency. It thus falls within Tasioulas' second category of mercy; namely where wrongdoing has occurred in a context which generates reasons for leniency because there were obstacles to law-abiding behaviour.[142]

Like desert itself, mercy is not a right or an entitlement. One cannot speak of a person having a 'right to mercy'.[143] Mercy is by its very nature a discretionary principle which will be extended to a defendant out of the goodness of the court's heart. The bar to relief of hardship is therefore discretionary and will be sparingly applied. It should be noted that the mercy extended is also limited in its scope: ordinarily, a defendant will still be liable to pay ordinary common law damages for breach of contract.[144] An exception to this may be where the defendant can rescind the contract. For example, *Blomley v Ryan* began as a purchaser's application for specific performance, but the vendor rescinded the contract as unconscionable.[145]

VI Conclusion

In conclusion, the defendant must disgorge net profit. This allows a number of expenses to be claimed by the defendant. The test for causation for disgorgement damages should be the 'but for' test, rather than any more generous test applied to fiduciary cases. There should also be explicit consideration of remoteness: that is,

[139] *Axelsen v O'Brien* (1949) 80 CLR 219 (HCA) 226 (Dixon J); *Francis v Cowcliffe* (1976) 33 P & CR 368; *Mountford v Scott* [1975] Ch 258 (CA).

[140] *Dowsett v Reid* (1912) 15 CLR 695 (HCA).

[141] ibid 705–07 (Griffiths CJ, with whom Barton and Higgins JJ agreed on this point).

[142] Tasioulas (n 51) 117.

[143] Feinberg (n 41) 86; Munzer (n 42) 260.

[144] Although see Chafee's comments with regard to 'lack of clean hands' above at (n 132).

[145] *Blomley v Ryan* (1956) 99 CLR 362 (HCA).

whether it would be fair to hold the defendant responsible for gains which were distant or unusual consequences of the breach, or which were more immediately caused by the defendant's non-wrongful conduct, the conduct of a third party or a natural event. Similarly, there should be opportunity for courts to make an apportionment between profits which were a direct consequence of the breach of contract and those which were not.

The allowance for skill and effort is recognition that the labour of the defendant deserves recognition in some circumstances. However, an allowance is not a right: it is something which the court has discretion to grant if it sees fit in the circumstances. In fact, allowances have been awarded in some cases where disgorgement damages have been awarded for breach of contract, and it is submitted that they were rightly awarded.

Finally, it is argued that the law should recognise the equitable bars to relief in relation to disgorgement damages: delay and acquiescence, 'lack of clean hands' and hardship. In effect, we have already considered delay and acquiescence when discussing the 'reasonable fee' cases in the previous chapter. The awards are reduced to a 'reasonable fee' in some cases because of delay on the part of the claimant in bringing a claim. The basis for this is desert: the claimant does not deserve the full profit if she has sat by and let the defendant make a profit, or if she has waited so long before bringing her claim that the defendant cannot access the facts he needs to defend the action. Similarly, the basis for the lack of clean hands defence is desert; the claimant does not deserve relief if she has abused the judicial process. General moral depravity will not suffice – it has to be related to the relief which is sought. Finally, the hardship defence should also extend to disgorgement damages, but the basis for this defence is not desert. The basis is mercy: that is, the defendant should not be punished unduly in the particular circumstances of the case.

8

Conclusion

This book has attempted to create a balanced analysis which considers the consequences to both the claimant and the defendant of granting relief. The eminent textbook authors Goff and Jones[1] and Carter and Mason[2] suggested in earlier editions that *any* wrong which results in a defendant obtaining a causally related gain should give rise to disgorgement. In light of this, it is hardly surprising that restitutionary analyses have been criticised for being too claimant-focused.[3] In the Court of Appeal decision of *Co-operative Insurance Society Ltd v Argyll Stores (Holdings) Ltd*,[4] Millett LJ made an observation which is pertinent in this context:

> It is always necessary to consider the consequence to the defendant of granting such relief as well as the consequence to the plaintiff of leaving him to his remedy in damages.[5]

In addition, there has almost been a tendency to see breach of contract as just another species of tort or wrong, but contract law must be distinguished from tort.[6] The aim of contract law is not simply to compensate the claimant for a loss, but to place her in a position as if the contract had been performed. Nonetheless, she will not always be entitled to actual performance of a contract, and often, expectation damages will be adequate to place her in a position as if the contract had been performed. Nor will a claimant necessarily have a 'legitimate interest' in the disgorgement of profits arising from a breach of contract, even if the breach of contract may have been 'cynical' or 'wilful'.

1 See, eg R Goff and G Jones, *The Law of Restitution*, 4th edn (London, Sweet & Maxwell, 1993) 723 (*cf* a later edition: R Goff and G Jones, *The Law of Restitution*, 7th edn (London, Sweet & Maxwell, 2002)); G Jones, 'The Recovery of Benefits Gained from a Breach of Contract' (1983) 99 *LQR* 443, 459.

2 K Mason, JW Carter and G Tolhurst, *Restitution Law in Australia*, 1st edn (Sydney, Butterworths, 1995) 619–21. (*cf* the later edition: K Mason, JW Carter and G Tolhurst, *Restitution Law in Australia*, 2nd edn (Chatswood, NSW, LexisNexis Butterworths, 2008)).

3 D Campbell and D Harris, 'In Defence of Breach: A Critique of Restitution and the Performance Interest' (2002) 22 *Legal Studies* 208, 234–35; D Campbell, 'The Extinguishing of Contract' (2004) 67 *MLR* 818, 830–31.

4 *Co-operative Insurance Society Ltd v Argyll Stores (Holdings) Ltd* [1996] Ch 287 (CA) (*Argyll Stores CA*). Majority decision subsequently overturned by the House of Lords in *Co-operative Insurance Society Ltd v Argyll Stores (Holdings) Ltd* [1998] AC 1 (HL).

5 *Argyll Stores CA* (n 4) 304 (Millett LJ dissenting).

6 SM Waddams, 'Breach of Contract and the Concept of Wrongdoing' (2000) 12 *Supreme Court Law Review* 1; SM Waddams, 'Gains Derived from Breach of Contract: Historical and Conceptual Perspectives' in D Saidov and R Cunnington (eds), *Contract Damages: Domestic and International Perspectives* (Oxford, Hart Publishing, 2008) 187, 194–96. Although I disagree with Waddams in the precise details as to how contract differs from other actions, I agree that it *does* have to be distinguished from claims in tort.

The availability of disgorgement depends upon two factors: the nature of the claimant's interest in performance of the contractual obligation, and whether a substitute performance is possible (whether obtained via an award of compensatory damages or through an award of specific relief). A defendant is 'free' to breach and pay expectation damages in situations where the subject matter of the contract is substitutable. Substitutability is at the heart of contractual remedies, because it looks to what the defendant must give the claimant in order for her interest in performance to be vindicated. The common law presumes that the default remedy is the least intrusive remedy to the defendant (ie expectation damages). However, it remains sensitive to the possibility that expectation damages will not be adequate to recognise the claimant's performance interest, and as such, courts are increasingly ready to award specific relief in order to give the claimant what she actually bargained for.

Disgorgement damages only have a place in contract law where expectation damages are inadequate to recognise the performance interest, specific relief is no longer available and the defendant has made an *actual profit*. Then, where there is a second sale or an agency problem, disgorgement damages may be awarded so that the concept of *pacta sunt servanda* is given teeth.

I also suggest that disgorgement ranges from partial disgorgement to full disgorgement. I relabel the troublesome category of 'restitutionary damages' as a form of partial disgorgement damages. This helps explain the overlap of the 'reasonable fee' cases and the 'expense saved' cases more convincingly than a restitutionary analysis. Whether the claimant is awarded partial or full disgorgement depends upon the reasons why specific relief was not awarded by the court: whether it *could not* because it was impossible, or whether it *would not* for discretionary reasons. This recognises that there may be situations where we wish to effectively apportion the gain between the claimant and the defendant by carving out an objective 'reasonable fee' award for the benefit of the claimant from the defendant's actual profit. Finally, the presence of desert-based bars to relief and allowances for skill and effort ensure that the defendant's interests are recognised where necessary, and that any conduct on the part of the claimant which suggests she does not deserve relief is also recognised. Hardship also recognises that there may occasionally be extraordinary cases where the courts should show mercy.

So, while the rationales of disgorgement damages are deterrence and punishment, my theory carefully crafts the remedy so that it is not overly deterrent or overly punitive. Practically, we want to allow *some* breaches of contract, and in order to do so, contract law must not be overly inflexible. The remedy is nuanced according to the particular circumstances of the breach.

As stated at the outset, Professor Stephen Smith outlined four criteria by which to assess the success of an interpretive theory:[7]

[7] S Smith, *Contract Theory* (Oxford, Oxford University Press, 2004) 5; A Beever and CEF Rickett, 'Interpretive Legal Theory and the Academic Lawyer' (2005) *MLR* 320, 324. Against S Hedley, 'The Shock of the Old: Interpretivism in Obligations' in CEF Rickett (ed), *Structure and Justification in Private Law – Essays for Peter Birks* (Oxford, Hart Publishing, 2008) 205 for criticisms of interpretive theory.

1. **Fit** (the extent to which the theory 'fits' the data it is trying to explain);
2. **Coherence** (the extent to which the theory is consistent and intelligible);
3. **Morality** (the extent to which the theory justifies the law's claim to be a legitimate or morally justified authority); and
4. **Transparency** (the extent to which the theory explains the legal reasoning of legal actors themselves).

My theory has attempted to fit with the existing case law as much as possible, and to be coherent with existing private law doctrines such as contractual remedies and breach of fiduciary duty. I have also identified the moral imperatives behind an award of disgorgement damages, namely deterrence and punishment. However, the law is still lacking in transparency. Prior to *Attorney-General v Blake*,[8] courts have tended to hide awards of disgorgement under constructive trust analyses, by unduly stretching the concept of fiduciary and by disguising awards as 'compensatory' by expanding the concept of loss. Even after *Blake*, courts in the UK have found it difficult to apply Lord Nicholls' 'legitimate interest' test, in part because of confusion as to how the test should operate. My aim with regard to this book is to provide an analysis which will assist courts in applying the law, and to encourage courts to openly acknowledge when they are awarding remedies which effect disgorgement. In this way too, parties to a contract will hopefully be able to predict with reasonable accuracy the remedy a court will award if they breach their obligations.

[8] *Attorney-General v Blake* [2000] UKHL 45, [2001] 1 AC 268 (HL).

BIBLIOGRAPHY

1. Articles/Books/Reports

Anderson, J, 'Account of Profits for Breach of Contract' [2000] *New Zealand Law Journal* 415

Aristotle, *Nichomachean Ethics* (T Irwin tr, 2nd edn, Indianapolis, Indiana, Hackett Publishing, 1999) Book V [trans of: 'Ηθικά Νικομάχεια]

Atiyah, P, *Promises, Morals and Law* (Oxford, Oxford University Press, 1981)

——, *Essays on Contract* (Oxford, Oxford University Press, 1986)

Austen-Baker, R, 'Difficulties with Damages as a Ground of Specific Performance' (1999) 10 *King's College Law Journal* 1

Ayres, I and Klass, G, 'Promissory Fraud Without Breach' [2004] *Wisconsin Law Review* 507

Bar-Gill, O and Ben-Shahar, O, 'An Information Theory of Willful Breach' (2009) 107 *Michigan Law Review* 1479

Barnett, K, 'Comment: The Midas Touch – Profits from the King's Gold Piano' (2010) 18 *Restitution Law Review* 83

Barrett, RI, 'The "Most Wrong" Equity Cases 1990–2003: *Attorney General v Blake*' (presented at the Supreme Court Judges' Conference, 24 August 2003)

Beatson, J, 'The Nature of Waiver of Tort' in J Beatson, *The Use and Abuse of Unjust Enrichment – Essays on the Law of Restitution* (Oxford, Clarendon Press, 1991)

——, 'Courts, Arbitrators and Restitutionary Liability for Breach of Contract' (2002) 118 *Law Quarterly Review* 377

Becker, L, Property Rights – Philosophic Foundations (London, Routledge & Paul, 1977)

Beever, A, 'The structure of aggravated and exemplary damages' (2003) 23 *Oxford Journal of Legal Studies* 87

—— and Rickett, CEF, 'Interpretive Legal Theory and the Academic Lawyer' (2005) 68 *Modern Law Review* 320

Bell, M, 'After *Tabcorp*, for Whom Does the *Bellgrove* Toll? Cementing the Expectation Measure as the Ruling Principle for Calculation of Contract Damages' (2009) 33 *Melbourne University Law Review* 684

Bennett, C, 'The Limits of Mercy' (2004) 17 *Ratio* 1

Benson, P, 'Disgorgement for Breach of Contract and Corrective Justice: An Analysis in Outline' in J Neyers, M McInnes and S Pitel (eds), *Understanding Unjust Enrichment* (Oxford, Hart Publishing, 2004) 311

Berryman, J, 'The Case for Restitutionary Damages Over Punitive Damages: Teaching the Wrongdoer That Tort Does not Pay' (1994) 73 *Canadian Bar Review* 320

——, 'The Specific Performance Damages Continuum: An Historical Perspective' (1985) 17 *Ottawa Law Review* 295

Birch, J, 'Exemplary damages for breach of fiduciary duty' (2005) 33 *Australian Business Law Review* 429

Birks, P, 'Restitutionary Damages for Breach of Contract: *Snepp* and the Fusion of Law and Equity' [1987] *Lloyds' Maritime and Commercial Law Quarterly* 421

——, *An Introduction to the Law of Restitution*, revised edition (Oxford, Clarendon Press, 1989)

——, 'Profits of Breach of Contract' (1993) 109 *Law Quarterly Review* 518

——, 'Civil Wrongs: A New World' in *Butterworth Lectures 1990–91* (1992) 55

——, 'Property in the Profits of Wrongdoing' (1994) 24 *University of Western Australia Law Review* 8

——, 'Equity in the Modern Law: An Exercise in Taxonomy' (1996) 26 *University of Western Australia Law Review* 1

——, 'Misnomer' in WR Cornish, R Nolan, J O'Sullivan and G Virgo (eds), *Restitution: Past Present and Future* (Oxford, Hart Publishing, 1998) 1

——, 'The Law of Restitution at the End of an Epoch' (1999) 28 *University of Western Australia Law Review* 13

——, 'Annual Miegunyah Lecture: Equity, Conscience and Unjust Enrichment' (1999) 23 *Melbourne University Law Review* 1

——, 'The Law of Unjust Enrichment: A Millennial Resolution' [1999] *Singapore Journal of Legal Studies* 318

Blake, G, *No Other Choice* (London, Jonathan Cape, 1990)

Bottrell, A, 'Contractual Performance, Corrective Justice, and Disgorgement for Breach of Contract' (2010) 16 *Legal Theory* 135

'Breach of Contract, Restitution for Wrongs, and Punishment: Review of Discussion' in Andrew Burrows and Edwin Peel (eds), *Commercial Remedies – Current Issues and Problems* (Oxford, Oxford University Press, 2003) 129

Brien, A, 'Mercy Within Legal Justice' (1998) 24 *Social Theory and Practice* 83

Buckland, WW, 'The Nature of Contractual Obligation' (1944) 8 *Cambridge Law Journal* 247

Burrows, A, 'No Restitutionary Damages for Breach of Contract' [1993] *Lloyd's Maritime and Commercial Law Quarterly* 453

——, 'We Do This At Common Law But That In Equity' (2002) 22 *Oxford Journal of Legal Studies* 1

——, *The Law of Restitution*, 2nd edn (London, Butterworths, 2002)

——, *Remedies for Torts and Breach of Contract*, 3rd edn (Oxford, Oxford University Press, 2004)

——, 'Remedial Coherence and Punitive Damages in Equity' in S Degeling and J Edelman (eds), *Equity in Commercial Law* (Pyrmont, NSW, Lawbook Co, 2005) 381

——, 'Are Damages on the '*Wrotham Park* Basis' Compensatory, Restitutionary or Neither?' in D Saidov and R Cunnington (eds), *Contract Damages: Domestic and International Perspectives* (Oxford, Hart Publishing, 2008) 165

Calabresi, G and Melamed, AD, 'Property Rules, Liability Rules, and Inalienability: One View of the Cathedral' (1972) 82 *Harvard Law Review* 1089

Campbell, D (ed), The Relational Theory of Contract: Selected Works of Ian Macneil (London, Sweet & Maxwell, 2001)

——and Wylie, P, 'Ain't No Telling (Which Circumstances Are Exceptional)' (2003) 62 *Cambridge Law Journal* 605

——, 'The Treatment of Teacher v Calder in AG v Blake' (2002) 65 *Modern Law Review* 256

——and Harris, D, 'In Defence of Breach: a Critique of Restitution and the Performance Interest' (2002) 22 *Journal of Legal Studies* 208

——, 'The Extinguishing of Contract' (2004) 67 *Modern Law Review* 818

Cane, P, 'Corrective Justice and Correlativity in Private Law' (1996) 16 *Oxford Journal of Legal Studies* 471

——, 'Exceptional Measures of Damages: A Search for Principles' in P Birks (ed), *Wrongs and Remedies in the Twenty-First Century* (Oxford, Clarendon Press, 1996) 301

——, 'The Anatomy of Private Law Theory: A 25th Anniversary Essay' (2005) 25 *Oxford Journal of Legal Studies* 203

Card, C, 'On Mercy' (1972) 81 *Philosophical Review* 182

Chafee Jr, Z, 'Coming Into Equity With Clean Hands – Part I' (1949) 47 *Michigan Law Review* 877

——, 'Coming Into Equity With Clean Hands – Part II' (1949) 47 *Michigan Law Review* 1065

Chambers, R, 'The Importance of Specific Performance' in Simone Degeling and James Edelman (eds), *Equity in Commercial Law* (NSW, Lawbook Co, 2005) 431

Chapman, B and Trebilcock, M, 'Punitive Damages: Divergence in Search of a Rationale' (1989) 40 *Alabama Law Review* 741

Chen-Wishart, M, 'Consideration: Practical Benefit and the Emperor's New Clothes' in J Beatson and D Friedmann (eds), Good Faith in Contract Law (Oxford, Clarendon Press, 1995) 123

——, 'Restitutionary Damages for Breach of Contract' (1998) 114 *Law Quarterly Review* 363

Choi, A and Triantis, G, 'Completing Contracts in the Shadow of Costly Verification' (2008) 37 *Journal of Legal Studies* 503

Coase, R, 'The Problem of Social Cost' (1960) 3 *Journal of Law and Economics* 1

Cohen, G, 'The Fault that Lies Within our Contract Law' (2009) 107 *Michigan Law Review* 1445

Conaglen, M, 'The Nature and Function of Fiduciary Loyalty' (2005) 121 *Law Quarterly Review* 452

Cope, M, Equitable Obligations – Duties, Defences and Remedies (Pyrmont, NSW, Lawbook Co, 2007)

Coote, B, 'Contract Damages, *Ruxley*, and the Performance Interest' (1997) 56 *Cambridge Law Journal* 537

——, 'The Performance Interest, *Panatown*, and the Problem of Loss' (2001) 117 *Law Quarterly Review* 81

Cooter, R, 'Price and Sanctions' (1984) 84 *Columbia Law Review* 1523

——and Freedman, B, 'The Fiduciary Relationship: its Economic Character and Legal Consequences' (1991) 66 *New York University Law Review* 1045

Cowan, D, Edmunds, R and Lowry, J, 'Lister & Co v Stubbs: Who Profits?' [1996] *Journal of Business Law* 22

Craswell, R, 'Contract Law, Default Rules and the Philosophy of Promising' (1989) 88 *Michigan Law Review* 489

——, 'When is a Willful Breach "Willful"? The Link Between Definitions and Damages' (2009) 107 *Michigan Law Review*1501

Cunnington, R, 'The Measure and Availability of Gain-Based Damages for Breach of Contract' in D Saidov and R Cunnington (eds), *Contract Damages: Domestic and International Perspectives* (Oxford, Hart Publishing, 2008) 207

——, 'The Inadequacy of Damages as a Remedy for Breach of Contract' in CEF Rickett (ed), *Justifying Private Law Remedies* (Oxford, Hart Publishing, 2008) 115

Cunnington, R, 'The Assessment of Gain-Based Damages for Breach of Contract' (2008) 71 *Modern Law Review* 559
——, 'Changing Conceptions of Compensation' (2007) *Cambridge Law Journal* 507
——, 'A Lost Opportunity to Clarify' (2007) 123 *Law Quarterly Review* 48
——, 'The Border Between Compensation, Restitution and Punishment' (2006) 122 *Law Quarterly Review* 382
——, 'Should punitive damages be part of the judicial arsenal in contract cases?' (2006) 26 *Legal Studies* 369
——, 'Equitable Damages: A Model for Restitutionary Damages' (2001) 17 *Journal of Contract Law* 212
Dagan, H, 'The Distributive Foundation of Corrective Justice' (1999) 98 *Michigan Law Review* 138
——, 'Restitutionary Damages for Breach of Contract: An Exercise in Private Law Theory' (2000) 1 *Theoretical Inquiries in Law* 115
——, *The Law and Ethics of Restitution* (Cambridge, Cambridge University Press, 2004)
Dawson, J, *Unjust Enrichment: A Comparative Analysis* (Boston, Little, Brown & Co, 1951)
——, 'Restitution or Damages' (1959) 20 *Ohio State Law Journal* 175
De Long, S, 'The Efficiency of a Disgorgement as a Remedy for Breach of Contract' (1989) 22 *Indiana Law Review* 737
Dodge, W, 'The Case for Punitive Damages in Contracts' (1999) 48 *Duke Law Journal* 629
Doyle, S and Wright, D, 'Restitutionary Damages – The Unnecessary Remedy?' (2001) 25 *Melbourne University Law Review* 1
Duggan, A, 'Exemplary Damages in Equity: A Law and Economics Perspective' (2006) 26 *Oxford Journal of Legal Studies* 303
Easterbrook, F and Fischel, D, 'Contract and Fiduciary Duty' (1993) 36 *Journal of Law and Economics* 425
Edelman, J, 'Unjust Enrichment, Restitution and Wrongs' (2000) 79 *Texas Law Review* 1869
——, 'Gain-Based Remedies for Wrongdoing' (2000) 74 *Australian Law Journal* 231
——, 'Restitutionary Damages and Disgorgement Damages for Breach of Contract' [2000] *Restitution Law Review* 129
——, 'Non-compensatory Damages for Breach of Contract and Torts' (2002) 76 *Australian Law Journal* 238
——, Gain-Based Damages – Contract, Tort, Equity and Intellectual Property (Oxford, Hart Publishing, 2002)
——, 'A "Fusion Fallacy" Fallacy?' (2003) 119 *Law Quarterly Review* 375
——, 'Gain-Based Damages and Compensation' in A Burrows and Lord Rodger of Earlsferry (eds), *Mapping the Law – Essays in Memory of Peter Birks* (Oxford, Oxford University Press, 2006) 141
—— and Bant, E, *Unjust Enrichment in Australia* (Oxford, Oxford University Press, 2006)
——, 'The Meaning of Loss and Enrichment' in R Chambers, C Mitchell and J Penner (eds), *Philosophical Foundations of the Law of Unjust Enrichment* (Oxford, Oxford University Press, 2009) 221
——, 'When Do Fiduciary Duties Arise?' (2010) 126 *Law Quarterly Review* 302
——, 'The Measure of Restitution and the Future of Restitutionary Damages' (2010) 18 *Restitution Law Review* 1
——, 'Money Awards of the Cost of Performance' (2010) 4 *Journal of Equity* 122
Eisenberg, MA, 'Actual and Virtual Specific Performance, the Theory of Efficient Breach, and the Indifference Principle in Contract Law' (2005) 93 *California Law Review* 975

——, 'The Disgorgement Interest in Contract Law' (2006) 105 *Michigan Law Review* 559
——, 'The Role of Fault in Contract Law: Unconscionability, Unexpected Circumstances, Interpretation, Mistake, and Nonperformance' (2009) 107 *Michigan Law Review* 1413
Elias, G, 'Explaining Constructive Trusts' (Oxford, Clarendon Press, 1990)
Erbacher, S, 'An Account of Profits for a Breach of Contract (Attorney-General v Blake)' (2001) 29 *Australian Business Law Review* 73
Farnsworth, EA, 'Your Loss or My Gain? The Dilemma of the Disgorgement Principle in Breach of Contract' (1985) 94 *Yale Law Journal* 1339
Feinberg, J, 'Justice and Personal Desert' in J Feinberg, *Doing and Deserving: Essays in the Theory of Responsibility* (Princeton, Princeton University Press, 1970) 55
——, 'The Expressive Function of Punishment' in J Feinberg, *Doing and Deserving* (Princeton, Princeton University Press, 1970) 95
Finn, P, 'The Fiduciary Principle' in TG Youdan (ed), *Equity, Fiduciaries and Trusts* (Toronto, Carswell, 1989) 1
Fox, D, 'Restitutionary Damages to Deter Breach of Contract' (2001) 60 *Cambridge Law Journal* 33
Francis, A, 'Property: A knotty problem' (2010) 160 *New Law Journal* 484
Fried, C, *Contract As Promise – A Theory of Contractual Obligation* (Cambridge, Mass., Harvard University Press, 1981)
Friedmann, D, 'Restitution of Benefits Obtained Through the Appropriation of Property or the Commission of a Wrong' (1980) 80 *Columbia Law Review* 504
——, 'Restitution of Profits Gained by Party in Breach of Contract' (1988) 104 *Law Quarterly Review* 383
——, 'The Efficient Breach Fallacy' (1989) 18 *Journal of Legal Studies* 1
——, 'The Performance Interest in Contract Damages' (1995) 111 *Law Quarterly Review* 628
——, 'Restitution for Wrongs: The Measure of Recovery' (2000) 79 *Texas Law Review* 1879
——, 'Economic Aspects of Damages and Specific Performance Compared' in R Cunnington and D Saidov (eds) *Contract Damages: Domestic and International Perspectives* (Oxford, Hart Publishing, 2008) 65
Fuller, L and Purdue, W, 'The Reliance Interest in Contract Damages' (1936) 46 *Yale Law Journal* 52 and 373
Gardner, J, 'The Purity and Priority of Private Law' (1996) 46 *University of Toronto Law Journal* 459
Giglio, F, The Foundations of Restitution for Wrongs (Oxford, Hart Publishing, 2007)
Gleeson, J and Watson, J, 'Account of Profits, Contracts and Equity' (2005) 79 *Australian Law Journal* 676
Glover, J, 'Is Breach of Confidence a Fiduciary Wrong? Preserving the Reach of Judge-Made Law' (2001) 21 *Journal of Legal Studies* 594
Goetz, C and Scott, R, 'Liquidated Damages, Penalties and the Just Compensation Principle: Some Notes on an Enforcement Model and a Theory of Efficient Breach' (1977) 77 *Colombia Law Review* 554
Goff of Chieveley, Lord and G Jones, *The Law of Restitution*, 7th edn (London, Sweet & Maxwell, 2007)
Goldberg, V, 'Relational Exchange: Economics and Complex Contracts' in V Goldberg (ed), *Readings in the Economics of Contract Law* (Cambridge, Cambridge University Press, 1989)
Goodhart, W, 'Restitutionary Damages for Breach of Contract: The Remedy that Dare Not Speak its Name' [1995] *Restitution Law Review* 3

Gordley, J, 'The Purpose of Awarding Restitutionary Damages: A Reply to Professor Weinrib' (2000) 1 *Theoretical Inquiries in Law* 39

Graham, M, 'Restitutionary Damages: The Anvil Struck' (2004) 120 *Law Quarterly Review* 26

Grantham, R and Rickett, CEF, *Enrichment and Restitution in New Zealand* (Oxford, Hart Publishing, 2000)

Gronow, M, 'Restitution for Breach of Confidence' (1996) 10 *Intellectual Property Journal* 219

Grundmann, S, 'The Fault Principle as the Chameleon of Contract Law: A Market Function Approach' (2009) 107 *Michigan Law Review* 1583

Gudel, P, 'Relational Contract Theory and the Concept of Exchange' (1998) 46 *Buffalo Law Review* 763

Hampton, Jean, 'The Retributive Idea' in Jeffrie Murphy and Jean Hampton (eds), *Forgiveness and Mercy* (Cambridge, Cambridge University Press, 1988) 111

——, 'Correcting Harms Versus Righting Wrongs: The Goal of Retribution' (1992) 39 *UCLA Law Review* 1659

Harder, S, Measuring Damages in the Law of Obligations – The Search for Harmonised Principle (Oxford, Hart Publishing, 2010)

Hardie, WFR, *Aristotle's Ethical Theory*, 2nd edn (Oxford, Clarendon Press, 1968)

Harding, M, 'Justifying Fiduciary Allowances' in Andrew Robertson and Tang Hang Wu (eds), *The Goals of Private Law* (Oxford, Hart Publishing, 2009) 341

Harris, D, Ogus, A and Phillips, J, 'Contract Remedies and the Consumer Surplus' (1979) 95 *Law Quarterly Review* 581

Harris, JW, *Property and Justice* (Oxford, Clarendon Press, 1996)

Harrison, R, 'The Equality of Mercy' in H Gross and R Harrison (eds), *Jurisprudence: Cambridge Essays* (Oxford, Oxford University Press, 1992) 107

Hedley, S, '"Very much the wrong people": The House of Lords and publication of spy memoirs (A-G v Blake)' [2000] 4 *Web Journal of Current Legal Issues*

——, 'The Shock of the Old: Interpretivism in Obligations' in CEF Rickett (ed), *Structure and Justification in Private Law – Essays for Peter Birks* (Oxford, Hart Publishing, 2008) 205

Hegel, GWF, *Philosophy of Right* (transl TM Knox) (Oxford, Clarendon Press, 1952) [trans of: *Grundlinien der philosophie des rechts*]

Hestevold, HS, 'Justice to Mercy' (1985) 46 *Philosophy and Phenomenological Research* 281

Holmes, OW, *Common Law* (Boston, Little, Brown & Co,1881)

——, 'The Path of the Law' (1897) 10 *Harvard Law Review* 61

——and Sir Frederick Pollock, *The Holmes-Pollock Letters: The Correspondence of Mr Justice Holmes and Sir Frederick Pollock 1874–1932*, Vol 1, M De Wolfe Howe (ed), (Cambridge, Mass., Harvard University Press, 1942)

Hutchinson, A, 'The Importance of Not Being Ernest' (1989) 34 *McGill Law Journal* 233

Jackman, IM, 'Restitution for Wrongs' (1989) 48 *Cambridge Law Review* 302

Jackson, H (ed), The Fifth Book of the Nicomachean Ethics of Aristotle (Cambridge, University Press, 1879)

Jaffey, P, *The Nature and Scope of Restitution* (Oxford, Hart Publishing, 2000)

——, 'Efficiency, disgorgement and reliance in contract: a comment on Campbell and Harris' (2002) 22 *Legal Studies* 570

——, 'Disgorgement and "Licence Fee Damages" in Contract' (2004) 20 *Journal of Contract Law* 1

Joachim, HH, *Aristotle: Nicomachean Ethics* (Oxford, Clarendon Press, 1951)

Jones, G, 'The Recovery of Benefits Gained from a Breach of Contract' (1983) 99 *Law Quarterly Review* 443

——, 'The Role of Equity in the English Law of Restitution' in EJH Schrage (ed), *Unjust Enrichment: The Comparative History of the Law of Restitution* (Berlin, Duncker & Humblot, 1995) 147

Kant, I, The Metaphysical Elements of Justice (John Ladd trans, Indianapolis, Hackett Publishing, 1965) [trans of: Metaphysische Anfangsgründe der Rechtslehre]

Kennedy, D, 'Distributive and Paternalist Motives in Contract and Tort Law, with Special Reference to Compulsory Terms and Unequal Bargaining Power' (1982) 41 *Maryland Law Review* 563

Kessler, F and Fine, E, 'Culpa in Contrahendo, Bargaining in Good Faith and Freedom of Contract: A Comparative Study' (1964) 77 *Harvard Law Review* 401

Kimel, D, From Promise to Contract: Towards a Liberal Theory of Contract (Oxford, Hart Publishing, 2003)

Kirby, M, 'Equity's Australian Isolationism' (2008) 8 *Queensland University of Technology Law Journal* 444

Kleinig, J, 'The Concept of Desert' (1971) 8 *American Philosophical Quarterly* 71

Kreitner, R, 'Fault at the Contract-Tort Interface' (2009) 107 *Michigan Law Review* 1533

Kronman, A, 'Specific Performance' (1978) 45 *University of Chicago Law Review* 351

Kull, A, 'Disgorgement for Breach, the "Restitution Interest," and the Restatement of Contracts' (2001) 79 *Texas Law Review* 2021

Laycock, D, 'The Death of the Irreparable Injury Rule' (1990) 103 *Harvard Law Review* 687

——, 'The Scope and Significance of Restitution' (1989) 67 *Texas Law Review* 1277

Lee, P-W, 'Contract Damages, Corrective Justice and Punishment' (2007) 70 *Modern Law Review* 887

——, 'Cases and Comment: Responses to a Breach of Contract' [2003] *Lloyd's Maritime and Commercial Law Quarterly* 301

Leng, TK and Leong, SHS, 'Contractual Protection of Business Confidence' [2002] *Journal of Business Law* 513

Linzer, P, 'On the Amorality of Contract Remedies – Efficiency, Equity and the Second *Restatement*' (1981) 81 *Columbia Law Review* 111

Loke, A, 'Cost of Cure or Difference in Market Value? Toward a Sound Choice in the Basis for Quantifying Expectation Damages' (1996) 10 *Journal of Contract Law* 189

Loughlan, P and Parkinson, P, 'The History and Nature of Equity' *The Laws of Australia: Equity* (Sydney, Butterworths, 1993) vol 15

Macneil, I, 'The Many Futures of Contracts' (1974) 47 *Southern California Law Review* 691

——, 'Contracts: Adjustment of Long-term Economic Relations under Classical, Neo-classical and Relational Contract Law' (1978) 72 *Northwestern University Law Review* 854

——, *The New Social Contract* (New Haven, Yale University Press, 1980)

——, 'Economic Analysis of Contractual Relations: Its Shortfalls and the Need for a Rich Classificatory Apparatus' (1981) 75 *Northwestern University Law Review* 1018

——, 'Efficient Breach of Contract: Circles in the Sky' (1982) 68 *Virginia Law Review* 947

——, 'Values in Contract: Internal and External' (1983) 78 *Northwestern University Law Review* 340

——, 'Relational Contract: What We Do and Do Not Know' [1985] *Wisconsin Law Review* 483

——, 'Relational Contract Theory: Challenges and Queries' (2000) 94 *Northwestern University Law Review* 877

Mahoney, P, 'Contract Remedies and Option Pricing' (1995) 24 *Journal of Legal Studies* 139
Mason, A, 'Themes and Prospects' in PD Finn (ed), *Essays in Equity* (NSW, Lawbook Co, 1985)
Mason, K, Carter, JW and Tolhurst, GJ, *Mason and Carter's Restitution Law in Australia* (NSW, LexisNexis Butterworths, 2008)
McDermott, J and Skinnon, J, 'Restitution for Breach of Contract' (2001) 6 *Deakin Law Review* 112
MacDonald, E, 'The Inadequacy of Adequacy: The Granting of Specific Performance' (1987) 38 *Northern Ireland Legal Quarterly* 244
McCamus, J, 'Disgorgement for Breach of Contract: A Comparative Perspective' (2003) 36 *Loyola of Los Angeles Law Review* 943
McGregor, H, 'Restitutionary Damages' in P Birks (ed), *Wrongs and Remedies in the Twenty-First Century* (Oxford, Clarendon Press, 1996) 203
McInnes, M, 'Unjust Enrichment: A Reply to Professor Weinrib' (2001) 9 *Restitution Law Review* 29
——, 'Restitutionary Damages for Breach of Contract: Bank of America Canada v Mutual Trust Co' (2002) 37 Canadian Business Law Journal 125
——, 'Account of Profits for Common Law Wrongs' in Simone Degeling and James Edelman (eds), *Equity in Commercial Law* (Pyrmont, NSW, Lawbook Co, 2005) 405
——, 'Account of Profits for Breach of Fiduciary Duty' (2006) 122 *Law Quarterly Review* 11
——, 'Gain, Loss and the User Principle' [2006] *Restitution Law Review* 76
McKendrick, E, 'The Common Law at Work: the Saga of *Alfred McAlpine Construction Ltd v Panatown Ltd*' (2003) 3 Oxford University Commonwealth University Law Journal 145
——, 'Specific Implement and Specific Performance – a Comparison' (1986) *Scots Law Times* 249
——, 'Breach of Contract and the Meaning of Loss' (1999) 52 *Current Legal Problems* 37
——, 'Breach of Contract, Restitution for Wrongs and Punishment' in A Burrows and E Peel (eds), *Commercial Remedies – Current Issues and Problems* (Oxford, Oxford University Press, 2003) 93
Meagher, RP, Heydon, JD and Leeming, MJ, *Meagher, Gummow and Lehane's Equity Doctrines and Remedies* (Sydney, Butterworths, 2002)
Miller, D, *Social Justice* (Oxford, Clarendon Press, 1976)
Mitchell, C, 'Remedial Inadequacy in Contract and the Role of Restitutionary Damages' (1999) 15 *Journal of Contract Law* 133
Mitchell, C, 'Causation, Remoteness, and Fiduciary Gains' (2006) 17 *Kings' College Law Journal* 325
Morgan, D, '*Harris v Digital Pulse*: The Availability of Exemplary Damages in Equity' (2003) 29 *Monash University Law Review* 377
Munzer, S, *A Theory of Property* (Cambridge, Cambridge University Press,1990)
Murphy, J, 'Mercy and Legal Justice' in J Murphy and J Hampton, *Forgiveness and Mercy* (Cambridge, Cambridge University Press,1988) 162
'Note to Philadelphia Ball Club Limited v Lajoie' (1902) 90 American State Reports 627
Nussbaum, MC, 'Equity and Mercy' (1993) 22 *Philosophy and Public Affairs* 83
O'Dair, R, 'Remedies for Breach of Contract: A Wrong Turn' [1993] *Restitution Law Review* 31
——, 'Restitutionary Damages for Breach of Contract and the Theory of Efficient Breach: Some Reflections' (1993) 46 *Current Legal Problems* 113
Okeoghene, O and Virgo, G, 'Inadequacy of Compensatory Damages' [2009] Restitution Law Review 112

—— and ——, 'Remedies for Breach of Statutory Duty' (2009) 68 *Cambridge Law Journal* 32

Ong, D, 'Non-Financial Loss Resulting from Tort and Breach of Contract' (2002) 22 *University of Queensland Law Journal* 20

O'Sullivan, J, 'Reflections on the role of restitutionary damages to protect contractual expectations' in D Johnston and R Zimmermann (eds), *Unjustified Enrichment: Key Issues in Comparative Perspective* (Cambridge, Cambridge University Press, 2002) 327

Palmer, IGE, *The Law of Restitution* (Boston, Little, Brown & Co, 1978)

Patfield, F, 'The Modern Remedy of Account' (1988) 11 *Adelaide Law Review* 1

Pearce, D and Halson, R, 'Damages for Breach of Contract: Compensation, Restitution and Vindication' (2008) 28 *Oxford Journal of Legal Studies* 73

Perillo, J, 'Misreading Oliver Wendell Holmes on Efficient Breach and Tortious Interference' (2000) 68 *Fordham Law Review* 1085

Phang, A and Lee, P-W, 'Restitutionary and Exemplary Damages Revisited' (2003) 19 *Journal of Contract Law* 1

—— and——, 'Rationalising Restitutionary Damages in Contract Law' (2001) 17 *Journal of Contract Law* 240

Polinsky, AM and Shavell, S, 'Punitive Damages: An Economic Analysis' (1998) 111 *Harvard Law Review* 870

Pollock, F, *Principles of Contracts* (London, Steven & Sons, 1911)

Pomeroy, JN, *Equity Jurisprudence* Vol 4, 4th edn (San Francisco, Bancroft-Whitney, 1919)

——, Treatise on the Specific Performance of Contracts, 3rd edn (Albany, Banks & Co, 1926)

Porat, A, 'Questioning the Idea of Correlativity in Weinrib's Theory of Corrective Justice' (2001) 2 *Theoretical Inquiries in Law* 161

Posner, R, *Economic Analysis of Law*, 8th edn (New York, Aspen Wolters Kluwer, 2011)

——, 'Let Us Never Blame A Contract Breaker' (2009) 107 *Michigan Law Review* 1349

Rabin, R, 'Law for Law's Sake' (1996) 105 *Yale Law Journal* 2261

Rainbolt, G, 'Mercy: An Independent, Imperfect Virtue' (1990) 27 *American Philosophical Quarterly* 169

Raz, J, 'Promises in Morality and Law' (1982) 95 *Harvard Law Review* 916

Remington, C, 'Intentional Interference with Contract and the Doctrine of Efficient Breach: Fine Tuning the Notion of the Contract Breacher as Wrongdoer' (1999) 47 *Buffalo Law Review* 645

Richardson, M, 'Breach of Confidence' in P Parkinson (ed), *The Principles of Equity*, 2nd edn (Sydney, Lawbook Co, 2003) 436

Rickett, CEF, 'Punitive Damages: The Pulse of Equity' (2003) 77 *Australian Law Journal* 496

Ritchie, DG, 'Aristotle's Subdivisions of "Particular Justice"' (1894) 8 *Classical Review* 185

Rotherham, C, '"*Wrotham Park* damages" and accounts of profits: compensation or restitution?' [2008] *Lloyd's Maritime and Commercial Law Quarterly* 25

——, 'The Conceptual Structure of Restitution for Wrongs' (2007) 66 *Cambridge Law Journal* 172

Rowan, S, 'Protecting Contractual Expectations: An Australian Perspective' (2009) 68 *Cambridge Law Journal* 276

Saidov, D, 'A Further Step Towards Protecting the Performance Interest' [2009] *Lloyd's Maritime and Commercial Law Quarterly* 295

Saprai, P, 'Restitution Without Corrective Justice' (2006) 14 *Restitution Law Review* 41

Schwartz, A, 'The Case for Specific Performance' (1979) 89 *Yale Law Journal* 271

Seavey and Scott, A, 'Restitution' (1938) CCXIII *Law Quarterly Review* 29
Seddon, NC and Ellinghaus, MP, *Cheshire & Fifoot's Law of Contract*, 8th Australian edn (NSW, LexisNexis Butterworths, 2002)
Sharpe, R and Waddams, SM, 'Damages for Lost Opportunity to Bargain' (1982) 2 *Oxford Journal of Legal Studies* 290
Shavell, S, 'Why Breach of Contract May Not Be Immoral Given the Incompleteness of Contracts' (2009) 107 *Michigan Law Review* 1569
Shiffrin, S, '*Could* Breach of Contract Be Immoral?' (2009) 107 *Michigan Law Review* 1551
——, 'The Divergence of Contract and Promise' (2007) 120 *Harvard Law Review* 708
Shiner, R, 'Aristotle's Theory of Equity' in S Panagiotou (ed), *Justice, Law and Method in Plato and Aristotle* (Edmonton, Academic Print & Publishing, 1987) 173
Siems, M, 'Disgorgement of Profits for Breach of Contract: A Comparative Analysis' (2003) 7 *Edinburgh Law Review* 27
Simons, K, 'Justification in Private Law' (1996) 81 *Cornell Law Review* 698
Smart, A, 'Mercy' (1968) 43 *Philosophy* 345
Smith, C, 'Recognising a Valuable Lost Opportunity to Bargain when a Contract is Breached' (2005) 21 *Journal of Contract Law* 250
Smith, L, 'The Province of the Law of Restitution' (1992) 71 *Canadian Bar Review* 672
——, 'Disgorgement of the Profits of Contract: Property, Contract and "Efficient Breach" ' (1995) 24 *Canadian Business Law Journal* 121
——, 'Constructive Trusts-Unjust Enrichment-Breach of Fiduciary Obligation: *Soulos v Korkontzilas*' (1997) 76 *Canadian Bar Review* 539
——, 'Restitution: The Heart of Corrective Justice' (2001) 79 *Texas Law Review* 2115
——, 'The Motive, Not the Deed' in J Getzler (ed), *Rationalising Property, Equity and Trusts: Essays in Honour of Edward Burns* (Oxford, Oxford University Press, 2003) 53
Smith, S, 'The Idea of Private Law' (1996) 112 *Law Quarterly Review* 363
——, 'Performance, Punishment and the Nature of Contractual Obligation' (1997) 60 *Modern Law Review* 360
——, *Contract Theory* (Oxford, Oxford University Press, 2004)
——, 'Substitutionary Damages' in CEF Rickett (ed), *Justifying Private Law Remedies* (Oxford, Hart Publishing, 2008) 93
Spry, ICF, *The Principles of Equitable Remedies*, 8th edn (NSW, Lawbook Co, 2010)
Stevens, RS, 'Involuntary Servitude by Injunction' (1921) 6 *Cornell Law Quarterly* 235
Stevens, R, *Torts and Rights* (Oxford, Oxford University Press, 2007)
——, 'Damages and the Right to Performance: A *Golden Victory* or Not?' in Jason Neyers, Richard Bronagh and Stephen Pitel (eds), *Exploring Contract Law* (Oxford, Hart Publishing, 2009) 171
Stewart, JA, Notes on the Nicomachean Ethics of Aristotle (New York, Arno Press, 1973)
Stiglitz, J, 'principal and agent (ii)', entry in S Durlauf and L Blume (eds), *The New Palgrave Dictionary of Economics*, 2nd edn (Basingstoke and New York, Palgrave Macmillan, 2008)
Stoljar, S, 'Restitutionary Relief for Breach of Contract' (1989) 2 *Journal of Contract Law* 1
Stone, M, 'On the Idea of Private Law' (1996) 9 *Canadian Journal of Law and Jurisprudence* 235
Swadling, W, 'The Vendor-Purchaser Constructive Trust' in S Degeling and J Edelman (eds), *Equity in Commercial Law* (NSW, Lawbook Co, 2005) 463
Tasioulas, J, 'Mercy' (2003) 103 Proceedings of the Aristotelian Society 101
Thaler, R and Sunstein, C, *Nudge: Improving Decisions About Health, Wealth and Happiness* (New Haven, Yale University Press, 2008)

Thel, S and Siegelman, P, 'Willfulness Versus Expectation: A Promisor-Based Defense of Willful Breach Doctrine' (2009) 107 *Michigan Law Review* 1517
—— and——, 'You *Do* Have to Keep Your Promises: A Disgorgement Theory of Contract Remedies' (2011) 52 *William and Mary Law Review* 1181
Tilbury, M, 'Restitutionary Damages' in *Civil Remedies* (Sydney, Butterworths, 1990) vol 1
——, 'Fallacy or Furphy?: Fusion in a Judicature World' (2003) 26 *University of New South Wales Law Journal* 357
Todd, S, 'A New Zealand perspective on exemplary damages' (2004) 33 *Common Law World Review* 255
Treitel, GH, Remedies for Breach of Contract – A Comparative Account (New York, Clarendon Press,1988)
Twambley, P, 'Mercy and Forgiveness' (1976) 36 *Analysis* 84
Ulen, T, 'The Efficiency of Specific Performance: Toward A Unified Theory of Contract Remedies' (1984) 83 *Michigan Law Review* 341
Virgo, G, *The Principles of the Law of Restitution*, 2nd edn (Oxford, Oxford University Press, 2006)
——, 'Restitutionary Remedies for Wrongs: Causation and Remoteness' in CEF Rickett (ed), *Justifying Private Law Remedies* (Oxford, Hart Publishing, 2008) 301
Waddams, SM, 'Restitution As Part of Contract Law' in A Burrows (ed), *Essays on the Law of Restitution* (Oxford, Clarendon Press, 1991) 197
——, 'Profits Derived from Breach of Contract: Damages or Restitution' (1997) 11 *Journal of Contract Law* 1
——, 'Breach of Contract and the Concept of Wrongdoing' (2000) 12 *Supreme Court Law Review* 1
——, *Dimensions of Private Law* (Cambridge, Cambridge University Press, 2003)
——, 'Gains Derived from Breach of Contract: Historical and Conceptual Perspectives' in D Saidov and R Cunnington (eds), *Contract Damages: Domestic and International Perspectives* (Oxford, Hart Publishing, 2008) 187
Waluchow, WJ, 'Professor Weinrib on Corrective Justice' in S Panagiotou (ed), *Justice, Law and Method in Plato and Aristotle* (Edmonton, Academic Print & Publishing, 1987) 153–57
Webb, C, 'Performance and Compensation: An Analysis of Contract Damages and Contractual Obligation' (2006) 26 *Oxford Journal of Legal Studies* 41
Weinrib, E, 'The Fiduciary Obligation' (1975) 25 *University of Toronto Law Journal* 1
——, 'Aristotle's Forms of Justice' in S Panagiotou (ed), *Justice, Law and Method in Plato and Aristotle* (Edmonton, Academic Print & Publishing, 1987) 133–52
——, 'The Gains and Losses of Corrective Justice' (1994) 44 *Duke Law Journal* 277
——, *The Idea of Private Law* (Cambridge, Mass., Harvard University Press, 1995)
——, Restitutionary Damages as Corrective Justice' (2001) 1 *Theoretical Inquiries in Law* 1
——, 'Correlativity, Personality, and the Emerging Consensus on Corrective Justice' (2001) 2 *Theoretical Inquiries in Law* 107
——, 'Deterrence and Corrective Justice' (2002) 50 *UCLA Law Review* 621
——, 'Punishment and Disgorgement as Contract Remedies' (2003) 78 *Chicago-Kent Law Review* 55
——, 'Corrective Justice in a Nutshell' (2002) 52 *University of Toronto Law Journal* 349
——, 'Two Conceptions of Remedies' in CEF Rickett (ed), *Justifying Private Law Remedies* (Oxford, Hart Publishing, 2008) 3–32
Williamson, O, 'Transaction-Cost Economics: The Governance of Contractual Relations' (1979) 22 *Journal of Law and Economics* 233

Witzleb, N and Carroll, R, 'The Role of Vindication in Torts Damages' (2009) 17 *Tort Law Review* 16

Worthington, S, 'Reconsidering Disgorgement for Wrongs' (1999) 62 *Modern Law Review* 218

——, *Equity*, 2nd edn (Oxford, Clarendon Press, 2006)

Wonnell, C, 'The Contractual Disempowerment of Employees' (1994) 46 *Stanford Law Review* 87

Yorio, E 'In Defence of Money Damages for Breach of Contract' (1982) 82 *Columbia Law Review* 1365

——, 'A Defence of Equitable Defences' (1990) 51 *Ohio State Law Journal* 1201

Young, PW, 'Account of Profits for Breach of Contract' (2000) 74 Australian Law Journal 817

——, 'Perhaps Equity is Beyond Childbearing' (2003) 77 Australian Law Journal 221

Zweigert, K and Kötz, H, Introduction to Comparative Law, 3rd edn (T Weir trans, Oxford, Oxford University Press, 1998)

Other Sources

American Law Institute, *Restatement of Restitution* (1937)

American Law Institute, *Restatement of Contracts* (1932)

American Law Institute, Restatement (Second) of the Law of Contracts (1981)

American Law Institute, Restatement (Third) of Restitution and Unjust Enrichment (2011)

Oxford English Dictionary, 2nd edn (Oxford, Clarendon Press, 1989) Vol XIX

United Kingdom and Northern Ireland Law Commission, *Aggravated, Exemplary and Restitutionary Damages*, Report No 247 (1997)

Wildman, R, 'Sonny Bill Williams set to make Toulon debut against Saracens' *The Telegraph* (18 August 2008) www.telegraph.co.uk/sport/rugbyunion/club/2580942/Sonny-Bill-Williams-set-to-make-Toulon-debut-against-Saracens---Rugby-Union.html

INDEX